innovative women poets

innovative

women poets

AN ANTHOLOGY

OF CONTEMPORARY POETRY

AND INTERVIEWS

EDITED BY *Elisabeth A. Frost* AND *Cynthia Hogue*

UNIVERSITY OF IOWA PRESS, IOWA CITY

University of Iowa Press, Iowa City 52242
www.uiowapress.org
Copyright © 2006 by the University of Iowa Press
All rights reserved
Printed in the United States of America

Design by Teresa W. Wingfield

The University of Iowa Press is a member of Green Press Initiative and is committed to preserving natural resources.

Printed on acid-free paper

Library of Congress Cataloging-in-Publication Data
Innovative women poets: an anthology of contemporary poetry and interviews / edited
   by Elisabeth A. Frost and Cynthia Hogue.
      p.   cm.
   Includes bibliographical references and index.
   ISBN-13: 978-1-58729-507-2; ISBN-10: 1-58729-507-5 (pbk.)
   1. American poetry—Women authors.   2. American poetry—20th century.   3. Women
poets, American—20th century—Interviews.   4. Women—Poetry.   5. American poetry—
21st century.   I. Frost, Elisabeth A. (Elisabeth Ann), 1963–.   II. Hogue, Cynthia.
PS589.I66 2006
811'.60809287—dc22   2006044574

06   07   08   09   10   P   5   4   3   2   1

to

gloria evangelina anzaldúa

and

barbara guest

—in memory

CONTENTS

ACKNOWLEDGMENTS

The editors are grateful to all the scholars, critics, and poets who gave their time generously, sharing their conversations, and in some cases, reading as well as writing drafts of the introductions and offering their insights and feedback. We are grateful to our research assistants—poets and critics in their own right—Sarah Vap, Elizabyth Hiscox, and Ken Monteith for their crucial help at every stage of the preparation of this collection. We thank our respective departments of English for the funding support they have offered for travel, research, leaves, and permissions that have helped us to complete the work on this book. To our students in several seminars over the past two years, thank you for reading some of these interviews and poetry, helping us to see that the combination is indeed very instructive! And finally, our thanks to Sylvain and to Derek for unflagging support.

Grateful acknowledgment is given to the following sources for permission to reprint material:

"Barbara Guest and Kathleen Fraser in Conversation with Elisabeth Frost and Cynthia Hogue" by Elisabeth A. Frost and Cynthia Hogue. Copyright © 2004 by Elisabeth A. Frost and Cynthia Hogue. Expanded by Cynthia Hogue. Reprinted by permission of Elisabeth A. Frost and Cynthia Hogue.

Selections from "Etruscan Pages" and from "Wing," "Electric Railway," and "Bresson Project" from *Il Cuore = The Heart: Selected Poems, 1970–1995* by Kathleen Fraser. Copyright © 1997 by Kathleen Fraser. Reprinted by permission of Wesleyan University Press.

"Spirit Tree," "Turret," "Petticoat," and "Noisetone" from *Miniatures and Other Poems* by Barbara Guest. Copyright © 2002 by Barbara Guest. Reprinted by permission of Wesleyan University Press.

"Parachutes, My Love, Could Carry Us Higher," "An Emphasis Falls on Reality," "The Rose Marble Table," and selections from "Türler Losses" from *Selected Poems* by Barbara Guest. Copyright © 1995 by Barbara Guest. Reprinted by permission of Wesleyan University Press.

"An Interview with Alice Fulton" by Cristanne Miller. Copyright © 1997 by the Board of Regents of the University of Wisconsin System. Updated by Cynthia Hogue with permission of Cristanne Miller. Reprinted by permission of the University of Wisconsin Press.

"Fuzzy Feelings," "The Permeable Past Tense of Feel," and selections from "My Last TV Campaign: A Sequence" and from "Give: A Sequence Reimagining Daphne and Apollo" from *Cascade Experiment: Selected Poems* by Alice Fulton. Copyright © 2004 by Alice Fulton. Reprinted by permission of W. W. Norton and Company.

"An Interview with Susan Howe" by Lynn Keller. Copyright © 1995 by the Board of Regents of the University of Wisconsin System. Reprinted by permission of the University of Wisconsin Press.

Selections from "The Nonconformist's Memorial" in *The Nonconformist's Memorial* by Susan Howe. Copyright © 1993 by Susan Howe. Reprinted by permission of New Directions Publishing Corporation.

"An Interview with Harryette Mullen" by Elisabeth A. Frost. Copyright © 2000 by the Board of Regents of the University of Wisconsin System. Expanded by Cynthia Hogue and Elisabeth A. Frost. Reprinted by permission of the University of Wisconsin Press.

"An Interview with Leslie Scalapino" by Elisabeth A. Frost. Copyright © 1996 by the Board of Regents of the University of Wisconsin System. Reprinted by permission of the University of Wisconsin Press.

"as – leg" and selections from *Crowd and not evening or light* by Leslie Scalapino. Copyright © 1992 by Leslie Scalapino. Reprinted by permission of the author.

"A Risk and Trust: An Interview with C. D. Wright" by Charles Jensen and Sarah Vap. Copyright © 2004 by Charles Jensen and Sarah Vap. Reprinted by permission of Charles Jensen and Sarah Vap.

Selections from *Deepstep Come Shining* by C. D. Wright. Copyright © 1998 by C. D. Wright. Reprinted by permission of Copper Canyon Press.

innovative women poets

INTRODUCTION

If, as C. D. Wright has recently remarked, scholars tend "to treat so-called theoretical questions as if they had a value in themselves, independently of any *practice*,"[1] poets necessarily consider questions of form, vision, and concept as integral to a living poetic practice emerging from, and rooted in, the world. In conceptualizing our book, *Innovative Women Poets: An Anthology of Contemporary Poetry and Interviews*, we wanted to reflect this conviction and to offer a different approach to the works than that of a traditional poetry anthology or essay collection by going to the source—to the poets' words themselves. This volume combines selections of the poets' writings with full-length literary interviews, providing a passage to poets' texts through the voices of the writers, as they reflect on their work, its role in the world, and the nature of their poetic practice.

We started this project with the awareness that over the last forty years, innovative women writers have shared a commitment to exploration—aesthetic, political, philosophical, spiritual, or all of these—even as their formal methods and thematic preoccupations have varied widely. We wanted *Innovative Women Poets* to reflect this range of formal and aesthetic orientations. Some of these writers have yet to receive the critical attention they deserve; others are frequently aligned only with a particular group or aesthetic—a categorization asserted more often by scholars than by the poets themselves. When a poet speaks of her writing in her own words, she usually resists the insularity of such categories, having a more fluid sense of her aesthetic explorations than such taxonomies convey.

We contend that the works of these poets speak to common issues in ways that have yet to be fully explored. In bringing them together in this volume, we hope to foster dialogue among varying poetic "schools." This same ambition also led us to highlight the idea of conversation (the interviews) within these pages. Most broadly, in representing an unusual range of poetic forms and modes of address, *Innovative Women Poets* attempts the textual and social practice that Erica Hunt calls "contiguity." Hunt describes an oppositional reading and writing practice that acknowledges "a field of related projects which have moved beyond the speculation of skepticism to a critically active stance against forms of domination." It is timely to recall the ground of Hunt's own inquiry: her sense in 1990, just at the start of the first Gulf War, that the Western construction of "peace" at "home" masked repressive and oppressive Western policies promulgating protracted but remote violence. An awareness at that time among dissident artists of "the submerged, disconnected and violent character of contemporary life," Hunt noted, has now irrefutably surfaced for a broader public as well. Thus, this anthology joins other efforts that consider, as Hunt puts it, "variance between clusters of oppositional writing strategies with respect for what has been achieved by each and a sense of the ground that holds it in place."[2] We aim for this book to be relational, to open lines of connection and interest, dissonance and dissidence, interchange and debate. The importance of "contiguity" is that it promotes a sense of common interests (both ethical and aesthetic) and shared space (both public and literary). It creates a place where writers of differing dissident and aesthetic practices meet, initiating—or in some cases furthering—exchange among both writers and readers.[3]

Our project, like others, grew out of the last decade's dramatic interest in women's experimental poetry. During this period, several important anthologies and books of criticism, as well as an abundance of new poetry collections, were issued by university and commercial presses. At the same time, major academic conferences were exploring experimental women's writing.[4] Such efforts have broadened our understanding of our own cultural moment. We hope that this anthology will contribute to this ongoing work, in particular the effort to limn a more diversified and historicized understanding of women's innovative poetics.[5] The debates among writers and critics about the nature of the poetry itself—the formal structures, voice, matter, history, and politics of innovative writing— have been vigorous and illuminating. But another aspect of contiguity is that it attempts to address previous oversights. For example, if considerations of innovative poetry emphasize formal elements of the work (techniques like "fragmentation, parataxis, run-ons, interruption, and disjunction," as Juliana Spahr usefully summarizes[6]), less often examined are crucial cultural contexts, without an understanding of which the experimental elements of the poetry can be missed. As Hank Lazer argues, there is a danger in being too prescriptive: "profoundly innovative and idiosyncratic writing . . . barely receives attention because it evades the principal contemporary groupings and taxonomies."[7] Lazer is addressing a broad issue in the field that surfaces in editing practices based on formal similarities or group affiliations alone. The result is that some male and many female poets have not gained significant visibility, in spite of attempts to redress past exclusions.

As regards women poets, we suggest that such oversight results from the ways in which much poetry by women is received, reviewed, and anthologized. Anthologization practices fall roughly into three common methods of categorization. Some anthologies include an exhaustive number of women writers of a given period (tending to privilege the already canonized); some emphasize feminist engagements and stylistic accessibility as primary criteria for inclusion (often underrepresenting formally challenging and analytical-political work on the basis of "inaccessibility"); and still other collections opt for a definition of "experimentation" that makes formal disruption the primary criterion of the work or artist (thus minimizing cultural contexts). Entering into a rich conversation about women's poetry, we choose to follow vectors of connection that help us to reconsider poetic form, voice, cultural context, and subject position. In particular, we hope that this anthology, and the differing hybridity of its selections, will deepen appreciation of innovation in a broadly multicultural context. Our inclusion of interviews—the poet's own voice in a medium other than poetry—is one means toward this end, since the poets themselves add illuminating personal insights, intentions, and historical contexts to readings of their work.

Our foundational editorial premise has been that innovative poetry can be defined in terms of both formal attributes (work that challenges dominant artistic conventions) and cultural stance (speaking from, or about, the margins or borders of power).[8] We wish to focus attention on the role of cultural activism in innovative poetry, to provide a forum for investigating various formal experiments—of "identity-categorized" poetry, for example—in dialogue with an avant-garde and visual poetics that is equally, albeit differently, a poetics of dissent. Through this forum we hope to foster discussion not only about constructivist experiments but also about the radical shifting of poetic substance, of what is expressed and expressible. Our aim is to expand understanding of the innovative endeavors women poets have engaged in and to do so by bringing together a broader range of poetic voices, values, and contexts than can be gathered from either a narrowly formalist approach or a set political agenda.

To that end, we have taken the notion of "innovation" in a necessarily (if not unproblematically) broad sense, as formally and conceptually exploratory.[9] Since we assume that challenging, contemporary writing by women need take no single form, the poems in the collection illuminate a variety of ways women poets today reflect on our culture, politics, art, and language. All the poets included in this volume search for forms in which to embody a new awareness or knowledge. Some find analogies in music or the visual arts, while others propel the notion of spoken voice into unmapped terrain, verging on the register that Julia Kristeva termed the "semiotic chora": the elements of poetry that have to do with sound but not signification—elements nonsignifying yet meaningful.[10] The poets included here trouble existing generic borders and readerly expectations, even as their methods differ. By bringing into contiguity works by poets not usually read together, we assert the importance of formal experiments that represent a range of not only cultural and political positions but also concepts of form itself.

A number of aesthetic movements in the last half of the twentieth century are reflected, and refracted, in the pages of *Innovative Women Poets*—including the New York School, the Black Arts movement, Black Mountain (extending the Objectivists), Language writing, and the front lines of second-wave feminist poetry. We have selected works that reveal surprising affinities, unexpected parallels. The writers we chose are too often associated only with a given group or category, which inevitably fails to describe their artistic projects and their evolution over many years. In the interviews included here, for example, Kathleen Fraser, Barbara

Guest, and Alice Notley recall their early impressions of, and participation in, the first and second generations of the New York School. Yet all three of these writers have long since transcended the label of "New York School" poet, developing highly original and idiosyncratic poetries that diverge both from one another and from the period and place. Similarly, Susan Howe and Rachel Blau DuPlessis, along with Fraser, emerged as poets at the time when the Objectivist George Oppen was returning to poetry in the 1960s and Charles Olson, a founder of the Black Mountain School, was exploring what has come to be known as "field poetics." The proximity of these women poets to one another in this volume helps us to appreciate the ways in which they build on the poetic practice, political engagement, and visuality of the works of those mentors.[11] Along with Mei-mei Berssenbrugge, Harryette Mullen, and Leslie Scalapino, these poets all share artistic affinities with avant-garde Language poetics—an at once experimental and political practice—without considering themselves members of the historical 1970s gathering of Language writing. We also are aware that the intensified interiority of Scalapino's and Berssenbrugge's works—their commitment to developing a contemplative poetics (influenced in Scalapino's case by her interest in Buddhism)—resonates with Alice Fulton's sharply detailed analytic lyric.

Other associational relations emerge around the jazz-blues poetics of the groundbreaking poetry of Jayne Cortez and Sonia Sanchez, along with that of the younger Mullen. These poets wrote during, or in communion with, the first and second generations of the Black Arts movement, although early on they developed multiple sources and preoccupations that, by the end of the 1970s, could be distinguished from that movement's political and aesthetic agendas. Their presence establishes an affinity with poets like C. D. Wright, who acknowledges her roots in gospel; Susan Howe, whose work, while it takes place in a visual field of the page, is also profoundly sound based; and Gloria Anzaldúa, the music of whose poetry expands the substantive terrain of the Mexican *corrido* (ballad).

And finally are the poets we have loosely associated with the political awakening of second-wave feminism. Alicia Ostriker, along with Anzaldúa, DuPlessis, and Fraser, came of age during the early years of second-wave feminism's social, political, and aesthetic flourishing. These poets have acknowledged what this movement made it possible for them to say and have themselves crucially contributed to its theoretical advances, but the ways that they diverged from or built on that movement are worth noting. Ostriker was until quite recently an oppositional poet of often personal, feminist lyrics. Then came her extended meditation on Judaic patriarchal tradition, which became, in the manner of the Hebrew prophets, a collaged and at times fragmented, fractured poetic argument with God. Among the first theorists of border poetics, Anzaldúa broke ground by taking issue with white feminism's heterosexual and racial blind spots, as well as with its "English-only" preferences, pioneering interlingual, cross-genre forms. Further, Fulton and Wright both acknowledge their feminist roots, but the innovative elements in their work have received less attention, perhaps because their projects are rooted in redefining lyric tradition. We emphasize that these writers share a fierce individualist poetics and a commitment to expansive innovation, evidenced in an engagement with visual composition, a range of poetic and scientific discourses, and a subversion of the first-person narrative mode.

Instead of typifying "movements" then, our selections address previous exclusions and suggest each poet's contiguous relation to the others, highlighting each writer's poetics, while at the same time challenging predominant modes of reception and artificial borders. We believe that each poet herein offers rich possibilities for recasting the "innovative." Anzaldúa's work affords a way to consider the intersections of ethnic identity and language in relation to poetic theory and history. Berssenbrugge's poetry links formal and linguistic experimentation to multicultural poetics in astutely theoretical ways and is, at the same time, highly attentive to poetry as an intimate as well as phenomenological practice. Like Berssenbrugge, whose work is both multicultural and collaborative, Cortez stresses interarts poetics as *itself* a radical cultural politics. Involved in avant-garde traditions and women's cultural locations, as well as with highly theoretical and experiential investigations of "poetry as a mode of thought or speculation," as she remarks in the interview, DuPlessis is central to our recent history of feminist avant-garde poetics. Fraser and Guest—together in conversation as well as in each writer's work—have devoted years to charting the modalities of the innovative in their work, with particular attention to the visual arts and to gender identities. Similarly emerging from a resistance to voice-based lyric, Fulton's poetry, from the 1970s on, explores language as a cultural and philosophical construct. Howe creates intersections between a highly abstract and aural sense of the word with a deeply embodied, spiritual inquiry, while Mullen's playful poetic experiments emphasize center stage cultural shifts in subject position, language use, and political realities. Notley's mature poetry highlights gender issues in the New York School, as well as the spiritual (and gendered) role of the poet. By contrast, Ostriker's comments on the ethical in poetry and on the retention of the "I" in the lyric allow us to afford space to a humanist vision that places faith in personal voice as a medium for social action. Scalapino's meditative, serial poetics engages with a range of avant-garde traditions and genres in a dialogic, yet utterly original, form. Finally, Wright's complex and layered writing explores women's voices in poetry that might well be seen as inheriting and combining Guest's visually exploratory writing with Ostriker's feminist ethics.

Since we have taken special care to include a range of aesthetic and formal concerns, we also hope that readers will notice among these voices some unexpectedly shared preoccupations. For example, we note the spiritual, philosophical, and ethical inquiry that variously informs the writing of DuPlessis, Fulton, Howe, Ostriker, and Scalapino; the engagements with the visual arts evident in Berssenbrugge, Fraser, Guest, and Wright; the commitment to cultural hybridity that informs the works of Anzaldúa and Mullen. We have deliberately chosen work that experiments with text, image, and uses of the page or line as visual elements of composition, apparent in selections by DuPlessis, Fraser, Howe, Sanchez, Scalapino, and Wright. At the same time, we attend to the performance poetics, musical influences, and pursuit of pure sound in the work of Cortez, Howe, Mullen, Notley, and Sanchez. Berssenbrugge's use of abstraction can be said to "cross-pollinate" with Mullen's cultural allusions; and Ostriker's daring bodily poetics—as well as her stance as feminist activist and scholar—exists side by side with Fulton's and Howe's elliptical, conceptual, and equally feminist poetics. It was also to redress limitations in critical reception and categorization that we believed it essential to include poetry by Anzaldúa. Anzaldúa is well known as a Chicana activist, a novelist, and a nonfiction writer (editor of the groundbreaking anthology *This Bridge Called My Back*, a collection that remains a crucial resource twenty years after its first appearance); but she is rarely acknowledged for her experiments with cross-genre form or for her innovative interlingual poetry. Anzaldúa's untimely death (during the preparation of this volume) makes her inclusion here particularly significant, as a homage to her own poetry of witness.

Selecting these divergent voices, we seek to avoid labels; thus, we choose not to divide *Innovative Women Poets* into subheadings or aesthetic groupings. The poets are listed in alphabetical order—a recourse to randomness that pleases us. The one exception to this arbitrary convention is the placement of the conversation between

Fraser and Guest at the close of the collection. We position this interview, one of the last Barbara Guest gave before her death in February 2006, as a tribute to this innovative poet who has only begun to receive adequate critical attention. While not seeking to associate Fraser solely with Guest, we do want to pay tribute to these two poets' intergenerational exchange and friendship, which exemplify the frequently unacknowledged conversations that take place among women artists.

Finally, we note that the interviews are central to this volume. Along with brief introductions,[12] an in-depth literary interview accompanies the selections of each poet's work. Some were conducted especially for this volume. Others we deemed important to collect from other sources; these we updated or expanded where possible, and edited lightly for length and consistency.[13] In this way, information about each poet's interests, influences, and biography is made accessible to readers, and we are able to juxtapose each writer's work with something only a well-conducted interview can provide: a direct experience of the poet's approach to poetry, from her own perspective and in her own words.[14] Too often the poet's voice—the conversational mode so different from that of writerly, formal statement—is eclipsed by critical or editorial voices and, if available at all (in important but often underread periodicals and magazines), it rarely survives in book form accompanied by samples of that same writer's work. We hope that this volume will redress that lack, contributing toward a fuller understanding and a more contextualized reading of these innovative poetries.

Notes

1. See C. D. Wright, *Cooling Time*, 5.
2. Erica Hunt, "Notes for an Oppositional Poetics," in Sloan, 681 and 687.
3. In this sense of furthering the exchange of ideas and aesthetic approaches, such editorial ventures as that of the journal *XCP: Cross-Cultural Poetics*, online journals like *jacket* and *How2*, and listserve discussions—for example, the Buffalo Poetics List and "Wom-Po"—inform our effort in the cross-cultural, the dialogic, and the contiguous.
4. In addition to *Moving Borders*, see also O'Sullivan, Rankine and Spahr, Keller and Miller, Hinton and Hogue, Frost (*Feminist Avant-Garde*), Kinnahan, Simpson, and Vickery. Major conferences have included "Where Lyric Meets Language," detailed in n. 6.
5. See Fraser's comments in relation to her collection of essays: "I have been interested in the observation of my 'cultural moment' in ways that I hoped might extend the reader's understanding of the necessity behind the pursuit of innovation; how and why one felt

compelled to imagine new terms for the next poem; something that could take one beyond the familiar and well-digested." *Translating*, 3–4.

6. Indeed, Spahr's comments are taken from a volume that emerged from the groundbreaking conference "Where Lyric Meets Language," organized by Claudia Rankine and Allison Cummings at Barnard College in 1999. See introduction to Rankine and Spahr, *American Women Poets*, 1–17.

7. See Lazer, who has in mind, among others, John Taggart, Will Alexander, and Hannah Weiner.

8. The historical avant-garde movements (as well as more recent movements) defined themselves in terms of the meeting of radical artistic innovations with radical politics. See Frost (*Feminist Avant-Garde* xiv–xviii) for a discussion of debates in definitions of the avant-garde in artistic form and political mission.

9. Even the term "innovative" is problematic, given debates about the nature of avant-garde, experimental, and postmodern writing. We choose the term "innovative" as less theoretical than "avant-garde"; less redolent of form alone than "experimental"; and less academic than "postmodern." For contrast, see the introductions to Frost (*Feminist Avant-Garde*), Hinton and Hogue, and Simpson, for discussions of the vexing question of terminology.

10. See Kristeva for a discussion of this term and its implication for a "revolutionary" poetics.

11. We thank Kathleen Fraser for her careful reading of and feedback on an earlier draft of this introduction. This comment paraphrases an insight that Fraser expressed in an e-mail to the editors, August 24, 2004.

12. Bracketed words ending with "(—ed.)" indicate material added by the current editors for this book. Bracketed words without such a note were original to the text.

13. The introductions to Gloria Anzaldúa, Mei-mei Berssenbrugge, Rachel DuPlessis, Alice Fulton, and Susan Howe are adapted from pieces written by the interviewer or were co-written by the interviewer.

14. In collecting interviews, we chose to focus not on the formal "artist's statement" favored by some editors (as in Sloan, Rankine and Spahr, and Finch) but rather on a mode more common to the artist's catalog than the poetry anthology: the wide-ranging, spontaneous conversation that interviews can provide. In this, we are grateful to such precursors as Tate, among others. We feel that the cross-pollination between work of art and artist's voice is quite underrepresented in the field of poetry, perhaps for the very reason that formalist concerns have been in the forefront of editors' projects in recent years and that poststructuralism questioned a poetics of presence extending to the practice of the interview.

gloria evangelina anzaldúa

INTRODUCTION

Born in the Rio Grande Valley of south Texas to sixth-generation mexicanos, this self-described "Chicana, tejana, working-class, dyke-feminist poet, writer-theorist" was punished in grade school for her inability to speak English "properly" and shamed for her differences from other children. Yet as Anzaldúa indicates in the following interview, she used these experiences to develop alternate forms of individual and collective identity that acknowledge each person's multiplicity and interconnectedness with others (both human and nonhuman). Anzaldúa's expansive redefinition of Chicana/Chicano identities, her innovative use of code switching (linguistic shifts between standard and working-class English, standard Spanish, Chicano Spanish, Tex-Mex, Nahuatl-Aztec, and other languages), and her sophisticated explorations of border issues and mestizaje[1] identities have significantly influenced contemporary U.S. literature and queer theory. Anzaldúa's writings, which are frequently anthologized and cited, have also challenged and expanded previous views in American studies, composition studies, cultural studies, ethnic studies, feminist theory, and women's studies. As editor or coeditor of three multicultural anthologies, Anzaldúa also played a vital role in developing an inclusionary feminist movement.

Drawing on and revising precolonial Toltec and Nahuatl worldviews, Anzaldúa develops a performative poetics that links social change with personal/communal healing. As she indicates in this interview, her shaman aesthetics unite imagination with soul, facilitating the perception of "interlapping universes." Anzaldúa describes writing as "making face, making soul" to underscore its transformational potential. She employs complex, visceral metaphors and concrete language designed to effect physiological, emotional, and psychic change in herself and her readers.[2]

Anzaldúa is best known for *Borderlands/La frontera: The New Mestiza* (1987), a hybrid collection of poetry and prose that was named one of the 100 Best Books of the Century by both the *Hungry Mind Review* and the *Utne Reader*. Blending personal experience with cultural history, Anzaldúa enacts a new genre or what she calls "autohistoria-teoría": women-of-color interventions into and transformations of traditional Western autobiographical forms.[3] This synergistic blend enables Anzaldúa to shift fluidly between what she describes in the following pages as "the personal I" and "the collective we." *Borderlands/La frontera* is divided into two parts: the first consists of seven mixed-genre essays that combine personal narrative with history, social protest, poetry, and revisionist myth. The second consists of thirty-eight poems in six sections. The poems, which include graphic descriptions of Anzaldúa's writing process, depict a wide range of topics: revisionist mythmaking, storytelling, racism, spirituality, sexuality. Almost all the poems include code switching, and ten are written entirely in Spanish.

Although scholars praise the innovative poetic dimensions of *Borderlands/La frontera*'s mixed-genre prose chapters, they rarely examine the second half of the book and almost entirely ignore the poetry in the first half. However, Anzaldúa strongly identified herself as a poet. Indeed, *Borderlands/La frontera* originated as a manuscript of poems and only later grew to include the opening mixed-genre chapters.[4] More importantly, Anzaldúa's poetry often attains levels of intimacy and brutal honesty even greater than those found in her prose and offers crucial elaborations of many key themes.

Anzaldúa's published works also include *This Bridge Called My Back: Writings by Radical Women of Color* (1981, coedited with Cherríe Moraga), a groundbreaking collection of essays and poems widely recognized by scholars as the premiere multi-cultural feminist text; *Making Face, Making Soul/Haciendo caras: Creative and Critical Perspectives by Feminists of Color* (1990), a multigenre collection edited by Anzaldúa, which is used in many university classrooms; *Friends from the Other Side/Amigos del otro lado* (1993) and *Prietita and the Ghost Woman/Prietita y la llorona* (1995), two bilingual children's books; *Interviews/Entrevistas* (2000), a memoirlike collection of interviews; and *this bridge we call home: radical visions for transformation* (2002, coedited with AnaLouise Keating), a collection of essays, poetry, fiction, and artwork that examines the current status of feminist/womanist theories and calls for new forms of theorizing and alliance making. Anzaldúa received numerous awards, including the Lambda Lesbian Small Book Press Award, an NEA Award, and the American Studies Association Lifetime Achievement Award.

The following conversations with the critic AnaLouise Keating took place at the University of Arizona on October 25 and 26, 1991, during Anzaldúa's residence as a Rockefeller visiting scholar, in which capacity she presented a series of lectures and workshops. We had planned to update this interview, but Anzaldúa passed away unexpectedly in May 2004 of diabetes-related complications.

AN INTERVIEW WITH GLORIA EVANGELINA ANZALDÚA
by AnaLouise Keating

ANALOUISE KEATING: In "En Rapport, In Opposition,"[5] you discuss the importance of spirituality to women of color. How do you integrate spirituality with your politics?

GLORIA ANZALDÚA: I think that most of us, all of us men and women of all colors, go around thinking that this is who and what we are, and we only see maybe three-quarters or not even three-quarters of ourselves. There's a component that is very much part of the unconscious—part of the spirit world—that's also part of us, but we've been told it's not there, so we don't perceive it. A little child is taught what to see physically. If we were taught to see differently, we would probably see people from other dimensions sitting in the armchair, you know. Interlapping universes. But we're not taught to see that way. In some spiritual traditions—like shamanist traditions—you actually learn to experience the interpenetration of those other worlds. According to the Olmecs, the Toltecs, the Mayans, the Aztecs, and others, this physical reality is one facet or facade of the spirit world. This is a mask for the spirit world, so that you and I are masks for the spirit. We're just the costume; we're just the clothes. If you can take the mask off or go behind the mask, you are let into a connection with this other reality, of the spirit.

With me it always happens with a traumatic shock of some kind that opens me so brutally—I'm just cracked open by the experience—that for a while things come inside me, other realities, other worlds. Like when I was mugged, I became aware of things that had to do with the landscape and the trees and the particular ravine where it happened. I could almost hear their vibrations (because every living thing has vibrations, a speed of vibrating). Somewhere really, really, really far back in our history I think someone got very scared of this connection with the spirit and the spiritual world, put down the wall, and concentrated on using our hands rather than our imaginations. So like in the poem "Interface," Leyla can achieve things with her imagination. She doesn't need a crane to move dirt. We went a technological rather than a spiritual route. If you want to move from here to New York, you get on a plane. But had we gone in the other direction, all we'd have to do is think, "I am now in New York between Third and whatever," and there we would be. This is why shamanism is so intriguing to people and intriguing to me, because you achieve that through your imagination, through your soul. Your soul is actually there. If you're dreaming about Manhattan—it's really there. And then you travel back to your body.

So here we go as feminists wanting to be practical and wanting to make a difference and wanting to make some changes, and we're looking at everything that gives us strength: having roots, having a historical past that we can connect with and say, "This is the route that my particular group has walked and I can see how what happened in the past has affected the present and therefore affected me and who I am and how I feel about myself." So we've dug into the past for a history and models and women and stories that can give us some sort of ground to walk on, some sort of foundation, some sort of place to take off from, and also to find positive stuff that will feed and inspire us.

When you start connecting with your past racial history and your own childhood personal history, you have all these ideas about feminism and the rights of women, the rights of all people, trying to make the world a little cleaner and a little safer and stop the destruction. You want it so badly that the desire opens you up to being exposed to things that will give you the strength to survive and accomplish this. As these pathways open—in these channels, tunnels, cracks, whatever you want to call them—you come up against an awareness that the universe is alive. It pulsates; everything's alive: nature, and trees, and the sky, and the wind.

Once you connect with that, you feel like you are part of interconnecting organisms—vegetable, animal, mineral—and they all have some kind of consciousness. If this pulsating rhythm, vibration, is some kind of awareness, of aliveness, then that's a consciousness. So you start looking at rocks in a different way—at birds and when they appear and when they don't appear. You let your imagination act as a brain, as a center (like in a computer there's a center that connects and sorts through all the data and comes out with what you want). And you see these things as part of this force that pulsates, that's everywhere. That's the spirit and spirituality, and it's real and you know it. Sometimes it comes through you as a result of a shock. Sometimes it comes as a result of a dream or something you read. But it's such a popular thing right now, in California anyway, that some people pretend that they've experienced this, and they go through what I call this pseudospiritual New Age awareness—the pseudowitches, but it's just a performance. And then there are other real people who in some way have seen the hidden part of their personality, the spiritual part, the unconscious part. They don't need to go through any of those fancy retreats and elaborate rituals, drumming, ecstatic states. They just all of a sudden see it. It's like turning around and looking at your shoulder and realizing that you'd only been seeing half an arm. Does that make sense to you?

ALK: Definitely.

GEA: But right now in the academy with high theorists, it's very incorrect to talk about that part because they're afraid that part is something innate and therefore they'll be labeled essentialists. Because the women who talk about spirituality a lot of times will talk about la diosa, the goddess, and how women are innately nurturing, and how they're peaceful. But they're not. It's all learned. Right? So they equate that kind of essentialism with spirituality, and I don't. Maybe in the past there is that in my writing . . .

ALK: Can you say more about the interconnection between "masks," physical reality, and the spirit world?

GEA: Well, my concept is slightly different from the Olmecs and the Toltecs and the Mayans. Their concept of the mask is their philosophy of life, their belief that the human is the adornment for the spirit. Behind this mask—this outer reality, this house, my clothes, my face, me—is a spiritual entity. To me, the masks are no longer necessary. We recognize that our flesh is spiritualized. The ancients believed in a separation: over here is the so-called real world, and there's a wall—a partition; then over there is the world of the spirit and of ideals, which is totally noncorporeal; we're the corporeal manifestation of *that* world. In *Prieta* I'm trying to do away with the separation and say it's here and now, and at the blink of an eye.[6] In "El Paisano Is a Bird of Good Omen," the roadrunner blinks, and Andrea (who's now Prieta) blinks and suddenly she's not sitting there on the fence post but is over in the lagoon. When she's watching those little kids playing with the lizard and the horned toad—in the blink of the eye she *is* those lizards and that horned toad and those ants and she's feeling the bites. I don't think that we need that partition. Does that make sense to you?

ALK: Yeah. It's not that the "spiritual" is somewhere else; it's *here*, but right now we don't see it because of the way we're looking.

GEA: Because of the way we have been taught what reality is and what reality is not.

ALK: Right. Because *what* we've been trained to see influences what we believe and therefore how we act.

GEA: Yeah. A very large percentage of our brain goes unused, a very large percent of the reality that we could take in through the senses is not used. And so the people who can see like this are either crazy or they're shamans or creative people.

ALK: That's similar to what I believe. . . . There's this tree I communicate with, and I really resist it. What'll happen is that as I resist it when I'm working, my writing . . . I can't write. Or things will start to go wrong around the house, and I'll say "okay" and I'll go outside and just sit there and say—

GEA: "Talk to me."

ALK: Yeah. The rational side can always say, "Oh, this is just yourself talking to yourself," but the other part says, "Well, yes, it could be that, but it just seems like something more."

GEA: I think that that self is extended to the tree. The self does not stop with just you, with your body. The self can penetrate other things and they penetrate you. Your remark that you can't prove it—it's not rational, it's not scientific—goes back to the concept of objectivity, which has been one of the ruling models of our lives, even before science. But it started with science, that you have to test it. It has to show some kind of physical manifestation or else—

ALK: —it's not real.

GEA: And that theory of objectivity which has been proven false over and over by its own scientists makes us separate because it privileges the eyes, the visual, and causes distance and separation. So the other part of yourself that's objective says, "Oh no. You can't be experiencing this. It's just you talking to another part of you. It's just your imagination taking off." So here come other people that say what happens in your imagination is just as real as what happens when you walk down the street. What happens in a fantasy, *that* reality has as much validity as external reality. When you're working at creating a story, what happens to those people and the setting is just as *real* as what happens to your mother and your brother. That's *one* of the points that I try to make in *Prieta*: there's not just one reality; there's all these different realities, and why should one reality—which is external life—be privileged over the others? Some cultures really pay a lot of attention to their dreams and rituals and the imaginative part of their lives, which is considered other dimensions of reality. But they are being killed off, like the Aborigine in Australia that have their dreamtime. It's just us that privilege the mechanical, the objective, the industrial, the scientific.

At a recent conference I took the pamphlet entitled "Alternative Responses to the Columbus Sesquicentennial" with a map of the U.S. and Mexico and South America, and I got up in front of the crowd and I turned it over and said, "Who's to say that up is up and down is down? We're whirling on an axis but we're also going around the sun. So why should the U.S. and Canada be upstairs—top—and South America and Africa and Australia be down here?" Just like why does the U.S. take it upon itself to call itself America?

I feel the same way about waking life—which is external reality plus some other alternate states. You can be sitting there and go off into fantasies, memories, thinking about things that have nothing to do with external reality. When you're writing, for example, you go off in alternate states. What's to say that on the other side, the dream eagle—the dream self—is not looking at external reality as the dream and the dream as real? Sometimes to me the dreams make more sense in the way they connect, associatively like a poem, than this outer reality.... It's getting too wild, right?

ALK: Not at all. Well, I don't think so. But some people object to spirituality; they see it as passive. If you're going to say there's all these other realities, someone could take the step of saying, "So external reality doesn't matter; oppression doesn't matter because you have all these other worlds." And you don't do that. You have definite spiritual beliefs yet maintain a very strong political agenda, and I think that's very rare. How do you manage to do this?

GEA: I look at us and we're flesh and blood. We occupy weight and space, three-dimensionally. We're not some kind of disembodied thought energy. We're embodied in the flesh. So there must be a purpose to this stage we're living in, to this corporeal stage which we lose after we die and we don't have before we're born. The things that we really struggle with and need to work out, we need to work out on the physical plane. We can't escape. Just because those other realities are there, we can't just say, "Oh, this is just a play on some kind of stage and it doesn't really matter." It might be a play on the stage, but it's a matter of life and death.

ALK: Also, if there's this kind of interconnection that goes with the spiritual, that's another way that people who are so different in so many ways can connect, through this other level. Does that make sense?

GEA: Sí.

ALK: I think I picked that up from your writing.

GEA: Yes. What I call "almas afines." That we're kindred spirits.

ALK: In *Borderlands/La frontera* you claim that your lesbianism is chosen; for some it is genetically inherent, but you *"made the choice to be queer."* Cherríe Moraga, in a review of your book, interprets this statement to refer to your political decision to identify yourself as lesbian, and her view makes sense. But I hadn't interpreted it that way when I first read your essay. So what did you mean, what kind of choice were you referring to?

GEA: I was thinking back to how much are we born with: How much of the basic personality, the basic self, is there genetically? And how much of it has been taught, especially about sexuality and being female, being Chicana, being white, being whatever class? Since I wrote *Borderlands*, I started thinking that there's got to be a middle road. There has to be a middle way; you can't get polarized between being born into this world as a blank slate and everything that's written on your body has been put there by society, including your sexual preference, and the other extreme that you are born female and therefore you're nurturing, giving, and peaceful; you don't kill, you don't violate. I wasn't a dumb person: I knew who was getting the strokes and who was getting the slaps; the boys would always be privileged. Heterosexuality was a patriarchal institution and the woman would always have to constantly struggle, even if she was coupled with a very progressive feminist-oriented male. His training would be to be the macho, and however much he would fight it some of it would bleed through, just like we fight against the passivity and all the things we were told we were. As a thinking woman, I looked at the model of the heterosexual couple. I would never be able to put up with that kind of shit from a man. Or if I did put up with it, I would be very ashamed of myself and feel very bad about myself.

So the only viable choice for me was lesbianism. In lesbianism there would be some power things—if my lover happened to be white, she would have some privilege; if I was older, I'd have some power—but I had more of a chance to have a meaningful relationship with a woman than I would with a man. This is common sense. You look at all the countries on the planet and how the heterosexual model is the ruling model and how some men have four or five wives and the wife never has power unless she's an upper-class woman, and then she has to do other things to keep that power—manipulate and conform. Or a businesswoman who's an executive has to play the game in order to obtain that position. So the women who've become equal to men in terms of power, it's been at a great cost to them, and they negate a lot of stuff. Sometimes they repress feelings, you know? They get ulcers . . . not that the men have it that easy, but across the planet heterosexuality benefits the male, so isn't it logical for you to want a different relationship?

ALK: Definitely.

GEA: If desire is something that you're not born with, but something that you acquire—that sexual hunger to connect, to touch somebody, to be touched by somebody—if that can be learned, it can also be unlearned and relearned. If there are political lesbians out there (a lot of political lesbians came out in the seventies because that was a viable alternative), there were other lesbians like Cherríe who at a very early age were attracted, lusting, after women. With both types, there was a resistance to the teaching that we should desire men. But with people like Cherríe, that took on a very emotional kind of manifestation very early on. They got turned on by girls. And with the political lesbian you were a lesbian in your head first and then you started looking at women differently because of these theories about sexuality: Is sexuality learned? Is heterosexuality learned? Is lesbianism learned? And through the theory you got to the body and the emotion and the closeness with women.

After *Borderlands* came out, I got to thinking that yes, some of us do choose. It's a very conscious thing: "I'm going to give up men; I'm going to go to women; I'm going to come out of the closet and declare my lesbianism." With other people, it's very unconscious. They don't even know they've made the choice. They think it's just natural to be a lesbian or to be a heterosexual woman, but there have been processes and decisions made all along the way that you're not even aware of, that you don't remember. Okay, so here we are now in 1991, and I don't think a person is born queer; I don't think every person is born queer. I think there may be some genetic propensity toward most things: music, having a good ear for music. I don't know if there are any queer genes, but if there are, they'll be discovered. So some of it might be biological; some of it might be learned; and some of it might be chosen. My position will probably change in a year or two, but that's where I'm at with it. Did I give you the analogy of the train and the tracks and the terrain as being the self?

ALK: No.

GEA: The train will stop at this way station, which might be Boston, and stay a few years and then get on the road again and stop at another way station. In this way station you were a heterosexual; in this way station you were a lesbian. You look back down the tracks and you look at your past and all the events in your life and your friends, and you're now looking at them through lesbian eyes. So you're reinterpreting the past.

When I became a lesbian, I looked back at my life and realized that all along I'd had these signals that I was one of them too. So, when I became a political lesbian and believed I had chosen that, had I really chosen it or had I been one all along but repressed it? When I was writing *Borderlands*, I had the lesbian perspective, but my thinking had not evolved to the place where I believed that when you realize that you like women, that you want to have primary, carnal relationships with women, that you can still make the choice to stay with men. Many of us have done that. You can become a lesbian and be a lesbian for twenty years and then decide that you want to be sexual with a man. I don't know if that changes your lesbian identity, but . . . you make a choice. If you know you're a lesbian and you're married and have kids, you say, "Okay, I'm going to be with my husband and I'll be a straight woman as much as I can and be with my kids." Or you can say, "I'm going to leave my husband; I'm going to come out as a lesbian and take this path," depending on how much courage you have. But I think that there are only certain places where you can make that choice, and those are the places of ambiguity, of change, where you're in nepantla—you can go either way. Once you're on this track, you're pretty much a lesbian and you think like a lesbian and you live with lesbians and your community is lesbians, and the heterosexual world is foreign and that's the path you and I—well, I don't know about you—but that's the path I'm on.

But I will get to these nepantla places where I have the choices. I can say, "I'm not going to be political anymore; I'm just going to retreat into my writing." I don't think I'll ever be that way, but people have made that choice. It's not that I'm invalidating what I said in *Borderlands*. That was my thinking then and I was in that particular track, but the train has kept going and I've stopped at other way stations. The last way station had to do with my class changes, going from a campesino working class into an intellectual, academic, artistic class. With the money and royalties and speaking engagements, I am now entering a middle class, which was like the nepantla space with the Coatlicue state right in the middle of it; it was so agonizing. And at the next way station I will look back at our conversation, and at *Borderlands* and *Prieta* and *Bridge* and *Haciendo caras* and whatever other books I write, and I will say, "I am now this identity." The old identities are still part of me: the straight woman is in me; the white woman is in me; the nonpolitical woman is in me. But basically my personality has always been a resisting personality, going against what's not fair. It wasn't fair the way my culture treated girls. It wasn't fair the way the white culture treats ethnic groups. So there's a strong sense in me that I'm going to fight against something because it's not fair.

ALK: You have the poem ["Del otro lado"] where you talk about "the other side"—always being on the other side—in *Compañeras*.[7] You also use that metaphor in *Borderlands*. What can you say about that?

GEA: It's almost like the differences in me from other women started at a very early age. When I was three months old, I started menstruating. The effect wasn't just psychological; it was also biological and physical. My body suffered. I was in pain. I had breasts when I was six years old—these same breasts that I have now—which my mother would wrap up so the little kids wouldn't notice. She would tie a little rag in my panties, so that if I bled it wouldn't be all over the place. And I had to make excuses at P.E. that I couldn't bathe with the other kids because they would see that I had pubic hair. So I was marked very early, and it was very painful for me to be so different because I already felt different because of my race and being a farmworker. In the valley if you worked the fields, you're a much lower Chicana than if you worked in a department store or in an office. It was a class thing. So there are already differences among women and between the different ethnic groups and white people. Those differences are painful. With me they really went all the way to the bone, the body. And because I was wide open as a child everything came in. People would say something in the wrong tone of voice and I would take it so personally that I would be devastated for the rest of the week. (I have a poem called "La vulva es una herida abierta/The Vulva Is an Open Wound." I'll give you a copy. I was going to include it last night at the reading, but when I decided that I wanted the audience to laugh rather than to cry, I decided not to use it. They would have gone away real sad.) I had very thin skin; everything came in.

ALK: How does your childhood go with being on the other side?

GEA: When I went to school, I saw that I was so different from the other kids—en masse—because I could pick up knowledge. They called me "the brain." I was a dumb Mexican who was smart. It was such a shock to the teachers because I was supposed to be dumb like the other kids. I always felt separate in school, and this was like a hundred percent Chicano with only the teachers being white. I already felt on the other side.

ALK: Separate, different? Not belonging?

GEA: Yes. Not belonging. Always on the other side. When I got to high school, it happened literally because I was placed in accelerated classes, and all the other Chicanos except one guy were in different classes. The only time we got together was in P.E., homeroom, and Health. But the white kids never spoke to me and the teachers never spoke to me. I'd sit in one corner, or in the middle, or in the front, or the back, and it didn't matter.

ALK: You were always on the other side.

GEA: I was always on the other side. The kids that would have been there for me in high school I couldn't really be friends with because I didn't spend the majority of my classes with them. I had a few peripheral friends, and I went to a consolidated school where people from the county were bussed in, so they were all strangers except for the kids who lived in the town. But then I went to college in an all girls' school—Texas Woman's University—where I first witnessed a lesbian experience: two women making love to each other. There were two dorm rooms with a connecting bath, and one day both of the bathroom doors were opened and there they were making out on the bed, two women naked. I was shocked and ran out of the bathroom. Then I had my first experience with an epileptic. I didn't know my roommate was an epileptic, and one day she just fell on the floor and was doing these strange things. But before she fell, she started coming toward me with her hands shaking and this *really* funny energy coming from her and this look in her eyes; I thought she wanted to strangle me. Nobody had explained it to me; I hadn't seen an epileptic before. All in the course of the same semester.

So I started looking at both kinds of queerness: the queerness of making love with another woman and this strange energy that a person could go into convulsions. I started connecting with differences then. I no longer felt like I was the only one on the other side. In some way I had an affinity to the queer women and to the epileptic woman. I realized that I wasn't the baddest little girl in the world. Before I thought that I was the worst, that there was something really wrong with me, that I must be so sinful to have this happen to me, that I must *deserve* to have this kind of pain and problem and that there was nobody else like me. Then I realized that there were other people not exactly like me but that had these so-called sicknesses; I started feeling better about being on the other side because now there were a few others on the other side. I already knew about the race and class stuff by then, but you can be working-class, middle-class, upper-class, and you can be sitting there and look perfectly healthy and normal; it's invisible. The epilepsy is also not noticeable until a person is going through it, and two lesbians walking down the street can pass. You can't tell unless they were making love or declared it in some way through their clothes or their lifestyle. But I always felt like my difference was visible, even though it was hidden—that somehow people could see I was marked, abnormal, subhuman, or whatever. And that mark, that seña, everybody could see—it was agonizing. So if I'm before an auditorium and I'm speaking, I still feel like I'm on the other side, even though I try to get rid of the lectern and not to have any barriers, and I try to be as open as I can. There's a little part of me that feels that I'm different.

ALK: You do have a certain vulnerability when you speak.

GEA: Some people choose to cloak themselves in a self-defensive way and act real cool. Or you can just be honest and say, "I'm vulnerable." We're all vulnerable up there on stage; it's just that some of us wear armor and some of us do not. I want to take as much of it off as I can. I know that I still have my shields.

ALK: Paula Gunn Allen describes homosexuals as "perverse" and defines "perversity" as "transformationality . . . the process of changing from one condition to another—*life-long* liminality."[8] It seems that you see homosexuality in a similar fashion: as *difference*, and because it's different, you can make these changes.

GEA: Sí. It's like saying, "Okay. If I am queer and I am different, then I'm going to make those differences strengths and not liabilities." It's going to be a pleasure, not a chore.

ALK: And because you're outside of certain cultural inscriptions, change becomes more possible?

GEA: Yes. It's almost like, "If I'm going to be hung, I might as well be hung for multiple deeds." Once you've transgressed—once you've crossed the line, broken the law—the punishment is the same if you do it for a few things or if you do it for many. (Probably it's not, but that's my rationalization.) If I've already broken one inscription, gone against one law and regulation, then I just have to gather up my courage and go against another one and another one and another one.

ALK: Allen also claims that dykes have both masculine and feminine energy. You say a similar thing in *Borderlands*, when you talk about homosexuals as being "hieros gamos," both male and female.

GEA: The hieros gamos comes from alchemy . . . an inner marriage of what they called the masculine force and the feminine force; the marriage of the two was called the "inner marriage, the hieros gamos." I'm not sure if there's such a thing as masculine and feminine energy now. And I'm not so sure that that's an essential thing we're born with; we're socialized into having male energy and female energy. We're socialized into believing in assertive "male" ways—a male way of walking, a male way of *thrusting* into space—and female ways of being receiving and nurturing and giving and all that. With us the femininity didn't take completely. Sometimes if the situation warrants for you thrusting out—forcing your words out because you're being excluded or oppressed—you have the energy to do it. And in other situations you will have the energy to be a receptacle, to just take things in. Right now women privilege the feminine and say the aggressive masculine is all bad. The men say femininity is inferior and *they're* superior. I think they're both wrong. It takes the two.

ALK: You're rejecting that either-or thinking.

GEA: Yeah. It's like my theory of identity: all these people are on the stage, and they take turns being center. In certain situations you don't need certain kinds of energy, you need other kinds. But when you're short and get in lines—like with me, I was always ignored by the white person or the man behind the counter. I had to learn to say, "EXCUSE ME. I WAS HERE FIRST." You don't do that in my culture; it's very bad for a woman to do that, but I've learned to go and ask.

ALK: In one of this week's workshops you distinguished between an "individual we" and a "collective we." What did you mean?

GEA: Because we're seen by the dominant culture as generic people, as a generic tribe, we've begun to see ourselves that way too—as a representative of a group rather than as individuals. When you're seen like that all your life, when you speak (at least when I speak), I find myself going from the personal I to the collective we. I know that it's politically incorrect to be representing other people, but in this particular chapter of my dissertation, "The Poet as Critic, The Poet as Theorist," I talk in more detail about why this is true. One reason is because there are so many people—women especially—who identify with the ethnic writer because that ethnic experience is not represented in the dominant literature. Women of color never see ourselves in these books; we don't see ourselves represented. So along comes Cherríe Moraga or me or any of the other Chicanas, and the Chicanas say, "Oh, that's *me* you're writing about," or "That happened to my mother." They really identify. What happens is that they start getting a sense of who we are, our mission, and the political work we have to do by reading women of color. We no longer look toward the so-called politicos—the politicians, the left-ists—the *guys* that before were telling us what's wrong with the family, or with capitalism, or the economic system. Instead, the women are looking at women of color, and not just Chicanas but also Audre Lorde, Leslie Silko, Paula Gunn Allen, the Asian writers. If we have commonalities with them, if we've had similar experiences we *identify*, so part of the reading process is formulating an identity for the reader. Also, if we don't happen to agree, to identify with certain passages of a book or with certain people or with certain books—we *dis-identify*. Dis-identifying is also a way of formulating an identity . . . by saying, "That's not me." We find ourselves represented or not represented. I am a reader as a well as a writer, and that process happens to me; it happens to all women who read. So as a writer and as a reader I know that when I say "we," sometimes it's a singular "we" that I use in order to make a connection with the readers. But sometimes it's a plural "we."

ALK: Meaning speaking for?

GEA: For *them*. Speaking to them and for them and with them. It's much more speaking *with* them, than *for* them.

ALK: Doris Sommer has done some work on that—in Third World testimonials the women speak *within* rather than *for* the community.

GEA: Yes. I see it more as a dialogue between the author, the text, and the reader. And then if the reader happens to write about the reading, it's a dialogue between the author, the text, the reader, and the reader-as-writer.

ALK: And do you learn as you're writing?

GEA: Yes. That's when I get insights. Sometimes I get them when I'm speaking, but mostly when I'm writing. I discover what I'm trying to say as the writing progresses, and this is more true with fiction and poetry because I allow more freedom for those words to come. Whereas in a creative essay—yes, it's creative and I have some freedom, but also I know that I'm theorizing.

ALK: When you write a creative essay, do you know where you're going to end up?

GEA: No. And this is the problem with the graduate classes I've taken. They want an abstract, an idea, or an outline. I don't work that way. For example, in writing *Llorona* they expected me to finish one chapter at a time, and I said, "This is the way I write: I write all the chapters at the same time and bring them up through the second draft, the third draft all together." So I don't have just one finished thing because I don't know where things are going to go. They don't understand that process because they plan a book: they perfect the introduction, then the first chapter, then the second. . . . I don't work that way. All the pieces have to be on the table and I'm adding and subtracting pieces and I'm shifting them around. So there tends to be a lot of repetition in my work. I put the same thing in two or three chapters because ultimately I don't know where it's going to end up, and that frustrates them. So I made that a part of the process, I talk about the "repetition compulsion."

ALK: Would you say that it's repetition with variation by the time you get to the final draft?

GEA: Yes. You start at the center and you spiral around. When you come back to that point where that particular idea is mentioned, you touch on it, but you extend it in some way—you go off on another tangent, you elaborate on it; I might put it in Spanish, or whatever—so that it gets more and more complex. But because with a computer it's very easy to copy, I may have the exact same passage in another chapter, which I'll later rework to fit that chapter.

ALK: I do that too.

GEA: You do that too? And I thought I was one of the few who had that process because I do the same thing with the novel. It was hard for my publisher to understand. She understands that now. I can't really finish "She Ate Horses" until I finish some of the other stuff.

ALK: You're learning as you write; you have to figure out where things are going to go. It wouldn't work if you just tried to finish one thing. I think you get a better whole by doing it your way.

GEA: I think it becomes more integral, more of a single entity rather than disparate parts. The parts are still there but they're . . .

ALK: Different?

GEA: Yeah. And I have to have a central metaphor like La Llorona or Prieta. Within that central metaphor are these things like working with the interface between the different realities—nepantla space. Nepantla is kind of an elaboration of [the word] "Borderlands." The little "b" is the actual southwest borderlands or any borderlands between two cultures, but when I use the capital "B," it's like mestiza with a capital "M." It's a metaphor, not an actuality.

ALK: A metaphor that doesn't apply specifically to *one* thing but that can apply to many things?

GEA: Sí. I found that people were using "Borderlands" in a more limited sense than I had meant it. So to elaborate on the psychic and emotional borderlands, I'm now using "nepantla"—which is the same thing. But with nepantla there's more of a connection to the spirit world. There's more of a connection to the world after death and to psychic spaces like between air and water. As I mentioned before, there is the world of external reality and behind it is the other world—el mundo de mas allá—so there's more of a spiritual, psychic, supernatural, and indigenous connection to Borderlands by using the word nepantla.

Notes

1. Due to copyright concerns, we have followed the 1987 edition of *Borderlands* in italicizing all Spanish words that appear in the poems. However, it is important to note that in her later writings Anzaldúa no longer chose to italicize Spanish or other so-called foreign words, preferring not to mimic our culture's official ranking of one "majority" language over others. In accord with the poet's preference, we have not italicized such words and phrases in this introduction and in the following interview (—ed.).

2. See Anzaldúa's discussion of her writing process in Lunsford's interview, "Toward a Mestiza Rhetoric," and in *Borderlands/La frontera* (—ed.).

3. Writers of autohistoria-teoría combine cultural and personal biographies with memoir, history, storytelling, and myth, creating interwoven individual and collective identities. Anzaldúa discusses autohistoria-teoría in "now let us shift" in *this bridge we call home*. See also Neile's essay in Keating, *EntreMundos/AmongWorlds* (—ed.).

4. Linda Garber explains, "The book began as a straightforward collection of poems. . . . Setting out to write a ten-page introduction to the poems, Anzaldúa instead produced ninety-eight pages, . . . the 'poetic prose' masterpiece that is meant when reference is made to *Borderlands/La frontera*." "Spirit, Culture, Sex," 217.

5. Anzaldúa, *Making Face*, 142–48.

6. Anzaldúa here refers to a short story cycle she had been working on since the mid-1970s and had planned to publish in the near future. Prieta is the main character; *Prieta, the Dark One* was one of several working titles. These stories will be published at a later date and can be viewed at the Gloria Evangelina Anzaldúa Manuscript Collection in the Benson Library, University of Texas, Austin (—ed.).

7. See Juanita Ramos (—ed.).

8. Caputi, "Interview with Paula Gunn Allen," 56.

—*Cihuatlyotl*, Woman Alone

Many years   I have fought off your hands, *Raza*
father mother   church your rage at my desire to be
with myself, alone.   I have learned
to erect barricades   arch my back against
you   thrust back fingers, sticks   to
shriek no   to kick and claw   my way out of
your heart   And as I grew   you hacked away
at the pieces of me   that   were different
attached your tentacles   to my face and breasts
put a lock between my legs.   I had to do it,
Raza,   turn my back on your crookening finger
beckoning beckoning   your   soft brown
landscape, tender *nopalitos*.   Oh, it was hard,
Raza   to cleave flesh from flesh   I risked
us both   bleeding to death.   It took   a long
time   but   I learned   to let
your values   roll off   my body   like water
those I swallow to stay alive   become tumors
in my belly.   I refuse to be taken over   by
things   people   who fear that hollow
aloneness   beckoning   beckoning.   No self,
only race *vecindad familia*.   My soul   has always
been yours   one spark   in the roar of your fire.
We Mexicans are   collective animals.   This I
accept   but my life's work   requires autonomy
like oxygen.   This lifelong battle has ended,
Raza.   I don't need to flail against   you.
Raza india mexicana norteamericana,   there's nothing more you can chop off   or graft on me that
will change my soul.   I remain who I am, multiple
and one   of the herd, yet not of it.   I walk

on the ground of my own being   browned and
hardened by the ages.   I am fully formed   carved
by the hands of the ancients,   drenched with
the stench of today's headlines.   But my own
hands whittle   the final work   me.

—Del otro lado

She looks at the Border Park fence
posts are stuck into her throat, her navel,
barbwire is shoved up her cunt.
Her body torn in two, half a woman on the other side
half a woman on this side, the right side
And she went to the North American university,
excelled in the Gringo's tongue
learned to file in folders.
But she remembered the other half
strangled in Aztec villages, in Mayan villages, in Incan villages.

She watched her land made hostile
and she a stranger, an 80,000 year old illegal alien
Go back to where you came from, she is told.
She is spanked for speaking her natal tongue
She is laughed at for eating her mother's tortillas and chiles
She is ridiculed for wearing her bright shawls.
The ancient dances beaten back inside her,
the old song choked back into her throat

At night when no one is looking
she sings the song of the wounded
the wind carries her wails into the cities and the deserts.

The half of her that's on the other side
walks lost through the land
dropping bits of herself, a hand,
a shoulder, a chunk of hair.
Her pieces scattered over the deserts,
the mountains and valley.
Her mute voice whispers through grass stems.
She sings the song of the wounded,
she howls her pain to the moon
no time to grieve, no time to heal
Hers is a struggle of the flesh, a struggle of borders.
An inner war.

She remembers
The horror in her sister's voice,
"Eres una de las otras,"
The look in her mother's face as she says,
"I am so ashamed, I will never
be able to raise my head in this pueblo."
The mother's words are barbs digging into her flesh.
De las otras. Cast out. Untouchable.
"But I'm me," she cries, "I've always been me."
"Don't bring your queer friends into my house,
my land, the planet. Get away.
Don't contaminate us, get away."

Away, she went away.
But every place she went
they pushed her to the other side
and that other side pushed her to the other side
of the other side of the other side
Kept in the shadows of other.
No right to sing, to rage, to explode.
You should be ashamed of yourself.
People are starving in Ethiopia,

dying in Guatemala and Nicaragua
while you talk about gay rights and orgasms.
Pushed to the edge of the world
there she made her home on the edge
of towns, of neighborhoods, blocks, houses,
Always pushed toward the other side.
In all lands alien, nowhere citizen.
Away, she went away
but each place she went
pushed her to the other side, al otro lado.

—Don't Give In, *Chicanita*
para Missy Anzaldúa

Don't give in *mi prietita*
tighten your belt, endure.
Your lineage is ancient,
your roots like those of the mesquite
firmly planted, digging underground
toward that current, the soul of *tierra madre*—
your origin.

Yes, *m'ijita*, your people were raised *en los ranchos*
here in the Valley near the Rio Grande
you descended from the first cowboy, the *vaquero*,
right smack in the border
in the age before the Gringo when Texas was Mexico
over *en los ranchos los Vergeles y Jesús María*—
Dávila land.
Strong women reared you:
my sister, your mom, my mother and I.

And yes, they've taken our lands.
Not even the cemetery is ours now
where they buried Don Urbano
your great-great-grandfather.
Hard times like fodder we carry
with curved backs we walk.

But they will never take that pride
of being *mexicana*-Chicana-*tejana*
nor our Indian woman's spirit.
And when the Gringos are gone—
see how they kill one another—
here we'll still be like the horned toad and the lizard
relics of an earlier age
survivors of the First Fire Age—*el Quinto Sol.*

Perhaps we'll be dying of hunger as usual
but we'll be members of a new species
skin tone between black and bronze
second eyelid under the first
with the power to look at the sun through naked eyes.
And alive *m'ijita*, very much alive.

Yes, in a few years or centuries
la Raza will rise up, tongue intact
carrying the best of all the cultures.
That sleeping serpent,
rebellion-(r)evolution, will spring up.
Like old skin will fall the slave ways of
obedience, acceptance, silence.
Like serpent lightning we'll move, little woman.
You'll see.

   —TRANSLATED FROM THE SPANISH BY THE AUTHOR

—Interface
for Frances Doughty

She'd always been there
         occupying the same room.
It was only when I looked
         at the edges of things
my eyes going wide watering,
         objects blurring.
Where before there'd only been empty space
         I sensed layers and layers,
felt the air in the room thicken.
         Behind my eyelids a white flash
a thin noise.
         That's when I could see her.

         Once I accidentally ran my arm
through her body
         felt heat on one side of my face.
         She wasn't solid.
The shock pushed me against the wall.
A torrent of days swept past me
         before I tried to "see" her again.
She had never wanted to be flesh she told me
         until she met me.
At first it was hard to stay
         on the border between
the physical world
         and hers.
It was only there at the interface
    that we could see each other.
See? We wanted to touch.
         I wished I could become

pulsing color, pure sound, bodiless as she.
        It was impossible, she said
        for humans to become noumenal.

What does it feel like, she asked
        to inhabit flesh,
wear blood like threads
        constantly running?
I would lie on the bed talking
        she would hover over me.
Did I say talk?
        We did not use words.
I pushed my thoughts toward her.
        Her "voice" was a breath of air
stirring my hair
        filling my head.
Once Lupe my roommate
        walked right through her
dangling the car keys.
        I felt Leyla shiver.
I named her Leyla,
        a pure sound.

I don't know when I noticed
        that she'd begun to glow,
to look more substantial
      than the blurred furniture.
It was then I felt a slight touch,
        her hand—a tendril of fog—
on the sheets where she'd lain
        a slight crease, a dampness,
a smell between candles and skin.
        You're changing, I told her.
        A yearning deluged me—
her yearning.

That's when I knew
she wanted to be flesh.
She stayed insubstantial day after day
so I tried to blur
my borders, to float, become pure sound.
But my body seemed heavier,
more inert.

I remember when she changed.
I could hear the far away slough of traffic
on the Brooklyn-Queens Expressway,
the people downstairs were playing salsa.
We lay enclosed   by margins, hems,
where only we existed.
She was stroking   stroking my arms
my legs, marveling at their solidity,
the warmth of my flesh, its smell.
Then I touched her.
Fog, she felt like dense fog,
the color of smoke.
She glowed, my hands paled then gleamed
as I moved them over her.
Smoke-fog pressing against my eyelids
my mouth, ears, nostrils, navel.
A cool tendril pressing between my legs
entering.
Her finger, I thought
but it went on and on.
At the same time
an iciness touched my anus,
and she was in
and in and in
my mouth opening
I wasn't scared just astonished
rain drummed against my spine

turned to steam as it rushed through my veins
light flickered over me from toe to crown.
   Looking down my body I saw
   her forearm, elbow and hand
sticking out of my stomach
   saw her hand slide in.
I wanted no food no water nothing
   just her—pure light sound inside me.
My roommate thought I was
   having an affair.
I was "radiant," she said.
   Leyla had begun to swell
I started hurting a little.
   When I started cramping
she pushed out
   her fingers, forearm, shoulder.
Then she stood before me,
   fragile skin, sinews tender as baby birds
   and as transparent.
She who had never eaten
   began to hunger.
I held a cup of milk to her mouth,
   put her hand on my throat
made swallowing motions.
   I spooned mashed banana into her bird mouth,
hid the baby food under the bed.
   One day my roommate asked
who was staying in my room,
   she'd heard movements.
A friend recovering from a contagious
   skin disease, I said.
She ran out saying, I'm going to the Cape
   indefinitely. See you.
   We had the house to ourselves.
I taught her how to clean herself,

to flush.
She would stand before the mirror
        watching her ears, long and diaphanous,
begin to get smaller, thicker.
        She spent a lot of time at the window.
Once I caught her imitating
the shuffle of the baglady.
        No, like this, I told her.
Head up, shoulders back.
        I brought in the TV.
This is how humans love, hate, I said.
        Once we sat on the stoop
watching a neighbor sweep the sidewalk.
        Hello, he yelled, hello, I yelled back,
eh-oh, she whispered.
        Watch my lips, Ley-la.
Say it, Ley-la.
        Good. I love you.
Ah uff oo, she said.
        Soon Leyla could pass,
go for milk at the bodega, count change.
        But no matter how passionately we made
love
        it was never like before
she'd taken on skin and bone.

        Do you ever want to go back, I asked her.
No, it's slower here and I like that.
        I hate summers in NYC, I told her,
wish it was winter already.
        The temperature dropped 10 degrees 20
and when a chill wind began to blow in Brooklyn
        I told her to stop
messing with the cycles that affected others.
        I watched what I said

and let Leyla run the place.
  She had snow in the livingroom
and a tree in the bathtub.
  Nights I lit the illegal fireplace.
Once when reaching toward a high shelf,
  I wished I was taller.
When my head touched the ceiling
  I had to yell at her to stop,
  reverse.
How do you do it, I asked her.
  You do it, too, she said,
my species just does it faster,
  instantly, merely by thinking it.

The first time she rode the subway
  I had to drag her out.
I suppose it was the noise,
  the colors flashing by, the odd people
that held her open-mouthed gaze.
  I had to do a gig in L.A.,
speak at a conference, was short on cash,
  but she wanted to come.
She walked past the flight attendants
  didn't even have to hide in the lavatory.
She laughed at my amazement, said
  humans only saw what they were told to see.
Last Christmas I took her home to Texas.
  Mom liked her.
Is she a lez, my brothers asked.
  I said, No, just an alien.
Leyla laughed.

—Poets Have Strange Eating Habits
for Irenita Klepfisz

Dark windowless   no moon glides
across the nightsky
       I coax and whip the balking mare
          to the edge
            peel the scabs from her wounds
       Her body caves into itself
       through the hole
       my mouth

In the border between dusk and dawn
I listen to frozen thumpings, my soul
       Should I jump   face tumbling
       down   the steps of the temple
       heart offered up to the midnightsun

She takes that plunge
   off the high cliff
       hooves tumbling in the vagrant air
          head tucked between her legs
            a cold wind tugging at her back
cutting tears from my eyes
the obsidian knife, air
the nightsky   alone   alone

       She spreads out her legs
       to catch the wind
          rushes to fill *el abismo*
          the nightride has ripped open
          its hunger rimmed with teeth
       I feed it my throat   my hands
       let it glut itself on me

till it's pregnant with me.
       Wounding is a deeper healing.

Suspended in fluid sky
I, eagle fetus, live serpent
          feathers growing out of my skin
          the buffeting wind
          the rock walls rearing up
          the Earth.

I bend my knees, break the fall
      no arm snapping
      a stunned animal
I burrow deep into myself
pull the emptiness in
its hollows chisel my face
growing thin   thinner
eyesockets   empty
tunneling here   tunneling there
the slither of snakes
their fangs pierce my flesh

falling

into faceless air
Taking the plunge an act as
routine as cleaning my teeth.

The Earth parts
I hit the bottom of the chasm
peer over the edge
          coax and whip the balking mare
          take that plunge again
          jumping off cliffs   an addiction
flailing   pummeling

flesh into images
sticking feathers
      in   my arms
          slithering into holes
              with rattlesnakes

dark windowless no moon glides
across the nightsky
the maw opens wide   I slip inside
Taking deep breaths   eyes closed
me la tragó   *todita*

NOTE: *me la tragó todita*—I swallow it whole

42

mei-mei berssenbrugge

INTRODUCTION

The daring paradoxes of Mei-mei Berssenbrugge's writing position it among those postmodern poetries most difficult to define. It is an intensely lyrical poetry and yet reads like spare prose, the sentence and its sequence more formally dominant than the verse line. It is a poetry that is socially and culturally specific and yet refuses to celebrate any one cultural dogma or system of belief. It is entirely abstract and anti-autobiographical; and yet it is viscerally descriptive of the light upon western landscapes, empirically descriptive of the material body, and dramatically engaged with the intimacy of human relations.

These paradoxes are reflected in Berssenbrugge's unusual social and aesthetic positioning among contemporary American poets. Most readers would associate Berssenbrugge with her interest in poetic abstraction, as well as the relationship between visual abstraction and the avant-garde poetic movements that emerged through the New York School and the later Language movement. Traveling frequently to New York City, Berssenbrugge engaged in flourishing movements of abstract visual art, poetry, and performance art and became influenced by New York School poets John Ashbery and James Sherry, and, later, other New York School and Language poets, including Barbara Guest, Anne Waldman, Charles Bernstein, and the visual artist Susan Bee. She also enjoyed dialogue with West Coast avant-gardists like Leslie Scalapino, about whom she speaks with admiration in this interview. Yet Berssenbrugge is also profoundly connected to the multicultural poetry movement that began in the 1970s, and her professional associations and friendships with writers like Leslie Marmon Silko, Ishmael Reed, the theater director Frank Chin, and his wife, the political activist Kathleen Chang, led to many multimedia collaborations with artists in theater and dance.

Berssenbrugge identifies her single most significant experience as the move to the United States and "to English" as a one-year-old from her mother's native Beijing, where the poet was born in 1947. Cultural-linguistic dualism is complicated by the diverse family of academic achievers from which she comes: the daughter of a Harvard-educated Chinese mathematician, Berssenbrugge's mother was herself a mathematician (highly unusual for a woman of that epoch). Berssenbrugge's father was the American son of Dutch emigrants. He met the poet's mother in Chongqing while he was working at the American Embassy as a code breaker after World War II, and he went on to pursue graduate degrees in Far Eastern Studies at Berkeley and at Harvard (hence the family's move to the U.S.).

Berssenbrugge was raised in suburban Massachusetts. She received her B.A. from Reed College and her M.F.A. from Columbia University. She then settled in northern New Mexico. As she recalls in this interview, for a time she worked as a caretaker and companion for Georgia O'Keeffe. In 1984, she garnered an American Book Award of the Before Columbus Foundation for *The Heat Bird*. In 1987, Berssenbrugge married the multimedia artist Richard Tuttle; that same year, the two collaborated on *Hiddenness*. Since Berssenbrugge's marriage (and the birth of a daughter, Martha), her books reflect often on family life: *Sphericity* (with Tuttle, 1993), *Empathy* (1997), and *Nest* (2003). But while acknowledging the influence of family in her work, Berssenbrugge insists that her poetry does not reflect actual life conditions or domestic facts. She has developed a "collage" method of writing informed both by visual artifacts (pictures, photographs) and her readings in critical theory, art, and science. She cautions the reader against a false clarity or too-facile "understanding," for she is most interested in "the mysteries." It is perhaps within the tension between understanding and its impossibility, those "mysteries" unfolding in the drama of human perception, that readers might best experience Berssenbrugge's poetic focus and force.

The following conversations with the poet-critic Laura Hinton took place in New York City in June and October 2003.

TWO CONVERSATIONS WITH MEI-MEI BERSSENBRUGGE
by Laura Hinton

JUNE 3, 2003
We have just had lunch in my Manhattan neighborhood near 28th Street and Third, where conversation topics have ranged from dogs to desserts but not literature. The cassette player on now, I have just asked Mei-mei a question concerning the relation of Mei-mei's writing to Theresa Hak Kyung Cha and Cha's revolutionary prose-poem book, Dictée.

MEI-MEI BERSSENBRUGGE: I'm trying to remember when I read *Dictée*. Before writing *Four Year Old Girl*, I was reading some of the cultural identity texts about nomads and the subaltern. I think Theresa Cha wrote this work before such studies became fashionable. When I read *Dictée*, her passion attracted me, but also the sense that she was carving meaning with each word in the moment, in a way that was almost sculptural, a physical art. I was interested in how she seemed to do that. It may have helped that she was multilingual. English was not her primary language. So she had a kind of triangulation on it, making the passion into something concrete. Her persona of someone who experienced a loss of place and a loss of culture I thought was beautifully expressed and something I thought I could identity with.

LAURA HINTON: Speak a bit more about that identification, going back to your own origins. You were born in China?

MB: Yes, I was born in Beijing, where my mother grew up. I came to the U.S. when I was one. I feel very strongly that my first language was Chinese—my mother tongue. All the linguistic structures were warming up in Chinese. I believe one experience that made me into a poet was switching from Chinese to

English, because then you see everything is relational. I think of poetry as a set of proportions, equivalences. And you see that language consists of these equivalences.

LH: So at the base of language you perceived early on this essential tension: of it meaning everything and nothing, that language is a rather mobile frame, in terms of referentiality. You believe that you intuited these aspects of language at a very early age?

MB: I had to get that understood, because otherwise, I wasn't going to be able to express myself.

LH: Did you go through a period of a certain loss when you made that shift in language? Have your parents ever noted to you anything particular about this time?

MB: I don't think my mother noticed, because we were going through our loss at the same time.

LH: Let's talk more about your poetry's origins within the context of your own family of origin, and your early language discovery (and loss). Were you writing at a young age? How did you begin as a writer?

MB: My mother walked with me on the bank of the Charles River when I was three or four years old. The grass was thick with dandelions. I remember thinking, "These yellow dandelions are *like* a big yellow blanket." This was an important moment of revelation; I felt something amazing had just happened, which I can still feel today.

I identify with my Chinese family, a family of spirited academics. My maternal grandfather took the imperial examinations around 1912 and traveled to Boston to study at Harvard. His fellow classmates in Boston included Madame Chiang Kai-shek and Madame Sun Yat-sen. My grandfather eschewed politics and became dean of mathematics at Beijing University. He had given his land away before the revolution. My grandmother, from Suzhou, studied with her brothers at home and in the early 1900s insisted on a college education, for which she traveled quite far overland by herself. To protest Japanese occupation, my mother, a mathematician, walked two thousand miles from Beijing to Chongqing, where she met and married my father, who was in charge of the code room at the American Embassy at the end of World War II. After I was born, we came to Berkeley and then Cambridge, Massachusetts, where my father took degrees at Harvard.

I know I studied creative writing at Barnard, but the first poetry course I remember was with Galway Kinnell at Reed College. I think it was his first teaching job. He brought many poets to Reed, and they stayed at our [student residence (—ed.)] house. So we had quite a poetry education. We had Robert Bly, Robert Duncan. We cooked and gave parties after the readings. At Reed we were required to write a thesis, and I had a mental block against expository writing. So I submitted some poems to Michael Harper for a creative thesis. When he accepted them, something mystical happened, [realizing] that my poems could be received in the world. Or that they communicated on a certain wave. After that, I lived for poetry.

LH: This block about expository writing, can you say something more about that?

MB: I think it's against whatever my brain structures are. And I can't overcome that. I can't write a paragraph.

LH: Perhaps because expository writing represents a certain kind of linearity associated with a Western-type logic that your own style of poetry writing seems very much against?

MB: Yes, I think it's the linearity—and also the voice. But I'm also interested right now in a type of discourse that is very direct and clear—"like" expository.

My friend Leslie [Marmon] Silko gave me a Courtney Love song, "I Want to Be the Girl Who Has the Most Cake." It struck me as so clear and so simple.

LH: Leslie Silko, by the way, is one of my favorite narrative writers—certainly my favorite Native American writer. But your work is very different. It's very interesting that you two are friends.

MB: We've been close since the early 1970s. We have different aesthetics and different points of view. Very different experiences. She's gifted at humor. The pueblo culture in New Mexico is sophisticated and civilized, and one of their instruments is humor, often understated humor. A purpose is to keep knitting the group together.

LH: Her aesthetic is chiefly driven by the storytelling mode. It's plot centered and descriptive, engaging in those traditions of narration. I think of your poetry as dealing with perspective. There is some description there, but any description of "reality" is marked by the issues of perspective, the shiftings of perspective—as if you're dancing around different problems of perspective and never satisfied with one way of looking at a landscape or objects in space or relationships with people.

And that is quite a different thing than, say, a brilliant story about Native American life in a book by Leslie Silko.

MB: That's where I think changing from one language to another set me on my course. But Leslie is a major influence. We met at a writing conference when we were in our twenties. She describes an ethos with many different layers of reality and irony. Also, Leslie gave me my first book of philosophy, Wittgenstein's *Remarks on Color*, which she had received from her friend Larry McMurtry. She started me on a journey: first Wittgenstein, then twentieth-century French philosophy, then dialogues with Robert Nozick, and, later, Gayatri Chakravorty Spivak, with whom I studied. Parallel to these investigations was a passionate involvement with the light, culture, and landscape of northern New Mexico, where I have lived since the early seventies, and my experiences with Georgia O'Keeffe and Agnes Martin.

LH: One of the things that attracts me about your poetry *is* its interest in color and the ethereal desertscapes that appear and disappear, rise and fall with the light, desert which I became deeply connected to as a child growing up in the West. The subtle—and I would add, philosophical—registers of color of the desert permeate much of your poetry. There's this issue about light and color. It's almost as if you are making a visual effect, but it's a verbal one. I experience the visual that way in your poetry—almost in a primal way, not a "translation" effect, through language. This authenticity and yet complexity very much attracts me to your work.

MB: Looking at the landscape of New Mexico was central to me for a long time. In my book *Nest*, the visual is not as prominent, although I wouldn't mind if it came back.

LH: Let me now ask you a slightly different set of questions. In Rae Armantrout's essay "Feminist Poetics and the Meaning of Clarity," she argues against the idea that women writers are less experimental and more traditional by nature, that they supposedly need more plot and narration in order to describe the conditions of their social oppression. Rae argues against that point, which had been suggested by other writers—all of them men, I think—saying that women are actually very attracted to an experimental kind of writing that rebukes this set of conventions. She questions the "meaning of clarity." This has to do with the poetic discourses of the academy, the institution of "Creative Writing," people studying Contemporary Literature, the mainstream forms of modern writing. She suggests that women are instinctive "outsiders" to these conventions.

MB: Yes, I would even say that women have an essentially more fragmented approach to writing. Just being the outsider gives you more freedom to see the fragments. I remember years ago Kathleen Fraser saying that women with children have to do this and that—it's more natural for them to pay attention in fragments. I've heard people say that to portray fragments is actually more naturalistic. If we sit here, for example, and people walk by, talking, and you record what we say and they say in patches, that's actually more representational than a single narrative line.

LH: So going back to this issue of "clarity." Take the writing of Leslie Silko, for example. Her writing is following those traditional representational structures that are considered part of a "clear" reader-writer contract, right?

MB: I wonder if that, for her, is really part of her social commitment. She has a deep commitment to people without power. Also, I question the word "traditional" as applied to Leslie. The clarity of her narrative line may not be of a tradition we are familiar with.

LH: Well, that's the argument that Rae Armantrout is countering. She's actually responding to her friend Ron Silliman's argument, that women, like other oppressed groups of people, need the conventions of narrative to speak at all. She says that we, as women, have a connection to alternative rather than conventional terms of discourse, which may be patriarchally-ideologically infused and inescapably so. That women have a different relation to the symbolic. What is your own position on this? In your writing, where do you see yourself? Because I believe that you, too, are a socially aware writer, on many different levels. What you are doing with perspective is very political for me, because perspective is situational, and that shifting situation is the nature of politics, whether you're in a room of people in some kind of institution, or any group, or the family—maybe I'm answering my own question—

MB: I like what you're saying.

LH: Where do you position yourself with regard to "the group," politically? And what kind of relation do you wish to build with your reader?

MB: I have deep feeling for the group, deep longing, and I have inner drive for my work. Generally, I've let my inner drive dictate what the next moment will be. I trust that inner drive's assessment of the reader. At the same time, I want to be open to and express the situation of my culture. I feel that audience extends out like a web. A reader can carry the influence of my poem to another person without that person necessarily knowing the poem itself. I also feel karma works in the proliferation of one's influence or expression. But I don't think understanding is that important. I think there are mysteries. Things can set other things in motion that can set yet other things in motion. Without understanding.

OCTOBER 2003

Mei-mei Berssenbrugge has just given a public reading at the City College of New York, where I teach. Now we are sitting around two large tables, with about twenty other people, most of whom are young men and women, aspiring writers or teachers in New York City, students of my graduate class, "Experimental Women's Writing."

LH: One of the things we've been discussing, Mei-mei, in class, is the use of the term "experimental." It's in the title of our course here at City College. But how do we define "experimental"? A lot of us are bothered by this term—and yet we use it because we lack another term that can identify a writing that works against tradition. (The term "innovative" is sometimes used, but it also seems problematic.)

We read your book *Empathy* as a class assignment. Your work is an interesting case in terms of being "experimental." Which it is, and yet, the work doesn't fit neatly into any such category of "experimental" as currently available to us. In class, we talk about the way "experimental" writing really should confront readers with what we understand and do not understand. We spoke last time together about Rae Armantrout's essay on "clarity." She asks this brilliant rhetorical question: "Is the world clear?" No, the world is not very clear (it seems increasingly less so). When your work is included in classes like ours or in books that use the term "experimental" (like the book I coedited with Cynthia Hogue, *We Who Love to Be Astonished*, on experimental women's writing practice), do you feel the term properly registers some quality in the nature of your work?

MB: I'm generally delighted to be collected in these books because I like my company. But I had a friend who said, "I'm not an experimental artist because I know what I'm doing." I have a natural interest in new forms because I like to follow where the energy goes. If something loses energy, then you try to find a form that embraces where that energy went. Eventually, this kind of work will no longer be called "experimental."

One thing that would qualify my work as "innovative" is my interest in abstraction. I explore abstraction in poetry. Richard [Tuttle] was describing a Goya painting he saw the other day—the little boy in a red suit with a bird cage on one side and a cat on the other. There's a sense that this is a representational painting, boy, bird cage, and cat. But Goya selected and *placed* that bird cage. Why did he want that there? The cat and bird cage create a kind of abstraction. They are formally innovative objects you can recognize.

LH: Here's a question that one of my students would like me to ask: "Would it be possible to write a meaningful experimental poem today without dealing with a dichotomy of the self?" [The student, Mimi Allen, gives additional clarification, suggesting that her definition of this "dichotomy of the self" is an explicitly *female* self that has an interior and an exterior, which are not the same. This "split" in female identity is reflective, the student explains, of women's social condition.]

MB: You mean a kind of unity? I have an ideal that there exists a poem like that—the way a bird opens its mouth and sings. Even though I can't "sing," I imagine that's possible. But also with inside and outside, woman and not-woman—these don't necessarily need to be dichotomies. They can also be continuities.

LH: So what do you feel is the principal goal of your work in terms of this "unity," aesthetically?

MB: I would say the ethos and aesthetic of my poetry aspire to be holistic, continuous, or one thing. I intuit an unknown edge of alive language exploring a question, perhaps an existential question, but to which is attached strong feeling. And perhaps this can become a beautiful, formed energy nexus of a poem.

LH: This is going to lead me to a question that jumps well beyond my imagined trajectory of questions, which once had a linear logic—a false logic. I recently saw Leslie Scalapino in San Francisco.

MB: She is a good poet.

LH: I mentioned to her that I had been reading a lot of your work and that you had also told me once—maybe a year ago—that people had been telling you and Leslie that you had much in common as poets—

MB: —when we were young—

LH: —yes, and that you and Leslie encountered each other and told each other, humorously, that it wasn't true, that, in fact, you were very different kind[s] of poets.

MB: Yes, we said, "I don't think my writing's like yours!" [*Laughter.*]

LH: So in my recent conversation with Leslie, I said to her that I *do* think there's something in both writings that's evocative, one of the other. Yet I couldn't identify what it was. Leslie told me that she agreed, that both of your poetries are interested in perception, and that they suggest an "inside and outside" existing simultaneously at once, that there was a sense of simultaneity in the writing and its object. I thought to myself, Yes! *That* is a facet of the writing that makes both poetries so revolutionary, to a Western sensibility, at least.

MB: We are both influenced by Asian philosophy. [The non-Western] is something that we identify with. Also, we're interested in phenomena. I don't know if that's the same as perception. I think she's more explicit and, actually, successful [about her dealing with phenomena]. But we each also connect that phenomenology with Asian timelessness. Each of us is socially committed, so we put that in the work as well.

LH: Almost as if the work is produced out of this multiplicity of vision that refuses to be a commodity served up on the market menu. (This goes back to the issue of "clarity." What is "clear" is what we are *used to perceiving* as "clear," according to marketplace value.)

About the timelessness: there is that alternative sense of time and space that infects the structure of the poem/poetry series itself. To extrapolate a piece or a line from your work—in the work of either one of you—you just can't. It's part of the timelessness of the "series."

One fascination some of us writing scholarship have is hybrid genres, those kinds of poetries that can't be defined by traditional categories of lyric, or narrative, the ballad, the epic—which are supposed to be so distinct. I call this kind of poetry work "intergenre" writing, which is kind of a poet's prose, and yet more. Harryette Mullen has called it "the mongrel text." Mullen's idea of this kind of hybrid poetry is that there are different registers of language, cultures—high and low—spliced and interlaced together textually. For example, in her book *Muse & Drudge*, which our class just read, we noticed the use of the Roman poet Callimachus next to Sapphire (a figure from *Amos 'n Andy*), as well as uses of the Greek poet Sappho. And we noticed the movement in and out of languages and registers of discourse, like the blues.

Since your book *Empathy*, you also seem to be writing a kind of hybrid "poet's prose." The writing remains very lyrical and yet breaks from lyric tradition at the same time by these interruptions through hybrid texts. I am fascinated, for example, by your use of the word "et cetera" in your recent book *Nest*. It leaves "lyric" diction. And there are other colloquial, speechlike elements in your newer poetry. You pay attention to the way it might be spoken and heard. How do you perceive your poetry as "hybrid" text, as a type of writing breaking down/recombining literary genres and discourses?

MB: One of my subjects is culture, the textile of our experience of contemporary culture. I was close to the early multicultural movement in the 1970s. Ishmael Reed influenced me a lot. He championed using brand names and gossip in fiction. I learned to ask where is the inherent interest? Some things are just more interesting than other things. I guess I wouldn't call the poetry a hybrid, because I like to think of it as one kind of surface. Now people take parts of things and a text can take its meaning from its context or its intention. It's a more complicated world now.

LH: You're describing postmodernism in a very eloquent manner.

MB: Yes. I don't like to call it "post." There's something very complicated about textures, and they are not about a single set of values or a single point of view or a single voice.

LH: It seems in modernism there was still some kind of belief in the authenticity of the self or the singularity of self. As Mimi [the student] was noticing, in the poems we are reading, there's no longer a care for the authenticity of the origin or the beginning point. The voices are interwoven. In your work, by the way, there are many enticing threads of narrative that allude to "a self," very magical and very real, about perception and relationships, domesticity and houses.

MB: It's made up. There's the narrative, for example, in "I Love Morning," where everyone in the house is waking up, and there's a girl named Martha who has a cat. My daughter's name is Martha, and the story drives her crazy. She says, "Everybody's going to think I have a cat." I try to make a unity between thought and emotion, or, perhaps, expository and narrative, the lyric and the nonlyric. I feel that narrative is a sacred form with deep power. Technically, my poems are collages. The parts are appropriated. While reading, I copy down notes, then cut them out and put them together in a collage, smoothing out the grammar. So it interested me that a sick cat and a woman with large arms could come together as something resonant. That is the kind of narrative I deal with in *Nest*. I call it a linguistic surface. If you're going beyond modernism, in many ways you're going beyond a three-dimensional space. I don't like to call it hybrid, because I like to think of it as one thing, a continuum.

LH: With Arthur Sze in Santa Fe, in an interview from the early 1990s on videotape, you talked about your creative process. You talked about the way in which you use a collage method, including photographs, laid out on a big table. Are you still working in this manner, as, say, in *Nest*?

MB: I was interested in the minor mode when I started the poems in *Nest*, instead of a major, victorious tone. I was interested in the shadows, the not-quite-successful—to recast failure as convex, positive. There's a poem called "Audience" about a depressed Japanese anima artist. I had the urge to explore this minor key and also to include the audience. I used to think only of what I wanted to write. In *Nest*, I started to think about my audience, what I call the genius of the audience. It seems obvious that American culture is betting on this genius of the audience. It's a kind of commercial bet. I was interested in not looking down on that and seeing where I could go. I'm trying to discern what people like. Maybe that's what I call this "genius." Perhaps because I was trying to think about the audience in *Nest*, I used more narrative.

My process has evolved slowly. Everyone is busy; one can't just sit down and write with concentration. Or I couldn't find that concentration. So I'd first seek my idea for a poem, for example, for the title poem "Nest." I decided to write about how, in the margin, fertile things happen. When things are fixed, things can't grow. But in margins, things grow. Then I find books that are contingent to my idea. I like French philosophy, Gilles Deleuze, Derrida. I like Buddhist texts. Anything I read that strikes me as pertinent to my poem I underline. Then I print the notes and cut them out. I add pictures that seem to me pertinent in some way, without questioning too deeply. Sometimes I take Polaroids. It's an unconscious process. When I'm ready to write, I arrange these pieces of text, photos, notes across a big table and compose the poem. I used to appropriate texts directly. Now I tend to alter them. I work from a map of the poem, and I find it's a good way to get more breadth, more horizontality.

LH: Do you find you're walking around doing something, an errand, and you get a line in your head and you jot it down, and it ends up on your table?

MB: Not very often. Usually I consider all fragments the same as the whole, like holograms. But one day, looking at the horizon, I said, "Where sky touches the ground is not the same as the whole."

LH: I am fascinated by margins, and your idea of the productivity of margins, that in-between space you describe in the poem "Nest." Likewise, in the poem "Empathy," the beginning line, which reads in italics, says, "what touches me is where the inarticulate, the error or tension finds concrete manifestation and is recognized."

MB: That is a quote from a wonderful poet, Beverly Dahlen.

LH: You were saying that in the book *Nest*, as a whole, you were concerned about audience, and yet there's something in the breakdown of communication, or "rupture," like margins, that happens. And can't we just hang out in that space.

MB: It is *most* productive. I guess if you know what you're doing, you're not in a good space for art. I'm grateful for my profession. I don't think artists are happy with the world and they feel a need to make another world. So you're at the edge, trying to make this world. It's more about resonance, frequency, energy, movement, flux, dynamism, than any fixed object. So we call that margin of error or misunderstanding. But that's because human beings want to achieve. You could also take those qualities we find in shadows, in misheard remarks, and give them positive terminology.

LH: So you think there is a kind of pejorative understanding of margin or error or being the space that doesn't count—?

MB: —wandering.

LH: Certainly the model we live with is to march ahead and to imagine that everything is clear and also that everyone has universal value and understands everything the same.

MB: Fertility—that's not a pejorative word. And it's also a kind of unformed area of flux.

LH: So to use a culturally feminine model, fertility, is to feminize the margin or the error? In our class, we've been looking at how women themselves are appropriating that space of "error," the margin, and doing something different.

[Here another student asks a question about the importance of Mei-mei's life in New Mexico to her work.]

MB: New Mexico has been important to my work for a long time, since my early twenties. It helped me to think about the horizontal plane of meaning, because its landscape is so large. Also, it correlated with my interest in phenomena around me, because the light is always changing and you never get used to it. It's beautiful and spiritual. Also, I was a hermit.

In the late 1980s, I felt the need for a child. I started working on a book with Richard Tuttle at the Whitney Museum. I sometimes say I would have married anybody, but I was lucky. Richard and I are hermit personalities. When you're young, being a hermit allows you more concentration, which helps writing. On the other hand, as the great theater director Peter Brooks said, the most important things we learn in the presence of other people. It becomes a balancing act. I am Chinese, and my family is my essential life metaphor. Dialogue with Richard informs all my work since our collaborative book *Hiddenness* and has extended my experience of the visual more than I can say. Martha Tuttle [their daughter] bravely and indefatigably opens my view ahead. One of my themes is the possibility or impossibility of connection with others. Many poems show the richness of this possibility with my family.

LH: A final question. Much is being written today in critical circles about contemporary experimental writers' transformations of the lyric. Particularly about women's participation in that transformation. Do you feel that you, like many other contemporary innovative or "experimental" women writers, are contributing to a new form of the lyric? Or do you see more of a continuum, say, from the nineteenth-century Romantic tradition (that of Wordsworth, for example, or of Shelley) to the twentieth-century modernist tradition (represented in Anglo-American terms by Pound, Eliot, Williams, H.D.)?

MB: I don't identify with either of these traditions. If I had ever thought of my intent, it may have been about writing in a way where time is simultaneous across the surface of a poem. I might say I want to express the qualities inherent in my voice I was born with. Also, that I'm naturally inclined toward sensual beauty. Now, I suppose I am trying to find a resonance in a poem beyond the single author and beyond the outline of the individual poem.

—Chinese Space

First there is the gate from the street, then some flowers inside the wall,
then the inner, roofed gate. It is a very plain wall, without expressionistic means,
such as contrasting light on paving stones inside the courtyard to the
    calligraphed foundation stones.
My grandfather called this the façade or Baroque experience, rendering a
    courtyard transparent.
The eye expecting to confront static space experiences a lavish range of optical
    events,
such as crickets in Ming jars, their syncopation like the right, then left, then right
    progress
into the house, an experience that cannot be sustained in consciousness, because
your movement itself binds passing time, more than entering directs it.

A red door lies on a golden mirror with the fascinating solidity and peacefulness
    of the pond
in the courtyard, a featureless space of infinite depth where neither unwanted
    spirits nor light
could enter directly from outside. It lies within the equally whole space of the yard
the way we surrounded our individuals, surrounded by a house we could not
    wholly
retain in memory. Walking from the inner gate across a bridge which crossed
    four ways
over the carp moat, turning right before the ice rink, we pass roses imported
    from Boston,
and enter the main courtyard, an open structure like a ruin. This is not
    remembering,
but thinking its presence around eccentric details such as a blue and white urn
    turned up to dry,
although certain brightnesses contain space, the way white slipcovered chairs
    with blue seams
contain it.

The potential of becoming great of the space is proportional to its distance away
    from us,
a negative perspective, the way the far corner of the pond becomes a corner again
    as we approach
on the diagonal, which had been a vanishing point. The grandmother poses
    beside rose bushes.
That is to say, a weary and perplexing quality of the rough wall behind her gives a
    power of tolerance
beyond the margins of the photograph. Space without expansion, compactness
    without restriction
make this peculiar and intense account of the separable person from her place in
    time,
although many families live in the partitioned house now. The reflecting surface
    of the pond
should theoretically manifest too many beings to claim her particular status in
    the space,
such as a tigerskin in space.

After the house was electrically wired in the thirties, he installed a ticker tape
    machine connected
to the American Stock Exchange. Any existence occupies time, he would say in
    the Chinese version,
reading stock quotations and meaning the simplicity of the courtyard into a
    lavish biosphere,
elevating the fact of its placement to one of our occupation of it, including the
    macaw speaking Chinese
and stones representing infinity in the garden. This is how the world appears
    when the person
becomes sufficient, i.e., like home, an alternation of fatigue and relief in the
    flexible shade of date trees,
making the house part of a channel in space, which had been interior, with
    mundane fixtures
as on elevator doors in a hotel, a standing ashtray that is black and white.
The family poses in front of the hotel, both self-knowing and knowing others at
    the same time.

This is so, because human memory as a part of unfinished nature is provided
for the experience of your unfinished existence.

—Empathy

I

For me, the insignificant or everyday gesture constructs a choreography of parts
and what touches me is where the inarticulate, the error or tension finds concrete
manifestation and is recognized.

First, I see roses in the dark with him, a compaction of spare light,
then a road through the woods in pitch dark. How she perceives the corridor in
    the dark
is a space within the time in which they were moving,
as if perspective of a space in the dark constructed a hierarchy in her mind,
in reverse of how the contents of her wishes remain unchanged and timeless,
so the innermost nature of her wishes is as much known and unknown to them
    as the reality of the external world.
It is as incompletely presented by what she can see as is the external world
by communication with someone she wishes for.

In this way her interrogation of him appears instead as a dialogue pertaining to
    uses of power,
because she can only remember what has been consciously said to her,
so that her feeling of identifying with him is like a quick flash or a signal.
When it is intense, tormenting and continuous, it's using itself to construct a
    rhetorical story again.
This state of confusion is never made comprehensible by being given a plot,
in the same way a complicated plot is only further complicated by being
    simplified,
although connectedness may not always be an artifice,
for example, when it reveals ways in which she construes what she perceives

according to an internal connection which will announce its conflict in the plot,
a tension like his mistaken gesture which is interesting as a site of power
   formation.
It may well be where the feeling of mysteriousness occurs
in which she believes him, but she doesn't want to prove it,
because an appearance in the dark will not deceive after enough appearances
and everywhere, sooner or later, there will be a hint of a tree or space above a
   lake,
so describing something as it is could by precise reference gain a neutral tone,
but in this case adheres to his and her manner of asking
where is the space, instead of what space it is.
There occurs an interval of northern lights over their walk, whose circumference
   is inferrable,
but whose outermost region lacks any known form of registration,
such as before that and before that.

2

In an empty stadium they alternate the refrain of a song in Japanese. The light is
   harsh
on rows of seats like cells of a honeycomb under high magnification.
The entire stadium resembles a honeycomb or geodesic dome turned inside out
   and concave.
He is saying, I am here. She is saying, where are you.
Speech and thought arise simultaneously as an hysterical question. An idea is a
   wish.
As a descriptive stream or spontaneous reaction to him,
speech serves as a starting point for uncovering a story through translation from
   wish into desire,
but when thought becomes reflective, a problem of interpretation enters the
   stream of emotion itself.
The speaking becomes fixed, although there is no such thing as repetition.
The speaking is a constant notation of parallel streams of thought and
   observations

whose substance is being questioned in a kind of oral thought at once open and
     precise,
but with a tension between ideas and her sense of scandal at invoking a real
     person.
He makes a rift or glimpse, both generative and relative to the glimpse,
a liberty of interruption, or exclusion, inside the stadium
in light so bright she sees her eyelash as a golden line reflecting on the inside of
     her sunglasses.
In the same way the song must never be allowed to threaten the presentation of
     what takes place in the song,
so that she may try to develop empathy for what she really wants to happen to
     her,
instead of desire being the song.

3

Anything with limits can be imagined, correctly or incorrectly, as an object,
even some language in the way that it is remembered, if you consider
each repetition a fact or object of varying strength in various situations of
     frequency and quantity,
and although you can never vary an unconscious wish,
which can only reveal itself in the contingency of the words, sexualizing the
     words,
the way a shadow moves up a wall of trees growing intensely gold at sunset.
Her equivalent for this is a time-lapse photograph of lightning, in proportion
to each moment you are looking. It is her attempt to show him a lightning storm
or any interval of colored light on the plain as what is good in life, the person,
     and what is good,
so instead of saying what time it is, she is asking, where is the time, its ratio as
     an opened lens
on clear sky. It may be relevant to ask if this kind of autobiography limits formal
or object possibilities, meaning less neutral or less real within her empathy for
     what is good in life
from his point of view. From her point of view, feminizing an art of presence
such as moving or speaking, with its distinct kind of maneuverability

is akin to those collages that verge on trompe l'oeil. Only when she looks closely
does she realize that that head is really not the one connected to that body,
although everyday gestures or tensions accrete an intimacy she can recognize.
Be that as it may, real and constant luminosity of the parts can create
a real self who will remain forever in the emotion of a necessary or real person.
To deny this is to deny the struggle to make certain meanings stick.

—I Love Morning

I

We're in New Mexico.

It's summer—all morning to lounge in bed, talk on the phone, read the paper.

Martha pats her spiky, old cat, Manet, studies cat's cradle from a book.

Time is ethos, as if we're engendered by our manner in it, not required to be in
   ourselves.

With no cause to act on time, there's no pointing beyond, so he gets up and plays
   Scarlatti in his underwear.

Being together, like scrim, defocuses space.

Knowability (features) of her face, continually passing into expression, is
   detached from her, a para-existence beside mother, halo, unraveling.

Light increases toward the red spectrum of day.

She nurses her cat with a syringe supported against my large arm.

My body is a film on her preconscious of images she chooses to line
   conversation.

Its alterity becomes a nuance of our ineluctable situation of futons, dishes,
   books, with the potential of a destabilized surface of time, no outflow through
   pink walls.

Atmospheric presence soaks objects.

2

I'm making a puzzle of the New York subway map for her.

I replace each stop with a name from our family, pestering for more names,
   Schmidt, Laubach.

I should see family as bodhisattvas helping me on the path, but it's difficult if
   I'm not a bodhisattva myself, to recognize one.

Anyone entering by chance (UPS, neighbor child) sees synchrony, confusion
   emanate from our bodies of smiling individuals, as if photographed
   separately, then assembled.

Asymmetry of legs, human, animal, disjunctions among gestures are sheathed
   in rose light wafting around a physical promise of happiness.

She sets up a tent in our room, paints on the inside names of all the people she's
   known, like stars.

She cuts out paper flowers and scatters them on the floor of the tent, morning
   not interfering, even though flowers are immediate, universal.

I love to read newspapers.

Negative space enters my house like spirits, low pressure under a table, in the petals of a rose, like a person you love.

Maternal love is needed for spatial sense, which gives rise to infant laughter.

A ringing, overflowing sense of others collapses us, with no representable condition of belonging.

She interviews him on tape and he answers in the voice of a young girl.

She draws Manet as average, general, to protect him, then introduces many toy animals into the tent.

3

A common mistake of groups is requiring each one to compensate for lacks in the whole, to care at any cost.

Our coalescence around a sick pet overflows (like laughter), incommensurate with problems of sociality in her terrifying dream.

The dream is intermediary, unraveling a thing beside itself.

I should try to help her, whether or not I truly help.

—Honey

I

Walking in an arroyo, I mistake a rock in the distance for a person, which on approach emptied of him, denser than a mirage.

I fear an object can be negated by thinking, as it remains in sight.

Though I say, "It's basalt shaped like a man," his menace is seamless.

Walking, trying to assimilate speaking into breathing, as into shadow, cool cut in light suddenly all over the place, like honey.

The hiker is tall with spiky, white hair cropped after polling readers of her Web page on style options.

Now, I frame feeling in a story for them, intransigent, no natural breaks, for example, "blinded by tears," "can't express my helplessness."

I use the Web, and words leave no trace, like a bird in the sky.

The bird, time, is an internal sense, auto-affection, but their sentiment creates auto-affection more pure.

Monkeygirl links a photo of us looking in my bathroom mirror to a site about mirrors of Web personalities, "Something's going on here!"

I wrote, "There are things going on more personal than I usually log in."

"Why don't I put them somewhere private, a Word.doc or paper diary?"

Means are involved.

The chorus is the people who are moved.

2

Don't assume emotions are engaged in this.

You're distracted by the day, rudeness, a package not sent, and your emotion is passed onto a screen.

Readers take care of it.

That night, we stoked gossip with identical entries about losing a dog during fireworks, then finding him under a bench at a restaurant known for sixties décor.

One by one, Web visitors copied this onto their own sites, as if they'd lost a dog, too.

Others suspected code "just for cool kids."

I've no distance from the hearsay.

It's a broader situation in which protagonist belongs to narrative, the way an outcome may be full or empty.

One finds a sweet spot, reversal.

The illusion of a person in a wash doesn't create emptiness when I recognize a rock, at the same time feeling its presence, a cut, and my response extend, like a stain.

Then, there's the animate problem of a rock moving from one side of the trail to the other, at night.

Will it subject itself to strange, internal obligation it feels, beyond its level?

3

I had health problems and went to bed.

The doctor allowed my dog, a small poodle, to sleep with me.

Guido and his friend put camp beds in the hall.

My room felt drab, so I taped pictures of nieces and nephews on my bathroom
   mirror and became addicted to bidding on-line for antiques.

I found an Aubusson rug the right size, just trees, but Guido said it was a
   fragment, nothing to focus on.

Veined hands with blue nails apportioned eggs on Georgian silver he set
   formally.

Objects were symbols, not belonging to experience, the way a speaker is
   supposed to, re: distinctions between concrete and figurative, the vase empty
   or full, like conversation.

When my strength improved, I wanted my own space.

I embarrassed him by talking and gesturing with no one there.

I spoke to someone with whom I needed to correct things I'd said and done.

Collecting's not hearsay; you're not part of the narrative, the way friends became
   attached to my dog, carrying it, begging kisses.

How did that person get inside, to whom I exclaim, bargain, whom I initially
   isolate in my experience of a neighbor I meet, being "a stranger"?

4

Is the person not existing, when I mistake a cairn, his emptiness of entity,
   mirage, moon in water?

Analyze, using any neighbor.

When communication's difficult, think of honey, hard with no natural breaks, or
   all over the place.

You wish to communicate, the way light scatters inside you, an expanding zone revealed in the distance by constellations of objects of the wish.

I recognize your shadow ahead as sound in the mind of the listener, like knowledge revealed by a visitor in my dream.

Considering splits between sight and fear on the trail, front and back of surfaces, between missing you (bathos, synthesis) and one with whom I grapple, who seems to pull strings and elicit feelings not mine:

Dream total epidermal contact with the puppeteer, open as virtual.

Communication (transmission) dissipates, like an expanse of sky confirmed by emptiness.

It passes through the beam of her emotion refracted all over, evoking alienations of beauty on sociality.

Each time she begins is thought, a move.

Momentum with no beginning takes the form of communication in groups, except during his drive cross-country to live with her.

"Oh yeah, it's bad," she writes back. "I'm used to being able to check in, Webcam, Flighttracker, e-mail."

"Now there's nothing, except the phone at night; well, it seems like nothing."

jayne cortez

Long before the explosion of hip-hop and the new performance poetry, Jayne Cortez was crossing the borders between improvisatory music making and traditional poetic text. With a focus few other women poets take to this task, Cortez stresses interarts poetics as *itself* a radical cultural politics, though her work is rarely recognized for this achievement. In a forty-year career of work grounded in unflinching political commitment, Cortez has published over a dozen books—including *Jazz Fan Looks Back* (2002), *Somewhere in Advance of Nowhere* (1996), *Coagulations: New and Selected Poems* (1984)—and numerous CDs of her poetry. Cortez's first book, *Pissstained Stairs and the Monkey Man's Wares* (1969), embodied the militant style and radical politics of the Black Arts years: a poetics of dissent and rage, linked to that of writers Amiri Baraka, Sonia Sanchez, and others of the Black Arts movement. But even as Cortez bitterly portrays violence and grief in black urban life, many of these poems also celebrate the lives of black musicians, from Bessie Smith to Charlie Parker. Here Cortez first explored the relationship between musical structures and poetic form and line, a harbinger of her commitment to the connections between poetry and music—from folk blues to the African praise song to avant-garde jazz—which is discussed at length in this interview. In all her work, whether on the page or the stage, Cortez moves fluidly among the usually self-contained worlds of poetry publishing, performance poetry, and live or recorded music.

Born in 1936 in Arizona, Cortez was raised in Los Angeles. Having studied music early on, she became fascinated with performance. Cortez helped found the Watts Repertory Theatre Company (*Pissstained Stairs* was first written for performance by the company) and served as the group's artistic director from 1964 to 1970. In the 1950s, Cortez was married to jazz great Ornette Coleman, with whom she collaborated; their son, Denardo Coleman, became a drummer and has performed with his father's bands, as well as on his mother's recordings. For many years, Cortez's books and CDs were published solely by Bola Press, which Cortez founded in 1972 to control the production and presentation of her books and recordings; these include the books *Firespitter* (1982), *Mouth on Paper* (1977), and *Scarifications* (1973). Cortez's poems, widely anthologized, have been translated into twenty-eight languages, and her many honors include the American Book Award and two NEA fellowships.

But to list Cortez's books is in many ways to skim the surface of her significance as an artist. Dedicated to exploring the intersection of musical form and poetic voice, Cortez has performed her work in a wide variety of settings, from the Museum of Modern Art to the Arts Alive International Festival in Johannesburg, South Africa. She has recorded eight CDs (many of these with a band she created, the Firespitters), including *Taking the Blues Back Home* (1997), *Cheerful & Optimistic* (1994), and *Find Your Own Voice* (1996).

From the start, Cortez took African American life as her subject, including black feminist concerns that had received little public attention. At the same time, she has explored African American music not just as subject but as form, attending to the structures shared by the poetic line and the musical phrase (rhythm, repetition, breath or pacing, inflection, and notation). Most significantly, Cortez has fused these formal experiments with a cultural politics devoted to African American empowerment. It is in this light that, in conversation with the poet and editor Sascha Feinstein, Cortez discusses music, poetry, and African American traditions. The interview took place at Lycoming College on November 20, 1997, and it focuses on three jazz poems included here: "About Flyin' Home," "States of Motion," and "Bumblebee, You Saw Big Mama."

AN INTERVIEW WITH JAYNE CORTEZ
by Sascha Feinstein

SASCHA FEINSTEIN: We reprinted "A Miles Davis Trumpet" in the first issue of *Brilliant Corners*, so perhaps we could talk about others from *Somewhere in Advance of Nowhere*. This afternoon you discussed the dangers of simply echoing what other people have played, or even your own playing. Is that what inspired "About Flyin' Home"?

JAYNE CORTEZ: There was a celebration of the tune "Flyin' Home," and for tenor saxophonist Illinois Jacquet, who had recorded the tune with the Lionel Hampton band almost fifty years ago. When I was about ten years old, I heard the Hampton band at an afternoon concert in a baseball stadium in Los Angeles. The band played "Flyin' Home" over and over. It was a crowd pleaser. The people were especially excited by Illinois' solo and big honking Texas sound. My poem about "Flyin' Home" is about repeating something exactly as it had been recorded and how that something is no longer a release. I admire Illinois very much. He definitely has that big-time black Texas sound and energy.

SF: Several jazz musicians have been saddled with a famous tune—

JC: There are signature poems, signature tunes, theme songs, et cetera, but that has nothing to do with depth or art or spontaneity. A signature is a signal before an intermission or it means the gig is over and goodbye. It's nice to have famous tunes, especially if you get residuals or royalties. But if I had to read the same poem over and over, night after night, I would get no satisfaction.

SF: Your book is framed by "About Flyin' Home" and—I guess it's actually the penultimate poem—"States of Motion," which reads like a series of brief elegies.

JC: The poem "States of Motion" was written for the book *Fragments*, a collaboration with sculptor Melvin Edwards. Actually, I was responding to some of his sculptures when in walked "States of Motion" like a dream. A great surprise that

---

created its own sculpture: "Sun Ra left the planet traveling in a pyramid made of metal keys."

SF: Other poems of yours seem to be built in similar ways. Do you see poems as sculpture?

JC: No. I don't see poems as sculpture.

SF: There are a great many jazz musicians mentioned in the poem. They might dominate—

JC: I knew the musicians mentioned in the poem—

SF: Is that simply because there have been so many losses?

JC: There have been many losses. This project gave me an opportunity to respond to those losses, to creativity, creation, and creative people.

SF: There is a strong sense of cadence in "States of Motion," but it's not the same kind of cadence that you have, say, in "About Flyin' Home," where you return to a refrain. I can't think of anyone who uses the refrain as effectively as you do.

JC: The refrain might be expected but what the refrain is relating to is unexpected.

SF: It's so hard to do that well.

JC: There are always comings and goings. You go, you return, and in between there are internal and external changes, environmental changes, changes based on personal experience, based on information. There are no exact ocean waves. The refrain is a device to add the next layer of sound, next metaphor, next transformation.

SF: You've done that as far as I can remember, starting with *Pissstained Stairs*. Do you see substantial changes in your poetry in terms of the use of repetition or otherwise?

JC: I see changes. I use more repetition. I make use of more material from the subconscious, from dreams. I try to go to the other shore, or to let go of the other shore, and let whatever's in the deep water come up to the surface. I use those hidden elements, those impulses to develop poems and surprise myself, and to keep on wanting to write poetry. The work has changed because I've changed.

SF: Of course. But you've always worked from the subconscious, as all good artists *have* to—

JC: I would like to have no known references, let references pop up from the out-of-nowhere place in me. Just let it happen and write, or write and let it happen.

sF: Do you find that the majority of your poems come in one burst like that? Do you do a great deal of revision?

jc: A number of poems come like that. Sometimes I do revision. For example, the guitar poem ["The Guitars I Used to Know"] took me about three years to complete. I kept starting and stopping, revising and revising. I couldn't find the shape, the launch pad, the point of departure. When I started working on my CD, *Taking the Blues Back Home*, I felt that I had to have the guitar poem as a part of the project. There were two great guitar players [Bern Nix and Carl Weathersby] set for the session, so I rewrote the poem and finalized it during the rehearsal period. Maybe I needed that kind of pressure. Maybe it was the right time. But it took three years of tearing up a lot of paper for it to be what it is.

sF: What about "About Flyin' Home" and "States of Motion"? Did they come faster?

jc: "Flyin' Home" came flyin' out. I had an early relationship with "Flyin' Home." I knew the tune. I heard the Lionel Hampton band.

sF: Perhaps the poem was brewing for a long time without your consciously thinking about it.

jc: Maybe it was stored in the storage space of my mind. But I wasn't even thinking about "Flyin' Home" until the day that they were celebrating the fiftieth anniversary of the tune. I started thinking about routine, and what it leads to.

sF: You recently recorded "Bumblebee, You Saw Big Mama," a poem for [the blues singer] Big Mama Thornton. Did you have a relationship with her, too?

jc: I knew the music of Big Mama Thornton because I attended teenage dances where she would be singing with the Johnny Otis band in L.A. Later, I heard her at clubs, blues and jazz festivals, and once at the Cookery. In the 1970s and early 1980s, the Cookery was a spot in New York City where you could hear great women musicians like Mary Lou Williams, Nellie Lutcher, and Rose Murphy. When the owner of the Cookery rediscovered Alberta Hunter and she made her singing reentry, she became the only attraction. The Cookery was her home base in New York City. So hearing Big Mama there with pianist Sammy Price was a rare occasion. It was really nice for me because I had a chance to talk to her.

I liked Big Mama's sound. The way she produced her music, her deep spiritual feeling. She was so dynamic and unpredictable. I was very impressed. She was an aggressive singer, and obviously an aggressive person. She could play the drums, she could play the harmonica, she could sing, she had a band, she looked the way she wanted to look, she dressed how she wanted to dress. She was a person who seemed very free.

SF: Your description of her reminds me of Robert Hayden's poem for Bessie Smith, "The Empress of the Blues."

JC: Oh, yes. I always remember his poem about Bessie and Sterling Brown's about Ma Rainey.

SF: What did you talk about with Big Mama Thornton?

JC: We talked about the past, about certain people and clubs in Houston, Texas. And I reminded her of the teenage dances in L.A., how she sang in the band that also featured Little Esther Phillips.

SF: Big Mama Thornton isn't nearly as well known as she should be.

JC: No. She's not well known. And Big Maybelle is not well known. They didn't have the opportunity to express half of the music in their souls on record.

SF: Obviously individual poems don't create legacy.

JC: Right.

SF: But did you write and perform the poem in part to tell the world about this magical singer?

JC: I wanted to remember her, to retrieve something from my memory about her. The poem is about a creative person and the creativity in my community. It's about stinging and being stung. I wrote it because I was inspired by her and she was a magical singer. I don't know if the poem will make Big Mama famous. I don't know how many people will read the book or hear the CD or search for more information on Big Mama Willie Mae Thornton.

SF: Earlier today I mentioned how much I admired [the drummer] Ed Blackwell, someone you knew very well. Can you talk a bit about the relationship between, say, a brilliant drummer and a very musical poet?

JC: Blackwell was like a brother. I met him in Los Angeles around 1953 or 1954. I heard him play in many different spaces. He wrote a tune for my son called "Denardo's Dribbles." He would babysit and put those rattles in Denardo's hands and shake out some rhythm patterns. Maybe that's why Denardo became a drummer.

I read my work with Blackwell in the 1970s in concert with Wilbur Ware, Clifford Thornton, and Sam Rivers at a gig organized by Bill Cole at Amherst College. Blackwell sounded like a one-man African drum ensemble. My poem "Everywhere Drums" is dedicated to Blackwell, and we recorded that piece together with

Denardo and Ghanaian drummer Abraham Adzenyah in 1990. Blackwell was such a powerful inventor of sound, rhythm, and time. He sure could charge up the atmosphere. I can't think of Blackwell without thinking cymbals, drums, and drumsticks.

SF: In the same way, perhaps, that I cannot think of your work without thinking of percussion.

JC: Is that right? Well, that's a compliment.

SF: I was asking about drums and poetry because your work is so propulsive.

JC: I think all experiences and memories carry different rhythms, different conflicts, and are conflictive rhythms. Drumbeats accent and support various pitches, phrases. Denardo can follow me, converse with me, and play what I say on his drums. That makes the encounter rhythmically exciting. I like reading my work with an assortment of drums. Several of my poems about drums and drummers have been published—"I See Chano Pozo," "Everywhere Drums," "If the Drum Is a Woman."

SF: With your band the Firespitters, you've recorded eight CDs. What are some of the struggles inherent in creating a solid union between poetry and music?

JC: The definition and implication of words. The definition and implication of harmony and rhythm. The effort to combine speech and music. Finding the key set of words, the pitch, the direction, the tempo. At rehearsals, we talk about the subject, about what the images suggest in musical terms. I read, they play. We make up things. We listen to each other. We try to make connections. Getting the gig is a struggle. Never having enough money to pay for the space and time needed to experiment is a struggle. I started reading my poetry with music in 1964. I organized the Firespitter band with Denardo in 1980. Now the poetry is the focus. The musicians respond to the poetry.

SF: There must be times when things aren't going well.

JC: Anything can happen in a recording session. I'm usually in an isolated booth, and each instrument is usually isolated. Sometimes we can't see each other. We are depending on the engineer and on the headsets. The sound in the headset always needs adjusting. We usually do a recording session in one day. We are wired up. It's very intense.

In 1982, when we recorded the album *There It Is*, the setup in the studio was negative. There were no isolation spaces. I had to scream my lungs out in the middle of the room so the musicians could hear the words and respond.

SF: But now you have Harmolodic in place—.

JC: Denardo and his father have Harmolodic in place.

SF: And you have outstanding musicians.

JC: Yes, and good engineers. And I'm learning about that whole process.

SF: What connections do you see between your poems and spoken blues?

JC: My CD *Taking the Blues Back Home* had to do with investigating the blues from a different point of view, to focus in on the deeper levels of the blues, the political aspects of the blues. The blues has so many codes I wanted to investigate them. The musicians may be playing a twelve-bar blues, but I'm talking about the blues before it became those twelve bars.

SF: There's the suggestion in your title and in the poems themselves that the blues have been abused.

JC: The blues have been abused. The black people who produce the blues have been abused.

SF: Are you also criticizing contemporary blues, saying that it's watered down?

JC: In some cases it has been watered down. In some cases it's used by people who have no understanding of the language of the blues and of the blues people. They have no notion about where the blues come from or what they say. They're just mimicking, imitating, and minstrelizing. It sounds good to them in their voice, and they can get over, and that's all it is. Others are using the cornier lyrics of the blues, and they're just corny.

SF: Langston Hughes had clear distinctions in his mind between blues poetry to be read and blues lyrics to be sung. He tells that wonderful anecdote about singing his poems and some stranger coming up to him to see if he's ill. [*Cortez laughs.*] But there seems to be more crossover for you.

JC: Well, you know, I really can't sing. So I don't sing, but I may chant a little bit. There may be something that comes with the music that makes me do that.

SF: And you have a splendid sense of inflection and the musicality of phrases.

JC: Thanks.

SF: Are there poets writing about the blues whom you admire?

JC: I like the blues poetry of Sterling Plumpp and Raymond Patterson and the poetry and jazz fusions of Amiri Baraka.

SF: I'm not surprised that you focus on Baraka. I think the two of you have done a great deal in terms of blurring the distinctions between music and the musicality of language.

JC: I have many opportunities to read my work at music festivals around the world, and so does Baraka. We are very lucky.

SF: Al Young also works frequently with musicians.

JC: I haven't heard Al. I have heard other jazz poems by poets like Ted Joans, who is a jazz poet. I think that Bill Matthews did a nice job with the piece that he wrote about Bud Powell ["Bud Powell, Paris, 1959"]. There have been good jazz poems. But a number of poets today write about jazz musicians and jazz music because it's the hip thing to do. They know nothing about the music, the struggle, or the contribution, or why some musicians are against calling their music "jazz."

SF: That's been true for decades—ever since Vachel Lindsay, who didn't know anything about the music.

JC: He didn't know anything about it.

SF: A lot of poets just latch on to the term.

JC: And the media is good at latching on to something like that and pushing it forward [laughs].

SF: You've mentioned the difficulty of finding contemporary trumpet players who take risks, who play, as you put it, "out there." Now, your poems take a lot of risks, but that's not true of many if not most of the poets writing today.

JC: That's true. That's because people are very repressed. The whole reason to create is so that you are free. In art you have to be absolutely free. If you're not, then you shouldn't be in it.

SF: It's pretty stunning when you think of all the poets from, say, the dozens of black poetry anthologies from the sixties—how so few of them are anthologized today, how we don't see their work, hear their voices.

JC: That's right. There was really a move to blot out the sixties.

SF: Out of fear?

JC: The poems were militant. They reflected the desire for more freedom and liberation. They questioned the American dream. The poems explored African roots. The poems called for an end to exploitation, domination, and oppression. Now, thirty-two years later, we have rappers who give us watered down versions of those messages backed by drum machines and made available as part of the pop music scene. I have nothing against rappers. If they can communicate and survive by rapping, cool. However, I do think they lack understanding about what went on before they arrived to rap. In the sixties, people were protesting. They were open-ing doors, burning down cities, calling for justice. People were serious. The censorship that came as a result of the sixties caused a lot of folks to hide their true feelings and caused some poets to give up writing poetry.

SF: Your poems often dip into the music of the 1960s.

JC: It was a rich time. There were definite breakthroughs—politically and artistically.

SF: Do you miss that energy of the sixties?

JC: No, because I think I'm still breaking through [*laughs*]. You know, you just continue to deepen and develop. That was a very electrifying time. A great moment in history. More people became politically aware and we took that awareness to another level in the seventies and the eighties, and nineties. We are in a better position to confront contradiction and keep creativity alive. Evolution may be slow, but we do keep evolving.

Right now I'm having fun reading my work with music and creating art with other artists. It's great.

SF: It is great. And we're very grateful.

—So Many Feathers

You danced a magnetic dance
in your rhinestones and satin banana G-strings
it was you who cut the river
with your pink diamond tongue
did the limbo on your back
straight from the history of southern flames
onto the stage where your body
covered in metallic flint
under black and green feathers strutted
with wings of a vulture paradise on your head
strutted among the birds
until you became terror woman of all feathers
of such terrible beauty
of such fire
such flames
all feathers Josephine
This Josephine
exploding red marble eyes in new york
this Josephine
breaking color bars in miami
this Josephine
mother of orphans
legion of honor
rosette of resistance
this Josephine before
splitting the solidarity of her beautiful feathers

Feather-woman of terror
such feathers so beautiful
Josephine
with your frosted mouth half-open

why split your flamingos
with the death white boers in durban south africa
Woman with magnificent face of Ife mask
why all the teeth for the death white boers in durban
Josephine you had every eyelash in the forest
every feather flying
why give your beaded snake-hips
to the death white boers in durban
Josephine didn't you know about the torture
chambers
made of black flesh and feathers
made by the death white boers in durban
Josephine terror-woman of terrible beauty of such
feathers
I want to understand why dance
the dance of the honorary white
for the death white boers in durban

After all Josephine
I saw you in your turquoise headdress
with royal blue sequins pasted on your lips
your fantastic legs studded with emeralds
as you kicked   as you bumped   as you leaped in the
air
then froze
your body breaking lightning in fish net
and Josephine   Josephine
what a night in harlem
what electricity
such trembling
such goose pimples
so many feathers
Josephine
dancer of the magnetic dancers
of the orange flint pelvis of the ruby navel

of the purple throat
of the feet pointing both ways
of feathers now gone
Josephine   Josephine
I remember you rosette of resistance
southern flames
Josephine of the birdheads, ostrich plumes
bananas and sparkling G-strings
Josephine of the double-jointed knees
double-jointed shoulders   double-jointed thighs
double-jointed breasts   double-jointed fingers
double-jointed toes   double-jointed eyeballs
double-jointed hips doubling
into a double squat like a double star into a giant
double snake
with the double heartbeats of a young girl
doubling into woman-hood
and grinding into an emulsified double spirit
Josephine terror-woman of feathers   i remember
Josephine of such conflicts   i remember
Josephine of such floating   i remember
Josephine of such heights   i remember
Josephine
of so many transformations   i remember
Josephine
of such beauty   i remember
Josephine of such fire   i remember
Josephine of such sheen   i remember
Josephine
so many feathers   i remember
Josephine   Josephine

—If the Drum Is a Woman

If the drum is a woman
why are you pounding your drum into an insane
babble
why are you pistol whipping your drum at dawn
why are you shooting through the head of your drum
and making a drum tragedy of drums
if the drum is a woman
don't abuse your drum   don't abuse your drum
                don't abuse your drum
I know the night is full of displaced persons
I see skins striped with flames
I know the ugly disposition of underpaid clerks
they constantly menstruate through the eyes
I know bitterness embedded in flesh
the itching alone can drive you crazy
I know that this is America
and chickens are coming home to roost
on the MX missile
But if the drum is a woman
why are you choking your drum
why are you raping your drum
why are you saying disrespectful things
to your mother drum   your sister drum
your wife drum and your infant daughter drum
If the drum is a woman
then understand your drum
your drum is not docile
your drum is not invisible
your drum is not inferior to you
your drum is a woman
so don't reject your drum
don't try to dominate your drum
don't become weak and cold and desert your drum

don't be forced into the position
as an oppressor of drums
and make a drum tragedy of drums
if the drum is a woman
don't abuse your drum   don't abuse your drum
                don't abuse your drum

—Lynch Fragment 2
  Autumn in New York, 1972

I am bleed mouth nod
from an oath in sorrow

i command both rise and fall
through melancholy links
of refugee sweat

i succulent republic of swamp lips
push forward my head through
windshields of violence
to baptise in a typhoon of night sticks

Scream on me

i've gasolined my belly against suspects
and flown away tears across
the dry rust wings of a roach god

Attention all units

i call to the fumes
drawn back against steel
against invisible fuck of a cry

to remove its road block flesh of a flunky
and let that rotting become feast
on sapphire of my adobe fangs

i am zest from bad jaw quiver
of aftermath

Come Celebrate Me

—Rape

What was Inez supposed to do for
the man who declared war on her body
the man who carved a combat zone between her
breasts
Was she supposed to lick crabs from his hairy ass
kiss every pimple on his butt
blow hot breath on his big toe
draw back the corners of her vagina and
hee haw like a California burro

This being war time for Inez
she stood facing the knife
the insults and
her own smell drying on the penis of
the man who raped her

She stood with a rifle in her hand
doing what a defense department will do in times of
war
And when the man started grunting and panting and
wobbling forward like
a giant hog

She pumped lead into his three hundred pounds of
shaking flesh
Sent it flying to the Virgin of Guadalupe
then celebrated day of the dead rapist punk
and just what the fuck else was she supposed to do?

And what was Joanne supposed to do for
the man who declared war on her life
Was she supposed to tongue his encrusted
toilet stool lips
suck the numbers off of his tin badge
choke on his clap trap balls
squeeze on his nub of rotten maggots and
sing god bless america thank you for fucking my life
away

This being wartime for Joanne
she did what a defense department will do in times of
war
and when the piss drinking   shit sniffing guard said
I'm gonna make you wish you were dead black bitch
come here
Joanne came down with an ice pick in
the swat freak motherfucker's chest
yes in the fat neck of that racist policeman
Joanne did the dance of the ice picks and once again
from coast to coast
house to house
we celebrated day of the dead rapist punk
and just what the fuck else were we supposed to do

—About Flyin' Home

What would you say to yourself
if you had to lay on your back
hold up the horn
& play 99 courses of
a tune called Flyin' Home
exactly as you recorded it
55 years ago
& what would you think
if you woke up in the afternoon
& your head was still spinning with
voices shouting
Flyin' Home blow Flyin' Home
& what would you do
if someone whispered in your ear
hug me kiss me anything
but please don't play Flyin' Home
& what if a customer said:
tonight I'm having sex with
a person who has been up
in a flying saucer
so please funk me down good with Flyin' Home
& what would you think
if someone started singing
Yankee Doodle Dandy
in the middle of your solo on Flyin' Home
& what if you had to enter
all the contaminated areas in the world
just to perform your infectious version of
Flyin' Home
& what if you saw yourself
looking like a madman
with a smashed horn
walking backward on a subway platform

after 50 years of blowing Flyin' Home
& what would you think to yourself
if you had to play Flyin' Home
when you didn't have
a home to fly to
& what if Flyin' Home became
your boogie woogie social security check
your oldie but goodie way out of retirement
& was more valuable than you
I mean somewhere
in advance of nowhere
you are in here
after being out there
Flyin' Home

—States of Motion

Sun Ra left the planet traveling in a pyramid made of metal keys
Willie Mae Thornton sailed away in an extra large moisture-proof harmonica
Pauline Johnson flew off to the meeting in her brass trimmed telephone
Thelonious Monk withdrew seated in a space ship shaped like a piano
Art Blakey departed in a great wood & stainless steel bass drum
Esther Phillips bowed out in a nasal sounding chrome microphone
Charles Tyler, George Adams & Clifford Jordan reached another realm riding in
    receptacles constructed like saxophones
Okot p'Bitek shoved off in an attache case full of songs, books & whiskey
Leon Damas hit the road in a big black banjo
Audre Lorde departed while wrapped in her book jackets
Dizzy Gillespie zoomed off in a sweet chariot shaped like a trumpet
Miles Davis left in a magnificent copper mute
Marietta Damas vacated the terrain in one beautiful house filled with folkloric &
    electronic gadgets

Romare Bearden crossed over the rainbow in a blimp made of his collages &
   etchings
Norman Lewis pushed away from the shore in a vault shaped like a bicycle
Ed Blackwell concealed in an assortment of cymbals marched off to the Mardi
   Gras
Tchikaya U'Tamsi floated away in a big heart-shaped tuba
Vivian Browne departed draped in her painted forest canvases
Larry Neal went to the bush enclosed in two bookcases of poetry & Bebop tapes
Kimako Baraka evacuated the surface in a stone temple marked with Egyptian
   hieroglyphics
Wilfred Cartey got away from the hurricane in an ocean liner made of rum
   bottles
Johnny Makatini took off in a black, green & yellow rocket
Kathy Collins departed in a container made of unedited film clips
John Carter left in a fabulous silver clarinet
Evan Walker split in his boat that was shaped like a bird
Dumile Feni hurried to South Africa in one of his muscle-bound wooden
   sculptures
Peter Tosh reached the intersection in a bus filled with herbs & political
   newspapers
Bob Marley retreated away in a booming amplifier draped in African flags tied
   with dreadlocks
Ana Mendieta made her exit as a bronze Silueta
Michael Smith left for the forest in one huge audio cassette case
Elena & Jawa Apronti traveled from Accra in compartments made of ceremonial
   umbrellas
Bill Majors rode off into the sunset in a highly polished brass mercedes benz
Coco Anderson went to the festival in a fixture shaped like a yam wrapped with
   eight patchwork quilts
Franco L. Makiadi rolled off in a king-size purple guitar
Nicolás Guillén went to the rendezvous in a grand rumba cow bell
Tamu Bess traveled home in a queen-size computer plastered with eyeglasses
Flora Nwapa crossed the horizon concealed in pages of her new novel
Sarah Vaughan ascended in a misty glass recording booth
Gilberto de La Nuez disappeared into one of his paintings in Havana

—Bumblebee, You Saw Big Mama

You saw Big Mama Thornton
in her cocktail dresses
& cut off boots
& in her cowboy hat
& man's suit
as she drummed &
hollered out
the happy hour of her negritude
Bumblebee

You saw Big Mama
trance dancing her chant
into cut body of
a running rooster
scream shouting her talk
into flaming path of
a solar eclipse
cry laughing her eyes into
circumcision red sunsets
at midnight
Bumblebee

You saw Big Mama
bouncing straight up like a Masai
then falling back spinning her
salty bone drying kisser of music
into a Texas hop for you to
lap up her sweat
Bumble Bee

You saw Big Mama
moaning between ritual saxes

& carrying the black water of Alabama blood
through burnt weeds & rainy ditches
to reach the waxy surface of your spectrum
Bumblebee

You didn't have to wonder
why Big Mama sounded
so expressively free
so aggressively great
once you climbed
into valley roar
of her vocal spleen
& tasted sweet grapes
in cool desert
of her twilight
Bumblebee

You saw Big Mama
glowing like
a full charcoal moon
riding down
Chocolate Bayou road
& making her entrance
into rock-city-bar lounge
& swallowing that
show-me-no-love supermarket exit sign
in her club ebony gut
you saw her
get tamped on by the hell hounds
& you knew when she was happy
you knew when she was agitated
you knew what would make her thirsty
you knew why Big Mama
heated up the blues for Big Mama
to have the blues with you

after you stung her
& she chewed off your stinger
Bumblebee
You saw Big Mama

rachel blau duplessis

INTRODUCTION

Rachel Blau DuPlessis is a poet-critic par excellence. Yet, to call her a poet-critic may belie the extensive range of her critical and poetic enterprises. If poetry and politics often exist in an uneasy relationship with each other, DuPlessis's response to her need to do "cultural work" in both areas has been to take on critical projects intended to alter cultural institutions and practices quite directly and to write poetry such that the shards of social and political strife turn into inspired, word-driven language. Her ambition, in short, has been to remake culture, as well as poetry itself. DuPlessis began her career with the rise of the feminist movement and the insight that because of emerging gender critiques "*all* of culture would have to be changed." Broadening this critique in subsequent years to include issues of race, ethnicity, and class, Du-Plessis has immersed herself not only in diverse critical and poetic projects but also in the activist, poetic, and academic communities that give rise to them.

Born in 1941 in Brooklyn, New York, DuPlessis received undergraduate and doctoral degrees respectively at Barnard College and Columbia University. DuPlessis grew up in a nonreligious household, although one imbued in Jewish heritage, which she describes as involving "both a Yiddishkeit, a spoken word, through my mother, and allegiance to the Book, a written word, through my father and grandfather." Her grandfather, dead long before her birth, was a rabbi and essayist, and her father was a professor of American philosophy and religions, including American Judaism. Beginning with her first poem, "Memory," at age twelve, DuPlessis has dedicated her poetic explorations to a revisioning that "necessitates the multiple, forceful, and polyvocal invention of a completely new culture, and the critical destabilizing of the old."[1]

This revision has resulted in multiple critical books, beginning with the groundbreaking *Writing Beyond the Ending: Narrative Strategies of Twentieth-Century Women Writers; H.D.: The Career of That Struggle*; and most recently, *Genders, Races, and Religious Cultures in Modern American Poetry, 1908–1934*. She worked on the feminist journal *HOW(ever)*, edited by Kathleen Fraser and devoted to exploratory writing by, and research about, experimental modern and contemporary women poets. Other scholarship focuses on her poetry mentor, George Oppen (*The Selected Letters of George Oppen* and *The Objectivist Nexus: Essays in Cultural Poetics*, coedited with Peter Quartermain), and feminist activism (*The Feminist Memoir Project: Voices of Women's Liberation*, coedited with Ann Snitow). Mediating between her critical writing and her poetry are experimental essays, several of which are collected in *The Pink Guitar: Writing as Feminist Practice*.

In the last few decades, DuPlessis has concentrated her poetic writing on a project entitled Drafts, as ambitious and open-ended as Pound's *Cantos*. Drafts began spontaneously as the concluding work of her early volume of poetry, *Tabula Rosa* (1987), in which relatively traditional poems staging a feminist critique of poetry lead toward the end of the volume to the nontraditional "Writing" (excerpted here), a prelude to her first two drafts. "Writing" began DuPlessis's work in which the material manifestation of writing (including actual handwritten poems inscribed on printed pages) becomes the instigation for a processual and serial composition that folds back on itself. DuPlessis has composed some 65 Drafts to date and is planning 114 separate works, the most recent Drafts becoming ever more capacious in their deliberate inclusion of both critical and random gestures, as well as their sense of our lives as political. Drafts has resulted in multiple publications, most prominently *Drafts 1–38, Toll* (2001) and *Drafts: Drafts 39–57, Pledge, with Draft, Unnumbered: Précis* (2004).

This interview with the poet-critic Jeanne Heuving was conducted in spring 2000 in Seattle and concluded by e-mail in fall 2004.

AN INTERVIEW WITH RACHEL BLAU DUPLESSIS
by Jeanne Heuving

JEANNE HEUVING: You have accomplished what might be two or even three different impressive careers. How do you bridge the demands of creating critical work that is academically respected, on the one hand, and of writing innovative poetry, on the other hand? Or to use one of your own book titles, what has been "the career of that struggle?"

RACHEL BLAU DUPLESSIS: My joke answer is I don't watch TV, so I have time. My real answer is that I am driven by the force of the questions that take me on, grapple with me. No one could do all that critical and creative work without a conviction that one has to try to address the issues that present themselves as vital. Gender in culture was the instigator; another was the call to poetic practice. I could never give up either one. So I ended up with both. The "struggle" is to be able to think through the work and get it done while living in the material world. Many poets engage in the investigation of sources that could be called scholarship. Many poets work out intellectual and ethical problems that have cultural necessity. Blake's phrase "Mental Fight" seems germane.

JH: Yet part of accomplishing work in the material world is taking on its different apparatuses, learning them. It seems to me that the apparatuses of the academy and those of innovative poetry are rather different, if in fact, the word apparatus even applies to poetry. Have you experienced any conflict here, not just in terms of time, but of basic orientation?

RD: Peculiarly, my academic career has specialized in moments of newness, new perspectives, whether this was the paradigm shift involved in sustaining feminist and gender-oriented questions, the interest in putting poetry on the agenda as a mode of thought and speculation, or my writing of feeling-rich essays as forms of criticism, or my proposing a textually alert method for a culturalist

---

reading of poetic texts invested in issues of social location. All these are, or were at their times, counterhegemonic. As an academic, I've behaved more like a poet-critic all along. I shrug off, or somewhat withdraw from, apparatuses.

JH: The poem "Writing" in *Tabula Rosa* is a prelude to your Drafts and might even be described as an "ur" Draft. Could you discuss how this poem came about and its relation to the work that follows?

RD: Ron Silliman has a way of describing the phenomenon of this kind of poem, calling it a "portal poem." It is a door into a great territory. I think I spent many years looking for that portal, and then finally I found it and walked into the space. There is a stubborn quality of looking for that portal; this is another answer to how I got work done. In the poem "Writing" I absolutely quit the iconic poem, which represented the last bastion of the lyric for me, and I started to write noniconic works, called Drafts. This is why I sometimes date the inception of that project from 1985, the date "Writing" was finished, not 1986, the date Drafts actually began.

JH: You commented that the arrival of your daughter caused, or enabled, the breakthrough that led to "Writing." Indeed, that particular juncture seems really tremendous in your life. Your first critical book, *Writing Beyond the Ending*, was just being published, your daughter had arrived on your door stoop, and your writing was taking wing. Can you talk some about this time?

RD: I'm a nonbiological mother, and I could talk for hours about the very great complexities around pregnancy failure and adoption, including really bad adoption. I do understand that women who have babies early and in complicated situations also have many problems, not to mention lack of time. For me, motherhood was very generative, and that was a great gift. The poem "Writing" came out of that experience. As a serial poem in twenty-eight sections, every section begins with a period. And yes, there are some puns there. But besides menstruation, a period also marks the end of a sentence. Every single section is written as if after the end of conventional statements, so that the whole poem is in a certain sense conceptualized as existing on the other side of a period. Also in this poem—because of having two poems, handwritten and typeset, in some of the page space—things became marginal to each other. There was no central core. Every thing was happening on the side! So what is realism made of, I asked myself. The question became an aesthetic drive. "Writing" was also talking about women's experiences in a kind of splay—as fragmented and as serial. I would now say that the poem features a posthumanist subjectivity that is very dependent on gender for its articulation. The "I," the "seeing

I" in the poem, is fragmented and fissured in a positive way. It doesn't seek whole-ness, healing, all of the ideologies of closure that we are very familiar with from another mode of feminist poetry. I was trying to get this same kind of collage, of splay, in essays, written about the same time, in "For the Etruscans" and "Language Acquisition" [collected in *The Pink Guitar* (—ed.)].

JH: Two of your recent Drafts are being published in *Boundary 2* and *Feminist Studies*. "Draft 52: Midrash," in fact, meditates on Adorno's contention that "To write poetry after Auschwitz is barbaric." And "Draft 49: Turns, an Interpretation" provides a history of feminist struggles. Are these poems or criticism?

RD: As a mode of practice, poetry is capacious of genres. The essay-in-verse is at least as old as Pope and Dryden in Anglo-American tradition and as new as Ashbery, Bernstein, and [Jena] Osman. Poetry can explore many discursive spaces. And most importantly, a poem can be a path for thinking through mate-rial. Adorno's *sententia* presented itself to me first in "Draft 29: Intellectual Auto-biography," but then, as central to "Draft 52," as necessary for me to think through in a serial form that honored, rejected, returned to, resisted, became angry at, became sympathetic to the claim he made. A serial mode allows the conflictual vectors of thought and their nuanced gradations to be presented. It's a stark, stunned, and stricken poem on his intransigent statement. The "history" of con-temporary feminism and the impossibility of comprehending all the sociocultural "turns" of that history, even despite my being avidly attentive to it, was written in a form modeled on Louis Zukofsky's long poem "Mantis," which has a companion poem "Mantis, an interpretation." His poem tries to comprehend his politics; mine tries to comprehend mine. Both of us use the so-called interpretation con-ceptually. And both of those recent Drafts are indeed essayistic enterprises.

JH: Could you discuss how you started writing long poems?

RD: Drafts began with what I started to feel in 1985 as the formal and ideological inadequacy of lyric, of the short poem, especially given the gender positionality of the female figure. As a woman occupying cultural spaces, I had the potential to be the female figure in someone else's lyric, but not in my own. And I was saying "No"—I was not going to accept that cultural position. Therefore, I entered into a kind of cri-tique of the lyric, a gendered critique, which made me want no longer to write the lyric but to go beyond it in some way. Thus I jumped track in my own practice. This apparent rejection of the lyric is a tendentious position and certainly very debatable; certain contemporary writers—Barbara Guest is an example—get a lot from

embracing the lyric. Also, of course, the Drafts are "lyrical," as many people—
Nathaniel Mackey and Hank Lazer—have said, sort of chuckling. I'm not trying to
exclude "the lyric" from poetry because that would be truly a quixotic gesture. I
wanted to surround it, to build through it, and to rupture it—to break it up inside to
become something else. I wanted to break a monochromatic subjectivity, a limit in
tone, a smallness which builds one iconic object against the void and does not
acknowledge the void inside the text. And I am also rejecting poems that are centered
only in the private world, not a social and political world. This position was enabling
for me. There are any number of other interlocking reasons: awe, grief, astonish-
ment, the plethora, being overwhelmed. Then there is the whole area of cultural
ambition, to open up into the largest kind of space, the challenge of scope itself. I just
want to write a lot of women's words right now because, basically, there are so many
absent women in my generation, in generations past, and in all of culture.

JH: So in a sense, you are talking about the importance of magnitude for the
sake of magnitude because of a diminishment or absence.

RD: Both Dorothy Richardson and Gertrude Stein were doing the same thing:
writing a gigantic oeuvre, a mound of oeuvre, to separate themselves definitively
from all of the traditions of the novel, and—I don't know what to call Stein,
exactly—of thinking/writing that went before in order to start a new tradition.
And of course those were heroic acts. Virginia Woolf had the same general cultural ambition as those other two, to de-track culture as it was and to make something completely different. Poets such as Alice Notley and Susan Howe have also
indicated the need for a cultural responsibility to women by creating large and
encompassing structures with a female signature.

JH: In retrospect, it is easy to see how Richardson, Stein, Woolf were heroic.
Yet it was precisely a certain sense of the heroic they were working against. Do you
see your own efforts in Drafts as heroic?

RD: That is a word it would be uncanny to apply to oneself. For me Drafts are
compelled. The project is called—in the sense of vocation. Drafts are a poem of
desire, so I am a desirer. I work into the page that called me. And I think I am a
worker, a cultural worker, not a hero.

JH: How did you hit on the concept of "fold" exactly?

RD: I have made very few rules for this poem, and all have occurred heuristi-
cally, in process. Within Drafts, formally, each poem is autonomous. That is, each
poem has a beginning, a middle, and an end, although they close only to open

again into the next poem. So the challenge was how to make a structure so that each thing is autonomous but linked. At "Draft 19," all of a sudden it occurred to me, I could "begin again"—a Steinian move. By beginning again, I could construct a fold or crease across which the poems related. The fold involves any kind of connection between two specific Drafts, one of which I call "the donor draft." What I'm trying to do is sustain a continuous, generative folding of one work over another. "Draft 1: It" now relates to "Draft 20: Incipit" and "Draft 39: Split" and "Draft 58: In Situ." It's a modular and responsive building, always on this periodicity of nineteen. Why nineteen? I have no idea. A happy numerological accident? An important age for me? My mother's birthday, June 19? That was an answer only about the mechanisms of the fold. However, the deep feelings of the fold, or its epistemology, are harder to articulate. I have the sense that with folding and repetition, all parts of the work are involved with all parts, each touches on all. There is a topology of mutuality, even mutual pleasure and relatedness. By establishing "donor drafts," different poems become "muses" for each other. This avoids any "I/you" muses, with those well-worn gender ruts, and makes the pronominal interaction more like "she/it" in the poem as a whole.

JH: Will this poem end?

RD: That is a very fraught question, biographically and technically. As an outcome of the idea of a fold or continuous linking of poems, I recently worried about potential terminus and decided that the poem would be a grid of six units of 19 poems each or 114. My next response was precisely to violate or destabilize that grid, completing a sportive and serious poem "outside" of the structure. This work, called *Draft, unnumbered: Précis*, published in 2003 with Nomados in Vancouver, is a fifty-seven poem summary of all the Drafts in the first three groups of nineteen, written in quasi-sonnet form. This unnumbered Draft operates as a benchmark set at the apparent center of this project. But I am amused to know that there will always be one more poem than the apparent plan calls for. And maybe other things like that will happen.

JH: Throughout your Drafts there is a sense of a negative operating in relationship to language, say, as defined by Giorgio Agamben in his discussion of Hegel, namely that the word "this" is not the same as the referent to which "this" refers. Thus, he concludes that language itself constitutes a field of negation. While this sense of language can create a sense of diminishment or disconnection, actually for Agamben, it offers possibility, freedom, because of the ways that language can thereby be asserted to constitute existence. Do these ideas, in fact, correspond to your sense of language as it is developed in Drafts?

RD: "Draft 1: It" incorporated two written letters, an N and a Y, for No and Yes; the motif of No and Yes continues in the poem. I feel extremely aware of void, or the unexpressed, the inexpressible, the partial, and the oddness of language when I write. However, it's not clear I want fully to assent to the tricky idea of language as a "field of negation," just because of gap and slippage. For language is also "socio-twisty," filled with its histories of use, filled with etymology, filled with associations of sound that can set up many emotional reverberations. Plenitude is not the same as absence, but they are joined in a space which I am aware of, sometimes, in writing.

Drafts began with a sense of "It." It's all *It*. So the sense of language in the poems is, in part, deictic, and yet not affirmative, not part of affirmative culture. If I were certain we were using the words the same way, I'd say that Drafts is a poem of negativity, but not negation. However, on the third hand, the deictic function, just pointing, might be imagined to preclude sound and the music of poetry, to be just the dry "this."

JH: As your Drafts have gone on, they seem to have taken up ever more dark-ness into themselves, the darkness not only of the absences of language itself, but also of traumatic twentieth-century historical events. Some critics of your work have stressed the role of memory and loss in your work, yet it seems to me it is more often about apprehension and disappearance, as if our actual lives—in their very fragility in language, and their haunting through historical events—are hardly palpable enough for the rich reserves of memory as we typically under-stand it. Would you agree with this?

RD: This is a powerful way of putting it. However, it does not nullify the obser-vations of other critics. The poem has many threads.

JH: Can you talk more about the Jewish aspects of your writing? The idea of midrash is very important to you, for example. Could you discuss this?

RD: Midrash is a textual mode of perpetual gloss in Hebrew textuality. The peo-ple who did midrash are obviously only the trained, highly educated rabbis, and they did it only on sacred text. Women are excluded in the orthodox tradition, as you know, and even in some conservative traditions. But when I discovered midrash, it became a metaphor for what I was already doing, which is a perpetual gloss on secular text. So Drafts are built by a midrashic sensibility. The midrashic element of Drafts is the fact that similar lines or quoted lines come back in new contexts, and the poem is like a self-gloss mechanism. The conceptual word "midrash" comes in two times so far. "Draft 6," written in 1987 and 1988, is called "Midrush"—with a decided pun, having to do with the belatedness of the whole project of Drafts—that I was in a rush, I was in a mid-rush, it was in mid-life and midrush. In my newest book manuscript *Drafts 39–57, Pledge*, my "Draft 52" on Adorno's famous remark, in fact, bears the title "Midrash."

Fairly early on in writing Drafts, I was startled to see that motifs around my particular kind of attenuated Judaism really started coming in, especially key Biblical stories such as the near-sacrifice of Isaac, Jacob's struggle with the angel, or Jacob in the desert, Rachel sitting on the father's household idols that she has stolen from him in exiting from his household—the idols are a curiosity, of course, for monotheism. Now I'm a completely secular Jew; I had no religious training inside Judaism. So the emergence of these stories was unexpected, yet something I needed to honor. And then the long shadow of the Holocaust began to appear in the poem. It is just as the psychoanalysts Nicolas Abraham and Maria Torok propose: there is a transgenerational phantom in our century. I think it haunts modernity—you know, whether it's Native Americans, whether it's the Middle Passage, whether it's the Armenian genocide, whether it's the Holocaust, whether it's Rwanda. The Holocaust is only one horror among other horrors, although six million Jews is a lot of people, and there were others besides them. The unthinkable above another unthinkable. The fact that we've lived in a century of enormity. It's just . . . amazing to me . . . and that that's part of this void . . . the enormity and the void that started coming into my work. There was nothing that I could do about it one way or the other. I couldn't. . . . I was only careful not to claim more than I understood or knew, because of my poetics, really the ethics, of Objectivism.

JH: In introducing you at the Subtext reading series in Seattle, I described your writing as "vertiginous" or as producing a sense of vertigo. It seems that something in your writing tumbles over on itself, and then there's some kind of hearing and rehearing that's going on. The writing is both moored and unmoored in ways that I really like.

RD: That's fascinating. One central concern of Drafts has to do with being a little dot in a very big universe. I mean this sounds sentimental, but it's quite deeply felt—I wouldn't even say spiritual, because it's much beyond spiritual. It is ontological: there's nothing like us out there, so far as we can find out, and somehow we're here, and so you have this little teeny dot of a mark, which in Hebrew is called the yod. Here is this little yod, set in a vast universe in which anything could happen and it did—which is the motif of the Holocaust for me, and the other genocides that formed modernity. Then you look out there at the great arc of things, and you're this little speaking dot—it's most amazing. And that causes vertigo. The vertigo for me is continuous; it's what we're in and of. So in Drafts the scale changes from very big to little. It happens a lot in my work verbally, thematically, and formally.

JH: This seems to me based in a certain kind of experience with language which one senses in some poets and not in others.

RD: To me, it's a form of continuance. Just the sort of rush of trying to pack as much into a line, a word, a shift, as possible. To create an experience by juxtaposing elements. Some of what you are hearing comes from control of the line. Understanding that I could do whatever I damn pleased with the line was very liberating. I found that I could play with the line as a kind of accordion; it could be really long or really short. I have one-word lines next to ten-word lines. Just an enormous kind of variation. I have become more and more aware of the relationship of syntax and segmentivity, or syntax and line break, because how you situate or locate a phrase in the sentence and along the line can create all kinds of different effects in a poem. How you elect to deploy syntax and spoken emphasis, how you move statement across a line, and where you break a line are all incredibly important to me—the build, the timing of disclosure, and their relationship to the white page, the canvas. So that's part of how that feeling of vertigo, or rush, envelopment gets created in the poetry.

JH: So that it's pulsating. Is this pulsating in the writer or in the reader?

RD: It's in the writer. I work and work on sequencing of materials and movement. On everything, really. Revision for me is very much about the right word, which is the right sound, which is the right etymology of the word, which is the right history of the word, the right texture or weight of the word, the question is it a simple word, is it a complex word, is it a diction choice that shocks the poem, or is it a word of another kind. I really work at choice, so that when something's done, it's built. I think about these things all the time. Every single little choice is like a risk choice, fraught with potential meaning and resonance. And so every single mark is making meaning in a poem. Including a comma, a capital, everything. It's part of the great pleasure of writing, actually, playing with language like that. Waiting for the moment when language plays with you.

JH: But do you actually write out of a kinetic sense, as if you yourself are pulsating, or are you concentrating on manipulating the language to produce this effect in the reader?

RD: Both, everything. There's no one answer to that question, except I don't like the word "manipulating" in relation to writing. At a certain point in my writing, I needed to be very pure and lucid. I was very afraid of beauty, sensuousness, seeing them as part of a foundational cluster of the lyric. That was pretty poetry, pretty girl—the poetess and all that, and down the tubes. However, this rejection was somewhat inhibiting for my poetry. It was an ideological position that affected the actual writing—by blocking it. Sound was my way out of this dilemma. Sound is much larger than just beauty, just this tremendous force and resource in poetry. Now I have a symphonic sense about the poems of Drafts. They're on this vast stage and there's a lot of reverberation, a lot of symphonic sound that can be created.

JH: You are increasingly becoming known as a poet. Yet, for a long time, your primary reputation was as a feminist critic. Can you comment on why you think your reputation as a poet has lagged behind your career as a feminist critic?

RD: In my own eyes, I was a poet first. But my project as a critic came to public fruition before my project as a poet. This is related both to feminism and to gender, as I experienced them, and also because of blockage and the belatedness that come from misplaced "perfectionism." My first poetry book, *Wells*, was published in 1980, about fifteen years later than first books from poets in my age cohort. To some degree, this feeling of blockage was related to what I had intuited as the position of women in culture but had no way of describing until 1968 because I was, with most others, prefeminist. Also I was involved in an implicit debate about the nature of poetry. I wanted a very pure poetry, an essential poetry, a very fine, compressed, focused poetry. That was my partial, incomplete reading of Objectivist poetics at that time. These stylistic and rhetorical choices taught me a lot, but I was always stopping, not going on. And then the third thing: it was quite hard being a woman in the university and sticking it out. The university did not embrace us with open arms in the Vietnam era, when we entered as supercargo. Part of my struggle was to survive as a woman with a serious, income-producing career that I would have no matter what. So for a lot of reasons, my poetic career was relatively dormant.

JH: What changed these blockages for you?

RD: Until I realized my own kind of feminist project, I didn't understand the poems I had been writing. I could not read myself. Then I wrote a few poems transforming the myths of Eurydice and Medusa to tell "women's stories." This revisionary mythopoesis was generative at that moment of feminist thinking. In the early 1980s, I started writing poems called The "History of Poetry," where I wanted to write the poems of women poets, real or imagined, from prior historical periods. A project historically imperial, perhaps, but earnest and urgent. From this, emerged a poem called "Crowbar," which I'm still quite fond of, in which I speak as the female in trobar clus poems, prying that structure of feeling up with a feminist crowbar. In 1984, our baby daughter arrived after a lot of Sturm und Drang around children. That was very liberating, and then I wrote the poem called "Writing." That poem, as I already said, tipped me into Drafts. By then, at the age of forty-two, I was a late early mother and a somewhat late early poet.

JH: How is it that you came into contact with or were motivated by avant-garde practices that were not part of your immediate surroundings?

RD: Here I'd want to talk of four essential things—the poetry wars around The New American Poetry,[2] the Oppens, Montemora as a magazine, and the HOW(ever) nexus. From the beginning I had a serious attraction to field poetry, collage, and especially seriality. Very straight-up poetry was rewarded at Barnard College when I was there, by the figure of Robert Pack. At the time I was in college, The New American Poetry anthology had just come out, and I read it. It was taboo. It was the other side. I mean there really were sides. It was thus I read Robert Duncan's "A Poem Beginning with a Line by Pindar" and was stunned. Because there was the lyricism, the use of myth, the colloquial language, the historical, critical litany of the [U.S.] Presidents. It just blew me open about what poetry could be. The connection to tradition and the transformation of tradition, all of those things were very palpable for me. Obviously, I read Ginsberg's "Howl" and a little Charles Olson and Robert Creeley but it was really Duncan. The sound, and the scope of that particular work, the voracity and splay of it, the way he took in so much, the hypersaturation of the means were very inspiring to me. That poem was a benchmark. I was also interested in nonconformist fictional forms. Doris Lessing's The Golden Notebook was extremely inspiring, around late college into early graduate school, for its dynamic depiction of female lives and choices and for the dimensionality—psychic life, sexual life, and political life all addressed. William Carlos Williams's Paterson had just been published in England in 1964, and when I opened it, I was opening myself to the modern long poem, which was still quite underread at that point. Its enormous encyclopedic weirdness was a reading challenge. I felt, "I've got to know how to read this; I want to figure this stuff out," and so I became quite interested in Pound and Williams. I gave myself a grounding that has never gone away. I wrote my dissertation, *The Endless Poem*, on Pound and Williams.

JH: And the Oppens and Objectivism, could you talk more about these?

RD: I was most formed in poetry by Oppen's uncompromising commitment to exactness, sincerity, and social and existential focus, along with a brilliant and challenging use of segmentivity—line break and page space—and seriality—argument by vector and leap. Oppen's objectivism brings with it a concern for ethics and social insight that is also part of my engagement with poetry. I met George Oppen in 1965, and I became a cousinly visitor to George and Mary. George was so clearly a major and important figure. He was also incredibly funny, incredibly fun to be with, very wry, droll—like Groucho Marx as major poet. He was an amazing figure, and it was an education, a pleasure to be in any sense connected to him. I would show him poems, so did other people, and they generally came back with a lot fewer lines than they had started with, which made some people mad. I sort of took it. I learned a kind of poetic conscience from George that has never gone away, a sense of the necessity to say only what you must and to say it in a focused way. He taught one not to fake what you thought you knew. I remember writing this completely horrible poem about these people in New Jersey on the highway, which was an Oppenesque topos—and his attitude was, "Get off it. You don't know what these people are saying to each other in that car." And I realized, "Well, right, I don't." The criterion he taught me was sincerity. The testing of the words, the emotion, the feel of the work by a deep inner ethos and a deep inner ear. He also had a horror of un-won words and any moralizing.

So I began to learn to speak from the core of who I am, that is, being a woman, and this led right into the politics of the time: you don't organize where you're not, you don't organize other people, you organize where you are. From Oppen I learned, in effect, to be focused, not self-indulgent, and those lessons did not, in a young poet, lead to much writing. For a long time, I had George on my shoulder, the way Virginia Woolf describes having the angel in the house on her shoulder. I had Oppen with me all the time, and it was not always a great thing because he was a judgmental presence. So it took me a long time, but the lessons, the sense of the line, and the necessity of the work, of what the work could be, were ultimately liberating. One of the most astonishing experiences of my life was being confronted with an early version of "Of Being Numerous" and being asked to respond. I was able, finally, to say something that stuck with him. I asked him the question "Whether, as the intensity of seeing increases, one's distance / from Them, the people, does not also increase," and he put this question into the poem as the opening of section 9 and proceeded to answer it. I think his "answer" in that section—"I know, of course I know, I can enter no other place"—was the first time I understood that you could talk the most vital arguments directly into the page. That was what making a poem was all about. That was another insight into the poem as a practice of thinking and responding in your time and place: now. Oppen's scope and swing from the political to the spiritual in one vertiginous swoop was a challenge and a model. For him the stakes of poetry were as high and deliberate as possible.

JH: Did you ever feel that powerful mentor figures are potentially dangerous?

RD: I actually was very resistant to male mentors. I certainly was resistant to them in the university. The only way for a woman to survive in the university was to be mentored. But I really resisted being mentored. So I just wandered off in my own little spin. For some reason I could accept mentoring from George, under erasure, possibly because this mentoring concerned my poetry. He was mentoring what I wanted to have mentored! George was helpful because of his example. Because of the criterion of sincerity. And because he never traded on his name to get me anything. That was the great thing about George. That was the most supportive thing. He never said, "Oh well, I'll get you published here." And that was great, it was fabulous, because I retained this intransigent independence that in retrospect seems astonishing, even touching when I look back.

JH: What about *Montemora*?

RD: Being published in *Montemora* was crucial. I saw *Montemora* first up in Maine. The Oppens had a little library there. George had just been published by Eliot Weinberger. And I thought, "Oh, this looks like a good magazine; maybe I'll send some poems there." When Eliot liked my work and I got published there, I couldn't have been happier. I understood, with *Montemora*, that one could have a community of intention, spirit, and intelligence around a magazine. *Montemora* was a virtual community where writers challenged each other, even if they were not in on a scene together. *Montemora* was a magazine with an international sensibility, a global sensibility in the most productive ways.

JH: What about *HOW(ever)* and other feminist writers? What relation did these have to your poetry?

RD: When I went to France in 1970, I basically exited from Columbia Women's

Liberation, where I'd been very active, sat down finally to read Kate Millett's *Sexual Politics*, which had been her dissertation at Columbia, and we'd said, "Kate, Kate, this is going to be really important!" And it was. With that book and with Woolf's *A Room of One's Own*, I realized in this incredible flash, that out of feminism, *all* culture would have to be changed. The implications of feminism were not just for a political project, which of course I was for—not just a social or a legal project, a movement for equality—but that all culture, in both the aesthetic and anthropological senses, would have to be transformed. This flash is still with me. That's what I work out of.

Although, what then happened was that contemporary poetry by women opened and closed. The force of that project narrowed. You could write certain kinds of poems about women that were often anthologized early on, in, say, *No More Masks*,³ or some of the other anthologies. I tried to do this, but it didn't work. I couldn't do those poems, because they weren't saying all of what I wanted to say. I am a poet of polysemy, of negativity, of the poem as exploration and critique. The critique part did emerge in much of the early feminist women's poetry movement, but other aspects did not. Oppen had made me quite resistant to "right-thinking" poetry of any kind. So that particular mode of feminist poetry, however dynamic, was also blocking for me. The demand for cultural transformation got narrowed very fast to certain kinds of moves around identity that could be made by some people but not by me. I couldn't trade on those parts of me that could be "identity" in that sense—and thus I was a woman poet without being able to draw continuously, seamlessly upon that ideology of "woman's voice" that was so powerful in the late seventies, early eighties. I respected that ideology of voice and its declarative powers, but it was not my mode. I was an Objectivist-influenced poet, yet a feminist. Hence the paradox I lived for many years: I was too Objectivist for the feminists and too feminist for the Objectivists.

And that's the way it went, straight through to the very end of the seventies, when I was published in *Montemora*. Eliot Weinberger, in fact, published some of my early exploratory essays, written in the *Pink Guitar* mode. During this time, I also worked on the editorial collective of *Feminist Studies*, a major journal of scholarship that was sustained by the intellectual and cultural vision of its founder, Ann Calderwood, and after the first few issues, by its managing editor, Claire Moses, and the volunteer board. We were creating a climate and standards for a new field, a set of intersecting analyses, that to me was culturally vital. I was part of that collective for fifteen years. I actually instigated within *Feminist Studies* the publication of creative work by people associated with a radical poetics, but it did not have a large impact.

JH: How did you get connected up with *HOW(ever)*?

RD: I tried writing groups in my near neighborhood in suburban Pennsylvania, but that didn't really work. That's why *HOW(ever)* was so vital to me from its inception. Although I was three thousand miles away, I had an audience in the Bay Area, of Kathleen Fraser, Beverly Dahlen, and Frances Jaffer. I was close in different ways to each of them, and this was all quite merry and generative. These were very important bonds for me, from about the early eighties.

JH: How did you in Philadelphia develop relationships with women poets in San Francisco?

RD: Oh, most of it was through the mail. But I would visit. I went to the Bay Area a lot in those years. I would give readings and talks. I started working on the Oppen letters around 1981, so that brought me there, too. The *HOW(ever)* group was incredibly important as personal and poetic support—and as an intellectual project. It was Kathleen Fraser's genius to see that the great women modernists could be considered, must now be considered, the contemporaries of the present. They had never been culturally assimilated in the way they were being understood at this time, because of the advent of feminist criticism. I'm not trying to downgrade the reception of the twenties, but it got sort of attenuated. Then, for decades, it was, "Gee, honey, I lost women's writing." So the fact was that the whole of twentieth-century women writers, innovative writers of fiction and poetry, reaching back into the beginning of the twentieth century, became our contemporaries at the moment of *HOW(ever)*. It was the great declaration of *HOW(ever)* to make that so, to negotiate that. I felt that that *was* my community. Women innovative writers became my community, in ways that were both personally and poetically satisfying.

JH: That's very interesting. I had no idea *HOW(ever)* was that important to you.

RD: Absolutely. For example, reading Beverly Dahlen's *A Reading* was vital to the beginning of the project of Drafts.[4] There was a moment when it was, "Well, go ahead, you know? What are you waiting for?" Because it seems to me that Dahlen's project summed up, or entered into, the demands that Williams had articulated, to write with the force moving. And to write where you are. The poetics of Dahlen's work was particularly apt for a long project. I was struck by her ability to enter wherever she was and create a continuance. So you're here; this is it. Entering, to begin anywhere, is clearly a motif that comes out of this American, postwar, if you want to say postmodern, poetics. But begin anywhere. You're here. Begin. It's like the Creeley mode, it could be the David Antin mode, the Robin Blaser mode.

That was all very helpful and important to me without gainsaying the psychic excitement and buoyancy and the connection to the projects of other writers. I was just beginning to listen to certain Language writers in those years, especially to Rae Armantrout, Lyn Hejinian, and Ron Silliman. At the same time, I was a contributing editor to *Sulfur*, edited by Clayton Eshleman, a magazine of an often, although not exclusively, expressivist poetics. I published some of my essays there, including one on Duchamp.

JH: Did you ever wish that you did not have so many different things going, including two rather different careers, of being an academic and being a poet? Have you ever wished to be primarily or only a poet?

RD: This has got to be a trick question, since any answer is necessarily problematic! I am also not sure one is ever "only" one thing, particularly a poet. Let's simply say I made a vow to cultural critique with the rise of feminism. I have kept that vow in a number of genres and modes. I am proud to be one of a cohort of poet-critics who emerged in my generation and are active in the next generation, too. Poetry is the center of my writing at this moment, because I want to bring the project Drafts to as much clarity and finish as possible. That is, I want all the time I can have now for the work I need to complete.

Notes

Thanks to Ross Posnock and a Heilman grant from the English Department of the University of Washington for providing monies for DuPlessis's visit to Seattle and for the transcription of this interview and to Ezra Mark, a Seattle poet and member of the Subtext Collective, for an impeccable transcription of it.
  1. The quotation is from an unpublished manuscript called "Sidelights to a Career in Writing" (—ed.).
  2. See Donald Allen's groundbreaking anthology, *The New American Poetry, 1945–1960* (—ed.).
  3. Florence Howe's important collection of twentieth-century women's poetry (with a clear feminist orientation) was first published in 1973 (—ed.).
  4. See Dahlen's *A Reading 1–7* and *A Reading 8–10*, among other volumes (—ed.).

—from "Crowbar"

End of the dogwood
start of the greenwood
end of the greenword song
but time repeats its greens and browns
the clues it leaves declare.

     lay dee   hist! story
     l'idée   mystery
     lay dés   My hyster   y

who threw a ring who kept a ring
who caroled the rich greenwoody song
all MherY duplicity of gesture
a throw of the ring not
abolishing

the Nymph of the Fountain:
to pray the nymph for this her safe return
to stop up the crevices of the mountain
a little IUD of wire this nymph n-
ode   cannot stand it, inseparable
complicit and disgusted desire.

A crowbar of trobar
pow
it
tries
desire, "thou"
the fulcrum

pries open the cellular troping
nucleii and the ever
drowning dark abyss

My Lady   Me Lady.

—*from* "Writing"

[. . . . .]
.A wri-
ting marks the
patch of void
foggy reflecting
mist catches wet carlight

that everything tests   film
condenses   fine tip flairs
refracted silence   baby wipes
The cold rush up   khaki thread
the dark dark trees   nipples
Somnulent spots of travel

Letters are canal-
ized as white foams
zagging, a fissure on the
sheet,
    tangle of branches unorganized without the leaves
cock-eyed underbelly of
plenitude of

---

mark. *outtakes, can imagine conversations?*
conversions?
Long passages of satisfaction swallowed up
in darkness.

[...]
.The torso fleurie *wanting to have her book virtually nameless*
flying vagini under full sail
twirl out a leaf print *what is the most transparent name?*
the point, sweet business,
treads water *is everything, or enough — so that*
we are where

charging janus penis janus
thick right at the cusp
we are.

slowly cover the space
bright disc harken

what were the women like?
down down down *Evidence he wrote in The Vita Nuova: They*
by the orbiting ocean. *travelled together*
and commented incessantly on Dante's
red blotches
his leaning weakly against a wall
for love.

—Draft 27: Athwart
  November 1995, February 1996, June–July 1996

  1
There was an other side
      a space behind, in back,
an overmuch, an
            into which

where muffled voices throb without their names.
                    It, whatever the term,
          falls out of range
                    such regular registers
as corporations,
          justifications,
                    orchestrated bailouts—
          basically, what computes.

Screening odd stuff curled in the can
          all of it strictly rushes,
          it showed drive, but drifted into derive,
          hardly a "ray focusing"
                    anything to a point,
          hardly
                    what needed to be considered.
          Cheerfully "now," a callow vector,
with the before missing, the after inconsequent.
          Twenty years here,
                    twenty there
                              flare
                              and go frail.

2

Unsolicited mourning
                    floods this site
          a well of muted consciousness.
          Connaissance inutile.
                         Do you make it *useless knowledge?*
          helpless
                    understanding?
                    or *unthinkable recognition?*
Untranslatable it
          is the transverse torque
                    across this course.

A lost specificity:
            not documentary, not song,
but a wall;
        "the" evoked, but what's to point at—
            incomprehensible zero space?
            the ledger's incalculable underside?

An execution usually "over there,"
        some last words that
            frame the poisonous cavils
of the general listener
      who modifies and justifies
who disclaims and denies,
         but basically can't stop
           going along.

    3
Next day, cyclonic rains,
      from which the tree,
an oak of sixty feet
      and sixty years, fell down.
      A tilted force pushed through the winds of ferocity.
Its final muffled noise and muted rush
         were quick,
              a surprise how reverberant,
         how hard to assimilate.

            Ragge of verse
    buffeted by high roaring
              deep
       negation, hole/hold can sometimes split and pivot,
   can create subjunctive hope and affirming rhetorics
            that it may be protected! so provide
          a giant hand to dust tree off and root it deep again!
      from flake to shape remake irrevocable time!

Give us a shallow dent of dirt in which to prop!

There was a time
up thru November 10
wherein the tree
just was, its oakish life
as such.
One storm and
one thud. It's the work of a moment.
An "event."
Something live from the winds
that empties "is"
of its simplicities
and pours "it" as libation on the ground.

4
Within the concert of the known
an errant sort
gets thrown, whereupon
largo twists itself
into capriciousness.
The event lists,
for the soloist,
inside a labyrinth of forgetting,
can not fake it any longer.
His hands fall athwart.
His memory has emptied.

The lapse looms large adrift
belongside what should have
been unquestionable song.
Its cumbersome shadow
blots a round of Mozart.
His hands lift from the piano.

The others strung with visible notes
        their lyric loops of light
                and kept the music going on
                        about the absent sounds.

But they too stopped
        by the empty site
                and had to drop
one upon one, at the deepening spot,
                      and fall with him.

5

The social world, they said, "drained
Is writing the bringing of justice?   from the work" after
Is just light   the "conventional
justice?   icons of the 30's,"
                    the "standard fare
compromised.   of the time." Quote "in
                      1940, when he began
            to spend summers in Martha's Vineyard,
      the social world drained from his work." Unquote.

6

Narrow market-casting
        is meant to prevent
                feeling much, even any, of this.
        It sutures us to things
we will buy
        whatever, straight thru time
                and never look at shame. The process
has been graduated
        in the dispensary, has been stuffed
                with a fine calibration of insistence.
Ambient desires, flavors, and crunchy patenting of colors
            can tell their demographic riddles

to those with ears to harvest the nuances.

And the autumn wet and drear?
the blood-dark leaf?
the button fallen on the street, some "useless scrap its power"?
The flowering pear that
    went its route, a ruddy green, then full, then red, then gold
then god, then golem-brown, its planet balls of rust that
starlings eat?
      Ghosts. Ghosts of ghosts at the open fosse.

NOTE: "Connaissance inutile" [in section 2,—ed.] is Charlotte Delbo's phrase about knowledge gained in, and by virtue of, the Holocaust. "Ragge of verses" [in section 3,—ed.] is John Donne. "Useless scrap its power" [in section 6,—ed.] is Eliot Weinberger on Cecilia Vicuña. The citation about the artist [in section 5,—ed.] is from a *Times* review of Aaron Siskind (as in "Draft 14"). Related to "Draft 8: The."

—*from* "Draft 52: Midrash"

[This serial poem is a 27-section midrash on Theodor Adorno's famous statement from *Prisms*, "To write poetry after Auschwitz is barbaric" (trans. Samuel and Shierry Weber, Cambridge, MA: The MIT Press, 1981, 34). We are publishing only the final sections here, along with a few of the author's notes to this poem.—ed.]

25

In half-wounded syntax, grid, fragment,
chunk chord and collage, make
things to say things
by a "Venture into the dark 'flat' side of their harmony"

   suspicious intensities and political laceration
   with the investment one sees meditation scrupulous remnant
of twentieth century history I know
    what I wanted. It was the endlessly overwritten

erosions of the book,   specificities
of book, and the voice of the traveler-   detail
            poem by its edgy sentence
its ontological intransigence to Let
Be   austere hermetic readable urgency.
Smoke and billows   salient
shifting so that one is caught in
                        hypnogogic shakedowns
their whorled resonance,   their dark bars, even access blocked.

The beyond is in the surface.
Walking through the dead as partly dead
—it must only be
an impossible draft of half-built, half-crumbled
all-suspicious poetry.

    26

        Doomed to resonate in a "tricky faceted phrase"
the paper coming apart in one's hands
the pages blown
from the "it self," or loss.

        Forget transfiguration
forget frisson
while it is impossible, think you are going
beyond any pattern in the aesthetics we know

forget "point" or end
try maybe
gridded series of embeddings and strange angles;
prime the lines with bolts of dark.

        Over and over. While a portion of this may be called "art."
it is difficult to give a name to the rest of the portions.

27

"The slain are really slain."
The letters flew up into the sky
with a hot blast as the bodies lie
inert slips of light and dark
in the smoke
of the smoke
forlorn and helpless.

"The abundance of real suffering
permits no forgetting."
Yet memory does not work that way.
It works another way, halfway, a ground lens,
a great stark. One little scrap where something is.
Incommensurate.

March–July 2002
not dedicated

NOTE: From Adorno's essay "Commitment," a passage about two pages long that begins "I do not want to soften my statement that it is barbaric to continue to write poetry after Auschwitz; it expresses, negatively, the impulse that animates committed literature" (*Notes to Literature*, vol. 2, 87). The passage is very intricate. He agrees, for example, with the critique of his absolute position offered by Hans Magnus Enzensberger "that literature must resist precisely this verdict, that is, be such that it does not surrender to cynicism merely by existing after Auschwitz" (88). He further argues that it is unthinkable to engineer "transfiguration": "By this alone an injustice is done the victims, yet no art that avoided the victims could stand up to the demands of justice" (88). However, turning the victims into "works of art, [they are] tossed out to be gobbled up by the world that did them in," an ethical nightmare of the aesthetic. Adorno acknowledges the (disturbing) fact that one may get kinds of pleasure from the depiction of horror. Furthermore, he rejects the "dreary metaphysics" of a humanism (and presumably journalism) that "shows us humanity blossoming in so-called extreme situations"—a "cozy existential atmosphere" whose implications are happier for "the executioners" than the victims. Finally, he acknowledges that an artist should not produce straightforward political art, or art of commitment, but understand, rather, that the political has "migrated into" all art (93) and work with those facts and their implications. In short, this later passage may be called Adorno's own midrash on his earlier statement.

Section 25: "Venture into the dark 'flat' side of their harmony," David Wright, Nonesuch CD notes for Philip Glass, Symphony #3, modified. Section 27: "The slain are really slain," Horkheimer letter to Walter Benjamin, 1937, cited in *The Arcades Project* (Cambridge, MA: Harvard UP, 1999, 471). "The abundance of real suffering permits no forgetting," Adorno, "Commitment," *Notes to Literature*, vol. 2, 88.

alice fulton

INTRODUCTION

Alice Fulton grew up in upstate New York, and the language of some of her most colloquial lines captures the intonations of that region ("Hi Ma," one of her most recent books, *Felt*, closes, "I finished my book. / It cooled off nice"). But Fulton's work is no more circumscribed by regionalism than Emily Dickinson's poetry is. Fulton's poems are multiply layered, dense with an immediacy of presence and spontaneity of wit. They satisfy both the ear and the mind by the controlled, complex exuberance of the language. Fulton is known for defining a new sign of punctuation that she calls the "bride" sign and writes as a double equal sign (= =). The poem "Immersion," for example, begins with a Dickinsonian series of definitions: "It's sensual math / and untied railroad tracks = = / the ladder of gaps and lace / unlatched. It's staples / in the page and the swimmer's liquid lane." Soon, however, the activity of defining shifts attention to psychological process, moving into idiosyncratic perspective, as "one thought is occluded by another / no less celestial mention in your head = =." The poem ends with open first-person speech and an assertion of the speaker's closeness to the reader, yet with increasingly metaphorical analogies. Finally, the still-elusive double equal sign itself is the end punctuation, the final "word." This speaker is "immersed" in the ideas of the poem to the extent that identity is unrecognizable except *as* a perspective, as suggestive as "= =".

Strikingly flexible in their diction and manner, Fulton's poems often include puns and slang, but her topics are deeply serious, as the following interview with the distinguished critic-scholar Cristanne Miller confirms. The poems are epistemological in their concerns: What is it possible to know? How does scientific knowledge affect the perceptions of common sense? How do the powers of language relate to media culture, scientific discovery, imperialism, gender, and the petty inhumanity or graciousness of everyday feelings and events? Some of her most significantly innovative work has been in poetic series, particularly in terms of the way a Fultonian speaker's identity shifts in order to question the foundations of identifying constructions, like race, class, and gender. In this updated interview, Fulton discusses such issues at length in relation to the poems excerpted here from the series "Give"—which retells the Apollo and Daphne myth from the (possible) perspective of a black Daphne.

Fulton's sustained poetic method of allusive, associative leaps, collage, and quotation is effortlessly inventive. Deftly negotiating the "passional" analytic that underlies some of her most significant work, Fulton makes strikingly postmodern some of the foundational poetic experiments of modernism. She is among the few poets of her generation to contemplate the ethical value of immersion—the surfeit of feeling—which has come to be associated in her work with generosity of spirit and compassion. In her most recent poetry, she enjoins us to immerse ourselves, to risk the too-muchness of others' feelings or our own feelings for others (including, as in "Some Cool," other sentient, intelligent beings, like pigs taken to slaughter), from which we ordinarily try to protect ourselves—as "Fair Use," included here, implies, to *interfeel*.

Felt was awarded the 2002 Rebekah Johnson Bobbitt National Prize for Poetry from the Library of Congress and was selected by the *Los Angeles Times* as one of the Best Books of 2001. Her other books include *Palladium* (1986), which won a National Poetry Series Award; *Feeling as a Foreign Language: The Good Strangeness of Poetry* (1999), a prose collection of essays; and *Cascade Experiment: Selected*

Poems (2004). Fulton has received fellowships from the John D. and Catherine T. MacArthur Foundation, the Ingram Merrill Foundation, and the Guggenheim Foundation. She is Ann S. Bowers Professor of English at Cornell University.

This interview was conducted at Pomona College in Claremont, California, during a three-day visit, November 14–16, 1995, and was updated via e-mail in 2004.

AN INTERVIEW WITH ALICE FULTON
by Cristanne Miller

CRISTANNE MILLER: I'm interested in what you call "betweenness" [in *Feeling as a Foreign Language* (—ed.)]. You list "the quality of betweenness: what comes between two quantities, objects, people" or "the nature of being between categories" as an organizational category important to your work and later mention "Thirdness rather than binary thought." Do you see betweenness or nonduality as linked to voice in your poems?

ALICE FULTON: When I began writing in the seventies, everybody was writing voice-based poetry, and young poets were concerned about "finding their voice." One of the tests for whether you were a true poet was whether you had discovered your authentic voice. Right from the beginning, I decided that wouldn't be it for me, that I wasn't interested in finding this thing that spoke through me, or finding a persona that would be mine and would be steady. I was much more interested in language and what could be built of it. I wouldn't have said it in these words, but I was using language as a construct. And that's still how I think of making a poem.

In the newer, polyphonic poems, the voices are multiple. I use various tones and registers of diction and vocabularies as a means of creating a texture of multiple voices within one poem. And these shifting voices, by refusing to build into one steady character or personality, might be said to exist between identities. As for nonduality and voice, my poems that create a speaker without giving any gender clues are trying to disrupt the man/woman binary and suggest a third, less categorical way of being.

CM: You and I have talked a lot about gender in your poems and the fact that for quite a while, even in *Dance Script with Electric Ballerina* [1983], you have consciously not gendered some of the characters who speak in your poems. For example, in a poem from that volume, "Between the Apple and the Stars," you wrote, "the scientist passes / a hand like a wand," rather than "her" or "his" hand. Could you say more about how this connects to the notion of betweenness?

AF: I'm interested in "betweenness" conceptually because it's not a binary. There have to be more than two options. Why should there be only two? Plurality is more inclusive. At first, my decision not to have a male or female narrator or speaker or character in a poem was based on issues of power—not on a wish to be between categories but on a wish to question where power is located. So when I wrote the line you mentioned, I obviously didn't want to say whether the Godlike scientist was female or male. But through talking with you and thinking more, I've realized that if I use the article "a" rather than a gendered pronoun, the persona is inscribed as a man anyway. Today, if I were writing that poem, I would probably write "passes her hand." Otherwise, readers see a hand, and because of the prevalent image of scientists being men, they just inscribe "his" underneath the article "a." I thought I was making it ungendered, but I wasn't. In a way, I have to take affirmative action.

CM: But more recently, for example, in "Echo Location" [*Sensual Math*, 1995 (—ed.; all bracketed material in this chapter is from this volume's editors)], you also don't gender your subjects; don't you switch from "you" to "it" there precisely in order not to use a gendered pronoun?

AF: I made "Echo Location" ungendered because I didn't want either sex or gender to be burdened with the sadistic power the speaker wields at the poem's beginning. I didn't want either sex to be blamed. I used "it" as the pronoun because "Echo Location" thinks about dominance—and reciprocity. The poem describes the dominance of one person over another, of artist over art object, and religion over the aspirant. "It" can sound cruel—it objectifies whatever it refers to. This is how most people hear "it" when the pronoun is applied to a human being. But personally, I feel the pronoun "it" can elicit compassion when it refers to someone who has been stripped of humanity. James Weldon Johnson uses "it" this way, tenderly, in one stanza of "O Black and Unknown Bards": "what captive thing, / Could up toward God through all its darkness grope, / and find within its deadened heart to sing." One of the things I like about the notion of betweenness or third space—actually, it doesn't have to be third; it can be fourth, or fifth, or thousandth—is that it stands outside polarity and dualism. That's why at times I try to say "it" rather than "he" or "she." Most people find the absence of gender or sex disturbing, but it can be liberating. The pronoun "it" can be freeing—even God can be "it." In "Echo Location," "it" refers to the human, the subject, the spirit, the blur. Rather than just avoiding the male/female binary, the pronoun takes on a spectrum of associations.

CM: Do you think about other aspects of identity in the same way in your poems—that is to say, in attempting to avoid fixed notions of identity, like class or race? Not avoid them, but to avoid writing them deterministically?

AF: I began to think about class and race later than I did about gender because gender and feminism were my earliest interests. In "Give: A Sequence Reimagining Daphne and Apollo" [*Sensual Math*], Daphne could be read as a person of color. I'm aware of issues of appropriation, and that's one reason why race wasn't an issue in my earlier poems. I've thought about it a lot, but I'm suspicious of white writers who write novels or stories (more commonly than poetry) in the voice or about the experiences of, say, Native Americans. White writers often say freedom of speech is at stake: "I have the right to write about whatever I want." Well, you do constitutionally have that right; but the ethical question is still one that has to be dealt with. And the ethical question is the one that continues to bother me.

But I've begun to see that an unraced poem by a white writer is going to be read as white—and that wasn't what I wanted either. It was too exclusive, or elitist. I didn't want to write as if the "white world" were the only world, the true world. But I also don't think that people of color need white poets (like me) to speak for them.[1] Writers of color testify to the culture, worlds, experiences they've known and lived; they don't need me to do that for them. Then, too, the disenfranchised don't form a single or simple category. In *Felt*, I write about instances of abasement, cruelty, and suffering that are not necessarily based on race. For instance, "Duty-Free Spirits" alludes to race by referring to the hidden whiteness of dominant U.S. culture, but it's also angry about human pretentiousness and arrogance, angry about "emollients made of mammal fat" or the commodification and subjugation of animals. But that summary makes the poem sound polemical when it's oblique, acerbic, playful, bitter. It's a funny poem, self-mocking. Subjects such as equity, cruelty, et cetera, could be too grim, too oppressive without infusions of beauty and humor. I like the word "fair" [as in "Fair Use" from *Felt*] because it denotes both beauty and justice. I need to keep trying to see many sides of a given situation or subject, so that struggle to encompass can, I hope, help me to avoid exclusive or claustrophobically privileged assumptions.

So in "Give," the Daphne sequence, I suggest in a reticent way that Daphne could be read as a black woman or a white woman. If a reader is attuned to phrases like "dark matter," the Daphne sequence can be racially inscribed. In "Supernal," for instance, Daphne is described as "graphite, / darkling, carbon as the crow. . . ." I thought that people of color, especially, might read those words with race in mind. It seems to me that white readers in general are less attuned to the racial connotations of words such as "dark." "Dark" or "black" are, of course, often used as negative adjectives in English—as synonyms for sad or evil. But these connotations don't reflect upon the image of white people, and so they're less inclined to notice the insidious way in which these negative connotations might encourage prejudice.

In my work, I've tried not to use "dark" to mean anything unhappy. And I've used dark matter to imply the importance of the background—including people who have been consigned to the background. This includes white women, as well as people of color. Most of the universe is composed of dark matter, but attention until recently has centered on the foreground of the universe, the figure, if you will—which is luminous matter. If "dark matter" is inscribed racially, it makes the poem larger, I hope, by calling people of color to mind. By implying issues of power and culture, I hoped to write about disenfranchised people without essentializing. To essentialize is to represent something as an archetype: a steady and timeless entity. Of course, such renditions fail to do justice to the complexity of human experience (or the complexity of time). Rather than truth, essence veers toward the simplistic and stereotypical, forms of dishonesty. But if we allow ourselves (as writers) to complicate rather than simplify, things (and people) are less likely to be trivialized or misrepresented. My best poems seem quirky to me and quirkiness is perhaps the opposite of "essence."

CM: You write in your notebook [in *Feeling as a Foreign Language*] about the "blue note" as an example of betweenness—for example, its being between the major and the minor. I immediately linked that to the blues and to Daphne's mother in "Give." I thought it was wonderful as a kind of blurring effect in terms of this whole notion of dualities and who is placed where, especially since Daphne is such a between figure—nature/culture, human/not-human. . . . Winner/loser also, or maybe it's loser/loser, I'm not sure.

AF: I'd like to think maybe some day a winner. I liked your reading of the last poem in the sequence, where you found hope in the lines ". . . the record turns and turns into / the night." I saw that image as the last metamorphosis in this sequence of changes. The story or record was transformed at last into the dark matter of the night. Invisible. I see now that the lines can imply a shift of power. By turning into the night, the record becomes the story of those who have been silenced. And you pointed out that "the record," in the sense of an account, is still playing; the story is still being told.

CM: Does that mean she gets free from the tree?

AF: It's the future. We don't know. I didn't want to write a utopian feminist vision. If I had wanted to write something heroic, I could have revised the myth. It might have been helpful to turn Daphne into a heroic figure, but presenting a blue-sky, consoling story was not my intention. I worry that such stories are the opiate of the people, so to speak. Someone remarked that a myth is a cultural script. I like that because it reminds us that myths don't present essential or arche-typal truths. Mythology is timebound and culturally determined. Myths reflect the largest beliefs and patterns of a given culture. So I was trying to write culture as it is, not as it should be. Misogyny and the subjugation of women are worldwide phenonema. In this sense, I was writing about world culture and not just Ameri-can culture.

CM: Also I think that the dilemma seems more powerful when the poem con-cludes with it rather than pretends it no longer exists.

AF: Yes. I didn't want to pretend everything's OK. People use the word postfem-inism sometimes, and I always object because the term implies something is over that hasn't even happened yet. To my mind, feminism had hardly caught its sec-ond breath when people began to talk about postfeminism; few battles had been won. I guess I didn't want to write something that seemed to give false comfort. That's why Daphne is left trapped in the tree, where we don't know what her fate is going to be, but "the record" is still "turning into / the night." I wanted a pun on the record "turns" and "turns into" the night: it keeps on revolving, but it also is transformed into the night.

CM: But that space is also Daphne's world, right? The dark world—

AF: Yes, the record turns into Daphne's space, which is negative space.

CM: I'd like to stay with this notion of the between for just a while longer. Again, in your notebook excerpt [in *Feeling as a Foreign Language*], you describe your work as somewhere between highly experimental Language poetry and more mainstream verse. Do you see your new poetry as moving more in one direction than another?

AF: I won't be moving in either of these directions, I hope. But it might be helpful for me to define what I mean by the mainstream a little bit, because it's amorphous. It includes the Language poets in a certain way, because they're taught and they're talked about; in a sense, they're now part of the mainstream. They're not as marginal as they were twenty years ago.

When I say "mainstream," though, I mean a genre of lyric poetry that's very voice based, where the poet is speaking. There's little mixing of registers of diction as a rule, and there's a limited range of emotion. It tends to be humorless—that's one emotion that's missing, humor. Authority is not questioned, I would say. Today's generic poem seems to be the lyric-narrative; it's an emotive poetry, as lyric poetry is, and its autobiographical anecdotes foster the traditional range of emotions allowed in lyric poetry—loss, desire, mourning, grief, love. I include those emotions, too; in fact, I love the lyric tradition. I think most poets love Keats and Dickinson—and many of the Romantics. I don't want to lose all I value in them, and that's what makes me say that while I'm not quite in the mainstream, I take some of it with me. I think what I have in common with the Language poets is an interest in critical theory and philosophy—in ideas and linguistic issues, the powers of language, language as structure. Those become part of the subject, in my poems. And so I'm between two worlds. Neither-nor.

CM: For me, the most interesting aspect of that in-between space is your great care with formal matters in the poems that doesn't lead to an overall sense of clear or fixed order. There's pattern and design, but there's not a simple coherent narrative center, or I suppose vocal center would be another way to put it.

AF: At the moment, the line in American poetry has become very arbitrary. Poets are organizing their verse around units of thought or prose structures, such as the sentence or paragraph. The line has devolved into prose with wide margins. But the way I write the line—whether it's end stopped or enjambed—there is supposed to be a slight rest at the end: a pause or caesura. The line, for me, is a little sculptural unit. I would say very few American poets are using it this way right now. The usual way for poets in the English tradition to lineate is to end the line where there is a pause in the grammatical, syntactical structure of the sentence. In contemporary poetry, it's conventional to end a line on a noun or verb and begin the following line with a prepositional phrase, if the sentence lets you. Glancing down the flush left margin in poetry books, you'll see many lines beginning with "of" or other connectives. The beginning poets I teach, the students, also tend to lineate this way, which makes me suspect that it isn't a position arrived at after long thought.

I work against these tendencies sometimes, or not even against them but between them. I try to think freshly about the why of every line. What is the effect of ending a line on an article or preposition? When is this a desired effect? Once I answer such questions, I might end the line on a function word or use syntactic doubling. (Of course, I learned those wonderfully useful terms from your book on Dickinson, *A Poet's Grammar.*) For instance, in "About Face" [*Sensual Math*], the lines "or were they—surrendering— / what a femme word—feeling / solicitous— glimpsing their fragility" contain syntactic doubling on the word "feeling." If you read the line "what a femme word—feeling" as an isolated syntactical unit, "feeling" is a noun described as a "femme word." But when you go and connect the line to what follows, "feeling" becomes a verb modified by the [word] "solicitous." The poem's content also considers doubleness, the turn that is an "about-face." The form of that poem isn't mimetic overall, though. In other lines, the meaning shifts at enjambments without the end word in the line changing its part of speech.

Function words, as you know, are the little abstract connectives—the articles, conjunctions, prepositions. In "A Little Heart to Heart with the Horizon" [*Sensual Math*], the announcer says "Talks on the fringes of / the summit could eclipse / the summit itself." I guess I ended the "on the fringes" line with "of" because the content implies marginality, the edges blotting out the mountain, the lowly superseding the mighty. And "of" has this dangling, fringe effect at the end of the line. It is a syntactically invisible word, a nonentity of a word, placed in a position of weight. Those are only two examples. There must be infinite ways of lineating, and it's a pity to see empty convention overruling such a rich structure.

CM: I would imagine from reading your poems that stanzas are also important to you. You have very clear stanzaic units that are sometimes echoed and then altered within a poem and so on.

AF: Yes. Sometimes there's friction between the stanzas. Sometimes strong enjambment carries you through and sometimes they'll be end stopped. The stanza is another opportunity to do something with the form between the words.

The words can only do so much. The space between them, the white space, which is what creates the line and stanza, can create meaning too.

CM: Do you think of your interest, or your conception of poetry, in terms of the line, as stemming from any particular earlier poet? I think about Pound saying that poets should compose in the sequence of the musical phrase or Marianne Moore saying the stanza was her unit of composition. Williams strikes me more as a poet of the line.

AF: Although the music of language is very important to me, I don't think of the line as a musical phrase. That would place all the emphasis on sound and meter. I also like to consider the grammatical weight of the words and their meanings. So that ending a line on "of" gives a feathery quality to the right-hand side. Those little words give a deckle-edged effect when they appear at the end of a line. They're the stitching of language, anyway, and by placing them at the end of the line, it's as if you're letting the seams show. Some poets think it's like a slip showing—messy, unmade. Those prepositions and articles tend to leave the line hanging in midair. They leave the reader suspended.

Some poems in "Give" alternate long lines with very short lines. This presented two separate problems. In the long lines, I was trying for coherence despite the length of the phrase. Trying to knit the length of the line together. The short lines, sometimes only one word long, were assuming an enormous weight—the pressure of the white space around them. So the short lines had to be strong; the meanings important. For example, just glancing at "A New Release," I see the short lines in the first stanza are "spun," "amplify," "diamond-tipped," "reticence," "again," "invasive," "dark."

I compose with the line and the stanza as units. My sense of the line was probably influenced by A. R. Ammons, my teacher at Cornell [where Fulton received her M.F.A.]. And Williams probably influenced Archie [Ammons], so Williams might have come to me in a mediated way, through Ammons. Archie's sense of the line is structured and yet there's a jaggedness; he'll end on prepositions and small words. That's unusual. In fact, in workshops they'll say, "Why are you ending on 'the' or 'and'?"—as if there could never be a reason for it. Among other things, such endings can be used to throw the reader off balance, to disrupt equilibrium. I think that's one reason to end on a function word—to tip the balance a bit, placing more weight at the front of the line. While workshops always question lines that end on function words, they never say, "Why are you ending every line with a noun or verb and beginning every line with a conjunction or preposition?" Because that lineation is the norm.

CM: In your essay "To Organize a Waterfall" [collected in *Feeling as a Foreign Language*] you talk about "accident." In fact, you quote Ammons as having said "a mistake is obviously a point where originality can begin." And then you say that you have to be extremely alert as a writer to make sure that what you're dealing with is an oddity that will take you somewhere as opposed to sloppiness or carelessness. How do you measure those things?

AF: Well, mistakes are often made, and I'm not sure that I always do tell the difference; but one thing that's helped me has been that so many of my readers and critics have objected to even a small alteration that's a bit unconventional. Poets and critics in general are opposed to changes, and their displeasure acts as a check to balance me.

CM: There's a wonderfully vital element of surprise, or oddity, or impulsiveness in the diction you use. Do you find that some readers or critics are troubled by this aspect of your poetics, too? I imagine that some readers are more enthusiastic about the quieter, or more transparently single-voiced, poems you write and disturbed by what they might see as quirkiness, a kind of diction or formal structure that hasn't been introduced earlier and therefore might seem out of place in a traditional "well-crafted" poem.

AF: Oh, yes. I think the prevailing critical wish in U.S. poetry is for a quiet, transparent poetics. I don't know that I've ever written a poem that pleases people who really like that style, so even works that I think are lyrical—beautiful in the old sense, with a singing quality—even those don't please people who yearn for a very plain poem. What they object to, I think, in my work, is the mixing of tones, as you say, and dictions—which creates a mixture of emotions. They want a pure, filtered emotion, and in my work the emotion is more unfiltered, inclusive. I think my whole aesthetic tends to be inclusive; I want to embrace multiplicity and yet make the structure hold. I try for traces of collage and disjunction, along with enough synthesis to hold the poem together. For example, a poem that might displease people is "Fuzzy Feelings" [*Sensual Math*]. It's very strange—and that's why I like it, I have to admit. The odd tone begins in the title. "Fuzzy Feelings" are emotions associated with cuteness, with triteness.

CM: Isn't that the poem where the speaker's in the dentist's office, that semi-public space where everything is so consumerist, so cute?

AF: Exactly. The decor is cute. The title points to the poem's interest in that kind of banal surrounding, and it brings to mind the fuzzy numbness of Novocain, which deadens feeling. The man in the waiting room asks, "Do women need fuzzy feelings?" He invokes stereotypes when he asks, "Do women need texture and men / need sex?" One good reader was disturbed by the man's question because he thought I was agreeing with the man, that women do need texture, and so on. But of course I was trying to call that kind of stereotype into question while praising the richness and complexity of texture.

All this in a poem called "Fuzzy Feelings"—which also mentions my niece's funeral, an occasion of real, rather than "fuzzy" feelings. For me, the poem is about veneer and imitation. And it considers authority—including the authority of type. When I wrote, "Laura died last year," the words looked so final in type. I followed it with what I felt—that I hated the type's authority in that line. I hated to put it in writing because writing, especially typeset writing, makes things more real—more authoritative and official.

CM: And then to complicate things even more, the poem ends with the notion of grace.

AF: Yes—of grace and what it means. Is grace a blessing bestowed through no will of our own, or is it a veneer we create and assume? Does it come from outside the self like a blessing, or is it a quality, a polish, we contrive ourselves? You know, being gracious often means that one replaces actual feelings with imitation feelings in order to smooth a social situation. This imitation of feeling can be kind, altruistic in effect. Or it can be false, even self-serving. "Fuzzy Feelings" is about authenticity, in a way: authenticity, authority, what we construct, what's from without, what's from within. The last line of "Fuzzy Feelings" is "Right now I'm trying to open wide," and when I wrote that in 1993, it seemed like an ars poetica. But "Fuzzy Feelings" is a love poem, too, in a way.

CM: I've never seen anyone write about love as a concern of your poems, and to me it seems so importantly there.

AF: Yes. I think maybe my love poems are a bit odd. They're not just saying to a particular man "I love you."

CM: Or to a woman. They're not about desire for a particular other, but they're certainly about relationship. Also, as you said in talking about mixed feelings, your love poems have mixed subjects. For example, "A Little Heart to Heart with the Horizon" includes somebody actually talking to the landscape, commentary on the [first] Gulf War and more generally on international politics, and then questions of what it means to "stand up" for hope, thanks, love—

AF: I'm afraid that it's a corny ending, actually.

CM: It's a very powerful ending. Here's a poem that's about politics, but not only about politics; it's about love, but not only about love; it's about language—as it asks, why not hold "horizon" meetings, on the level, as it were, rather than "summits," if peace is really what nations want? It's all about ways that language constructs and is constructed by notions of power—how it reveals the kinds of power brokering going on. The speaker says, "Go figure!"

AF: Exactly. What "figures" and what doesn't, what's low profile—like the horizon—and what's upright—like a summit. I will "figure" for a while, and then I'll be part of the background. The end of the poem is probably as sentimental as I get. I talked to a friend recently about being sentimental, and he said, "That's something you don't have to worry about." His tone wasn't exactly complimentary. I think I'm generally seen as being completely unsentimental. Part of the risk, for me, in *Sensual Math* and *Felt*, was to allow feeling without falling into gushiness. But talking about love and thanks and hope raises, I think, some possibility of sentimentality.

CM: "Sentimental" has become such a pejorative word. It's been so tainted by earlier twentieth-century poets' notions of value, but you could certainly reaffirm sentiment without being sentimental, in that implied cloying way.

AF: Yes, but when you try to affirm sentiment—especially emotions like thanks, hope, love, loss—then you risk sentimentality. And the only thing that can save the poem is language. Language is a way of retrieving the poem from cliché. It seems to me that sentimentality comes from clichéd rhetoric and dictions. One of the things I try to do in my work is make room for emotions that are excluded from the lyric, like embarrassment. I find peripheral emotions interesting. Embarrassment has a different sort of eroticism, a different sort of intimacy. Though it sounds odd, some emotions are more culturally constructed than others. What's embarrassing in our culture is not embarrassing in another and vice versa. All cultures seem to mourn the loss of a beloved, so grief seems less affected by cultural factors. Embarrassment leads to this deeper, darker stuff. It's embarrassing, in a certain sense, to be a poet and write about going to the dentist or about having veneers. Maybe we all have too much; or maybe this is a personal critique of my own poetry—maybe I felt it was getting too polished, too controlled.

One way to counter that is to rip off parts of the mask and let yourself risk a little embarrassment. Of course, the poems would be unbearable if all they did was expose the poet. I don't much like poetry that exists to confess. I want a poem to be more evasive, more elusive, more oblique. Lately, I've been interested in emotions between names—states so nuanced or neglected they aren't named in English. And I'm thinking of emotions that seem to be frozen out of poetry.

CM: Are there other examples?

AF: Let me think. Newness. The experience of newness is an emotion in itself. Newness is exhilarating. And the uncanny—the prickling and shivering we feel in the presence of the *unheimlich*. Sadomasochism. To my surprise, I found I was writing about sadism toward the end of *Sensual Math*, in "Echo Location," for instance. And in "Some Cool" there are the awful images of slaughter and of the surgeon putting the hand inside the chest—that intrusion into the body, the pain, the looking away, the unfeelingness. Some of my poems are about the wish to avoid certain areas of knowledge as a means of avoiding feeling. People are unwilling, for instance, to know about the suffering of animals—the way we conveniently assume their Otherness—since that knowledge might make it harder to eat meat. My poems seem to specialize in inconvenient knowledge. By "inconvenient" I mean to suggest the sort of knowledge that asks us to change our lives. Of course, changing comfortable habits is hard. "Cruelty is convenient, / that's the thing" ["Split the Lark" in *Felt*]. "The Permeable Past Tense of Feel" [in *Felt*] includes the cruelty of slaughterhouses as well, a very inconvenient knowledge. I mean, how many slaughterhouses do we see as compared to the number of hamburgers we eat? In ethical terms, eating meat is a form of sadism practiced by people who never think of themselves as cruel. And I've done it, too, so I'm not exempting myself. After raising some ethical questions, the poem says, "How have I inconvenienced myself / in service to this feeling? / Felt is ideal for padding and sealing. / How have I left the earth / uncluttered with more me?" Self-implication is key to the ethics of my poems. In fact, it was important to me that the poet-speakers of "Some Cool" and "The Permeable Past Tense of Feel" be implicated in the suffering the poems expose. "Split the Lark" considers this, too, and it ends with a line of self-reproach. I think it's best to direct moral critiques toward oneself rather than toward others. We might not be able to change anyone else, but we sometimes can change our own behavior. And since everything is interconnected, by changing ourselves we change the world.

I think each of my books contains some poems about loss, but I've tried to avoid lyric pain, which often considers loss of love or loss through death, and write of the suffering imposed on an animal or on another. The worldwide subjugation of women and animals are ethical areas that engage me—perhaps the areas to which I feel I can write with most authority at the moment. I didn't feel tentative when I wrote about these subjects [in *Sensual Math* and *Felt*]. I did feel the need to think deeply and at length. I've written about the infliction of pain in circumstances that are not romantic and the emotions that pain evokes. In some poems, the speaker has agency and inflicts pain, and in others the speaker is in a more passive position. In *Felt*, I tried to exhume and face up to various denied or difficult truths—without becoming dreary or didactic. More than ever, I wanted a sense of closure that opened, last lines that were oblique yet connected and suggestive. I kept going back to certain poems till the endings seemed to have the right degree of self-implication, eccentricity, and deviance.

CM: I'd like to pursue the notions of exposure and fiction. You said that there are many distinct voices in your poems, none of which are yours. At the same time, there are experiences in the poems that could recognizably be identified as yours.

AF: They could be. My sense of poetry is that it's all a construct, even if some of it happens to be true. By the time I've constructed the poem, the experience has become a fiction. Parts of the poem are true, parts are fictionalized, so it would be wrong to take it as slice-of-life. I know you know this, but very often people read poems autobiographically.

CM: This topic is interesting in your work because it seems to involve contradictions. You use dedications in several poems or explanatory introductory lines that relate your speakers or subjects to yourself—for example, you've written poems to Hank [De Leo, Fulton's husband], your grandmother, your father, your mother, your sister, your nieces. You place yourself there—one might assume that your mention of relatives includes some factual basis. There's a coming in and going out of what is or isn't "you" as speaker or perspective.

AF: Yes, you're right. There are certain things I would never fictionalize in a poem. When I've read poems about my nieces who died, members of the audience have come up and asked if it was true, and I've said, "Yes, I'd never make that up." In that case, I rely on the reader's taste—that's an old-fashioned word—the reader's aesthetic sense to know that there are matters about which one doesn't lie.

One of them would be the deaths of your sister's children. It would be completely gratuitous to make up such an event. But it isn't gratuitous to make up other things that may seem autobiographical and to write them in the first person.

I wanted to write something other than the lyric-narrative-confession—which can be written in different ways but is resolutely autobiographical. The pure lyric tends to avoid cultural artifacts in its wish to be universal. The language of lyric poetry today is full of hearts, desire, light, wings, angels. Not full of doughnuts, condoms, Elvis, photons, duct tape, electromagnetic fields, and greasepaint. Then, too, it seemed narcissistic to focus solely on my own experience. Lately, though, I have to admit I'm interested in writing about my life—but not in a confessional way. I'm trying to write a poetry of experience that is also a poetry of ideas.

CM: I want to go back to the flip side of your poetry and ask you about faith. This is another issue that comes up in all of your volumes and in poem after poem. In *Sensual Math* and *Felt*, the particular turn that your work seems to have is that you refer frequently to disbelief or to nonbelievers. The speaker of "Some Cool," for example, writes "for the born-again infidels / whose skepticism [. . .] / [. . .] climbs the body, / nerve by nerve," and the speaker in "Fair Use" [in *Felt*] asks, "What lowercase god sent this / = = immersion = = / to test my radiance threshold?"

AF: Yes. A perfect skepticism questions disbelief. A faith can be the way you live your life from day to day; it can be your stand in the world. As I said in "Cascade Experiment" [*Powers of Congress*], "we have to meet the universe halfway." Faith can be a belief that things aren't quite as nasty as they can seem: that people aren't inherently evil, that good and evil are maybe a fifty-fifty split. The great religious questions endure. I have notions of trying to believe; I move toward belief. There's a spirituality in human beings that, I think, is in me, and I try to call upon it. Maybe it's connected to human goodness, the better traits in people. Maybe it's the spark that's good within us that makes us see "it" as "us," "the other" as "me." And that seeing, which refuses division, dissolves binaries. I'd like to replace boundary with fusion. But as I've talked with scientists, they've pointed out—and they're absolutely right—that we need boundary and division. They're inherent in physicality. So the question becomes "how can we live and be spiritual and good knowing that there will always be otherness?"

CM: I would have thought that in science there is less boundary and division than there is in constructed notions of the world. One of the things you talk about, for example, in a poem like "Cusp" [in *Powers of Congress*] is the lack of physical boundary where we assume there is one. We think solid surfaces collide when we touch, but instead it's atoms, with space between them, that we dislodge when we touch something. Science would seem to me to be saying there is no boundary.

AF: In "Cusp" I'm talking about the deep interweaving at the quantum level. But so often science will say two things at once; it argues with itself. Even at the atomic level there is boundary, I think, because atoms are discrete units. Boundary exists and is necessary in the immune system, to use another example; it's deeply embedded in our physicality. Without a perception of boundary we wouldn't be able to fight off infection. When, say, we get a cut and bacteria enter the skin, antibodies rush to the site because the body is saying, "I've been invaded; this is not me." That's all about otherness; it's embedded in us—the need to say "this is not me." And it actually allows us to survive.

But it also has its awful side. When applied to culture, it leads to war and all sorts of territorial nastiness. As I thought about this, I wondered whether there was a way I could write about the existence of boundary without being negative, without boundary being something that leads to war, and so on. That's partly what I was thinking when I wrote about the orchid in "My Last TV Campaign." The bee orchid incorporates aspects of the bee into its body and lives—and lives better! The bee orchid is the opposite of the body's allergic reaction—which tries to fight the outsider off. The bee orchid literally incorporates the Other into the self as a means of evolving. In human terms, it implies that we can reach out to all sorts of othernesses and, by incorporating them, become more successful entities in the largest spiritual sense.

CM: You've started experimenting with long poems: "Give"—the Daphne sequence—in *Sensual Math* and "About Music for Bone and Membrane Instrument" in *Felt*. Would you say something about what has been leading you in this direction of the longer poem, or sequence?

AF: I think it's something that came from a worldview, in a certain sense. I have this wish to include, and that leads to longer poems. Writing the Daphne poem, I felt many things needed to be said in order to rewrite the myth, a myth being a big imagining. I began with Ovid; I did a close reading and dismantled his version— line by line. I would think, there's a whole poem I could write just from that one phrase or sentence. And, I wrote them all. I was also researching the history of the Roman wedding. I read Mary E. Barnard's book *The Myth of Apollo and Daphne,* and it got me thinking about how the myth had been reimagined by others. She points out that myths often had humor; they questioned authority by means of travesty.

CM: You mentioned to me recently that you were turning more to open expression of emotion.

AF: I'm not sure I would ever be open, because I'm interested in the hinge moment that opens and closes, revealing and concealing. But I am drawn to emotion, wayward as well as lyric—uneasy mixes of emotion.

CM: So when in the double equal sign poem [= =] in *Sensual Math* you say that poetry "contests the natural," do you ensure that poetry contests the natural by going toward the thing that is more difficult for you to do at the moment?

AF: What a marvelous connection! Why should I want to make things harder for myself? Maybe because poets can become facile, too good at writing a particular type of poem, and difficulty can prevent this rote or habitual approach. It isn't just "the fascination of what's difficult," because there's something perverse about that, and I'm really not a punishing kind of person; I like work to be fun. There are things in my work that do come readily or naturally that I wouldn't want to change. But I don't want to lose the ability to write a short structure, because that matters to me in poetry. I wonder what possibilities exist within the short poem— for me, particularly. I've written more long poems lately, and so I'm more familiar with their possibilities.

CM: That makes sense. Do you ever think you'll go back to writing sonnets?

AF: I might write a fourteen-line poem, but I'm not sure it would be a sonnet. Actually, fourteen lines seems a little too short for my sensibility. I'm thinking more of the thirty-line poem. In *Powers of Congress*, there's a double Shakespearean sonnet that is also an acrostic ["Cause Célèbre," which is part two of "The Gilt Cymbal behind Saints"]. I look back on that as a kind of madness, something I felt compelled to do. Now I'm much more interested in spontaneity and the rough edge; I'm interested in accident and in allowing things to show—maybe things that people don't want to see or wish they hadn't seen, things I never thought I would reveal. At the same time, I want a textured rather than transparent surface of language. I don't like poems that try to be transparent, though I am interested in creating a surface that combines areas of sheerness with more opaque areas. I want to write a many-textured poem, in which the language shifts, not just between flatness and richness, but between the almost infinite shades and tones available.

CM: In your essay "To Organize a Waterfall" you say that "linguistic structures are most powerful when least evident." I'm curious about your sense of strategy in experimentation or play with language and formal structures.

AF: That quotation refers to my belief that the hidden persuasions of structure are the most difficult to undo or contest. Until very recently, for instance, the pronoun "he" stood for everyone, men and women. No one consciously saw the pronoun as male, but subconsciously everyone was given to understand that the universal was male. The subject, the One, was male—and the difference, the deviance, or Other was female. Using the male pronoun to mean everyone is a reticent yet pervasive assertion of a worldview. As a strategy, its power depends on its invisibility. It was so accepted a usage that no one saw it or questioned it for a long time.

The same could be said for the adjectives I mentioned earlier—"dark" and "black." Why should sad or bad things be called "dark"? I've found piercing, sunny days to be quite painful. Unremitting sun is a sad, really an unbearable thing. And as I've said somewhere, light is a nihilist. Light is corrosive. So the negative connotations of "dark" seem arbitrary. But how firmly entrenched they are! That "dark" can mean bad is taken as natural; it seems so self-evident that few people even think about it. This is the power I was referring to—the power of a belief so firmly held that it becomes unquestioned, an invisible assumption.

I like to say something feral, something that's outside the realm of the genteel or assumed. I like the outlaw. When I use that term, it sounds a little too flaunting or self-praising. I'd like to think of a word that means uncalled for, unexpected, and perhaps impolite. As you know, I included handwriting in the margins of "Point of Purchase" [*Powers of Congress*], and I'd like to do more with script and text. In an age when "digital" means sound and thought reduced to a binary code of ones and zeros, the eccentricity of handmade things becomes more dear. The handmade exists outside the neat, clean either/or of the digital world. The handmade comes from the realm of the human, where things get messy.

CM: This gives us a wonderful sense of your work. Thank you.

AF: Thank you for thinking about my work and for helping me to think about it.

Note

1. Portions of Alice Fulton's discussion of writing a poetry that contemplates (among other issues) race, class, and what she terms "inconvenient knowledge" were updated by Fulton to include her more recent collection *Felt* in an e-mail to Cynthia Hogue dated June 19, 2004, and edited at this point into the text of the original interview (—ed.).

—= =

It might mean immersion, that sign
        I've used as title, the sign I call a bride
after the recessive threads in lace = =
the stitches forming deferential
                space around the firm design.
                It's the unconsidered

mortar between the silo's bricks = = never admired
                when we admire
the holdfast of the tiles (their copper of a robin's
    breast abstracted into flat).

        It's a seam made to show,
the deckle edge = = constructivist touch.
        The double equal that's nowhere to be found
                in math. The dash
        to the second power = = dash to the max.

It might make visible the acoustic signals
of things about to flame. It might

                let thermal expansion be syntactical. Let it
add stretch

                while staying reticent, unspoken
as a comma. Don't get angry = = protest = = but a
comma seems so natural, you don't see it
when you read: it's gone to pure
transparency. Yes but.
                The natural is what

poetry contests. Why else the line = = why stanza = = why
meter and the rest. Like wheels on snow
that leave a wake = = that tread in white
without dilapidating
mystery = = hinging
one phrase to the next = = the brides.

Thus wed = = the sentence cannot tell
whether it will end or melt or give

way to the fabulous = = the snow that is
the mortar between winter's bricks = = the wick that is

the white between the ink.

—Fuzzy Feelings

Is beige a castrate of copper, pink, and taste?
Does lace add blush to any situation?
Do you want novocaine?

I've been staring at the ceiling's
stucco moonstuff for three hours, grateful
for the prickly little star
someone's inked onto a lattice strip.
This light means business, like a xerox

of the sky's allover glow.
I'm seeing nonexistent rainbows
outside, transparency split
into the true colors it hides behind
its see-through guise.

Is the universe an imitation?
Are the cat's tabby cables
a mimicry of snake? How can you tell
a natural emerald from the flux-grown fakes?

Inside it's all beige
partitions, latex gloves, lace tiebacks
and prints of ducks in love.
The drilling decor and rock
make me think I'm in a bodyshop
through which a boudoir's wandered.

Metaphor is pure immersion. Pure sinking
one into another and the more
difference that's dissolved the more = =

often I'll sink
into a book that swimless way.
Some volumes turn out to be wallpaper
or boxes for valuables. Simulants

tend to be flawless, while natural
emeralds have defects
known as inclusions, imperfections
with a value all their own.

I'm faking Lamaze and ancient mantras. I'm having
new veneers. The dentist talks about a relative
who boasted over 364 girlfriends
and seduction rooms in every shade.
He was in air conditioning
and smoked himself to death
though he could hold his breath
longer than anyone else.
"My role model," the dentist says.

Do women need fuzzy feelings?
a man asked in the waiting room's
frayed *Glamour*. Do they need simulated intrigue
dinners, candlehours, cuddle-wuddle
teddy bears and wittle tittie tats?
Anything with ribbons on it,
an earthtone rainbow baby angel goose and floral bed.
Do women need texture and men
need sex? "To stick it through
the uprights," this guy said.

Scientists think the universe was smooth before it loomed
itself to a jacquard
of defects known as textures.
A texture is not localized.
It's an overall sensation, like being

enthralled or born, in love or mourning, growing
at the speed of light and leaving
its distinctive signoff on
the sky. Photons—lumps of glow—
gain energy by falling into
a texture after it unwinds.

"I hate rock," the dentist says,
changing the tape for its clone.
What does beige = = what does lace = =
what does pain imitate? The autopsy
of beige revealed a gelded rainbow,
upwardly mobile ideals. Lace
is a form of filth I hate.
As for the dying moan and gush

of the deer killed by hunters down the road—
I'd find it more tasteful

done in plastic or an acrylic
venison Christmas sweater.
I'd rather wear vinyl than hide.

I didn't mean what I said about lace.
Lace in a vacuum would be okay.
Even beige would have its place. It's context,
culture makes them = = wait, I'll take the novocaine.

When I get home, I'll fall into the immense rub
of a robe like a universe unwinding.
I'll talk to Sandy
whose daughter Laura died last year.
(I hate the type's authority in that line, the—
get it in writing.)

When a friend asked how Sand was doing
her husband said "She'll never be the same."
"What a relief it was—to never have to be
the same. I felt so grateful," she explains.
The return to a genuine, originary self
was—thanks very much—not to be

expected. Her imitation would see her through
another evening of held breath.
As we left the "slumber room"
she asked whom Laura most resembled.
I think she = = you, I said
in some wrong tense.

Before a party, she blends some body
veil into herself. Gets ready to flex
the verbal abs and delts and hopes
she won't be up till dawn

re-living how she broke into
emotion during her free pose.

Does "grace" mean alive and lucky
to be not writhing?
Or the ability to hide it
when you writhe?
The fissures = = vacancies inside

a natural emerald are known as its *jardin*.
I'll leave this place with a refined smile
outside a headache that makes me cry all night.
Right now I'm trying to open wide.

—*from* "Give: A Sequence Reimagining Daphne & Apollo"

UNDOING

Take:
her wish to be chaste. And exist in violent cloister.
To be unravished as a prime
of rainbow—a red or blue
unsplittable
through any prism. Take
the as-it-is-as-it-is—
the script. Use two hands and twist.

If you're a virgin, what are you doing
running around the woods, getting raped?
Curving every which way
in nonconjugal space.
Don't you know the best manners are the least
obtrusive? Your presence pursues its own undoing.

Just asking for it: Just use two hands and twist.
As it is as it is: your femaleness naturally
says take. Says this rape has your name on it.
Your beauty provokes
its own dominion, whose no can never mean no.
How does that one go? TO OPEN
SCRIPT PUSH DOWN WHILE TURNING

While spinning her negative charge
she has—like a wave—no single location.
If pushed through a slot, her velocity
compounds. Take
a hue outside the spectrum,
an unchromatic octave
higher than the eye can see,
a singular—unravished shade. Name it she.
Her color, name it nevergreen.

As to her bareness and her glance,
he wants to array it in flame
sandals and flame veil, a white tunic
with a double-knotted sash.
Give it an iron ring.
Put on its high-heeled sneakers—put
its wig-hat on its head. Its dress
of a fine smooth textile
made in filament and staple form
from wood pulp
solutions extruded through
spinnerets
and solidified in baths or air.

He wants to part her hair with a lance.
To make her rayon likeness,
evergreen as glance. His composite

new improved her. Cast her
in fibers of modified wood pulp found in
butcher linen or tire cords.

Prestige involves accumulation.
His desire to collect her
assumes a type—and others of the.
A kind—not one of a.
A whole forest to be had.
Let arrows stand for probabilities.

If he bored in close he'd find her bare
charge higher than it seemed == an infinite
beneath an infinite shield = = an infinite
that can't be split
by modifying in the middle.
Neither soft nor hard, dull nor
bright, she traveled fast and had no given.
The more he tied her down as to position
the less he knew of her
momentum. Always transported, always elsewhere
before he = = *who was she*

to tabernacle in the woods?
Place a minus sign in front of it.
Haze her
escape. TO OPEN—LINE UP ARROW
ON SCRIPT AND VICTIM
PUSH SCRIPT UP WITH THUMB.

No matter how many of her he gathered together
in his name, she would not
be the natural he could cultivate.
Though cast as lady or grotesque,
as hectic membrane in the flesh,
she would be neither-nor.

Apollo pulls a cloud back like a foreskin
             on the sky that is his body.
His laserscope will amplify
             the available starlight,
zero in on the nymph
      in her stealth boots
             that leave no helpful scent.
Daphne—who is graphite,
      darkling, carbon as the crow—

             is out of breath.
If only the stars would tire,
      she might find cover.
If only they would empathize.
      But who will help a person
      on the wrong side of a god?
All largo, she turns to face Apollo.

Though she expected him
             to wear blaze orange, supernal
as the sun, he tracked her down in camo-
      skin, which "disappears in a wide variety of terrains."
He owns every pattern in the catalogue.
      After considering *Hollywood Treestand*
             ("all a nymph sees is limbs")
      and *Universal Bark*

             ("a look most guys relate to")
      he chose a suit of *Laurel Ghost*,
      printed with a 3-D photo of the forest,
             which "makes you so invisible
      only the oaks will know you're there."
Even his arrow's shaft is camo.

Only his ammo jackets gleam
                    like lipstick tubes.

Is it any wonder, when his wheel-bow
            has been torture-tested
to a million flexes,
                            his capsicum fogger
fires clouds that can cause blindness,
                his subminiature heat detector
finds the game by the game's own radiation,
                and the tiny boom mike in his ear
lets him hear a nymph's grunt from 200 yards—

any wonder—when the ad said
                        "Put this baby to your eye
and see if she's worth harvesting" and
            "See the hairs on a nymph's ass,
                up close and personal"—
that he turns the housing, gets her
            on the zeroing grid,
and now his snout at her fair loins doth snatch?

Who can she turn to, the monastic, almost
                    abstract Daphne?
The stars are tireless. She decides—
            no, winds up—
            pleading, in extremis, with her father:
                        ". . . I am not like
them, indefatigable, but if you are a god you will
not discriminate against me. Yet—if you may fulfill
            none but prayers dressed
            as gifts in return for your gifts—disregard the request."

That's when her father makes her
                into nature, the famous green novation.

And Daphne—who was hunter and electron—
                        is done with aspiration.
Did you see it coming? You're a better man than she.
                With no one to turn to—
                        she turns to a tree.

—The Permeable Past Tense of Feel

                        Let the barbaric flowers live, I'm living.
            I'm liking the meadow blobbed with bird's-foot trefoil,
                    with earth-gall and the creeping wheatgrass
                        anciently known as felt. I mean nonelites
                    that live in disturbed soils, nuisance shrubs
            whose fragrance exceeds exaggeration. Isn't it green.

                            These days everyone wants
                two acres gated with herbicide. Everyone wants
                    to eat high on the food chain while—

Contain yourself. We need less
impervious surface per person

        beginning with the mind.
        Oh, the blisters sustained
        while blaming others. The indignation of!
        Only the sky has a right to such
        disdain. Isn't it blue, my companion
        animal said. And doesn't the body extend

                    into other endowed stuff. Feeling things
                    with blue irises and pink or brown
                        fleshy hairless ears
                        enrobed in fat and skin

that chew and breathe and joy themselves
by twisting, aerodynamic, when they jump.
That have soulweight and intestines.
That like Mozart,
which is played to calm them since calm
things are easier to kill.

Felt comes from "beat" and from "near."
= = As hooks pass through, the fibers entangle
till our presence is a double-dwelling = =

Why must I say they are like
us whenever I say let them live? Speak eco-speak
like eat no flesh and save the watershed, like
maybe the whole blue-green.

How have I inconvenienced myself
in service to this feeling?
Felt is ideal for padding and sealing.
How have I left the earth
uncluttered with more me?

The inhabitant cleans and wipes,
eats and spasms. Cruelty exasperates
reason. At the top of its range,
ah is the only sound
the human voice can make. So felt
takes on the shape of flesh

beyond resemblance
into same, a thou-art-that that oscillates
through pollen-throwing and clasping devices,
ovaries and arms. So lid and lash
close over iris and pupil, dissecting tables drain
into our sweet spot.

The century heaves. Nowever. Who has time?
With primates to raise, important hearts
to hold down.

= = When the box is full, hammers beat the felt,
which turns to present a new surface
before it's struck again = =

Lovers, givers, what minds have we made
that make us hate
a slaughterhouse for torturing a river?

As prescribed burn begins, I see the warmth
sculpture rise higher, twisting from the base.
And though the world consists of everything

that is the case, I know
there must be ways to concentrate
the meanings of felt in one

just place. Just as this flame
assumes the shape of the flesh it covers.
I like to prepare the heart
by stuffing it with the brain.

susan howe

Distinguished especially by her revisionary engagement with historical archives and by her daring, multivocal manipulations of the visual page, Susan Howe has been a key contributor to American experimental poetics since the 1970s. "Is a poetics of intervening absence an oxymoron?" she muses in "Submarginalia" (*Birth-mark*). The question limns Howe's own project: her writing embodies absence in its elliptical and disjunctive character and in its use of page space. Absence is a thematic preoccupation as well, particularly in Howe's concern with voices that have been silenced, figures who have been erased, or, more recently, those dear to her who have died. While sometimes mimetic, the absences of her poetry are also interventions. Given that "Language surrounds Chaos" (*Europe of Trusts*), Howe's painstakingly arranged words and spaces give definition and even voice to what might otherwise have remained inapprehensible, incoherent, lost.

Paradoxically, then, her poetry provides eloquent testament though it is filled with silences. It sings in subtle harmonies while it confronts the violence and the repressions of history.

Born in 1937, the daughter of an Irish actress and a Harvard scholar of American history, Howe did not begin writing poetry until relatively late, after exploring possible careers in the theater and in the visual arts. Her earliest poems, since collected in *Frame Structures: Early Poems, 1974–1979*, were published by small presses in the mid-1970s. Her first book of literary criticism, *My Emily Dickinson*, appeared in 1985. By the mid-1990s, when Lynn Keller conducted this interview, Howe's poems were gaining wider distribution. In 1990, Sun and Moon collected several works from the 1980s in *The Europe of Trusts*, and Wesleyan University Press published *Singularities*; in 1993, *The Nonconformist's Memorial* (poems) appeared from New Directions, and *The Birth-mark* (essays) was issued by Wesleyan in 1999. Despite fears voiced in the interview that she would never be able to write poetry again after her husband's death in 1992, Howe has since produced two new books: *Pierce-Arrow* (1999) and *The Midnight* (2003). Her interest in the visual remains as central to these poems—which incorporate photos, copies of old manuscript pages, and reproductions of book illustrations into their design—as to her earlier works.

Howe combines in her writing, as in her genealogy, an Irish love of the word's rich music, its wealth of allusive and personal association, with a New England intellectual's passion for documentation, tradition, and the quest for truth. "History," she reminds us, "is the record of the winners." Her response is to bring to light other stories, to "tenderly lift from the dark side of history, voices that are anonymous, slighted—inarticulate" ("Statement"). Her critical essays, like some of her poems, place in new perspective figures who have been marginalized as eccentric, wild, liminal, such as Anne Hutchinson and Mary Rowlandson. *My Emily Dickinson* counters received readings of Dickinson as the idiosyncratic "madwoman" by revealing the intertextual dimensions of her poetry, placing it firmly within the literary culture of her era. The Dickinson who emerges is—like Howe herself—a radically innovative writer, but one richly responsive to America's literary traditions. A voracious "library cormorant," Howe uses the scholar's tools respectfully but deliberately resists the restrictions of academic paradigms.

Although family connections have kept her close to academia throughout her life—her companion of twenty-seven years, David von Schlegell, directed the sculpture program at Yale—Howe did not begin university teaching until 1988. She is a professor at SUNY–Buffalo and a chancellor of the Academy of American Poets.

Keller conducted the following interview in March 1994 while Howe was a visiting scholar at the University of Wisconsin–Madison.

AN INTERVIEW WITH SUSAN HOWE
by Lynn Keller

LYNN KELLER: You were once a painter. Can you tell me about the kind of painting or visual art that you used to do and the relationship you see between that work and the kind of poetry you write?

SUSAN HOWE: I graduated in 1961 from the Boston Museum School of Fine Arts, where I majored in painting. I used quotation in my painting in the same way that I use quotation in my writing in that I always seemed to use collage; sometimes I made a copy in the painting of some part of another painting, another form of quotation. Collage is also a way of mixing disciplines. Those were the early days of Pop Art, when it was common practice among artists to move around from one medium to another—it was a very exciting time. I moved to New York in 1964. Then I began living with a sculptor, David von Schlegell. He was involved with the group around the Park Place Gallery, which I think Paula Cooper was running at the time. There was lots of really interesting sculpture during those days and lots of interesting writing about the work in *Art Forum* magazine. Barbara Rose had written some really good pieces on Ad Reinhardt, there was Reinhardt's own writing, Don Judd and Robert Smithson were busily producing manifestos. Richard Serra, Joan Jonas, Don Judd, Eva Hesse, Ellsworth Kelly, Robert Morris, Carl Andre, John Cage, Agnes Martin . . . the work of these artists influenced what I was doing. There was the most extraordinary energy and willingness to experiment during the sixties. Painters, sculptors, dancers, filmmakers, musicians, conceptual artists were all working together and crossing genre boundaries, sometimes with appalling results, more often wacky and wonderful events. I remember a show Agnes Martin had at the Greene Gallery—small minimalist paintings, but each one had a title—it fascinated me how the title affected my reading of the lines and colors. I guess to me they were poems even then. Eva

Hesse's show at the Greene was also an inspiration, it was so eccentric. Daring and delicate at once.

David's work was very important to me as well, though he wasn't verbal and he didn't write about what he was doing and he was shy. This put him at a disadvantage in those very wordy times. He was an extraordinary builder. In those days his medium was aluminum and wood. He constructed his own pieces, thus going against the grain of prevailing minimalist dogma though his sensibility was minimalist. Now I can see minimalist art of the sixties and seventies as an American movement rooted in Puritanism. I was inspired by the craft *and* the poetry of space in David's work, by how the two things were inseparable. He was very influenced by boat design—New England has produced some wonderful yacht designers; David grew up on the Maine coast. He and the sculptor Robert Grosvenor were obsessed by boats; they were always going off to boat shows and discussing which boats they would buy if they could. Bob liked old military engineering manuals, and so did I. David had been a pilot in World War II; shortly before that he worked at Douglas aircraft. All of us would search out books with photographs of Herreshoff boats or ones with pictures of early submarines. I guess it was about that time I began to connect writing and drawing in my mind. This is important because if a boat sails fast it usually *looks* beautiful. As if the eye has some perfect knowledge that *is* feeling. Some enduring value, some purpose is reflected in the material you use. The mysterious link between beauty and utility is, for me, similar to the tie between poetry and historical documents; although it would take me years to explain what the connection actually is, I know it's there. Or rather than explain it, I show it in my writing. David understood the connection by instinct.

Anyway, I began to make books—artist's books are different from poet's books. These books I made were not books of poetry or prose; they were objects. I would get a sketchbook and inside I would juxtapose a picture with a list of words under it. The words were usually lists of names. Often names of birds, of flowers, of weather patterns, but I relied on some flash association between the words and the picture or charts I used. Later I did a series of watercolors with penciled lines, watercolor washes, and pictures and words—I always left a lot of white space on the page. Around that time (1968 or 1969), through my sister Fanny, I became acquainted with Charles Olson's writing. What interested me in both Olson and Robert Smithson was their interest in archaeology and mapping. Space. North American space—how it's connected to memory, war, and history. I suppose that's the point at which it began to dawn on me that I needed to do more than just list words. I was scared to begin writing sentences. I'm not sure why. But it just gradually happened that I was more and more interested in the problems of those words on the page than in the photographs I used or the watercolor washes.

We left New York City and moved to Connecticut in 1972 because David had a teaching job at the Yale School of Art and we had two small children so to commute seemed impossible at the time. We found this place, Guilford, right on Long Island Sound that reminded David of Maine. So we settled there. For a couple of years I kept a space in part of Marcia Hafif's loft on Crosby Street and went down one or two days a week to work there. Before we moved out of New York, I had started making environments—rooms that you could walk into and be surrounded by walls, and on those walls would be collage, using found photographs (again a kind of quotation). Then I started using words with that work. I was at the point where I was only putting words on the walls, and I had surrounded myself with words that were really composed lines when a friend, the poet Jed Greenwald, came by to look at what I was doing and said to me: "Actually you have a book on the wall. Why don't you just put it into a book?"

At the time, Marcia, whose work I have always admired, was filling small sketchbooks with repetitive pencil strokes. She would start one at the top left corner page 1 and continue until the end, so there were no actual words but the page was filled the way it might be in a printed book. For some reason her books set me off, and I started in a different way with the standard 4" x 6" ("Classic Sketch Book" is the brand name). As the pages are blank and the cover blank (black), there is no up or down, backwards or forwards. You impose a direction by beginning. But where Marcia was using gestural marks, I used words. It was another way of making word lists but now in a horizontal rather than vertical direction so there was a wall of words. In this weird way I moved into writing *physically* because this was concerned with gesture, the mark of the hand and the pen or pencil, the connection between eye and hand. One reason I like the drawings of Joseph Beuys so much is that it seems to me he is doing both things at once. There is another more unconscious element here of course: the mark as an acoustic signal or charge. I think you go one way or another—toward drawing or toward having words sound the meaning. Somehow I went the second way and began writing. Ever since, I have used these little black books as a beginning for any poems I work on. Though my work has changed a lot, those books the poems begin to form in have not. I've never really lost the sense that words, even single letters, are images. The look of a word is part of its meaning. The meaning that escapes dictionary definition or rather doesn't *escape* but is bound up with it. Just as a sailboat needs wind and water.

LK: Do you still do painting or other visual art?

SH: No. I can't believe I stopped, because I really worked very hard at it, and I was all caught up in color. I loved using color. But I just completely stopped.

LK: Your interview in the issue of the *Difficulties* devoted to your work, conducted by Janet Ruth Falon, ends with your statement that if you had to paint your writing, "It would be blank. It would be a white canvas. White." I wondered if you could explain.

SH: Well, that statement springs from my love for minimalist painting and sculpture. Going all the way back to Malevich writing on suprematism. Then to Ad Reinhardt's writing about art and to his painting. To the work of Agnes Martin, of Robert Ryman, of Marcia Hafif and then to a particular group of David's wooden sculptures and to his late paintings. I can't express how important Agnes Martin was to me at the point when I was shifting from painting to poetry. The combination in Martin's work, say, of being spare and infinitely suggestive at the same time characterizes the art I respond to. And in poetry I am concerned with the space of the page apart from the words on it. I would say that the most beautiful thing of all is a page before the word interrupts it. A Robert Ryman white painting is there. Or one of David's late paintings. It's like the sky, because—though the sky has color and white isn't the absence of color anyway—it's clear, infinitely open, with anything possible. Malevich writes: "Under suprematism I understood the supremacy of pure feeling in creative art." These days the word "supreme" is a bad one but I don't care—I was born in another time. This pure feeling is connected to silence. Any mark or word would be a corruption of that infinite purpose or purposelessness.

LK: Let's talk about some of your pages that do have marks on them. In poems where lines appear on angles and sometimes cross over each other, almost obliterating some of the words—for instance in the "Eikon Basilike"—what are you thinking about as you arrange those lines? What determines their position and orientation? Are you thinking about the overall design of the page? Is it the meaning of each line that determines its position?

sH: In the "Eikon Basilike," the sections that are all vertically jagged are based around the violence of the execution of Charles, the violence of history, the violence of that particular event, and also then the stage drama of it. It was a trial, but the scene of his execution was also a performance; he acted his own death. There's no way to express that in just words in ordinary fashion on the page. So I would try to match that chaos and violence visually with words. But a lot of what determines the arrangement is subconscious. First I would type some lines. Then cut them apart. Paste one on top of another, move them around until they looked right. Then I'd xerox that version getting several copies and then cut and paste again until I had it right. The getting it right has to do with how it's structured on the page as well as how it sounds—this is the meaning. I suppose the real answer to your question, "Did you stop doing any visual art?" is "no." I'm still doing it, but I'm doing it on pages like that with words.

lk: Pages 6 and 7 of "The Nonconformist's Memorial" [pages 177 and 178 this volume (—ed.)] provide one example of a near mirroring of text. I wonder if you could talk about where the impulse for the mirroring came from.

sH: The mirroring impulse in my work goes way back. It's there in my first book, *Hinge Picture*, and in *Secret History of the Dividing Line* [reprinted in *Frame Structures*], then in "Thorow," even in *Articulation of Sound Forms in Time* [reprinted in *Singularities*]. I was very interested in Duchamp's *Large Glass* and the book that went with it, *The Bride Stripped Bare by Her Bachelors, Even*. Duchamp was an inspiration to me when I was beginning to shift from painting to writing. At first when I used mirroring in my writing, I was very sedate about it and it involved repetition in a more structured way. But with "Thorow" I had done one scattered page and made a xerox copy and suddenly there were two lying on my desk beside each other, and it seemed to me the scattering effect was stronger if I repeated them so the image would travel across facing pages. The facing pages reflected and strengthened each other.

lk: So, mirroring reinforces the power of the visual design. It fascinates me that your reading of your poetry is so dramatic in that you use many different voices and paces and that these are not necessarily scripted on the published page. Are those voices in your ear as you're composing?

sH: Well, in spite of all my talk about the way the page looks, and particularly in regard to these pages constructed as if they were a sort of drawing, strangely the strongest element I feel when I am writing something is acoustic. For example, the pages in "Eikon" and in "Nonconformist's Memorial" we have been talking about are in my head as theater. I hear them one particular way. I think that comes from my childhood and very directly from my mother. Even now, when she's eighty-nine years old, the theater is her greatest passion. She was always fascinated by voice, by accents, and she very early passed on to me that feeling for the beauty of the spoken word. Then, too, of how people moved on the stage, of how you blocked out a scene if you were directing it. Sometimes I think what I'm doing on the page is moving people around on stage.

I've been thinking a lot about voice now because of an essay I have been writing on the work of French documentary filmmaker Chris Marker. Marker is so interesting, he leads you into all sorts of places; while I was trying to discuss his use of sound effects, I somehow wandered over into Olivier's movie of *Hamlet* and theater as opposed to cinema and I realized that I am a product of radio days. My childhood imagination was shaped by listening to *The Lone Ranger, The Shadow, Grand Central Station*, and then to records of actors like Olivier—not VCRs, not just music as on FM radio now, but drama, news, all popular culture. We talk a lot about the shift from cinema to television and from silent movies to talking pictures but less about the shift from radio to television. In the days of radio you connected people with their voices not their looks. It didn't matter what they looked like—you could imagine that by simply listening.

LK: When you move from publishing fine small-press editions of your poems to more mass-market editions you lose, not this arrangement on the page, but certainly a lot of the space on the page. And more than that: I noticed, for instance, that when *The Liberties* was transferred from *Defenestration of Prague* to *Europe of Trusts*, the page that has "crossing the ninth wave" on it was omitted.

SH: You know why? Because I had to cut. I was allowed fewer pages. That was David's drawing, too; I loved that. If I could ever get that book done again, I would want it back. I love that drawing. It's part of the poem.

LK: So when they said to you, "Look, we only have this many pages; you have to cut," you said, "Well. This doesn't have words on it, so I guess it'll go"?

SH: Well, technically that illustration was not part of the writing. We couldn't find the original and that was a problem too. When it came to Wesleyan and *Singularities*, they were adamant about numbers of pages. I had a lot of trouble with spacing, et cetera. For "Thorow" I sacrificed three quotations concerning his name. They were amusing and interesting and helped to explain my title, but technically they weren't part of the poem, so when I simply had to cut something, I cut them and it was a mistake. Whenever I read the poem, I put them back.

LK: So someday you would hope to reprint it differently.

SH: Yes. And I wish I could reprint the drawing of the ninth wave. When I first set up *The Liberties*, I was working with Maureen Owen, who edited Telephone Books. Maureen was wonderful to work with because she was open to any adventure. I showed her what I wanted and then we worked it out, though it was a mimeo edition and she had almost no money and naturally ran into trouble getting small-press grants. She has daring and vision, and Telephone Books, the magazine and the press, is where many people got into print for the first time. Of course, it stopped being funded, as is the case with so many interesting small-press magazines. She had to stop, and she was a gifted editor.

LK: Do the poems in *The Nonconformist's Memorial* look as you wanted them to look?

SH: Peter Glassgold, my editor at New Directions, was wonderful. In "Melville's Marginalia," it was desperately important to have the space around individual sections. By and large, if I'd say I had to have something alone on a page, Peter would allow it. Look, for instance, at this page [p. 21]. I love that page, and they got it right. They went to a place that did one wrong version after another, had a hell of a problem with the typesetter, but they kept at it. Sadly, if that were ever to be anthologized, the space will get lost; space always gets lost.

LK: Perhaps as you get more known, you have more power and have more input.

SH: No. As you get more known, you tend to get anthologized, which means your work gets jammed together. Of course, it's possible that there's something precious about all that white space around the page, especially now that so many people are doing it—it's become self-conscious.

LK: But you do care about it.

SH: I do. I started as a visual artist. I can't erase that.

LK: I'd like to talk about Language writing and experimental writing. Perhaps partly because of your close association with Charles Bernstein from your teaching at SUNY–Buffalo, you are often identified as a Language poet. But several times, I've heard you say you're not *really* a Language poet. How is your work different from Language writing? What makes you want to say, "I'm not really a Language poet?"

SH: Well, for one thing I'm older than most of the people I consider to be Language poets. By the way, that is a small group. Most of them are in their mid- to late forties now. As I have said, I came to poetry through my art, and my sensibility was very much formed in the sixties. I seem to have been led into writing by accident, the same way my writing then led me into textual scholarship, and now I find myself writing something you might call film criticism. I have never followed an agenda or a program. Also, much of my inspiration as a poet comes from modernist writers. At first Charles Olson (a late modernist or first postmodernist) gave me a certain permission. The early edition of the *Maximus Poems IV, V, VI* published by Golliard was crucial. I would open it up, and what he was doing with the space of a page and with history would set me off. *Finnegans Wake* is another work that was necessary to me. And then there was John Cage and what he did with *Finnegans Wake*. For a couple of years I had a correspondence with Ian Hamilton Finlay because I had written an article for the *Archives of American Art Journal* about artists and poets (Ad Reinhardt, Robert Lax, and Ian Hamilton Finlay). Finlay is one of the great letter writers. He had me following all sorts of leads and all of them very much affected what I was doing. These people all influenced me on a formal level. Virginia Woolf and Emily Dickinson were there as the two completely necessary guides in ways that were immediate—absolutely necessary, not at a remove but in me.

LK: And this seems to you different from what lies behind most Language poetry.

SH: Absolutely different. I wasn't reading the Russian formalist critics. I had no Marxist background, having never been to any university. I suppose I got some of these ideas because they were all around, but I got them first through artists' writings—through people like Reinhardt, Finlay, Judd, Smithson. Of course, they were probably reading Jacobson, Adorno, Lukacs—people I'd hardly even heard of at the time. Most of the Language poets were in universities during the late sixties and their work is fueled by the political rage and the courage of that period. I can understand it and identify with it but at a remove. However, I feel these writers are my peers, and I care what they write and what they think about what I write. So it's complicated. There isn't an easy answer.

LK: When I think of the major spokespeople for so-called Language poetry, they are men: Charles Bernstein, Ron Silliman, etc. If the women who are associated with that movement were the main voices we were hearing as spokespeople, would they be saying something different from what the men are saying? Partly I'm asking how gender seems to affect the production of language-centered writing.

sh: I don't think it's fair to say that gender affects the production of language-centered writing in a bad sense. Or rather, I would say that gender affects *all* writing that attempts also to be theoretical or to state a position. Why accuse Language poets of something that is omnipresent? Lyn Hejinian is a key figure in that group—as editor and publisher of Tuumba Books, as editor (with Barrett Watten) of *Poetics Journal*, as translator of Russian poetry, above all as a poet—and I think she would tell you that she has received encouragement, intellectual companionship, equality, fraternity, sorority, from writers classified as Language poets. She has written essays and taken a critical position. It's not necessarily the fault of the men in this group; rather it says things about our culture. I think that women who take a theoretical position are allowed to take a theoretical position only as long as it's a feminist theoretical position, and to me that's an isolation. I would be extremely wary of being put in the category of writing about "women's problems," because then you get, I think, shifted out. I don't know whether Lyn is bothered by these things or not; I can't speak for her. But I'll say there's no question in my mind that Lyn Hejinian is an indispensable, essential figure in what is "the main group that was."

lk: You say, "The group that was." Do you think that things are moving on from Language writing just at the moment when the academy seems ready to say, "Oh, there's this thing: Language writing."

sh: That's the sign it's over.

lk: Let me read you a statement by Marianne DeKoven and get your response. DeKoven identifies "the purpose of experimental style, whether in writing signed by woman or by man" as being "to assist in changing culture by charting alternatives to hegemonic structures of consciousness." Do you think that all experimental writing does have as its purpose cultural change and "charting alternatives to hegemonic structures of consciousness"?

sh: I think her idea is a good idea, but when you say "all," it bothers me because there is such tremendous variety.

lk: Do you feel that *your* work is invested in cultural change or "charting alternatives to hegemonic structures" (leaving aside how grandiose that sounds)?

SH: I always go back to the fact that Wallace Stevens is my favorite poet of the twentieth century—poems like "Auroras of Autumn" or "Notes toward a Supreme Fiction" or "Credences of Summer." I don't know if that kind of poetry is changing culture or changing hegemonic consciousness, but it certainly changes my consciousness, and it's tremendously beautiful, and moving, and philosophical, and meditative, and all the things that words have the power to be, which is ultimately mysterious. If only I could write a poem like that—that's what I'm saying! And the same thing goes for *Four Quartets* or *Trilogy*. That would be my goal, something perhaps more selfish than changing society—if I could just write something that was of that caliber, that would be enough. Certainly my essays are often angry, and the drive that propels me is some kind of feeling of righting a wrong. But then language has its own message. For individual poets to be able to bring whatever it is that they feel is their deepest necessity to express—I'm thinking of "expression" in broad terms, in terms of space, in terms of sound, in terms of all those things— that's what we're here to do. It's our ethical obligation.

LK: You need to pursue your gift, in a sense.

SH: Yes, and to pursue it to its nth degree, until it's possible it won't reach other people—and yet you have to reach a reader. Although I may feel just writing is enough, we do live in a world where it appears we need to communicate.

LK: People objecting to experimental writing sometimes complain that whatever claims are made for its social engagement or Marxist perspective or its changing "hegemonic structures of consciousness," that, in fact, the audience it reaches is a very narrow, highly educated one, that the reader has to have tremendous intellectual confidence even to grapple with these texts. What do you think? Does that concern you?

SH: No. The objection offends me. I think it is part of a really frightening anti-intellectualism in our culture. Why should things please a large audience? And isn't claiming that the work is too intellectually demanding also saying a majority of people are stupid? Different poets will always have different audiences. Some poets appeal to younger people, some to thousands, one or two to millions, some to older people, etc. If you have four readers whom you truly touch and maybe even influence, well then that's fine. Poetry is a calling. You are called to write and you follow.

LK: Can you talk about the relationship between your prose and poetry? Take, for instance, "Melville's Marginalia." Why did that take the form ultimately, or predominately, of poetry? It starts out in a way where it almost could have been one of the essays in *The Birth-mark*. But then it moves into more definitely poetic sections.

SH: It didn't start with the essay. It started with the poetry. I was in Philadelphia writing an essay called "Incloser," which is about Thomas Shepard. I had already written the essay once, and it had been published in this book Charles Bernstein edited, *The Politics of Poetic Form*. And it wasn't right; I was still working on it, and I was teaching in Philadelphia, and I had some extra time, and all of a sudden—I started writing parts of that essay. They were the parts about women in the early conversion narratives. At the time I was up for a job at Buffalo and initially I didn't get it, and I thought: Okay, it's all up with academia. I'd been trying to do the right thing, I'd been nervous about my writing of essays because I knew I needed a job. And I felt: it's over, forget the job. Also, I'd just seen these Shepard manuscripts. I just decided, to hell with it: I need to speak, I need to write a certain way about Shepard and about these narratives. So I started writing the essay exactly as if I were writing a poem. It shifted to a completely poetic language. I started rearranging, obsessing over lines and words, as opposed to paragraphs or pages. I included a soliloquy that I made up, Anne Hutchinson speaking or thinking. A dramatic soliloquy doesn't usually occur in an essay, a soliloquy in the form of poetry. It was as big a change for me as when I wrote *Pythagorean Silence*. With "Incloser" I found my own voice as an essayist. Even though I'd already written the Rowlandson essay and the Dickinson book.

So then I came to Melville. I was in Philadelphia for another semester the following year teaching again at Temple. It's strange because though I was very lonely there and very worried about David's illness because I was away from home, each semester I was there I seemed to have extraordinary inspirations for my writing. I chanced on *Melville's Marginalia* at Temple Library, two huge volumes collated and edited by Wilson Walker Cowen. What I did was to randomly go through the book and light on something—sort of chance operation without discipline. I would pull a line from one of the portions he had marked and then use it to make a poem. More and more the whole issue of marginalia began to interest me.

LK: This was before you figured out that Clarence Mangan was the model for Melville's Bartleby.

SH: Yes. I was struck by the fact that Melville owned a book by Mangan because Mangan was part of my Irish background and childhood memories from there. What Melville had chosen to mark interested me. So one of the poems in the series had Mangan in it. A year later when I went to Paris as part of some poetry festival, I was struck by the fact that Dominique Fourçade, the French poet who was translating, didn't bother to translate the poem with Mangan in it. It's amusing because Mangan was an insatiable translator. He even made up languages so he could translate them. I was interested that they didn't notice that one. The following summer I was interested enough in the subject of Melville's marginal notations to go to the Houghton Library [at Harvard University] and see his actual books and the marks he really did make in them rather than relying on Cowen's transcription. There I saw the Mangan edition and how heavily it was marked and it made me more curious about Mangan, so then I was off on that trail. At this point the poem seemed to turn toward being an essay, and I went with it. I was convinced and still am by the Mangan-Bartleby connection; though no one takes me seriously, I am serious. But Mangan would like that because his whole career is a sort of joke or pun. He is an untranslatable translator. The interesting thing is that now I see how my interest in marks in books goes back to Marcia Hafif's books and my beginning to write at all. Marginal markings are on the cusp between drawing and writing. You say something with a gesture.

LK: What about your composition process? Do you write essays and poems in a similar way?

SH: In some ways similar and in some ways not. Writing poetry, I feel completely free. It's meditative. I lay out all the pages on the desk and it's quiet and I have books and I can go where I want, do what I want. I'm just free, at peace. Writing an essay, I want to say something specific. I can't figure out how to say it. I'm very nervous about my scholarship; I'm very anxious to be scholarly correct. At the same time, my favorite essays are generally essays by writers about writers. Then there is sound. The power of sound never changes between poetry and essays. More and more, as I write essays I seem to be—as in the Marker essay I'm doing now—obsessing that every line is right. I started working that way in the Shepard essay. I worked line by line, which is a problem for essays; it can make them jerky and fragmented. I would say that, for me, the big similarity is sound. When I revise it's as if I were taking dictation, but who the dictator is I do not know. I will change something if it doesn't read right. Most scholars wouldn't do that. I wouldn't change a fact, of course, but I couldn't leave a sentence be if the acoustics weren't right. So the essays are acoustically charged just as poems are, but they originate more from fear, from a feeling of needing to write or say something but having no idea *how* to say it. They are stutters.

LK: When your father wrote his scholarship, he was confident? Was he fearful?

SH: I don't know since I never talked to him about it. I think he was very worried about making scholarly mistakes, very worried about being thorough, but he did not have an exciting writing style—my mother had the ear as a writer. The interesting thing about my father was, he was *obsessed* by footnotes. You could say the marginalia idea is something about letting footnotes take over the text. I grew up with my father's "So-and-so wrote a very bad footnote" or "That footnote was wrong" or "The way the English put footnotes on the page is much better than the Americans'"—with frantic worry over footnotes and bibliographies. Yet I love the *play* of footnotes (though I can't write a correct footnote). That's one of the things I have such fun with in *Melville's Marginalia*; in a sense, it's one huge footnote, and I love that idea, and I think Melville was playing with that idea a lot in *Moby-Dick*. Certainly Mangan has an uproarious and subversive way with footnotes. This is also one of the things in Chris Marker's film *Sans Soleil* that most appeals to me. In many ways it's a film about editing and quotation and footnoting (in film)—and then his name Marker is an assumed name, and what is marking if not marginalia?

LK: When you were reading the other night, you suggested there was a close connection between "Submarginalia" and *Melville's Marginalia*, one of which appears in a book of essays and the other in a book of poetry.

SH: Right. I was writing them both at the same time, and I had an August deadline for both (and if you teach a full schedule as I do, summer is the only chance you have to write at all). Terry Cochran at Wesleyan told me I needed an introduction to the essays in *The Birth-mark*. I thought the essays were like separate poems and could just be put together and left to connect by chance or proximity. The reader's reports backed him up; they seemed to assume there *was* an imminent introduction. I chanced on the Coleridge citation about marginalia in a section of the lengthy and wonderfully informative introduction to the volume of the Princeton edition related to his marginalia. I was using the volume in reference to the poem for the New Directions book [*Nonconformist's Memorial*]. The essays were on one table, the poems on the other, so I was going across the room from each to each, and Coleridge's paragraph on himself as a library cormorant proved to be what I needed to set me off on the nonexistent introduction—it just took off and then I had a hard time stopping. Really both the "Submarginalia" section of the introduction and *Melville's Marginalia* are a play with footnotes. I wish the two were in one book.

LK: Perhaps I already know the answer to this question, because of what you just said about the peace you find in poetry, but I'll ask anyway: This year, I know you've had no time . . .

SH: No peace.

LK: . . . to write poetry. Does that drive you wild?

SH: Yes. David died on October 5, 1992. I haven't been able to write poetry since then. I have been teaching. And working on the essay on Chris Marker's work, a Andrei Tarkovsky film called *Mirror*, and two films by Dziga Vertov. It has been an enormous challenge because I have never written about film. Of course, it is turning out to be eccentric or poetic. I am very worried though about whether I will ever have the heart to write another real poem.

LK: I suppose that's true for anybody who stops writing for a while.

SH: Yes. But this isn't merely a question of writer's block. David was like a wall against the world to me. I felt I could do anything as long as the shelter and nurture he provided was there.

LK: So that sense of freedom you described a few minutes ago in writing poetry—you're afraid that some of that may have been made possible not by writing poetry, but by David.

SH: Absolutely. And it wasn't only his companionship and love but his work and his nature. He was of the sea. He was a wonderful sailor, and toward the end of his life when he couldn't sail because of the pain he was in, he could still row. He always had some kind of boat, and they were always beautiful ones. Now I feel that the sea went with him. The sea and poetry—actually for me they are one and the same. My favorite pieces of his resemble boats. After he died, I discovered some plans he had been working on for a boat that we could live in. He designed a desk for my computer, a place he would work, and we would just take off in it and escape. But he never showed it to me. There was something utterly unique about David—his students knew it—a way of thinking about the world and about art that was generous and strong. We each worked all day at our art (when we weren't teaching); we didn't discuss our work much together, but we were living and thinking together. We agreed without having to explain.

LK: You were very lucky. I'm sorry you lost that.

I gather from some things you've said that sometimes theorists have provided a kind of space for you. I'm thinking of your comments about Foucault or Benjamin, that they have provided impetus or reinforcement for your work. Who are you reading now?

SH: Walter Benjamin. I would call some of his essays poems. I love his interest in very short essays, his interest in the fragment, the material object, and the entrance of the messianic into the material object. I find some theorists are helpful in teaching nineteenth-century American literature: Kristeva, Benjamin, Levinas, Blanchot, Derrida, Foucault.

LK: And feminist theorists—have they helped your poetry?

SH: Not my poetry, no. But I like to read some Hélène Cixous. And Kristeva, who influenced the way I wrote about Mary Rowlandson. Irigaray sometimes. And there are American women who are scholars who work in the field of Early American Studies who are very important to me. Of course, there are women writers who have helped my poetry.

LK: H.D., Stein . . .

SH: Virginia Woolf. Not Stein so much, though I admire her; she's definitely helped me write essays. She is a great permission giver. Dickinson, obviously. It's important to me to read Lyn Hejinian's work and Leslie Scalapino's and Anne-Marie Albiach's poetry.

LK: Where do you see your vision parting from a poststructuralist view? This came up yesterday in the context of whether there was some historical "truth."

SH: Rather than attempting to talk about poststructuralism, I'll answer in terms of truth. I think there is a truth, even if it's not fashionable to say so any more. I do think it's urgently necessary to bring Dickinson's manuscripts to light. I believe there are stories that need to be told again differently. I believe with Walter Benjamin that the story is in danger of being lost the minute someone opens one's mouth to speak; but you've got to open your mouth to speak, and there *is* a story, and it's probably going to be lost anyway, but whatever that story is, whether you call it fact or fiction, or an original version, it's something real.

LK: What are your expectations of your readers?

sh: Freedom. It goes back to Joyce again, because you know how he was so obsessed with revision; he'd spend a day thinking about whether to put a period in or take it out.

lk: What hell.

sh: Yes. Well, I tend to do that, too. There's an absolute precision to his writing. At the same time, there's incredible play and freedom. I don't know what his point of view would have been, but I think the writer is commanded and commanding. Poetry has acoustic demands—and yet that's where the mystery begins. The thing that reminded me about Joyce—or Pound, say—is you pull out a word or a sentence or a fragment and go with it; you let it lead you somewhere. That's the way I begin to write a poem anyway. I write the way I read. I wouldn't want the reader to be just a passive consumer. I would want my readers to play, to enter the mystery of language, and to follow words where they lead, to let language lead them.

lk: In discussing *Pythagorean Silence* with my students, you admitted that it contained a great deal of personal and autobiographical material. But you were quite definite about not wanting to reveal that material in any specific way. I wondered where that comes from. It occurs to me that there may be a gender issue. Women poets in particular are often read in a very reductive way according to biography—or specious biography. Dickinson would be a stunning example. Keeping your biography out of view could be one way to avoid that kind of trap. Alternatively, I can see this reticence as having to do with principled notions about what's important about poetry or with ideas about what constitutes the speaking subject on the page. Or it could just come from a sense of privacy. But it does seem to raise questions again about what the reader takes away from the poetry, because you might say that the personal material is there so as to suggest patterns that others would be able to recognize or identify with. Or you might be content to have those aspects of the poem remain indecipherable, inaccessible to your reader.

sh: It's the whole problem of biography. There are a lot of people—including professors in the academy—who would say biography is not important. The work is its own thing isolated from history, isolated from biography. But when I'm teaching, I like to concentrate on writers rather than movements. Take Language poetry: they're all individuals. And Romantic poetry: Shelley is not the same person as Wordsworth and is not at all the same person as Byron. They may have been friends, but they're different. I'm interested in details of difference. I'm always curious about biography. And you can't say you don't bring your own story to whatever you write, even in ways you might want *not* to bring it. But I do not like confessional poetry. These days, in America, confession is on every TV program, let alone in most poems. By now it's totally boring, or maybe it's my Yankee sense of decorum. Yet if a reader really loves a writer—and if he or she doesn't love a writer, it doesn't matter—but if he or she does love a writer, that reader will probably do some research. He or she will look for a biography.

And yes, yes, yes, I think it's a gender issue, because women tend to get lied about, and exaggerated stories are told about them, if they are not obliterated. So I think it's important to find a story, to save a story, but I don't think it's important to bray a story.

LK: You have said that as a poet you feel you're taking dictation. This would be at the opposite extreme from the biographical, I think—your sense that as a poet you act as a medium. Can you elaborate on that? When you talk about dictation, it's not that there are voices.

SH: No, no. I don't hear voices (though I'm always scared I might). You don't hear voices, but yes, you're hearing something. You're hearing something you see. And there's the mystery of the eye-hand connection: when it's your work, it's your hand writing. Your hand is receiving orders from somewhere. Yes, it could be your brain, your superego giving orders; on the other hand, they *are* orders. I guess it must seem strange that I say poetry is free when I also say I'm getting orders. It can become very frightening. That's what Melville's so good on in *Pierre* and *Moby-Dick*, that once you're driven onto this hunt, you can't stop until you're told to stop. It connects to blasphemy and to the sacred for me. It connects to God. That's why I like George Herbert and *Four Quartets* and Stevens. Being a poet is a calling. You are called and you must listen.

LK: For some reason these questions about compositional process and where art comes from are particularly mystifying with composers: Mozart, for instance, what he could do in his head!

SH: And why is it that a person who's not Mozart can't do it? But if you're Mozart, or even Bobby Fischer playing chess, it's grace. You've been granted some grace.

—*from* The Nonconformist's Memorial

20.15 Jesus saith unto her, Woman,
why weepest thou? whom seekest
thou? She, supposing him to be the
gardener, saith unto him, Sir, if thou
have borne him hence, tell me where
thou has laid him, and I will take
him away.
16 Jesus saith unto her, Mary. She
turned herself, and saith unto him,
Rabboni; which is to say, Master.
17 Jesus saith unto her, Touch me
not; for I am not yet ascended to
my Father: but go to my brethren,
and say unto them, I ascend unto my
Father, and your Father; and *to* my
God, and your God.
18 Mary Magdalene came and told
the disciples that she had seen the
Lord, and *that* he had spoken these
things unto her.

—The Gospel According to St. John

Contempt of the world
and contentedness

Lilies at this season

other similitudes
Felicities of life

Preaching constantly
in woods and obscure

dissenting storms
A variety of trials

Revelations had had
and could remember

far away historic fact

Flesh become wheat

which is a nothingness
The 1 *John* Prologue

Original had no title
Ingrafted onto body

dark night stops suddenly
It is the last time

Run then run run

Often wild ones nest in woods
Every rational being

The act of Uniformity

ejected her

and informers at her heels

Citations remain abbreviated

Often a shortcut

stands for Chapter

1.

nether John and John harbinger

In Peter she is nameless
Actual world nothing ideal

headstrong anarchy thoughts
A single thread of narrative

She was coming to anoint him
As if all history were a progress

As if all history were a progress
She was coming to anoint him
A single thread of narrative
headstrong anarchy thoughts
Actual world nothing ideal

In Peter she is nameless
The nets were not torn

The Gospel did not grasp

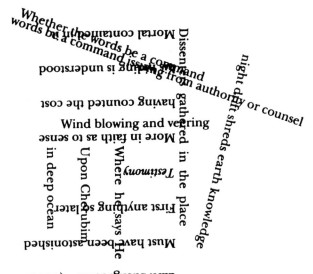

Whether there
words be a command
Mortal contained in
Dissent
Issuing from
night day or counsel
Nothing is understood
gathered
having counted the cost
shreds earth knowledge

Wind blowing and veering
More in faith as to sense

in deep ocean
Upon Cherubim
Where he
Testimony
First anything so later
says
He
in the place
Must have been astonished

dark background   (Gardener

Pure Sacrosanct Negator
I John bright picture
What are
suddenly unperceivable time from place to place
All other peace   Effectual crucifying knowledge

I John bright picture

dark background (Gardener

Must have been astonished

First anything so later

Testimony

More in faith as to sense

Having counted the cost

his hiding is understood

Mortal contained in

a state of separation

Where he says Hound

Upon the Cherubim

and in deep ocean

Baffles consuming daggerel

The skull's ascension

In the Evangelist's mind

it is I absolutely I

Word before name

Resurrection and life are one

it is I

without any real subject

all that I say is I

A predicate nominative

not subject the I is

the bread the light the door

the way the shepherd the vine

Stoics Academics Peripatetics

and liturgical fierce adversity symbol

Hazard visionary ages foursquare

She ran forward to touch him
Alabaster and confess

Don't cling to me
Pivot

Literally the unmoving point around which a body
    Literally stop touching me
turns

We plural are the speaker

Came saw went running told

Came along

Solution continuous chaos

Asked told observed

Caught sight of said said

Wrapped lying there

Evangelists refer to dawn

The Three Day Reckoning

Alone in the dark to a place of

execution

Wording of an earlier tradition

Disciples are huddled together

We do not know

The Evangelist from tradition

He bent down

Mary was standing

In the synoptic tradition Mary

enters the tomb

The Narrative of Finding

One solitude lies alone
Can be represented

where the capture breaking
along the shock wave

interpreted as space-time
on a few parameters

Only in the absolute sky
as it is in Itself

word flesh crumbled page edge

The shadow of history
is the ground of faith

A question of overthrowing

Formulae of striking force
Vision and such possession

How could Love not be loved

Disciples are huddled together
They do not know

Retrospective chronologies
Synoptics speak

Revelatory Discourse Source
The Feeding Narrative in Mark

Rough messenger Trust
I studious am

Would never have stumbled
on the paved road

What is that law

You have your names

To do and to settle
Spirit of Conviction

Who wounded the earth

Out of the way of Night
no reason to count

Crying out testimony

Paths of righteousness
Love may be a stumbling

out on the great meadows
Prose is unknown

You have your names

I have not read them

Coming from a remote field
abandoned to me

The motif of fear is missing
The motif of searching

Historicity of the scene
Confused narrative complex

Two women with names
followed by two without names

Distance original disobedience

Against the coldness of force
Intellectual grasp

Scene for what follows
Do not touch me

It is by chance that she weeps
Her weeping is not a lament

She has a voice to cry out

No community can accompany her
No imagination can dream

Improbable disciple passages
Exegetes explain the conflict

Some manuscripts and versions

Her sadness

was out of enclosure

Transfiguration.

Out of enclosure She

So many stumble

going out of the world

Come then!

Feet wrapped in hay

I stray to stray

her knowledge of Me

Hearers of the Face Discourse
Happy to be in peace
know next to nothing
She drank a tumbler-full of water
Often singing
Her body trembled like a leaf

harryette mullen

Harryette Mullen is known for her innovative, "mongrel" lyric poetry (as she puts it in a 1996 interview, "We are all mongrels"[1]), which has gained increasing attention in recent years. Mullen's primary concern is to diversify the predominant aesthetic of accessibility that characterizes contemporary African American poetry and criticism. Her work, with its myriad sources, allusions, and humorous leaps, is a poetic hybrid that takes the forms of both the short lyric and the long poem, all the time investigating the diverse lexicons of a "miscegenated" global culture.

As she notes in the discussion that follows, Mullen has crossed the lines between often-isolated aesthetic camps, pioneering her own form of disjunctive lyric that combines a concern for the political issues raised by identity politics with a poststructuralist emphasis on language. Her influences range widely, from the Black Arts movement to Language writing to rap. *Trimmings* (1991), for example, assumes an open-ended, serial form that takes Gertrude Stein's *Tender Buttons* (1914) as a point of departure, weaving it with more recent threads of popular culture and feminist theories. Looking at *Tender Buttons* through the "cool dark lasses" of a black feminist perspective, Mullen creates a dialogic text about women's clothing—"girdled loins" wrapped in Steinian "tender girders" (*Trimmings*)—complete with everything from dress shields to gowns. On occasion Mullen even rewrites passages from *Tender Buttons*, implicitly critiquing Stein's politics even as she pays tribute to her innovations. The poems from *Trimmings* originally appeared on separate pages. Here, we separate them with a bullet.

Still more allusive, Mullen's *Muse & Drudge* (1995) is a long poem in lyric fragments, spliced together in unpunctuated quatrains here separated with a bullet to show the separate pagination of the original, as are the poems from S*PeRM*K*T. In this sampling of diverse sources and cultural references—from Sappho's lyre and Bessie Smith's blues to Anita Hill and Clarence Thomas—Mullen forges densely punning, spliced-together phrases. In the process, she creates musical effects ranging from scat to rhyming toasts, underlining the ancient origins of the poetic text in song. *Sleeping with the Dictionary* (2002) continues Mullen's linguistic experiments, employing generative devices invented by the French avant-garde group Oulipo. The book as a whole is an example of the form abecedarian: the series of poems (and also often the lines of the poems) proceed in alphabetical order. Using this and other playful devices to highlight the importance of language and its structures, Mullen shapes poems that are feats of poetic game playing merged with stinging critiques of the politics of language and so-called dialect, especially as these relate to race and ethnicity in the U.S.—as poems like "Bilingual Instructions" make clear.

Born in Alabama, Mullen grew up in Texas, the daughter of teachers and the granddaughter and great-granddaughter of Baptist ministers in the still-segregated south. She earned a B.A. in English at the University of Texas at Austin and a Ph.D. from the University of California at Santa Cruz. She now teaches African American literature and creative writing at the University of California at Los Angeles. Her works include six collections of poetry, most recently, *Sleeping with the Dictionary*. In addition to *Trimmings* and *Muse & Drudge*, other volumes include *S*PeRM**K*T* (1992) and a collection of early work, *Blues Baby* (2003).

This interview, conducted by the poet-critic Elisabeth A. Frost, took place at the Modern Language Association meeting in Toronto in December 1997, where

Mullen was giving a poetry reading in conjunction with a scholarly panel devoted to her work.

AN INTERVIEW WITH HARRYETTE MULLEN
by Elisabeth A. Frost

ELISABETH FROST: I'd like to start with the fact that we're meeting for this interview at the MLA convention. You write both scholarship and poetry. Is there a sense of competition between the two?

HARRYETTE MULLEN: This is a good time to celebrate that they definitely have come together in a positive way. When I was a graduate student, there was a weird trepidation about one interfering with the other.

EF: Did you find your research making its way into your poetry?

HM: I wrote my dissertation on slave narratives. That research has definitely influenced my thinking about not just poetry but a lot of things. It gave me a deeper sense of where I have come from, individually and collectively. I can remember reading some of the slave narratives and just weeping and thinking, "Whatever is wrong with my life is nothing compared to theirs." These people went through so much just so that we could exist. It has really become the bedrock for everything else—that grounding in history, a collective experience.

EF: I'm interested in your articles that deal with the interplay between orality and literacy. That issue makes its way into your poetry, too, because there is so much play between the oral and the visual, in almost every line.

HM: I am writing for the eye and the ear at once, at that intersection of orality and literacy, wanting to make sure that there is a troubled, disturbing aspect to the work so that it is never just a "speakerly" or a "writerly" text. When we talk about orality, most of the time we are really talking about a mimetic representation. Poetry does come out of song. If it gets very far from song, it's difficult for many people to connect with it. So I'm always experimenting with how to be in that space, where it's neither completely spoken nor completely something that exists on the page.

EF: Do you feel that this is also a problem in the way poetry is conceptualized? People are pegged—you are either a speech-based poet or a visual poet, for example.

HM: I think so, partly because there are different social scenes that people are participating in. People in one camp don't necessarily even meet people in the other camps. In Los Angeles, for instance, I can go to some poetry readings and see basically the same people, and I can go to other venues and there will be a whole different cast of characters who don't participate in this other literary world. I like traveling. I enjoy the different perspectives—I've always done that, out of necessity, since my childhood. That's how I feel most comfortable.

EF: You say out of necessity. How do you mean that?

HM: I started in childhood. My family moved around. They were from Pennsylvania. I was born in Alabama, and I grew up in Texas. I lived in New York, now I am living in California, and I lived a little while in New Mexico. My family lived in one neighborhood and went to church in another, and we went to school in a third. I couldn't play with my school friends because none of them lived near me. People in my church didn't live near us. And people in my neighborhood were rapidly moving out because we were black and they were white. You have to find your community wherever you can.

EF: Your poetry deliberately crosses camps—it defies expectations. Would you talk about some of the strands in your work, that you are stitching together?

HM: Well, you know that I have been influenced by hanging around with the Language crowd. It was their interest in Gertrude Stein that made me want to go back and read Stein again after I was kind of frustrated with her. I think that because I had been listening to a lot of experimental, engaged, innovative poetry, her writing began to make more sense to me and I felt more comfortable reading it. I really was interested in the idea of writing a prose poem. I thought that I would treat the sentence as if it were a line and not worry so much about grammar or punctuation, but just use the grammar and the punctuation in the service of the rhythm of the sentence. That liberated me to try a lot of things I wouldn't have tried otherwise. I was also very much influenced by a certain black tradition, particularly having taken folklore courses with Roger Abrahams at the University of Texas at Austin. We couldn't take Afro-American literature courses at that time. This was in the 1970s. I took African and Afro-Caribbean literature courses, as well as folklore courses. Now I realize that what was being taught was the folklore of the street culture, and I can remember in some cases feeling really alienated, because the folklore that I knew was the folklore that you know if you go to church, if you are on the school playground, if you are leading a very sheltered, lower-middle-class life in a black community. The folklore that was being taught was collected in prisons, pool halls, or on the street corners. It was the lore of the men on the streets. No wonder I didn't understand it. I didn't know about "Shine and the *Titanic*." A piece I published in *Callaloo*, "She Swam on from Sea to Shine," is based partly on a toast which is a folk epic about Shine, a legendary character, who supposedly survived the wreck of the *Titanic*. That is very much a genre of oral recited poetry that men perform in black communities, and Abrahams did collect material in prisons, from poor and working-class black men. But I had been working with the idea of folk tradition even before I really knew what it was, because I have a folk tradition—the jump-rope songs and the formulaic greetings that kids have. That was always part of how I experienced poetry.

I have always felt that what I wrote was somewhere between what I heard and what I read. What I have heard has influenced my sense of rhythm very strongly. Music has always been fundamental to me, as well as folklore and poetry, and the church—Psalms and Proverbs, the gospels, the spirituals, and all the preaching. My grandfather and my great-grandfather were Baptist preachers; there are two generations of them. So we had a book culture (my maternal grandfather had a shelf of philosophy books and my paternal grandfather was a printer), and my mother and my father's mother were teachers. All my immediate relatives had jobs that required literacy—teaching and preaching, doing office work, or social work. There was the street or the playground on one hand and home, school, church, and books on the other. There are always different camps, including the people that don't care about books but want to be able to deal with you face to face. You have to have your wits about you because people are always testing you; if you are walking down the streets in any black community, people just talk to you, in these conventionally formulaic ways, to break the ice. Somebody throws one of these little zingers at you, and you have to be able to bounce back with something. I was never all that good at it, but I certainly could appreciate what other people were able to do, and I could think of things to say later on, which is why I am a writer.

EF: How old were you when you started to write?

HM: At a very young age I was writing the stuff that kids write—I made cards with lines of verse for everyone's birthdays or holidays and comic books. I would illustrate and make little stories, invent board games and give them to my friends, with a story that unfolds as you play the game. I created my own alphabet. I was really into the world of symbolism, whether it was a secret code, or coats of arms, or all kinds of riddles or alphabets. We had an encyclopedia that had the history of each alphabet since the beginning of the letter. I wanted to unlock everything that was there, the history. I felt that way about words. Words belong to families, like people.

EF: That's a wonderfully empowered attitude toward language, as opposed to learning in school that a certain way to use language is "correct." You got a strong dose on both sides, a very spoken life and a very written one.

HM: I have read drafts of my grandfather's sermons. He wrote them, but he didn't preach them as they were written. We used to say, some preachers just preached the gravy, but he would preach a sermon with both meat and gravy. I think about that for myself too. You have the gravy, but you can't just live off the gravy; you need the meat as well.

EF: You use a lot of different sources, materials, voices, especially in *Muse & Drudge*, which is so allusive. For me it gets more so every day, as I teach it, because every stanza comes into being as I'm informed about references I might not know. How do you feel about what I might call the politics of allusion?

HM: That's a good question. On the one hand, I feel that because *Muse & Drudge* is so fragmentary, wherever parts of the text came from really doesn't matter because it is really not a complete thought about anything. It is very much a book of echoes. Some of the fragments rhyme and some don't, and that is basically the principle of the book—the recycling of fragments of language. For example, all the Sappho references come from a translation by Diane Rayor—we were at Santa Cruz together when she was beginning her career as a translator of ancient Greek. Her book title, *Sappho's Lyre*, is echoed in the first line of my book. I begin, "Sapphire's lyre styles / plucked eyebrows / bow lips and legs / whose lives are lonely too." But in fact, in the whole book, there is only one direct quotation, and it was kind of a joke for me to do that because the one thing that was quoted was from a comic book: "fool weed, tumble your / head off—that dern wind / can move you, but / it can't budge me." That's from a Krazy Kat comic. There are several things that are taken from Krazy Kat comics, but that one is a complete quotation. Almost nothing else is. I could put quotation marks around everything, from the folk tradition, or blues songs, or whatever theory I was reading—particular theories of representation. There are also a lot of quotes from my family.

But I really like the idea that the only thing that needs quotation is the line from the comic book. George Herriman is a fascinating figure. He was an African American man from Louisiana, whose family had moved to California and passed as white—really, they became white people. Herriman was the creator of Krazy Kat, a comic that I knew about because my mother sometimes called me Ignatz, the name of the mouse that was in love with Krazy Kat. "Hairy man" puns on Herriman's name: "black cat in the family tree / hairy man's Greek to me." Since Herriman rarely spoke of his family or his background, friends and acquaintances speculated on the basis of his appearance that he was Greek or that he was French because of his Louisiana Creole heritage. Reading the comics one might think he was Jewish since the characters often sprinkle Yiddish words into their speech. Herriman was a melting-pot American. The Hairy Man is an African American folk character similar to the bogeyman in stories told to scare children into correct behavior. The issue of lost kinship, of lineage and the denial of relationship in "passing" is evident in Herriman's story. There's a quatrain that plays on that idea—"mutter patter simper blubber / murmur prattle smatter blather / mumble chatter whisper bubble / mumbo-jumbo palaver gibber blunder"—with homophones of *mother, father, sister, brother.* Readers find different meanings in the multivalent references.

EF: So the language comes out of both shared knowledge and very private knowledge. Where does that put the reader for you?

HM: The reader is getting whatever the reader can get. Just as I do when I'm reading. This is about me reading too, getting what I get and passing it on. What I really love, when I read this poem or when someone else reads it and tells me about the experience, is that different people get different things. If I'm in a room with an audience, sometimes the young people are laughing, and the old people just stare. And vice versa—the old people will hear things that they know that the young people don't know. Black people get certain things, and Spanish speakers get certain other things. There are people who recognize Sappho lines or Bessie Smith lines.

EF: That's why I love teaching this book. The group experience of going through this text is totally different from reading anything else. It's a sort of collective reading process. It's confusing for some students, because they're used to the idea that there is an authoritative reading. Some of them run with it, but others are intimidated. So we brainstorm and come up with all kinds of stuff, and that becomes very fun.

HM: That's how it should be. I think that there is always a danger of poetry being remote, even painful. People have this fear and anxiety about being wrong, and in this case it is not really about being right or wrong, because the poem allows you to come in and leave at various points. There are times when people will hear something very clearly and know exactly where it came from, and other times sections are obscure. That's OK, because someone else is going to have the same experience, but with different parts being clear or obscure. In fact, some of the things that I wrote, I had just found out myself. I was learning as I wrote *Muse & Drudge*. It came out in 1995, and I probably began at least a little bit of it around the time *S*PeRM**K*T* came out in 1992. So between 1992 and 1995 there was probably one six-month period when most of it was written, and then I did a little bit here and there along the way. When I was busy, I didn't write as much. When I was really going, I was writing every day, and everything seemed to rhyme. I would hear something every day, or I would read or remember something that really seemed to fit into the poem. I think that readers should feel free to use whatever competence they have, and I'm really delighted when people tell me about their reference points. I may have gotten something from one particular source— for example, the phrase "the other side of far" for me comes from Zora Neale Hurston. For other people it comes from Larry Neal. It's both; Larry Neal may have gotten it from Zora Neale Hurston originally—I don't know. Or a line that I heard in a blues song someone else has heard in a country-western song.

EF: When we read the lines "you must don't like my peaches / there's some left on the tree," my students say, "Oh, Steve Miller Band!" That metaphor comes much earlier from Ma Rainey.

HM: Most of what I'm using doesn't really belong to any one person or group. Some material I think of as African American, and I'll go somewhere else and find out it's Irish, or German, or Italian! I think that it's mine. And I realize that I have to share it.

EF: So it's about claiming what's yours but also allowing it to be possessed by others.

HM: This whole book is about being possessed by others. It is very much made up of the voices themselves—words of others that I've read, heard, or overheard. I knew this book was not going to be about me; it's about black women primarily, and I am a black woman, so some of those voices could be mine, but I was not writing about myself. The individual and the collective merge, as in the blues.

EF: When did you decide you didn't want to use the traditional first person, the lyric "I"?

HM: Well, I hadn't done that for the two books before, *Trimmings* and *S*PeRM**K*T*. In both of those books, it's the culture that's speaking, definitely.[2]

EF: At the end of *Trimmings*, you mention that a word like "pink," for example, signifies femininity in the dominant culture, but "pink" and "slit" apply equally to a sewing catalog and a girlie magazine. You write that as "a black woman writing in this language, I suppose I already had an ironic relationship to this pink and white femininity. Of course, if I regard gender as a set of arbitrary signs, I also think of race—as far as it is difference that is meaningful—as a set of signs. Traces of black dialect and syntax, blues songs and other culturally specific allusions enter the text with linguistic contributions of Afro-Americans to the English language" ["Off the Top" (—ed.)].

HM: I wanted *Trimmings* to be a feminist exploration of how femininity is constructed using clothing, how the clothing itself speaks to, or is emblematic of, certain kinds of constraints on women's bodies. That is one of the issues I wanted to deal with: the overlap at that time of pornography and fashion, the kind of photography that was very trendy in fashion magazines. The other thing had to do with the critique by black women and other women of color of the very way that feminism was constructed around the needs of white women without always considering the sometimes very different needs of women of color who were not middle class or working-class white women who also had problems with academic feminism. I was thinking about the dominant color code for femininity. It is pink and white. English literature is full of the "blush." I felt that I had to include images of black women. *Trimmings* grew as well from my response to Stein. One of my poems even cannibalizes Stein's "Petticoat" poem [from *Tender Buttons*].[3] My reading of Stein's "Petticoat" poem also brings Manet's "Olympia" into the picture. I had an insight that she might have also been thinking about that painting, with her "Petticoat" poem.

EF: Would you read that passage from your poem?

HM: "A light white disgraceful sugar looks pink, wears an air, pale compared to shadow standing by. To plump recliner, naked truth lies. Behind her shadow wears her color, arms full of flowers. A rosy charm is pink. And she is ink. The mistress wears no petticoat or leaves. The other in shadow, a large, pink dress."

I use the language of Stein. She has a "light white," "an inkspot," "a rosy charm." So I put those words into my poem. Then I expanded to give the reader an image of Manet's painting of the white nude with the black woman in the shadows who's obviously a servant. Manet contrasts the white woman's body and the black woman's body with the white woman's body constructed as beautiful, feminine, seductive, also a little outrageous. The black woman is basically just a part of the decor, but her presence seems to enhance the qualities that are attributed to the white nude. In a way, the whole book is really built around this: both my active and my somewhat critical engagement with Stein, my problematic relation to the Western icon of beauty and the black woman's relationship to that, and my interest in representation itself, whether it is a visual representation or a representation in language. I didn't think it was enough just to have that, so I put some other things in here that were definitely meant to investigate alternative female images. I put in the Josephine Baker poem and the "bandanna" poem because it was unsettling to me just to investigate this white femininity without some kind of black experience being represented as well. There are also "cool dark lasses" wearing their shades, maybe jazz divas, someone like a Billie Holiday.

This book is connected to *Muse & Drudge* because *Muse & Drudge* is a book about the image and representation of black women, and *Trimmings* has more to do with the representation in the dominant culture of white women, although there are black women here and there. *Muse & Drudge* is intended to think about folk representations, popular culture representations, self-representations of black women, and to think about how to take what is given. There is a whole set of codes, a whole set of images that we really don't control as individuals. They are collective and cultural. The problem as a writer is how do you write yourself out of the box that you are in? *Muse & Drudge* is an attempt to take those representations and fracture them, as I try to do with breaking up the lines and collaging the quatrains together, sometimes from four different sources. It was an attempt to use this language as representation, to use it in a self-conscious way as code, as opposed to taking the code as something that is real. The body exists, but there is a way that your body is interpreted based on a historical and social context. I take that and use it as material, as opposed to saying, well, that defines you; that's what makes you who you are. I have a certain faith as a writer that we can use language in a liberatory way to try to free ourselves. I had to take things and riff on them, as a musician improvises on a melody and really creates a new song.

EF: Can you talk a bit more about code switching in *Muse & Drudge*, the significance of including black dialect with the simultaneous invocation of Sappho as the poem opens?

HM: With "Sappho and Sapphire"? Because Sapphire has been a pejorative figure for black women ever since the old *Amos 'n Andy* television comedy and before that, a radio program with white men doing their version of black dialect. So it was actually an extension of the minstrel tradition where "black face" was done linguistically instead of in a visual way. Later black actors performed these stereotypes in the television comedy. So the black woman, Sapphire, was a loudmouth, aggressive, the image of the supposedly emasculating black woman with the husband who is henpecked. She was a shrill harpy, and she always dressed in grotesque outfits as well, with hideous hats. So in the sixties, when people were reversing the signification of these pejorative terms, black women reclaimed Sapphire as an assertive, vocal black woman who stands up for her own opinions. You know, just take that negative stereotype and make it positive. Sapphire is actually an entry in the *Feminist Dictionary* with a discussion of this process of inversion. I definitely wanted to think about Sapphire singing the blues and Sapphire as Sappho, singing the blues. If we think of ancient lyric poetry, we have to think of Sappho. This is a place where a woman is actually one of the forerunners and foremost practitioners of the art. So I'm honoring this woman, and I'm also thinking about the blues tradition and Diane Rayor's translations, because she is trying to bring Sappho into a very contemporary American language. It seemed to me that Sappho is singing the blues. That was the conceit that allowed me to go on with this poem and to investigate my own connections with this tradition, which was actually called into question by people like the Language poets, who feel that the lyric poem is too much entangled with a subject they want to deconstruct. I have a certain attachment to the lyric subject, but the lyric subject in this poem is multiple, not singular.

EF: Are there aspects of the blues that are particularly important, which you draw on?

HM: Well, there are so many women that have made their mark. Some particular women *are* the voice of the blues—Bessie Smith is a good example. She is the blues; she lived it and died it. And blues women were very influential and admired as artists before black women were admired on their own—that is important to me. Also, the blues is something that I can identify with even though I didn't grow up with it. We were one of those religious families who thought, "Ooh, this is the devil's music!" I had to develop my appreciation later in life. My family in that way was very old-fashioned. At home we listened to gospel music, spirituals, classical music. We heard blues and R&B music when we were getting our hair done or on the jukeboxes in the soul-food restaurants in the black community. (I'm talking about the period before my sister and I developed our own tastes. This was the influence of my family.) I never realized, until much later, that my mother had been in the high school band with Ornette Coleman. It never occurred to her to mention it.

EF: The woman on the cover of *Muse & Drudge* looks like a gospel singer.

HM: Gil Ott, my publisher, had some photographs that a friend of his had taken. She's actually not a performer; she is a woman who attended a public hearing in a big, crowded municipal building—I think it was a hearing about access for people with disabilities—and she is actually in a wheelchair, but you can't see that in the picture. She was participating in a public protest. I liked it because it looks like she could be praying, singing, or clapping. Her eyes are closed, her hands are together. It's an ambiguous image, which I liked. She looked very soulful to me. She definitely looked like a black woman. I put the photo on the Xerox machine and made it bigger, used black marker to crop it, and blacked out everything around her. She kind of shines out of the black background. She just seemed right.

EF: I like the the visual pun on blues and sapphire in the background color.

HM: I knew that it had to be a black and blue cover.

EF: I'm curious what you think about the debate in recent years about the blues as an expression of black culture. The Black Arts movement rejected the blues because the songs were seen as focused on oppression and not enough on rage. It is hard for me to believe that you would agree, but it is interesting to see how the blues has been troped.

HM: I think it depends on which kind of blues you listen to, because there are so many different kinds of blues and many different kinds of people who sang it and continue to sing it. People are revising and editing the blues now. The blues we are hearing now is probably not the same as when it was sung by people with a living memory of slavery. When you don't feel so oppressed, you sing differently. So the blues has evolved.

It reminds me of Alice Walker's Meridian, a character who stopped going to church as she became politically active. I can remember sitting in the black church singing, "Wash me whiter than snow," with no irony whatsoever. This character in *Meridian* goes back to the black church and says, "The music sounds different. It has changed." That is happening in all forms of black music. Blues was always an improvised music, and the lyrics have always been shuffled into different combinations. People felt free to make their own custom version out of the parts of a particular blues song.

EF: I wonder about your epigraph to *Muse & Drudge*, from Callimachus. It reads, "Fatten your animal for sacrifice, poet, / but keep your muse slender."

HM: That comes from another one of Diane Rayor's books, *Latin Lyric and Elegiac Poetry*. It is his advice to a poet. It has to do with the economy of poetry. I'm very interested in the tropes that people use—here, the idea of sacrifice, fat and slender beauty. When you think about a black woman in this culture, which one is she going to be? She could be either one, the black woman as a beast of burden or as a postmodern diva. There's the black woman who is out of her place, a Josephine Baker, or the supermodels who are admired even as other black women are still being oppressed. That is where the title *Muse & Drudge* comes from. Also, as a woman writing poetry, you are seen as someone else's muse. So there is tension in that as well.

EF: One of the motifs that recurs is about the female body, the black female body.

HM: And the body as an instrument.

EF: Like the lyre. A lot of the images in the beginning, especially Sapphire's lyre, cut both ways. Using the body as an instrument is a kind of feminine strategy—exalted on the one hand, yet undervalued as art. But the substitution of that bodiliness for another kind of self-expression becomes tragic.

HM: That's how I thought about it, even in terms of the jazz-blues tradition, where the men are playing the instruments and the women are singing. Yet the men are the ones who are usually regarded as geniuses, because singing is supposed to be less of an art—it's seen as more natural, more intuitive. The same thing is also said about instrumental jazz musicians, that they were just born with it, that music just comes out of them.

EF: It interests me that Callimachus is affirming the lyric, the economy of poetry, as you said. At the same time you've written in the form of a long poem.

HM: I think I realized that somehow I could have both in one—very brief lyrics that I could write in the moment. It's a serial lyric that accumulates the thematic concerns of a long poem.

EF: The page is not necessarily a unit in the book, at least according to my reading. Things stop and start very differently in different sections.

HM: There is one whole page about birds; it begins, "sauce squandering sassy cook / took a gander bumped a pinch of goose." And there is one whole page about my mother. There is one whole page of Hollywood's image of black people, and there is a whole section that has to do with a transition in my life. Because it was such a flexible form, I found that I could piece lines, couplets, quatrains together and sometimes have a unit expand into a page, or two pages, or more.

EF: Do you like the idea of someone just opening it at random, starting anywhere?

HM: Someone pointed out to me that you could just read the first page and the last page and that would help you to understand the body of the poem.

EF: Especially since Sappho frames it. The final quatrain, "proceed with abandon / finding yourself where you are / and who you're playing for / what stray companion," echoes a Sappho fragment.

HM: Yes. I knew the structure, but I did not know which parts would be where. When I wrote the last lines, I probably knew that they were going to be the last lines, and I think I knew what was going to be on the first page. Everything else just kind of moved around.

EF: Did it feel really different to be writing quatrains, compared to prose poems?

HM: It felt wonderful because it is such a flexible form. A lot of it is already given—some of the rhymes from the blues songs. It is so ingrained, either quatrains or couplets. A lot of the materials that I am dealing with are already in that form. It allowed me to pluck material from all over the place. I thought when I chose the quatrain that it would help me. As I went through it, I thought, "I could do this forever!" I could find two lines and then find two more lines. And I could find different ways of writing. Not all of them are *ab*—I could do four *a*'s, or I could do whatever I wanted. I could rhyme *reel* and *leer*, *girl* and *gal*, *radio* and *cielo*, *rubia* and *nubia*. I could rhyme things for some obscure reason known only to myself. There are little motifs that do repeat—birds repeat throughout the whole book, actually. The idea of the bird and the head, all those African masks with the bird coming out of the brow, that fascinates me. And the idea of dreams and imagination, with the bird, the head, the hat, the hair. There is that upward motion that takes you away from the body. The body has a head, but the head is dreaming, the head is imagining. The head is flying, like a bird. I began to discover that motif, and I worked those elements into the poem. It is also in a lot of the material because it is an African motif.

EF: There is also a lot about hairdos.

HM: Well, if two black women are together long enough, they will talk about hair. Human beings are obsessed with hair. It's so meaningful. It's such a cultural signifier. All the things we do to our hair, and our feelings about it, are part of who we are.

EF: I was thinking about the relationship between hair and clothes, because of the two meanings of "ironing" and "pressing." There's the stanza "my head ain't fried / just fresh rough dried / ain't got to cook / nor iron it neither."

HM: Yes. People say that you get your hair "pressed," and there's the "curling iron" and "pressing iron," and when we wash our hair and it gets all crinkly, it's "rough dried," which is what you say when the laundry comes out, before it's ironed. Also at the turn of the century a common occupation for black women was laundress, and those black laundresses were among the first workers to organize a strike for higher wages. As much as I hate the hot comb, look at Madame C. J. Walker, who was a role model for working black women.

EF: There is another motif, not as pronounced. Some of the stanzas in *Muse & Drudge* have to do with media events. There is a sequence that I particularly like: "another video looping / the orange juice execution / her brains spilled milk / on the killing floor." We get Rodney King, then O.J., and a couple of stanzas earlier there's Tawana Brawley: "they say she alone smeared herself / wrote obscenities on her breast / snatched nappy patches from her scalp / threw her own self on a heap of refuse." And there is also, if I am getting it right, Anita Hill: "we believed her / old story she told / the men nodded at her face / dismissing her case." There is this quick progression of media constructions of black men and women as projections of some kind of fear.

HM: I actually wrote this before the O.J. trials, but I realized after the O.J. case that "orange juice execution" was going to be read as having to do with him. It refers to something that happened in L.A. before the Rodney King riots—when Latasha Harlins was killed for supposedly stealing orange juice from a store; a frightened Korean shop owner killed her. Her death was in the background of the riots. That's what I was thinking of, but the poem is made so that people can attach to it the things that are already in their minds when they come to read it. Anita Hill and Tawana Brawley came into my mind having to do with what happens when black women speak and create a new version of reality. People finally began to understand after the O.J. verdict that black people and white people often don't see things the same way. This was a revelation for a lot of people, but of course this has been going on for a long time. The poem partly is about a reality that is sometimes not credible. We are presented with a *construction* of what reality is, and some constructions can claim more authority than others.

EF: I wanted to ask you about the question of audience in your work.

HM: *Muse & Drudge* was written to create an audience. It was very deliberate. And when you talk about your class having a collective experience, I think that's great—that is exactly what I was hoping for. The first book that I published, *Tree Tall Woman*, attracted mixed audiences that I would read to, but definitely a good portion were African American women. But with *Trimmings* and *S*PeRM**K*T*, all of a sudden my audience was basically white people. Not that I am against that, but it feels very strange when I walk into a room to read my work, and I am the one person of color in the whole room. That seems odd to me. So I think, for some reason, this work hasn't really spoken to certain audiences. I believe it has something to do with the limited audiences and distribution networks for small-press books, although the Internet is expanding the possibilities. *Muse & Drudge* was written specifically to try to bring different audiences together. I wanted the book to invite more readers. That is one reason why there is a black woman on the cover. Usually the covers of books don't say, "Here is a black poet," but I have become very aware of the protocols, the blurbs, and what's on the cover. You can tell a black book fifteen feet away by the cover. The color is usually much brighter than other books', with maybe a Kente pattern in the design. Usually there is a black icon or a black person. There are signals that say this is yours or it is not yours.

Muse & Drudge was an attempt to use what Peter Hudson referred to as an "ocean of black signs" and also to go in directions that have to do with poetry generally. What people think of as "black poetry" is set aside from what people think of as "poetry," in terms of tradition, history, how language is used. People have a very specific notion of what black poetry is. I'm finding that more and more as I teach black students who object to or have difficulty with certain poets that I assign. People are so concerned with what is black and what is not black. And to some extent I am concerned with that myself. The question is how blackness is defined and who defines it. There are certain cliches of blackness that I have played with. I thought of this book as a way to use them and free myself from them at the same time.

But the conventional idea of what black people should write is too narrow. The tradition is broader, more eclectic, than people sometimes think, even within the realm of the folk tradition, the oral tradition, going back to African roots. Africa has been visited by everybody, and people who live in Africa have traveled too. They speak many different languages; there are many different religions, and they incorporate cultural influences from everywhere. And they don't feel that they will be less African if they do that. Here, because we are a minority, and because of our history, we fear we are always in danger of losing our identity. When I look in the mirror, I can see who I am. And whatever I do can be connected to that. I remember in the black community some people would say that you can't be a professor, because that is a white thing. You can play basketball. But there was a time when we weren't in basketball either. When did basketball become black? When black people were allowed to play basketball. We just have to do the things we want to do. And we can do them as black people and as human beings. There's this idea that a black person and a human being are not the same thing. People say, "This is not a black story, it's a human story"—and what they are really saying is that black is not human, even though that is not what they think they're saying.

EF: It happened yet again after Ralph Ellison died. The obituary in the *New York Times* said that *Invisible Man* is not a black story but a universal story, as a mark of praise.

HM: A human being always comes from a particular time, place, and culture and speaks a particular language. Why is a black person, or an Asian person, seen as anything less than universal? If anything, if we are talking about the earth here, the model should be the Asian woman, because that is who is most numerous.

EF: In all your work, but particularly *Muse & Drudge*, there's a balance between the assertion of identity and what I think of as hybridity—the cultural mixture, different influences occurring at once. There's sometimes tension, but there doesn't have to be.

нм: If you accept that they go together, the tension evolves into harmony. That's something that we learn from jazz. When Thelonius Monk creates a new sound with discordant notes, he allows us to hear a greater range of possibilities in his music.

ЕF: Tell me about the song settings of *Muse & Drudge*.

нм: They were composed by T. J. Anderson, who lives in Chapel Hill, North Carolina. He has reorchestrated works by Scott Joplin and written operas and concert music. He's not as well known as I think he ought to be. He was commissioned by a group that was celebrating the centennial of William Grant Still, an early African American composer, and T. J. wanted to use poetry in his piece. He wanted to use Nnenna Freelon, a jazz singer who lives in North Carolina. After two other poets had turned him down, my sister told him that I was a poet and that he could talk to me directly (the book was not published yet). He took seven pages and wrote his composition *Seven Cabaret Songs*. He composed a musical vignette for each one. It was performed in North Carolina in 1995, and I think at Wright University in Ohio around the same time. Then it was performed by the San Francisco Contemporary Music Players.

ЕF: How did it feel to hear your words set to music?

нм: I loved it. Nnenna Freelon has a very clear voice. T. J. wrote the piece for her vocal range. There's clarity and warmth in her voice—the clarity of Ella Fitzgerald with the warmth of Sarah Vaughan. Parts of the songs are spoken, and parts are improvised—she gets to do some scatting. Parts of it are jazzy, and parts of it are kind of bluesy. It has several different musical influences. The music is very allusive in the way that the poem is also allusive. I think they really understood what the poem meant as well.

ЕF: Would the experience have been different if you were writing something that you knew was going to be set to music?

нм: I don't know. I like to listen to music when I'm writing, and I felt that this was a poem that had a connection to music. But I didn't think that it was music— it's poetry. But now it's like a great evolution that it's set to music. It's really come full circle.

Notes

1. Bedient, "The Solo Mysterioso Blues: An Interview with Harryette Mullen" (—ed.).

2. In the next few exchanges, we have "spliced" into the conversation further comments Mullen made on the same topics in Hogue's interview in *Postmodern Culture* (—ed.).

3. One of the shortest "entries" in this serial work, "A Petticoat," reads in full on page 22: "A light white, a disgrace, an inkspot, a rosy charm."

—*from* Trimmings

Becoming, for a song. A belt becomes such a small waist. Snakes around her, wrapping. Add waist to any figure, subtract, divide. Accessories multiply a look. Just the thing, a handy belt suggests embrace. Sucks her in. She buckles. Smiles, tighter. Quick to spot a bulge below the belt.

.

Her red and white, white and blue banner manner. Her red and white all over black and blue. Hannah's bandanna flagging her down in the kitchen with Dinah, with Jemima. Someone in the kitchen I know.

.

A light white disgraceful sugar looks pink, wears an air, pale compared to shadow standing by. To plump recliner, naked truth lies. Behind her shadow wears her color, arms full of flowers. A rosy charm is pink. And she is ink. The mistress wears no petticoat or leaves. The other in shadow, a large, pink dress.

.

When a dress is red, is there a happy ending. Is there murmur and satisfaction. Silence or a warning. It talks the talk, but who can walk the walk. Distress is red. It sells, shouts, an urge turned inside out. Sight for sore eyes. The better to see you. Out for a stroll, writing wolf-tickets.

.

Girl, pinked, beribboned. Alternate virgin at first blush. Starched petticoat besmirched. Stiff with blood. A little worse for wear.

.

Clip, screw, or pierce. Take your pick. Friend or doctor, needle or gun. A dab of alcohol pats that little hurt hole. Hardly a dimple is soon forgotten brief sting. Stud, precious metal. Pure, possessive ring. Antibody testifying with immunity to gold, rare thing. So malleable and lovable, wearing such wounds, such ornaments.

.

In feathers, in bananas, in her own skin, intelligent body attached to a gaze. Stripped down model, posing for a savage art, brought color to a primitive stage.

.

Shades, cool dark lasses. Ghost of a smile.

.

Thinking thought to be a body wearing language as clothing or language a body of thought which is a soul or body the clothing of a soul, she is veiled in silence. A veiled, unavailable body makes an available space.

—*from* S*PeRM**K*T

Lines assemble gutter and margin. Outside and in, they straighten a place. Organize a stand. Shelve space. Square footage. Align your list or listlessness. Pushing oddly evening aisle catches the tail of an eye. Displays the cherished share. Individually wrapped singles, frozen divorced compartments, six-pack widows express themselves while women wait in family ways, all bulging baskets, squirming young. More on line incites the eyes. Bold names label familiar type faces. Her hand scanning throwaway lines.

.

It must be white, a picture of health, the spongy napkin made to blot blood. Dainty paper soaks up leaks that steaks splayed on trays are oozing. Lights replace the blush red flesh is losing. Cutlets leak. Tenderloins bleed pink light. Plastic wrap bandages marbled slabs in sanitary packaging made to be stained. A three-hanky picture of feminine hygiene.

.

Off the pig, ya dig? He squeals, grease the sucker. Hack that fatback, pour the pork. Pig out, rib the fellas. Ham it up, hype the tripe. Save your bacon, bring home some. Sweet dreams pigmeat. Pork belly futures, larded accounts, hog heaven. Little piggish to market. Tub of guts hog wilding. A pig of yourself, high on swine, cries all the way home. Streak a lean gets away cleaner than Safeway chitlings. That's all, folks.

.

Well bread ain't refined of coarse dark textures never enriched a doughty peasant. The rich finely powdered with soft white flours. Then poor got pasty pale and pure blands ingrained inbred. Roll out dough we need so what bread fortifies their minimum daily sandwich. Here's a dry wry toast for a rough age when darker richer upper crust, flourishing, outpriced the staff with moral fiber. Brown and serve, a slice of life whose side's your butter on.

.

Refreshing spearmint gums up the words. Instant permkit combs through the wreckage. Bigger better spermkit grins down family of four. Scratch and sniff your lucky number. You may already be a wiener.

—*from* Muse & Drudge

Sapphire's lyre styles
plucked eyebrows
bow lips and legs
whose lives are lonely too

my last nerve's lucid music
sure chewed up the juicy fruit
you must don't like my peaches
there's some left on the tree

you've had my thrills
a reefer a tub of gin
don't mess with me I'm evil
I'm in your sin

clipped bird eclipsed moon
soon no memory of you
no drive or desire survives
you flutter invisible still

.

honey jars of hair
skin and nail conjuration
a racy make-up artist collects herself
in time for a major retrospection

her lady's severe beauty
and downright manner
enhance the harsh landscape
positioned with urban product

mule for hire or worse
beast of burden down when I lay
clean and repair the universe
lawdy lawdy hallelujah when I lay

tragic yellow mattress
belatedly beladied blues
shines staggerly avid diva
ruses of the lunatic muse

.

why these blues come from us
threadbare material soils
the original colored
pregnant with heavenly spirit

stop running from the gift
slow down to catch up with it
knots mend the string quilt
of kente stripped when kin split

white covers of black material
dense fabric that obeys its own logic
shadows pieced together tears and all
unfurling sheets of bluish music

burning cloth in a public place
a crime against the state
raised the cost of free expression
smoke rose to offer a blessing

.

with all that rope they gave us
we pulled a mule out of the mud
dragging backwoods along
in our strong blackward progress

she just laughs
at weak-kneed scarecrow
as rainbow crow flies
over those ornery cornrows

everlasting arms
too short for boxers
leaning meaning
signifying say what

Ethiopian breakdown
underbelly tussle
lose the facts just keep the hustle
leave your fine-tooth comb at home

.

if your complexion is a mess
our elixir spells skin success
you'll have appeal bewitch be adored
hechizando con crema dermoblanqueadora

———

what we sell is enlightenment
nothing less than beauty itself
since when can be seen in the dark
what shines hidden in dirt

double dutch darky
take kisses back to Africa
they dipped you in a vat
at the wacky chocolate factory

color we've got in spades
melanin gives perpetual shade
though rhythm's no answer to cancer
pancakes pale and butter can get rancid

.

go on sister sing your song
lady redbone señora rubia
took all day long
shampooing her nubia

she gets to the getting place
without or with him
must I holler when
you're giving me rhythm

members don't get weary
add some practice to your theory
she wants to know is it a men thing
or a him thing

wishing him luck
she gave him lemons to suck
told him please dear
improve your embouchure

.

marry at a hotel, annul 'em
nary hep male rose sullen
let alley roam, yell melon
dull normal fellow hammers omelette

divine sunrises
Osiris's irises
his splendid mistress
is his sis Isis

creole cocoa loca
crayon gumbo boca
crayfish crayola
jumbo mocha-cola

warp maid fresh
fetish coquettish
a voyeur leers
at X-rated reels

.

they say she alone smeared herself
wrote obscenities on her breast
snatched nappy patches from her scalp
threw her own self on a heap of refuse

knowing all I have is dearly bought
I'll take what I can get
pick from the ashes
brave the alarms

another video looping
the orange juice execution
her brains spilled milk
on the killing floor

if she entered freely
drank freely—did that not mean
she also freely gave herself to one and all—
then when was she no longer free?

—All She Wrote

Forgive me, I'm no good at this. I can't write back. I never read your letter. I can't
say I got your note. I haven't had the strength to open the envelope. The mail stacks
up by the door. Your hand's illegible. Your postcards were defaced. "Wash your wet
hair"? Any document you meant to send has yet to reach me. The untied parcel
service never delivered. I regret to say I'm unable to reply to your unexpressed
desires. I didn't get the book you sent. By the way, my computer was stolen. Now
I'm unable to process words. I suffer from aphasia. I've just returned from Kenya
and Korea. Didn't you get a card from me yet? What can I tell you? I forgot what I
was going to say. I still can't find a pen that works and then I broke my pencil. You
know how scarce paper is these days. I admit I haven't been recycling. I never have
time to read the *Times*. I'm out of shopping bags to put the old news in. I didn't get
to the market. I meant to clip the coupons. I haven't read the mail yet. I can't get out
the door to work, so I called in sick. I went to bed with writer's cramp. If I couldn't
get back to writing, I thought I'd catch up on my reading. Then *Oprah* came on
with a fabulous author plugging her best-selling book.

—Bilingual Instructions

Californians say No
to bilingual instruction in schools

Californians say No
to bilingual instructions on ballots

Californians say Yes
to bilingual instructions on curbside waste receptacles:

Coloque el recipiente con las flechas hacia la calle
Place container with arrow facing street

No ruede el recipiente con la tapa abierta
Do not tilt or roll container with lid open

Recortes de jardín solamente
Yard clippings only

—Black Nikes

We need quarters like King Tut needed a boat. A slave could row him to heaven from his crypt in Egypt full of loot. We've lived quietly among the stars, knowing money isn't what matters. We only bring enough to tip the shuttle driver when we hitch a ride aboard a trailblazer of light. This comet could scour the planet. Make it sparkle like a fresh toilet swirling with blue. Or only come close enough to brush a few lost souls. Time is rotting as our bodies wait for now I lay me down to earth. Noiseless patient spiders paid with dirt when what we want is stardust. If nature abhors an expensive appliance, why does the planet suck ozone? This is a big-ticket item, a thickety ride. Please page our home and visit our sigh on the wide world's ebb. Just point and cluck at our new persuasion shoes. We're opening the gate that opens our containers for recycling. Time to throw down and take off on our launch. This flight will nail our proof of pudding. The thrill of victory is, we're exiting earth. We're leaving all this dirt.

—Zen Acorn

for Bob Kaufman

a frozen
indian acorn

a frozen
indiana corn

afro zen
indian acorn

afro zen
indiana corn

a zen fro
in diana corn

frozen fan
in zero canadian

indian corn for
arizona nonradiance

a narco dozen
faze an african

alice notley

INTRODUCTION

Alice Notley's early work was influenced by a range of writers and aesthetics: William Faulkner (Notley studied fiction at the University of Iowa Writers' Workshop), Blake, Dickinson, the late Robert Creeley ("the first contemporary poet whose work I liked"), Frank O'Hara, and Gertrude Stein, among others. As Notley remarks in the interview with poet Claudia Keelan, Shakespeare was also an influence, his language "awash all over me and I can still summon that spirit up if I need to."[1] Married to the second-generation New York School poet Ted Berrigan from 1972 until his death in 1983, Notley recalls that he was "the single greatest influence on my being a poet" but that she "found it difficult to be influenced by his style." In the interview, she speaks movingly of the artistic ethos by which they lived and she has continued to live since his death: the spirituality of the artist's poverty.

In terms of finding her poetic voice, Notley states that it was meeting second-generation New York School women poets Anne Waldman and Bernadette Mayer that was crucial: "There was no sound in American poetry that . . . corresponded to my experience; there was no poetry with motherhood as its subject. I had my first child in 1972, and there was virtually nothing there in the poetry to help me know who I was." Hearing Waldman's and Mayer's work gave her the means, Notley recalls, to "be included."

Notley's mature work is distinguished by its element of "diagnosis," a compositional practice that analyzes inequities in structures of gender, politics, poetry, and culture, without either removing the self from the scene or using the self to propose a false or fantasized cure. While it was Nietzsche who first called artists and philosophers "physicians of culture," Gilles Deleuze pushed the definition to question issues of composition and the manner in which literary work implies a way of living: writing's aim to bring life to a state of nonpersonal power. In his essay "Literature and Life," Deleuze focuses on the "detours" of syntax, of point of view in all issues of what we commonly call writerly style—issues pertinent to approaching Notley's poetry.[2]

Among her best-known works is the innovative feminist epic *Désamère*, the first section of which is included here, written after Notley and her second husband, the British poet Douglas Oliver, moved to Paris from New York in 1992. As Notley discusses at length, *Désamère* is a visionary poem that confronts environmental disaster and can therefore seem hopeless. But, she insists, the hopelessness isn't in the writing. She remarks of one of the poem's main characters, the French writer Robert Desnos, whose voice the poem reimagines, "I owe an apology to the French for coopting their Robert Desnos. . . . I found thinking of his life very moving, and I'd always liked his funny, luxurious poetry. His voice in my poem is oracular by reason of his known aptitude for dreaming, his life experience (including his death as a result of Nazi internment), and also his insouciance." Insouciance, Notley stresses, helps to sustain a lighter tone and carries with it "a freeing quality that can open poetry to truth."

Notley grew up in Needles, California, in the Mojave Desert, to which her most recent poetry scenically returns. She is the author of over twenty books of poetry, including *Disobedience* (2001); *The Descent of Alette* (1992); *Mysteries of Small Houses* (1998); and *"Close to me & Closer . . . (The Language of Heaven)" and "Désamère"* (1995). She is also the author of *Coming After: Essays on Poetry* (2005) and the editor of *The Collected Poems of Ted Berrigan* (2005), which she mentions in this interview as being in process. Notley continues to edit the journal *Gare du Nord* in Paris, founded with Oliver, who died of cancer in 2000. The following conversation with the poet Claudia Keelan took place via e-mail between September 2002 and December 31, 2003.

AN INTERVIEW WITH ALICE NOTLEY
by Claudia Keelan

CLAUDIA KEELAN: Reading you, I've come to see that you believe poverty is important. At the same time, I can't see that you share faith with the Franciscans, or have any allegiances to systems of thought or religious principles, do you? How did you come to believe that poverty is important?

ALICE NOTLEY: When I was young I attached great importance to certain ethical statements as received, viz., Blessed are the poor in spirit for theirs is the kingdom of heaven. . . . And everything else about poverty in New Testament Christianity. It bothered me a great deal that I was taught these things by people who didn't practice them (it still bothers me—look at the Christian billionaire President and his praying Christian cabinet: I just read that Condi Rice gets down on her knees to pray every night. . . . Blessed are the peacemakers, yeah). I am not a Christian, but I think the ethic of the Sermon on the Mount is a superior one. It got into my system. Poverty also suited my temperament from an early age on: I am inept and shy, and I hate to work for people doing things I don't understand. I preferred being on my own to having money and never got a summer job in Needles. Though I respected my parents' hard work and meditated constantly on why one might spend one's life selling auto parts: it required accepting cars and then auto parts, and I've never accepted cars. But I do accept the fact that my parents grew up very poor and this was a way not to be poor: I didn't think they should suffer.

I became a poet and fell in with Ted Berrigan, who believed that writing poetry was work enough and that he shouldn't have to do other work that wasn't connected to being a poet. Of course, *poet* is the world's most underpaid job, but it was years before I caught on that no one respected it anymore either and that hardly anyone really cared if there was poetry in the world or not and that was why it was underpaid. Still, I didn't want to work except for writing and a bit of teaching. I write every day. I read every day.

Living with Doug Oliver I began to think more about how being poor one doesn't use, or take, what the truly poor—people in sub-Saharan Africa, say— ought to have. I don't feel entitled to more than anyone else's share of the world's money or goods. Although of course I automatically have that even not having much by our society's standards. I have an Episcopalian Franciscan friend, a monk who has become a priest, and who took the vows of poverty, chastity, and obedience. He told me that by far the hardest of the vows was poverty, since, for example, even in the monastery he automatically had health care and the people in his parish—Bushwick in Brooklyn—didn't. I feel clearer not having much; I don't feel part of the infernal and illusory machine which churns out jobs, objects, and the walls of the visible world.

CK: You sound like a Christian to me. If you listen to Bush, his politics (poetics) are more attached to the Apocalypse, which was an added book, by dumb old John of Patmos. If Bush is a Christian, then Jesus sure wasn't. But that bit in the Sermon on the Mount about how to pray, by "going into the closet and begin newly, not with vain repetitions as the heathen do." Certainly your poems follow this?

AN: My mother always talked about going into the closet to pray except she quoted Paul. I always liked the idea because it meant I didn't have to bow my head in public with everyone else: I detested public prayer, saluting the flag, and singing the school song. I recently attended a poetry reading where parts of the audience were supposed to respond with particular words at points in certain poems: it was quite amusing but I couldn't do it. I can't participate in a group.

I am not a Christian because I don't believe in god and I detest the idea of the male religious leader and/or model. I am extremely hostile to all the major religions. However, my thinking has been influenced by Eckhart, the anonymous author of *The Cloud of Unknowing*, Buddhism to the extent I understand it (and given that I'm hostile to the Buddha), etc.

CK: I asked about your ideas of poverty and faith because your work, at least from *Désamère* is filled with children who live in the aftermath of their father's, or a powerful male figure's decisions. The tyrant in *The Descent of Alette* is both a businessman and a father-figure, isn't he? The brother is also prominent, isn't he? And the narrator, or leading figure in *Désamère* and in *The Descent of Alette* is a woman who wants to—is the word *remedy*? The sins of the father?

AN: The chronology of the work is as follows: first *Alette*, then *Close to me &*
Closer, then *Désamère*. The dominant male figure is that of the Tyrant, who is not at
all the same as the father. The Tyrant is the military-industrial-intellectual-artistic
complex; he is how the made objects of the word have found their shapes. The
father in *Alette* is the owl; a human transmuted into a purer nature by his death,
and so able to teach Alette how to combat the tyrant. In *Désamère* there is the
Satanic figure in the prose section, who is the Human as people sentimentalize it.
And there is Robert Desnos. The brother is always the victim, in *Alette* and elsewhere, being a soldier and having been turned into a killer despite his sensitivity.

CK: Your use of Desnos really interests me. He's somehow a channel, yes? Is it
Eckhart's mysticism, his direct connection to the divine that influences you? Is
that a stance you seek as a poet?

AN: *Désamère* was the first work I wrote after arriving in France—fall of 1992 I
believe, into winter 1993. For some reason, the minute I left the United States I
perceived the reality of the global warming crisis, which had not penetrated my
dim skull before. *Désamère* is my seeing that. I was very lonely and went to a zoo
here almost every day, the menagerie of the Jardin des Plantes. It is one of the
world's oldest zoos, very small, and I stared at the animals dreaming up *Désamère*.
I bought and read every book I could find on global warming and the greenhouse
effect. *Désamère* is my version of summing up the second half of the twentieth
century (like all the big-fat-tome male novelists; DeLillo's *Underworld* comes to
mind), bringing it into the global warming desert future, pinning it down into
specific lives, using dead Desnos to tell the story. Yes, he is a channel. I wanted
someone French, and the form of the third part is from him; the form of the first
part is from Marie de France.

I'm not sure I know how to answer the Eckhart question. I suppose it is his
connection to the divine. His heresy as perceived by the church was to make no
difference between himself and god (though he didn't think he was doing this, but
it was obvious to everyone else that he was). I go with that. It is what I mean by
being an atheist (which seems to me the only honorable thing to say one is right
now). I like the ways he uses god and Christ, especially the latter, as metaphors for
his experience—Christ is reborn in the individual soul each day. It sounds so
grotesque in certain passages, and I get a kick out of that. I have a workshop I
sometimes do where I lay out an Eckhart Sermon, Lawrence's "The Ship of
Death," and O'Hara's "Joe's Jacket" next to each other. Doug got a wonderful

poem out of this workshop the first time I did it called "The Soul as Crumpled Bedsheet," so now I do the workshop using Doug's poem too, which stands up.

CK: Emily Dickinson didn't see any difference between herself and God either; it seems to me the history of Protestantism—radical Protestantism—makes that case, i.e., to be Antinomian, to go without name or company, which is why both *Alette* and *Désamère* seem to be—well, descendants—of that kind of spiritual quest. I guess I'm trying to get you to make a connection between spiritual practice and poetics. I know you say in your short essay "Disobedience" that there can be "no doctrines"! But both those poems are epics. Could you talk about your take on the epic, on the "new" protagonist?

AN: I find out everything I believe through writing. Most of my significant experiences, and most of the things I "realize" are found out through the practice of poetry, specifically during the performance, the literal writing of it. My poems seem to have gotten longer as the so-called quest has become more detailed, more exact. *The Descent of Alette* was a conscious attempt to write a traditional epic, first of all—not a modernist one. But what I was finding out—well in this case I had had an epiphany outside the poem, an incredibly negative one, about two things. One, I'd begun to know how monstrous my brother's actions had been in Vietnam in the context of that country (he didn't do anything very bad by "army standard") and of his own sensitivity (he was not what you'd call a natural sniper, if there is such a thing) and my own implication, as an American and his sister, in these actions. Second, that not one thing in the world, not one object and not one practice or habit had been invented, as far as I could tell, by a woman. *Alette* is about those facts, though most obviously the second one—but I wouldn't have chosen epic if I hadn't had to deal in some part of myself with the fact of that war. In the course of writing *Alette*, I mean in the story of *Alette*, there is the black lake and there is Alette's enlightenment, which is tied to her acquisition of natural "owl" powers. I became, after having written the poem, obsessed with the lake. *Close to me & Closer* is me wading into the lake, the black lake the other side of which is infinity. *Désamère* confronts, again, the necessity for a political stance and tries to combine it with the knowledge of the lake—which in this case is not the lake but the desert. *Disobedience* idiomizes all these themes, uses a flip, of-these-times voice and material out of a life lived in Paris to pull everything together in a more overt way. I have two other manuscripts, "Reason and Other Women" and "Benediction," in which I continue the research.

CK: I'm intrigued by the detective in *Disobedience* and also by the notion of American-ness expressed in the first poem "Change the Form in Dream," where you write: "the only / thing American really worth bringing is the sense / that you must accept me, exactly. / Not as your woman." What do you mean here? Do you consider yourself an expatriate writer, and if so, what does your exile serve?

AN: The detective arose gradually out of a dream process. I first had the dream of the detective looking for the woman in the back room: he wasn't recognizable. Then a couple of other dreams fed into the construction of this figure as a character in the poem, including a dream of a childhood friend named Tommy Harward (now lives in Boulder City) whose name suggested the name Hardwood. But then I got to a point, simply writing, where the next words that came out of me, because they sounded right, were "oh sure I can, I'm Robert Mitch-ham." At that point I knew I'd be able to talk to him for a whole poem. He became my friend.

I was recently looking at those lines ["the only / thing American . . . (—ed.)], trying to remember exactly what I meant. They are addressed really to the French, not to Americans—to the place where I now live. I am saying that I am not a member of your French culture, but I will not be a member of American culture, here; I am an exact entity, exact person. I am insisting on my individuality as an exactness. But then I knew the poem would be read mostly by Americans and that the statement works in both directions.

Expatriate is a funny word; I don't know anyone here who uses it, except for certain magazine writers. I've never heard anyone say "I'm an expatriate" though I know many people who have been here for years, are French citizens. I'm not talking about writers particularly. You become part of an international community, Anglophones in Paris. I suppose I'm an expatriate at the moment—I've been here now for ten years. I don't feel that I belong either here or there, but it has become more interesting for me to write from here. My viewpoint is made more complicated by my being here, and my response to poetic language is shiftier. Language seems more substantial and less precise, more about texture and presence and less about meaning in terms of individual words. The experience of speaking and hearing French has made all language mysterious to me again.

CK: The more I read of your work, the more aware I become of your interest in what you call "the forgotten possibility," which seems to be a figure more animal, more mineral, than human. Humans are always evolving into animals and plants in your imagery. Do you think that what we call progress is misguided, that we should in fact get closer to becoming animal? Is it an idea you got out of reading?

AN: I'll try to answer your question about the animal, but the answer seems so obvious I don't know where to begin. It doesn't come out of reading at all. We (my sons and I and then Doug) had a cat for fifteen years, named Wystan, who was very ugly, witty, and "good." He was a good being. If there is an afterlife, I would hope to see him in it (this sounds so corny). Recently I dreamed I had three sons and one of them was a cat. But this doesn't get at any of it. I "know" that animals and plants and rocks are as important and knowledgeable as we are. I don't think they are anything like the descriptions of them biologists make. But most of the biologists I know love animals and use science as a way to hang out with animals. Theory of evolution drives me crazy because of its pointing toward "man"—and being dreamed up by a "man." How come man is carnivorous if apes aren't? Chimps are somewhat, but humans are obviously unmerciful, inferior, so aggressive. I love the wild eyes of wild animals and how they don't even bother with people. You can't make friends with them through the eye—have you ever looked at a duck's eyes? I finally had an experience of burrowing owls last summer in Needles and their eyes seemed to take me in but they were doing their dance of trying to keep me away from their nest, which was somewhere on the high school lawn. I loved going through this with them. My Aunt Margaret said we were scaring them, but I don't think so. They were doing their job. Burrowing owls are in danger, as are most animals, desert tortoises, common frogs. . . . It's so unjust. I feel so stupid because I'm fifty-seven years old and I know very little about animals and except for roaches and rats and mice—and coyotes—they're disappearing. They're so much less destructive than we are. Their ethics are generally better, and they're so mysterious.

CK: I guess what I was thinking about in the question was how writing, when you are really writing, you're becoming. Deleuze says: "writing is inseparable from becoming; in writing, one becomes woman, becomes animal or vegetable, becomes molecule, to the point of becoming imperceptible." Your writing seems dedicated to something like this . . . the whirling, morphic style of *Alette*, and her dismemberment, etc.

AN: What Deleuze says make me nervous. I dislike it when men talk about becoming women in writing: I have heard other French men say such things. It means they don't want to give up power to women. They would rather say they are them. One imagines many things in writing but I'm not sure one becomes what one imagines. I am not Alette or Désamère: they are the ones who become. The dismemberment of Alette—the dismemberment of a woman—is something I've dreamed many times—still do—in many different ways: I know the dream well, it's terrifying. It's part of what's happened to me, on several levels.

CK: The fact of dismemberment—how did it occur to you, on what levels, and did writing *Alette* help?

AN: Now that I'm pinning it down, it seems that I wrote about dismemberment, in *Alette* first, and then proceeded to dream about it at key times. I don't remember how it occurred to me, since I wrote *Alette* out of what I was dreaming and "seeing" and I "saw" the dismemberment. Later someone reminded me that that was a traditional shamanic initiation: the body is taken apart and put back together with some new parts. And I had read that literature somewhat, particularly Eliade. But I wasn't thinking about it at all—shamanism, my reading—when I wrote that sequence in *Alette*: it was logical and I saw it. Since then I have had a number of dismemberment dreams, as if this is happening to me over and over, I or someone is being torn apart, sometimes eaten by people, sometimes stabbed repeatedly, sometimes attacked by birds. I have a number of poems, in my unpublished manuscripts, that refer to these dreams. In the dreams the corpse is not given the grace of being put back together. After Doug's death, I had a feeling of being remade out of metal parts. I think the poet becomes more and more shamanic getting older, in the sense that so much happens to one, and there's nothing left but the poetry function, which is a healing, ecstatic function, as much as it is anything else.

CK: Since there seems to be a dearth of shamans everywhere I've ever been, that seems like good news to me . . . I'm hearing that you don't like—or maybe more accurately—don't purposely bring your reading to bear when you write poetry. Is that right? If it is, does your resistance to that kind of empiricism have a lot to do with the disobedience you've described? Do you think, unlike many writing now, that the poet can find the same or like-knowledge in writing as in reading?

AN: All of that and more. I haven't had to read the literary theoreticians/philosophers because I don't teach except for workshops; I escaped having to read them in college, by virtue of my generational placement. I think they're mostly a factor in the university environment. I know what the conversation is like, from a perhaps minimal exposure; I haven't the slightest interest in what the theory people have to say. I tend to think of them as more men telling me what to think (I know that about three of them are women). And I, after all, am the poet, I also think of the French theoreticians as people writing for French society out of the French language: I have a sense that Americans misunderstand where they're coming from, how they're educated and what situations they're really speaking to. I do an enormous amount of reading long poems, a lot of reading about Australian aborigines, and ancient Sumer, reading of Sumerian literature, plus books about owls, snakes, etc. My reading for *Désamère* consisted of a few books about Robert Desnos, the lais of Marie de France (whom I used as a former model for the first section), and everything about global warming I could get my hands on.

CK: I want to switch gears for a while. I'm in Mississippi now, going to read for the *Mississippi Review* this afternoon. The editor of the magazine, Angela Ball, asked me about you as part of the second-generation New York School. I know you lived in New York with Ted, and your sons live there now. To what extent do you see your project in conversation with say, Bernadette Mayer, Ashbery, Koch, O'Hara?

AN: I was probably part of the New York School until the mid-eighties and I remain of it, to some extent, through friendships and certain interests. In fact, I have a book of essays coming out from the University of Michigan Press called *Coming After*, which is largely about second-generation New York School people. I changed after Ted died, and then again after some other deaths in the late eighties, and I needed to become my own school, if you wish. I was obviously deeply affected poetically by Ted. I, in fact, learned to be a poet from him. But his sense of community was much wider than the New York scene and included such figures as Phil Whalen and Bob [Robert] Creeley, Anselm Hollo, certainly Allen Ginsberg, all of whom became my friends too. And all of whom have some New York School characteristics, such as humor, which I myself seem incapable of not having, no matter how I'm writing. I would define the New York School in terms of its relation to New York City, how those poets were or are affected by living in an international city which overwhelms one personally with its own story. In New York you construct a personal story or character for your poetry in accordance with how the city's going, with what the city tells you to say. I sometimes think of *Alette* as my last New York poem, since the first section of the poem reflects so strongly the presence of the homeless people in the city in the late eighties. In *Mysteries of*

Small Houses, I consciously tried to revive some of my New York School styles in order to reflect the times of my life I was commenting on. And certainly some of the verve is in the style of *Disobedience*.

CK: I felt your connection to the school in *Mysteries of Small Houses*—the sense of being in a present that has the past and future running right through it, like in O'Hara's "The Day Lady Died." I've always thought that the notion of time and its fluidity was one idea the poets of the New York School shared.

You talked about Ted helping you become a poet. . . . You've also talked about your resistance to men telling you what to do. . . . But your poems are full of owl-men and maintenance men and detectives who often give sound advice. Do you feel a split between your resistance and allegiance?

AN: Sometimes. But I have spent most of my adult life married, and am used to being in conversation with the golden partner—alas now not. I felt myself to be a sort of "school" with each of my husbands actually. Although Ted taught me how to be a poet, I did become his equal and he had no problem with that. He had a particularly selfless love for poetry itself. And with Doug, I engaged in a sort of internationally based school of narrative poetry, no problems. I like to talk to men. I think I believe, or have believed, in dialogue, and one person speaking being formed out of the two present, the way when you talk to someone and you're enjoying it you lose consciousness of individual self—are the conversation. If men and women were engaged with each other in this way habitually, in all levels of life, there wouldn't be problems of power.

Ted's favorite quotation from Whitehead was, everything that is going to happen is already happening. It is the basic belief behind *The Sonnets* and he applied it to his life as he was living it. He also used to teach Frank's poems such as "The Day Lady Died" as past time playing back in the present and rendered as present. With my sons, I am now editing Ted's *Collected Poems* for the University of California Press—a very big book.

CK: I'm curious as to how Ted taught you to be a poet.

AN: He was someone who was always being a poet so I too became someone who related everything I saw in life to my poetry. He had a lot of books, so I read all of his books. And we showed each other our poems, and he suggested changes (later I helped him). He also talked about forms, reading, further things to do. He quite literally taught me, though I never had him for a teacher at the Workshop. I hardly ever went to class in Iowa; I was sick of school by the time I got there. I feel as if I got my training from Ted after I graduated. I think I've said he was eleven years older than I was. He had already become this thing I wanted to be, but at great cost. He always said he couldn't have done it without pills—amphetamines—since he was a working-class guy from Providence; the pills had made his brain light up from the first time. I do believe that. I shared his predilections to a certain extent but my brain had actually started working when I was a kid in Needles and it didn't need that kind of stimulation. I was a liberated little girl and thought whatever I wished—somehow a possibility in the desert but not in Rhode Island where one behaves and thinks exactly as one's family always has and never ever leaves the state except to go to Massachusetts.

CK: In *Mysteries of Small Houses* there's reference to drugs a lot, and a sorrow about it in the later poems. Did you and Ted use drugs for vision in the shamanistic sense? Did it work? What's your take on it now?

AN: I don't think I've ever used drugs for shamanistic purposes. I've had my most interesting visions without them. I view drugs now as mostly destructive but not more so than anything else we're up to: I think I compare cars and pills in *Désamère*. I probably consider the average drug addict to be more "moral" at this moment than the President or any of his company. I'm interested in the idea of addiction. Americans are addicted to lots of things: power, righteousness, fear, money, possessions, as well as the usual alcohol, food, gambling, pills.

CK: At least one of addiction's appeals is changing one's sense of powerlessness to one of power. That propensity seems to be one you're protesting in many of your books, am I right?

AN: I think I listed power as one of the things that Americans are addicted to. In terms of drugs, the classic paradigm is less power than it is control: the addict, as in Burroughs'[s] *Junkie*, takes total control over his or her life. Drugs are then both a regulating principle and a schedule: your life makes sense! You always know what you're doing. And you can live a very long time in this way, as Herbert Huncke did (I think he was approaching eighty and still addicted when he died). As far as poetry goes, there is a lot of power-wielding in our world even though the territory is usually pretty small. A lot of poets are interested in power. I find it hard to say whether this is antipoetic or not. It isn't always cleanly outside the poem, either. Sometimes one is as good as the poem. I, of course, usually see all of this in terms of the male power bid; but there is also the mainstream poetry power bid, for example. This is the whatever-our-group-is power bid as well. There is also the sense that if one doesn't have any power, one can't do any good, can't even get published. As related to poetry, power is complicated.

CK: Earlier you wrote that "everything that is going to happen is already happening" was Ted's favorite quote from Whitehead. Do you believe this too and how does it make you feel? I mean, you've been with Hepatitis C for thirty years and didn't know it, Ted died from it, also without knowing it, and your brother was a sniper in a shitty war despite his goodness who later overdosed . . . and all the other things "already happening," both good *and bad*.

AN: I think I do believe this statement, but it's important that "what is happening" has a lot to do with what you personally have done and are doing. You can sometimes change what is happening. Ted used the statement, it was an amulet for self-recognition and actions (possible change). I got Hepatitis C from/with Ted—doing drugs—thirty years ago; he died of the disease without knowing that was what he had (I didn't know until last fall), but I was crossing forbidden boundaries—so in a sense I "knew." However, it is clear to me that I wouldn't know anything if I hadn't crossed forbidden boundaries, and knowledge is part of what is happening and the key to change. My brother was in a bad war, because men have believed in war for a long time; war has been happening for a long time. He had already gone to that war before he was born. Virtually every man I've been close to, including both my husbands, has done military service. He got a very bad war, because the military-industrial complex and twentieth century male politics were happening in their particular, very bad ways. So the big question is, how does one change what is happening? There are, I suppose, specific answers at specific points.

CK: That's a very good question. Your answer suggests that for you, changing what was happening involved knowing you were crossing forbidden boundaries, without fearing what the result or results would be. Has the achievement of knowledge always involved this dynamic?

AN: Not always directly. I've unfortunately learned so much from being near people who were dying, and then grieving for them later. But many of them had been "disobedient" and almost all the poets I know are disobedient—the vocation has that requirement somehow. No one wants you to be a poet; in being a poet one is disobeying society's wishes. But I've learned what I know from all the ways I've suffered, in disobedience and obedience, and that's the knowledge of my poetry. Society's interest is in having everyone who has disobeyed reform. I have only reformed very superficially: I'm loyal to everything I've done and all the people I've been close to. I'm loyal to Mitch-ham, the seedy detective, who is my Will in *Disobedience*. Finally, ideas like "the will" seem seedy in themselves, so why not have a dilapidated, not terribly good actor, represent that? All ideas are pretty seedy, aren't they?

CK: Not the good ones, which I admit are few. The necessity of disobedience is a profound idea and has informed all the poetry, social movements, and even architecture that I love, structures where a new kind of "reform" is made all right, but a reform in service of the disobedience which opens categories to a further inclusiveness. Blake and his "without contraries there is no progression," Williams'[s] *Spring and All*, the relationship of the civil rights museum's form in Memphis to King's notion of the "beloved community." All those structures "change what is happening," in conventional ideas of law, of beauty, of responsibility. I'm not thinking of "the idea" as Wallace Stevens did, as something that is conceived in an individual imagination and then foisted upon a reader in place of the world, but as something more related to the French use of the word—the *idée*, a plan, a suggestion, a dream—which participates with the world, not exclusive of it. You're right that ideas like "the will" seem seedy, or simply empty, but Mitch-ham's presentation of your Will in *Disobedience*, his pathos, is something I follow and therefore know more about how you view deterministic ideas such as "the will."

In *Disobedience* where Mitch is talking about "the slip" as trangression and Alice steps in and says, "I'm trying to be as clear as possible / as unfictional as possible / given that I have allowed 'fiction' in." What is your sense of the fictional? A lot of poets—I think of Stevens, [Robert] Duncan, Susan Howe, others— promote the inherent fictionality of the word/world. I don't feel that belief when I read you.

AN: A sense of our fictions is something I struggle with endlessly. I believe a fictional view of existence has been imposed upon us: that time and will and history are the result of other people's fictions taking over whatever the "everything" may be. I don't believe any of the stories I've been handed: the scientific story for example. And I'm not interested in what historical figures did: I don't think they did it like that. I believe the story my brother told me as I present it in *Mysteries of Small Houses*, but I omitted some events to make the events more streamlined and believable as art (can you feature that? More happened than even in the poem). I don't think my brother lived that so-called story as story. I think he lives it as shock and instances of—what—confrontation in chaos? But Mitch-ham is a total, bla-tant fiction, so I really enjoy his presence. In *Disobedience*, I posit, rather than story or narrative as reality, the "tableau." That is, the scene impregnated with event and time crisscrossing back and forth. This is based on my sense of how things "hap-pen" to me and also on the way my dreams operate. My dreams don't contain long stories, they contain these tableaux. Doug's dreams, however, were stories, and we used to discuss this, particularly when I was writing *Disobedience*. There may be a large gender difference, based on prevalent social perceptions and how one is brought up to be in "the story."

CK: So then, I'm hearing you do believe we operate in, or struggle inside of, fic-tions imposed upon us—patriarchal fictions, scientific fictions, historical adapta-tions—but that sometimes something (awareness of the fiction, personal fear or love or desperation) breaks through and time becomes real momentarily? What your brother lived through, for example, and how he understood it, how he told you about it. A tableau suggests a series, a seriality, which given in individual con-science, would delineate the individual's preoccupations. The recurrence, for example, of the caves in *The Descent of Alette* and *Disobedience*, and the first woman who reappears as soul in *Disobedience*. Caves and reclaiming a first woman . . . Fake male guides. Are you trying to write yourself out of the fictions when you write?

AN: Sometimes, but not always. This is very sticky. One thing I often think is that everyone operates as if she/he were in a novel. To this extent, I find the rise of the novel, the novel itself, something like a culprit (followed of course by the film). I think it would be a very good thing if the novel could be demolished, but not in a postmodern way where you just write another kind of novel. I love the narrative poem because it can create "extension" without all that psychological tyranny. In poetry words themselves lead you out of time and the story: they stop you or they say "this part of the so-called story can be gotten through very quickly because the important thing, after all, is the poem." And why should anyone identify with a "character" in a poem? I don't believe one escapes time by being within certain moments: I think it really isn't there. The first mother in *Alette* doesn't really corre-spond to the Soul in *Disobedience*. The first mother is the first woman—Lucy the African skeleton; the Soul in *Disobedience* is the narrator's soul. She isn't damaged as the First Woman is; she's whole.

With regard to seriality, tableaux are not necessarily experienced as serial and connective. In *The Descent of Alette*, the caves don't make a linear story together, they may be parts of something but they aren't all of them. Their order isn't terribly important (I had a music professor in college who compared a certain kind of medieval music to string beads). My brother didn't necessarily tell me his "story" in order—he told me these things that happened. My memory of what he told me imposed a second order (I have a set of notes from the meeting); then a third order was imposed by the writing of the poem in *Mystery of Small Houses*. When you're asked to think of everything, it tends not to come "in order." People who practice storytelling (in bars or professionally) give an order to events so they can remember them. Time becomes a mnemonic trick.

CK: I suppose it's their "underness" that connects Lucy and the Soul for me. Both exist in a fiction which would keep them under, if Alette in the one case, or the Soul herself in *Disobedience*, didn't keep "retrieving" her. Perhaps Soul isn't broken, but she's definitely in conflict with the story she finds herself in.

Isn't the tableaux of your dreams cinematic in the same sense film is? At least "serious" film? The tableaux in *The Descent of Alette* also remind me of Spenser and *The Faerie Queen*.

AN: The First Man and the First Woman are standard figures in myth. The First Woman is that kind of First Woman. I read a lot of Native American myth before writing *The Descent of Alette* and was quite influenced by it, particularly *Diné bahane'*, a translation/rendering in English of the Navajo creation cycle, by Paul Zolbrod. In Navajo and Hopi mythology there is an "emergence" of the first people through successive worlds—five in the Navajo story and four in the Hopi. My descending levels of reality in *The Descent of Alette* have more to do with this "emergence," reversed, than they do with, say, Dante. When I told my mother how *Alette* ends—how Alette kills the Tyrant—she said, that sounds just like an American Indian story.

As for the tableaux, they're not cinematic, they're dream-like. The caves in *The Descent of Alette*—and much of the material in *Disobedience*—come directly from either dreams or automatic (tranced) envisioning. The rule in *The Descent of Alette* was to take an element from a dream and then to "see" as quickly as possible whatever I "saw" with my eyes closed, to use it without judging it. That is, the initial element would trigger an automatic visionary sequence which would become a "cave." I've been studying my dreams for the past twenty years or more; much of my theorizing about time and tableaux is based on these dream studies. I've also thought about the traditional relating of myth to dream, that a myth is a dream become more wakeful and made useful to more than one person. I never think about film; I know there are a couple of films in the caves, but they are dreamed.

I've already mentioned that I read a lot of books by Mircea Eliade right before I wrote *Alette*. He says, over and over, that among indigenous peoples, when someone died, when something bad happens, the only thing to do is to sing the world back into creation: start over again at the very beginning. My books always seem to be about trying to find that beginning in order to start over. I think I should point out that in such cultures, one must think about time in an entirely different way. Eliade (who knows how much he knows?) speaks constantly of sacred and profane time. The Australian aboriginal life was geared almost exclusively toward sacred time; there were sacred stories always going on—one lived them and they were embedded in the landscape (as Shiprock, in New Mexico, is one of the monsters killed by the Twins in the Navajo cycle).

I haven't read much Spenser; it's gorgeous but a bit too late for my purposes. Happy New Year, Claudia! (We are starting over again.)

Notes

1. Keelan and Notley, "A Conversation: September 2002–December 2003."
2. See Gilles Deleuze, "Literature and Life."

—*from* Désamère

Amère and Desnos

Overhead at night, above the planet
Identity gone to sleep. . . Look what I've done
End of century, world so human
It may become a desert
Doesn't it feel like one anyway?
Approach a desert then, in a prophecy
An America now and later
Flat and cut with washes
What nondescript hardy little bushes!
In the distance treeless mountains
Then a campfire, someone's here
Small orange-haloed, a flame
People sit around it
Two, man and woman, well-lit
A third standing, distanced from the two,
Tending towards them nervously,
'I dropped the shell,' he says,
'But I'm not responsible for the misaim
Someone else set the sights—'
He's speaking to the woman
She's middle-aged, brown desert face
'I believe you,' she says
'When you die, I take it hard'
The man who sits with her's different
Wears glasses, a somewhat mid-century suit
His eyes are closed,
He seems to talk in his sleep
'You're both caught in times separate
From your condition now,' he says
'Still causing it, you can't leave your pasts

I'll try to dream you out of them'
Faceless people at the fire,
Further back from it, hard to see,
Murmur to each other, sometimes say things to the three
And one says to the dreamer, 'Who are you?'
'Robert Desnos,' he says, 'dead and happy
My intention is to be happy
Even if our world should disappear
I see you better than you do
Because I'm foreign and because I died
In nineteen forty-five,
The last time things seemed clear'
He's quiet now, and the others
Are focussed on the fire, waiting to hear
The voice of Desnos again
And wondering where the world is

[. . .]

'I know what an animal's like,' Desnos says,
'Sweet, educated, unassuming
A man fits out a Terezine:
Torture chamber, gas chamber, crematorium
Men destroy Laos and Cambodia'
'Brother's shaking again,' says Amère
'They rehabilitate Nixon, but he
Manages for only a moment
To be rehabbed before an O.D.'
'I dream,' says Desnos, 'night's blackness here
Is produced from the eyes of a Cambodian woman
Who's gone blind in refusal of sight—
Won't watch it any more, the
Extermination of her family
In a genocide of which Nixon's part-entrepreneur—
Bombs Cambodia, finances the Khmer Rouge—
He's in my dream too: as his advice

Is being asked, as he counsels politicians,
His published memoirs in front of him,
Cracks form in earth, trees wither,
But his face grows younger, hair actually
Lightens almost to blonde'
'I keep going AWOL,' Brother cries suddenly,
'That's why they give me a Dishonorable Discharge'
'Is there judgment for Nixon?' Amère asks
'In the judging of Nixon,' Desnos says,
'Perhaps everyone's judged, to the extent that
Everyone tolerates him:
Trees disappear, animals die, don't they?
The same laxness results in global warming,
In a world where it's difficult not to be guilty'
'Some people are more vulnerable, less
Free to be good,' Amère says
'I was vulnerable,' says Desnos, 'and I was free
Whole countries of freedom inside me
During my abduction by the Nazis, watching
The anonymous soldiers so unlike animals,
I knew everything, didn't I?
Auschwitz Buchenwald Floha Terezine
Reading the palms of the others
Foretelling for them long and happy lives
'*La passion de la liberté est une passion*
de l'âme'
To be free and to be good
Are almost the same
But why should only victims be free and good?'

'I dream,' says dead desert Desnos,
'When Kennedy sends the first Green Berets
Into Vietnam,' sixty-two,
White moon stains a lake, watery flower

You're young, Amère, you say
"This view is corny'"
'It's the sixties,' Amère says, 'I want a city
Soon it's the eighties, the city's ruined
Which person am I, am I ruined?
The rents so high, animals sleeping
Outside at night, drugged and dirty'
'In the sixties, behind the war
A building grows larger,' says Desnos
'The war's a transparent movie, the building's
Windowless, a double-black domino'
'Can't humans escape each other's
Exigencies?' asks Amère
'Who doesn't serve the building? It
Makes weapons, cars, appliances, jobs
In the sixties Reagan's its ad-man
While the young try to block entrance to it
Human products are more powerful than humans are
But I'm not really like a decade'
'So you say,' says Desnos, 'but anyone
Smokes when the others smoke'
A voice from the dark says,
'The sky's full of smoke, everyone smokes'
'Nineteen eighty-four,' says Desnos,
'Oh isn't a woman smoking?
Black woman in a log cabin, fashionable
Blue dress, gold earrings and bracelet
Smoking, furious, cigarette, cigarette
Black men parade past the open door
They tell her they're headed for
Twenty thirty thousand dollar jobs
She sucks a cigarette, shouts,
'What's a salary, without a future?
Our heroisms, agonies, gains in social justice,
Nothing without a planet

Reagan spends it
Squanders it sitting at a desk
Like everyone else'
'Am I ruined?' Amère repeats
'If it's ruined, is each person ruined?
Is there something that can't ever be ruined?'
'In a zoo,' says Desnos, 'in the nineties,
I see Przewalski's horse—
They live mostly in zoos now you know
I dream you're one, bare your teeth, try to speak
You want to say something about ruin: It's not that
Soul won't outlive you unless species does
Soul is what there is, swallows ruin
And yet, you strain to say,
I am ruined if species is ruined'
'I have such a sadness,' Amère says
'As when a husband dies, magnified
Till it replaces all that we were
There may never be nothing more
But this feeling, and then nothing'

'A Russian woman I knew of in America
Drew the blinds so Stalin wouldn't see her
In nineteen eighty-two,' Amère says
'See that strangely shaped creosote bush?
It becomes for a moment the
Man I was with then
We'd moved into the low-rent houses
On the edge of town, right in the desert
Not much professional world there
No junk bonds or corporate mergers
Or job that required a poet
Is that Reagan near our fire?'
Desnos says, 'No one's here who had power

240

I often dream of Reagan somber
Quiet, his face unlined, he wanders his
Future death emptily
Looks like someone just out of high school
Crewcut, short-sleeved cotton shirt'
'Dead animals haunt live ones,' Amère
Says, 'exacting tasks from them
They keep asking me to do their work
Though there's little work to being an animal
Forage and eat, groom a little
The other species don't have poverty
The dead forget poverty, tell you to go on'
'I dream' says Desnos, 'that in the eighties
The summers are one hot field
First a man dies, in a bed, on the ground there
Of accumulated poisons
"I die of my research," he seems to say,
"And good comes of it"'
'Grief also,' says Amère
'Soon after,' says Desnos, 'Brother begins his shaking'
'Delayed reaction to war, common,' Amère says
'And all around,' says Desnos,
'One sees parched grass and plants
Which then disappear leaving sand
Everyone everything has a fate
Now that people have invented fate
And extended its reach beyond the human world'
'But our knowledge of fate,' Amère says,
'Seems to come to us in pieces
Of the past and future blown together
Fragments of history and prophecy . . .
It's hard to make truth of tatters'
'One can't live,' says Desnos, 'as if deciphering
The truth's in you, there isn't very much to it
There's nothing to it—

ALICE NOTLEY   241

And perhaps nothing in America,
In a country with a name or leader, is it'

'See this piece of amber?' Amère says to Brother
'I give it to you for Christmas,
In nineteen eighty-three
So you can be buried with it five years later'
'It outlasts my body,' Brother says
'Outlasts the Human Era,' Desnos says,
'Civilization of rocks is what there might be'
'Yellow amber from the Baltic Sea—
This is when I'm *La Veuve*, the Widow,
Like a Tarot card,' Amère says
'I replay these times for their
Perverse richness—painful and lit with mystery
Before them I was part
Technological person
Pills but never cars, destroy own
Body, but not the world's
Are pills and cars really the same?'
Desnos says, 'The dream's of earth
Pills glide over it producing smoke
The pills eat black pills, earth's black beauties'
'Take a pill and talk to us,' Amère says to Brother
He just turns away
'*La Veuve*,' Desnos says, 'I see the label
Outside the animal cage, mute and
Sable-furred mammalian female'
'My cage was haunted,' Amère says,
'A man's voice would tell me, "Leave this room"
How leave a cage? The whole world's a cage
All that's left of the old world are beautiful voices
Voice on cage fire-escape sings a
Song that goes, "Ain't a body happy?"

Or another song, "From
The past to nowhere's where I go"'
'That's the human song,' says Desnos,
'From the past to nowhere, not even
Leaving amber, because of course
Amber leaves itself behind'
'The voice in my cage,' says Amère, 'says
"Blindness can come from nowhere and be
Accompanied by temporary insanity"'
Desnos says, 'You're condemned to <u>see</u>'
'Brother,' says Amère, 'Why are you and I
Like this . . . soldier, widow,
Why aren't we cars?'
'Because you grieve like animals,' Desnos says,
'Behaving as your species would
If it hadn't turned into cars
You're still the animals'

'I dream,' says Desnos, 'a woman dies
In the eighties, she might be Amère'
'Reagan-hater?' a voice says,
'That was to be like him too
That was your part in that movie'
'In my dream,' says Desnos, 'she's bare-breasted
In a bed, with covers to the waist
A nurse and doctor there, the nurse says,
"Others died, not her"
The doctor, shadowy man: "She's the country"
Blonde nurse: "Then I'm dead too—I have a
Right to drink, if you do"
She holds up a glass of white wine to
Counter his bourbon'
Amère says, 'I didn't die'
Desnos says, 'You emptied

When people you loved died of drugs
Harvesting consequences of the sixties—
Or died of traffic, Vietnam, etc
I dream now a President says,
"The statue of Stalin is broken,
Black blood flows from its mouth, but
What will we do with our Amère?
The Cold War's over, but she's dead
Won't learn computers, do video wars,
Write poems in the codes of
Careers, she's just dead
But isn't everyone more alive than ever?"'
'We go on and on,' someone says,
'Pretend the movie's somehow the same
Whatever we do, it's all right to continue
In almost the exact same way'
'After Amère dies,' Desnos says,
'Someone like her arises from her deathbed
Naked, but that doesn't matter, as if
There were no clothes in this no-world
No clothes because no one's inside anyone
Everyone has denied the angel so it's left them
Or is it, Amère, that you're naked with
Guilt, or old sorrow?'
'What I'm guilty of,' Amère says,
'Is being in a human culture—
But how can we have life without that?
Desnos, I want to be free like you'

Desnos says, 'I dream I don't die
Have somehow become a soldier, after
My death—I know I've died before—
While the French cling on in Indochina
The year is nineteen fifty-four

I'm supposed to be as patriotic
As when the Germans threatened my own *quartier*
In my Nam I lift in two hands
Water to drink, but it's bloody
I find I have the capacity
To divine things through the patterns
Blood makes in water, the swirls and currents
And layers of its spreading:
France's bloody reign in Vietnam,
Its one hundred years there become
A red tide of algae in the future
Multiplying on excess carbon dioxide
What's the connection? It's in the absurd
Ductility of human response
To phantom realities, colonial empires,
Communist and technological ones
But I, Desnos, have only ever
Responded to the empire of the spiritual
Why am I here in this grief, as if
My nationality, French or human,
Has dominion over me after death?'
'What do you do next?' Amère asks
Desnos says, 'I die at Dien Bien Phu, and my
First pure death is erased
I'm condemned to return in future deserts
Dreaming the truth for others, until
A more humble future is won for us'
'Is this dream the truth?' asks Amère
'Only partly,' Desnos answers, 'for
I am dead, and I am happy
I'm not French now, or an animal
With the lucidity of a jewel I trap thought
Change phantoms into figures so
You can see how they manipulate you—
I see now that saints are needed,

In the old way, to counteract leaders
To sit still, withstand
The onslaught of the phantoms
Burn to purity, turn to soul . . .
I dream someone walks towards
A flower which bears
A mane like the sun's rays
And searing dark center, a mouth
To enter, be eaten by
In which there's no Frenchness, Americanness
Human or beetle or rock
One finds a future in that mouth
By admitting that nothing is something, and
That all our contrivances are nothing . . .
The oldest truth of all'

'I dream now,' Desnos says, 'that same flower
Has tongues for petals which move and quiver
Out of its center a language comes
Indecipherable, melodic,
Which speaks from *l'âme de l'univers*
That language, implies my dream, is
Embedded in any poem
Speaks to more than people, more than any
Human Era—
That's why people despise poetry:
It isn't really addressed to them,
It makes them small—
But the flower seems to be calling out
And at the same time growing larger
Its center becomes all it is
A black disc on the horizon
It's large enough to enter
And you, Amère, walk into it'

'Where is that mouth?' asks Amère
'Anywhere,' says Desnos, 'and
Certainly in this desert'
'How change anything?' she asks
'I don't know,' he says, 'except that
Each being's all that there is
Infinity must be in anyone
If you should find it, that which is the base
Of our communality—how else are we
Like animals, rocks, and trees, except for existing
Out of the ground of infinity?—then
We might know what others are'
'Difficult,' says Amère, 'I'm not saintly'
'Change the definition of saintly
A poet may be a good saint because
He or she hears the word—the language
Spoken by the flower—and can repeat it'
'Who will take care of Brother?'
'The two of us, all these times, are dead'
'I'll take a new name,' Amère says,
'Part yours, to remind me to be happy,
My first change of definition of saintly:
My name is now St. Désamère—
I'll enter the desert alone'
'I dream,' says Desnos, 'that as we disappear
The fire goes out, the desert gets cold
You're left standing alone in an antiquated
Garment, a plain long robe—
Stars there're still stars
Then all that's gone, there isn't you
The dream says to me, "She's there but
Don't try to see her—There can't be
An audience at all"'

alicia ostriker

Alicia Ostriker opens her collection of essays on poetry, *Dancing at the Devil's Party: Essays on Poetry, Politics, and the Erotic,* with a bold comment that characterizes the importance of her own poetic project: "From time to time, some of us believe, poetry changes the world. . . . I have always enjoyed the work of visionary artists dissatisfied with the rule of 'things as they are.'" Among the defining concerns of Ostriker's work, from her development as a second-wave feminist poet and critic to her more recent feminist reconsiderations of Judaism, is the hope to help change the rule of structures of dominance and violence through art. Aligning in her concerns with other poets in this volume, most obviously Alice Notley and Alice Fulton, Ostriker speaks here of the challenge to remain life affirming despite the devastations of our times. Although she refuses to give way in her work to despair and grief, it is not wrong at times to subordinate art to history's horrors, in her view, but she urges us not to stop there: "the struggle [for peace and justice] can neither be won nor abandoned" ("Beyond Confession 35"). Her art significantly tracks one poet's struggle: the witnessing, the transmuting, the act of contemplative analysis that her poetry entails. These are places where the concerns of her poetics and ethics *fuse*, as she remarks in her discussion of these issues in the interview.

Ostriker acknowledges that her work risks an earnest compassion for others' feelings and experiences—what she has analyzed in conjunction with Allen Ginsberg's poetry in terms of the Jewish concept of *chesed*, akin to the Buddhist notion of *loving-kindness*. Linking the commentary on America in his poetry to the role of "prophet" as well as "poet" (as in Old Testament Hebrew prophecy), Ostriker argues that no full understanding of Ginsberg's tragicomic sensibility—the link between the book of Lamentations and "Howl," to take a specific example—is possible without taking into account Ginsberg's formative Jewishness. As this interview makes clear, the same should be noted of Ostriker herself. The poetry by Ostriker included here explores formally complex methods interweaving biblical midrash (commentary), modernist collage, nonlinear narrative, and in *The Volcano Sequence*, a furious subject confronting God in a spare, prophetic voice.

Ostriker's criticism advocates a poetry that has an "intensely engaged and engaging" speaking subject and has favored a performative, ritual poetry that "implies the possibility of healing alternatives to dominance-submission scenarios." Poetry is not "therapeutic" but "diagnostic" (a remark that Notley makes as well), an aesthetic language for understanding and addressing what's wrong. Discussing poetry that "suggests nonoppressive models of the conjunction between religion and politics, usually by re-imaging the sacred as immanent rather than transcendent" (*Dancing* 16–17), Ostriker is boldly writing a defense of poetry by excavating its archaic, shamanic function.

Twice a finalist for a National Book Award, Ostriker is author of ten volumes of poetry, most recently *The Little Space: Poems Selected and New, 1968–1998* (1998), *The Volcano Sequence* (2002), and *No Heaven* (2005). As a critic, she has authored the groundbreaking *Stealing the Language: The Emergence of Women's Poetry in America* (1986), and the controversial *The Nakedness of the Fathers: Biblical Visions and Revisions* (1994). Among her honors are fellowships and awards from the National Endowment for the Arts, the Poetry Society of America, the San Francisco State Poetry Center, the Rockefeller Foundation, and the Guggenheim Foundation.

The interview that follows took place over three hours on March 8, 2002, at the annual Associated Writing Programs Conference, held that year in New Orleans.

AN INTERVIEW WITH ALICIA OSTRIKER
by Cynthia Hogue

CYNTHIA HOGUE: You seem to have done the all-but-impossible. You have equally distinguished careers in poetry and in scholarship and criticism. Did you set out to do this, or has your career unfolded in ways that have surprised you?

ALICIA OSTRIKER: I never thought of myself as "a poet." I was a dreamy kid, a bright-eyed English major, a geeky Ph.D. student, an earnest assistant professor, a wife, a mom. I had never spoken the sentence "I'm a poet" before my first residency at MacDowell, pushing forty, with a book of poems, and a couple of chapbooks published. At a writers' and artists' colony, faced with thirty artists, writers, and composers at dinner, you have to answer two questions: "What's your name?" and "What do you do?" You can't say, "I'm an English teacher." When you have said, "I'm a poet," to thirty people, it suddenly sounds real. Meanwhile I'd actually been writing poems all my life, including when I was first teaching, when my kids were little, and insanity was breathing down my neck. I started out with two in diapers and about a million freshmen. The poetry was in the chinks. Life consisted of what my family wanted or needed me for and what I was getting paid for. Who cared if I wrote that next poem? Nobody needed that next poem but me. It took decades for me to arrive at the confidence to make time for poetry and to identify myself primarily as a poet.

The scholarship and criticism happened by accident. I went to graduate school because all I really wanted to do was teach college. Needed to get the piece of paper to do that. The degree. I pretty much hated it and went through as fast as humanly possible: two years of courses, a year writing my dissertation on William Blake, and there I was, a certified academic. Meanwhile I'd fallen in love with William Blake and wanted to convert everyone into being a Blakean. Blake was my guru. So I started out being an eighteenth-century man and discovered women's poetry in the mid-1970s, long after everyone else did. I'd published *Vision and Verse in William Blake* and finished doing 200 pages of notes for the Penguin edition of *Blake's Complete Poems*. Picked my head up out of that trance and realized there was a women's poetry movement going on. When I started writing about women's poetry, I bifurcated into scholar mode and critic mode. Scholar mode meant lengthy research, footnotes—the stance of authority. That was the necessary mode for *Stealing the Language*. Being a critic was different, looser, more personal. But when I began writing essays for *American Poetry Review* on May Swenson, Adrienne Rich, Anne Sexton, and H.D., and they published them, well, that was wonderful. I like that mode immensely, and it's mostly what I've done since.

CH: Why?

AO: Well, I have really paid my dues as a scholar. But you are so constricted in your expression when you're writing a scholarly article. You can be witty but you can't be playful, you can't be passionate, you can't be joyful or sorrowful or angry; you have to crayon inside the lines.

CH: Who are the writers and artists who have influenced you most profoundly? How?

AO: My mother was an English major, who poured Shakespeare, Tennyson, and Browning into my infant ears. The music of traditional poetry was always part of my life. The first poem I remember responding to for more than the music, as a child of eight or ten, was Rukeyser's "Effort at Speech between Two People," which I ran across in some anthology. I didn't actually understand the poem, of course. But something in me recognized this utterance of deep loneliness, something in me said, "Yes, that's how it is." The next time it happened was with Whitman. I was an adolescent, sitting on a patch of grass in Central Park reading "Song of Myself," ecstatic, thinking, "Yes, yes, that's how it is." It was one of those moments when a poet touches something that has existed just below the threshold of your own consciousness, brings it into language, and you simply affirm its truth.

So there was Whitman, and later Blake. Later there was Ginsberg. The great heterodox visionaries. When I was an undergraduate, it was John Donne, George Herbert, Gerard Manley Hopkins, John Keats. I memorized great stretches of these poets more or less unconsciously. And Auden. I wanted to be a combination of all of them. Of course, the poets we studied in school were virtually all men. And they all wrote in traditional forms. So did I. It seemed to me that was the only proper way to write. One year two fellow students, guys who were friends of mine—one a poet, one a novelist—ganged up on me. "Why don't you write as if you're in the twentieth century?" they asked. Meaning, why don't you change your diction and stop writing in stanzas? Well, I was furious, felt betrayed, attacked back. Got on my high horse. When they left, I was harrumphing to myself, "Anyone can write the kind of stuff they're talking about, it's nothing, it's so easy," and wrote my first poem in what I then called free verse. It was about my parents and my sister. I had never written about my family. Revelation! My language changed. Everything changed. Or, rather, the skills I had learned as a formalist poet became funneled into poetry of a quite different order, carrying the traditional along a path it never intended to travel. Or perhaps was meant to go? Actually, most of the great poets who work in open forms, from Whitman to Adrienne Rich, began as formalists.

But back to the question of models. At first my models were all men, then by the mid-1970s they were all women. Contemporary women at first, and then H.D. became for me what Blake had been, the great teacher.

CH: I'd like to ask you about that subject of teaching. It runs as a theme in your poetry from beginning to end. Take a poem like "The Class," for example, where you very specifically ruminate about the relationship a teacher develops with her students—the tragic leavened by the tragicomic [*reading*]:

We say things in this class. Like why it hurts.
[. . . . .]
The teacher hears tales from the combat zone
Where the children live, [. . .]
                         Like all draftees,
They have one job, survival,
And permit themselves some jokes.
Like my father hits the bottle . . .
And my mother.
[. . . . .]
The homosexual drummer tapping out
A knee tune, wagging his Groucho brows.
Hey, you ought to meet my mom real soon.
'Cause when I tell her, she's gonna die.
[. . . . .]
The teacher's job is to give them permission
To gather pain into language[.]

That's unusual counsel.

AO: In the early 1960s when I was writing my first poems about pregnancy and childbirth, I realized I was following Coleridge's advice to treat all life as raw material for art. That's what Whitman tells us also. So whatever is important in my life turns up in some form in the poetry. Since I've been teaching since the late Neolithic, teaching is an important recurrent theme, along with love and sex and family and politics and religion and art.

CH: You also seem yourself a consummate teacher. It's not just that you write about teaching and your students but that your poems have on some level a didactic element.

AO: Not preachy, I hope.

CH: No, I'm not saying that. In fact, I have called it a kind of ethics in your work.

AO: I loved your saying that. I think it's true. An embarrassing truth.

CH: Why is it embarrassing? Because the ethical is as contested and difficult an issue in poetry as the political? Should it be resisted as some poets argue the political should be resisted in poetry?

AO: What can it mean to be political but not ethical? The kind of politics I care about is totally continuous with ethics, which is continuous with compassion, which is continuous with passion. Going back to the panel this morning (On "The Lyric I"), you can't have passion if you don't have an "I" who is experiencing the passion. Without that, you can't have compassion, and without compassion your politics, including so-called progressive politics, is worthless.

CH: What I found in your work is the kind of ethics you describe in Allen Ginsberg, *chesed*, loving-kindness ["'Howl' Revisited," collected in *Dancing at the Devil's Party* (—ed.)].

I wanted to talk to you about that because you will say very directly in a poem like "Everywoman Her Own Theology," "Ethically, I am looking for / An absolute endorsement of loving-kindness."

AO: And to say that is embarrassing, so I follow it with a joke: "No loopholes except maybe mosquitoes."

CH: One of the ironies I've noticed in that wonderful poem in which you are so wittily caustic about poststructuralist theory and the subversion of the stable sub-

ject is that your pronouns are shifting, the "I" fracturing and morphing into
another throughout the poem [*reading*]:

—I Brood about Some Concepts, for Example

A concept like "I," which I am told by many
Intellectual experts has no

Signification outside of language.
I don't believe that, do you? Of course not.

If I kick myself, do I not
Hurt my foot, and if I fuck

A friend, or even if I masturbate,
Do I not come? Somebody does,

I think it's me, I like to call her "me,"
And I assume you like to call the one

Who comes (it is sweet, isn't it,
While birth and death are bitter, we figure,

But sexuality, in the middle there, is so
Sweet!) when you come, "me" and "I" also,

No harm in that, in fact considerable
Justice I feel, and don't you also feel?

Coito ergo
Sum, you remark. Good, so that settles it

With or without the words . . .

You're doing the very thing here that you are poking fun at.

AO: You can't poke proper fun at anything unless you have mastered it. What is the art of parody? If you want to parody Henry James, you must be able to write like Henry James.

CH: But the subject who speaks, "Ethically, I am looking for / An absolute endorsement of loving-kindness," and then shifts the tone in the next line, that subject is insistently present through your whole work (though destabilized by your irony). In your preface to *Dancing at the Devil's Party* you respond to Auden's claim that "poetry makes nothing happen" by claiming yourself, "Poetry can, as Rilke puts it, tell us that we must change our lives. From time to time, some of us believe, poetry changes the world. I am of this (perhaps dotty) persuasion." You are making fun of yourself even as you are writing of such ardent beliefs.

AO: As Martin Luther said, "Here I stand; I can do no other." Maybe it's a form of defensiveness: to laugh out of fear of being laughed at. A fear of being too earnest, too naked, too sentimental. On the other hand, laughter is a strategy. You don't want your readers to feel lectured at, so you need some levity. Levity sweetens any message you hope to transmit.

CH: Okay, so the levity and the lesson intertwine through your work.

AO: On the other hand, all the poets I love have an ironic edge. Irony isn't only a defense; it's a weapon.

CH: I notice you share that edge with Marianne Moore, who also has that ethical dimension to her work, and who has been criticized for the moralism in her later work, for not pulling back into the irony with which she leavened her earlier ethical strain.

AO: I do love the rapierlike wit of Moore's early work. Think of "To a Steam Roller" or the lines in "Critics and Connoisseurs," where she says,

> I have seen this swan and
> I have seen you; I have seen ambition without
> understanding in a variety of forms.

[Muriel] Rukeyser perhaps suffers from putting her ethics right out front, un-ironized. Another poet who comes under criticism is Denise Levertov, and not just for her political poetry, which was scorned by so many critics as mere propaganda. I think Levertov doesn't have the reputation she deserves because she writes pure lyric, in which ethics and aesthetics are always fused, and there doesn't seem to be an ironic bone in her body.

CH: When the context, the pressure of the historic moment falls away, all that passion, all that fervent emotion seems more exposed, and yet it doesn't happen in H.D.'s World War II poems. Those poems are high lyric but not ironic.

AO: Oh, I find plenty of irony in H.D.'s war poems. Last week teaching *Trilogy*, the poem in which H.D. came into her own as a great modernist poet standing shoulder to shoulder with Eliot, Pound, and Stevens, I was aware for the thousandth time how many factors converge to make a masterpiece and how irony is one of them. In "The Walls Do Not Fall," the irony takes the form of a struggle with self-doubt. In "Tribute to the Angels," she reads the biblical book of Revelation against itself, subverting its authoritarian voice; and after her dream of "the Lady," there's a deliciously ironic conversation with the interlocutor, who wants to explain her dream to her and whom she graciously dismisses. There's a sophisticated irony here that might embody a quarrel with the world or might embody an interior quarrel between two halves of her own mind, which Yeats said is what makes for true poetry. But whatever it is, it creates a levity that leavens the earnest liturgical dimension of the poem. And then when you get to "The Flowering of the Rod," you're actually in the midst of a comedy of manners. She's talking about redemption and salvation, she's redefining the entire meaning of spirituality, and she's doing it in the mode of comedy, using the figures of Mary Magdalene and the magus, Kasper.

By the way, there is an early letter from H.D. to Moore, in which she praises Moore as a swordswoman who cuts people's heads off so deftly that they don't even know they've been beheaded. Moore and H.D. both are radical enough to irritate some of their readers. They are both poets whose force is, in Moore's words in "The Steeple-Jack," "Disguised by what / might seem the opposite."

CH: Did you derive your method of intertwining impulses of lesson and levity—or maybe irony is a better word for that strategic move—from such influences, poets like H.D. and Blake?

AO: Blake especially, when I was starting out. Look at how "Songs of Innocence and of Experience" ironize each other, and the lightning irony in "The Marriage of Heaven and Hell." Or Donne, where the passion in his religious poetry is always intermixed with play.

CH: Another clear intersection of your critical and creative work is your study of Judaism, including *Feminist Revision and the Bible* and *The Nakedness of the Fathers: Biblical Visions and Revisions*. You have, for over a decade, been researching and writing about Judaism. This development in your work has made your poems more ambitious, expansive, it seems to me. How did you begin to use your poetry and prose to approach Judaism as a subject for your work?

AO: Judaism hit me in the mid-1980s the way women's poetry hit me in the mid-1970s. I fell off the cliff.

CH: In the same way? Differently? How did it inflect your poetry?

AO: Utterly unexpectedly, though in retrospect it seems inevitable. In 1985, I had just finished *Stealing the Language*, with its final chapter on what I call women's revisionist mythmaking. The book was in press, and I found myself one evening thinking, for no apparent reason, about the book of Job. I was musing about the way Judaism supports questioning and challenging authority, including the authority of God. When Job correctly, according to the story, accuses God of injustice, God ultimately does not punish but rewards him. This Jewish kind of wrestling intimacy between God and his creatures is unique, I was thinking, in world religions and cultures. But suddenly I remembered that when God gives Job back his health and his wealth, he also gives him ten new children to replace the ten he allowed Satan to kill off at the beginning of the story and the question surfaced: What would the wife of Job feel about that?

At this moment I felt something like a three-thousand-year-old scream rise in my throat and entered the only experience of automatic writing in my life. My pen flew across the page, but I was in some sort of trance. When I emerged, I saw that my pen had wondered what Mrs. Job would say to God when she gets the courage to talk back as her husband did. What my pen had written also fantasized about what Job's wife would accept as reparation, not only for her sufferings, but also for every injustice in history that God has apparently sponsored. I understood instantly that I was on one of those proverbial trains you can't get off and that for the foreseeable future I would be wrestling with the Bible and Judaism. My task was before me.

What I had not realized when writing about women's revisionist mythology was that, in looking at classical myth and fairy tale, I had omitted our living mythology, the stories of the Bible. What I thought was a conclusion was actually an introduction. Since then, I've done the two books you mentioned, and I'm working on a set of essays on what I call Biblical Countertexts. I've also written numerous poems brooding on various aspects of Judaism. I teach a course called

"The Bible and Feminist Imagination," my favorite course, and I teach midrash writing workshops.

CH: Explain midrash. I need a definition.

AO: Traditional midrash is originally an ancient rabbinic genre. You find it in Talmud and sermon literature. Midrash takes the compelling but compressed stories of the Bible and retells them, elaborating on them, filling in the gaps, making the stories spiritually and morally meaningful to the community in time present. Giving them a contemporary spin.

There is an explosion of midrashic writing today, in prose, poetry, and drama. Much of it is strongly feminist. The most popular example is Anita Diamant's *The Red Tent*, which retells the story of Dinah in Genesis. I personally think *The Red Tent* is kitschy, but who am I to argue with bestsellerdom? Among prose writers of midrash I would recommend Norma Rosen's *Biblical Women Unbound*, which is smart and savvy, and Jill Hammer's recent *Sisters at Sinai*, which is lyrical. In poetry I love Diana Hume George's *A Genesis* and Enid Dame's *Stone Shekhina*. Merle Feld has an extremely interesting and provocative play called "Crossing the Jordan," which intersplices episodes from Genesis with the intifada.

CH: Would you say there is a pedagogical and ethical element to midrash?

AO: Yes, always, both in the ancient world and now. For me there is also a theological dimension. We need to redefine God and our relationship to God. I try to do this both in *The Nakedness of the Fathers* and in my new book of poems, *The Volcano Sequence*. We know that the being we call God the Father swallowed God the Mother in prehistory. It's like the story of the wolf swallowing grandmother. Like the grandmother in the story, the Goddess doesn't die. She's just trapped in the belly of the beast. Part of my task is to help midwife that divine female who needs to be reborn into the world through our collective imagination. "The brain like a cervix," I call it in *Volcano*. So many writers are engaged in this task together; it alleviates the discouragement we all feel.

CH: In your recent work you increasingly confront the twentieth-century history of the Jewish people. Your wrenching poem about Shostakovich and also your personal poem, "The Book of Life," are both lyrical but also incorporate elements of collage: portions of Shostakovich's memoir, portions of the Bible, almost a newsreel account of the massacre of the Jews of Kiev. Can you say how you came to do this incredibly ambitious work? You built the foundation, but then it just seems to burst.

AO: Both "The Book of Life" and the Shostakovich poem, "The Eighth and Thirteenth," as well as the mastectomy poems in *The Crack in Everything*, were first drafted during a week I spent in retreat, six months after my surgery. We have a house in the Berkshires, up a dirt road, with no telephone, no electricity. I wrote there, accompanied only by books, a radio, wine. As for the bursting: you build up skills and strategies, then find new uses for them. Many poets I admire, for instance Adrienne Rich, work in collage form and in multiple genres. It is a way of including more of the raw material of life and also a way of incorporating silence into the poem. You leave gaps. You create spaces for the reader to jump into, which brings the reader into more of a transaction with the poem.

CH: Among the many things I find remarkable is your capacity to include shocking details in your poetry. Sometimes they are very personal, as when in the apparently autobiographical early poem "The Leaf Pile," a frustrated and tired young mother slaps her son hard:

I have shaken him, I have pried the sweet from his cheek
I have slapped his cheek like a woman slapping a carpet
with all my strength.[. . .]

You are saying things that are taboo. But in "The Eighth and Thirteenth," the description of Babi Yar also shocks the reader.

AO: Breaking taboos and crossing boundaries is a requirement of the art. You have to take a chance. Miles Davis says, "Don't be afraid of mistakes. There are no mistakes." Virginia Woolf somewhere says, "When you see a sign that says No Trespassing, trespass immediately." But political poetry must never be just about politics, so "The Eighth and Thirteenth" is also about music. Similarly, personal poetry must also be transpersonal and political, so "The Leaf Pile" is a poem about demystifying myths of maternity and about personal and historical memory. The poem should demonstrate how everything is connected to everything else, on this lovely planet we are so rapidly despoiling. I do hate the idiotic distinctions we make between poetry and politics, or between "us" and "them," or between mind and body.

CH: You write of bearing witness in your recent essay, "The Poetics of Postmodern Witness." Was the experience of writing *The Volcano Sequence* an act of bearing witness?

AO: In a sense. The poems were more or less channeled. They were very bleak when they began arriving, and I wanted to avoid censoring their bleakness. So I made a deal with the poems: If you agree to keep on arriving, I agree not to tell you what to say. The poems wrestle with the violence and pain of this world, through addressing a slippery "you" that is sometimes God, sometimes my mother, sometimes the Shekhina, who in Jewish mysticism is the feminine aspect of God. The tragedy is that they are divided.

CH: In that same essay ["The Poetics of Postmodern Witness"], in response to Adorno's well-known despair, you reject despair and choose joy. In fact, the notion of "joy" seems to run like a golden thread through your oeuvre. In the early prose poem "Cambodia," you write, "Our bodies and our minds shoot into joy as trees into leaves." Much later, the first poem in *The Crack in Everything*, "The Dogs at Live Oak Beach, Santa Cruz," ends with the image of the dogs leaping into the surf, "For absolutely nothing but joy." And yet you acknowledge that this is a "wounded / World that we cannot heal"; "that in this century / to survive is to be ashamed." Why insist on joy? Why persist in that constant struggle?

AO: As a drowning person struggles to get to the surface, to breathe.

—The Eighth and Thirteenth

The Eighth of Shostakovich,
Music about the worst
Horror history offers,
They played on public radio
Again last night. In solitude
I sipped my wine, I drank
That somber symphony
To the vile lees. The composer
Draws out the minor thirds, the brass
Tumbles overhead like virgin logs
Felled from their forest, washing downriver,
And the rivermen at song. Like ravens
Who know when meat is in the offing,
Oboes form a ring. An avalanche
Of iron violins. At Leningrad
During the years of siege
Between bombardment, hunger,
And three subfreezing winters,
Three million dead were born
Out of Christ's bloody side. Like icy
Fetuses. For months
One could not bury them, the earth
And they alike were adamant.
You stacked the dead like sticks until May's mud,
When, of course, there was pestilence.
But the music continues. It has no other choice.
Stalin hated the music and forbade it.
Not patriotic, not Russian, not Soviet.
But the music continues. It has no other choice.
Peer in as far as you like, it stays
Exactly as bleak as now. The composer

Opens his notebook. *Tyrants like to present themselves as*
patrons of the arts. That's a well known fact. But tyrants
understand nothing about art. Why? Because tyranny is a
perversion and a tyrant is a pervert. He is attracted by the
chance to crush people, to mock them, stepping over
corpses. . . . And so, having satisfied his perverted desires,
the man becomes a leader, and now the perversions continue
because power has to be defended against madmen like
yourself. For even if there are no such enemies, you have
to invent them, because otherwise you can't flex your
muscles completely, you can't oppress the people completely,
making the blood spurt. And without that, what pleasure is
there in power? Very little. The composer
Looks out the door of his dacha, it's April,
He watches farm children at play,
He forgets nothing. For the thirteenth—
I slip its cassette into my car
Radio—they made Kiev's Jews undress
After a march to the suburb,
Shot the hesitant quickly,
Battered some of the lame,
And screamed at everyone.
Valises were taken, would
Not be needed, packed
So abruptly, tied with such
Frayed rope. Soldiers next
Killed a few more. The living ones,
Penises of the men like string,
Breasts of the women bobbling
As at athletics, were told to run
Through a copse, to where
Wet with saliva
The ravine opened her mouth.
Marksmen shot the remainder
Then, there, by the tens of thousands,

Cleverly, so that bodies toppled
In without lugging. An officer
Strode upon the dead,
Shot what stirred.
How it would feel, such uneasy
Footing, even wearing boots
That caressed one's calves, leather
and lambswool, the soles thick rubber,
Such the music's patient inquiry.
What then is the essence of reality?
Of the good? The mind's fuse sputters,
The heart aborts, it smells like wet ashes,
The hands lift to cover their eyes,
Only the music continues. We'll try
For the first movement,
A full chorus.
The immediate reverse of Beethoven.
An axe between the shoulder blades
Of Herr Wagner. *People knew about Babi Yar*
before Yevtushenko's poem, but they were silent. And when
they read the poem, the silence was broken. Art destroys
silence. I know that many will not agree with me and will
point out other, more noble aims of art. They'll talk about beauty,
grace, and other high qualities. But you won't catch
me with that bait. I'm like Sobakevich in Dead Souls: *you can*
sugarcoat a toad, and I still won't put it in my mouth.

Most of my symphonies are tombstones, said Shostakovich.

All my poets are Jews, said Tsvetaeva.

The words *never again*
Clashing against the words
Again and again
—That music.

—About Time

Rather they are joy, against nothingness joy.

—LOUIS ZUKOVSKY

What we have been doing
The idea was—
The work of science. Of art.
The philosophical heart
Hardened. Timeless. If you strike it, it clangs. It
Beats time.

~

What you can't kill: the mud
And what is inside the mud
A spirit panting
Ma non troppo

~

The body's loop from clay to clay
Interrupted. Wrestled, made to gleam.

~

Under the garden
The world spirit panting
Slick, sour
Along with its worms
Each an individual
Produces a tunnel
Of air and crumbs

Humbly
       O artist
Humbly! awaiting their hour.

    ∼

Until then
Already
Not yet
Soon.

—*from* The Volcano and the Covenant

I am molten matter returned from the core of
the earth to tell you interior things—
—ANNE CARSON

1. the volcano breathes

coughs   coughs up

    ∼

if the subconscious is a *geniza*   like Cairo synagogue   piled attic
      twelve jars a shepherd finds in a cave   papyrus crumbs

repository [place of repose   in which to put/push/press/repress
          pinched   her moist red   disturbed
          rose there   her terebinth   grove misremembered but]

can't throw anything away
holy holy holy
holy god holy name holy demon same

the mind can't
throw anything holy away
let it stay let it be she   let it wait

~

oh god
yours and ours
it hurts

pain is the pressure of what attempts to be expressed and cannot be, oh shit, oh baby

            anguished impression is pressure to

she told them at the lecture the naked [failures] fathers
        what do you guess your pain and suffering mean
[she looked from the podium] looked round the room seated they were pretending
            no no pain no suffering

            not me insisted their eyebrows not my face I am
                a commercial for normal/eyes away
                    only   a few lashes flickered

~

dry crust in quiet   flame ready now
        your labor pains persist indefinite exacerbate until
oh dear god, maybe never [fear is your driver/your doctor]

            oh god, yours and ours, how they hurt so
                bring forth your uterine self? by yourself? is it time's nick? [time present]
            she so buried so erased so unlawful so forgot so swallowed

like wolf swallowing grandmother [the being
      called] god the father swallowed god the mother,
        the process required millennia
        you swallowed her down the hatch

    meanwhile in the text she kicks watch that

        to "raise the sparks" is metaphor is   imagination is!
        to speak the unspoken unspeakable   stems pierce asphalt
    lava through split stone, heaving water dividing
      razon, oh desire of god, your desire be done
let the waters break from the waters   fireflow rise

want to be a midwife to
   pull it out to dream

words of the mouth meditations of the heart
from the source the desire
is to flow without cease

I do have a heavy burden
and cannot wait to put it down

∼

to put it down is forbidden

2. psalm 37: the meek shall inherit the earth

try not to be angry
at the meanness of men, they fade like grass
in october, nothing of them remains

trust me to give you what you need
leave it to me, I will vindicate you
and give you whatever you want

the mean men will shoot themselves in the foot
all by themselves and even their children
will fail to thrive

the meek believed these promises
these deep whiffs of opium
once upon a time

while the arrogant went about their business
the words continued to be contrafactual
and very beautiful

they shall not hurt nor destroy
nation shall not lift up sword

3. I decide to call you   Being

a word with two contradictory
meanings   someone to wipe the blood
and dirty tears away through boundless love

someone able to punish listen wrestle
like a person but
larger

and *ein sof*   boundless
being   in the sense of pure existence   remote
abstraction more impersonal than zero

you exquisite
joke   you paradigm paradox
you absent presence   you good evil   shredding the eye

so that it can become a door
you are inexplicable   like a *koan*
running uphill barefoot
blowing   the door down

        you complete nothing

        you perfect nothing

～

everyone asks   are you the father or the king
or the mother or the snake   but to me
listen you are the hope of my heart
you are the quarrel in my art

you are the tangled quarrel in my art
like a married pair who will go to their graves
carrying resentments like suitcases of foreign coins

you are the sex in my art
whatever wants to faint under long kisses, whatever grapples
flesh to flesh, the nipple that reaches, the tongue that spills

4. interlude: the avenue of the americas

Above the tongues of taxicabs, the horns and buyers
the teeth of buildings grin at each other, the institutions
of media medicine publishing fashion

know how to
bite through human flesh
like hinged aluminum traps chopping the necks

of beavers, or like logging rigs, those saws
that go through a hundred-year-old
redwood in about three minutes

take out a thousand acres
of virgin oregon forest
annually because loggers need jobs

intellectuals need the special sections
of the New York Times stacked
on driveways

each rosy dawn, the Japanese need
the splinters these pines and spruces
finally get turned into

everybody needs what they can get
and more. Yesterday walking
between fifty-third and fifty-second

on the avenue of the americas at twilight on my way
to a good restaurant with good friends I passed
three beggars wrapped in plastic. Why not say

beggars?
Why invent novelty phrases like "the homeless"
as if our situation were modern and special

instead of ancient and normal,
the problem of greed and selfishness?
The beggars turned toward me

I put money in the woman's cup
though I didn't like her facial sores
her drowned eyes bobbed to the surface

as if they believed for a second
something new was about to happen
but nothing was

so the eyes sank rapidly back
like crabs into sand, and sorrow
pressed into me like a hot iron

after which I hurried through the hurrying crowd
sky overhead primrose and lilac, skyscrapers
uncanny mirrors filled with cloud bouquets

to overtake my friends who had strolled ahead
chatting so as not to be embarrassed
by the sight of charity

the rotting odor of need

~

[. . .]
the volcano and the covenant

as if one could cut a covenant
with a roaring volcano

imagine our souls
being birthed and destroyed

the way a flame
uncurls in one instant

and when the next passes, it is no more
yet is like a scorching white word

in the red ongoing song
then gray ash that crumbles

softly to nothing, oh to
burn like that

[. . .]

6. predawn

ruach, ruach, the language to say it
ruach, ruach, wind, spirit, breath
spirit of god on the deep's face
spirit of god moved on the face
of the deep, spirit
moved

spirit was moving, spirit was moving
ruach elohim
the face of the deep waters moved
first it was dark darkness was on it
the face of the deep darkness was upon it
then the spirit came the wind came
the breath came and it moved

it moved, the breath came
and it moved
ruach it
moved

~

what did the stars do
the stars sang for joy
what did the hills do
they leaped like young rams

what does the day do
it tells the next day
what does the night do
whisper to the next night

what shall I do

sonia sanchez

INTRODUCTION

A pioneer of the Black Arts movement of the 1960s, Sonia Sanchez has been writing, publishing, and protesting since before her first book, *Home Coming* (1969), announced the arrival of a politically potent new voice. Her earliest books were particularly important for being among the very first in the U.S. to explore and embody a black feminist consciousness. In the 1960s and 1970s, Sanchez skillfully and daringly negotiated the opposing terrains of militant black liberation, middle-class/white feminism, and the poetry establishment. She has also gone on to write movingly about other social issues in recent years, including the AIDS crisis. From the very beginning of her political and poetic career, Sanchez charted new directions: those of a formally innovative, passionately engaged, radical black poetry.

Indeed, Sanchez's social activism has always been inextricable from her poetry, not just in her chosen subjects but in the poetry's very form. Hers is a poetics devoted to truths passionately spoken, whether in the traditions of the strict forms of the page (haiku, rhyme royal, and sonnets) or in the aural traditions of jazz improvisation and what is now called "performance poetry"—a category that she in fact pioneered. As she notes in the following discussion, she eventually came to consider "the poem and the music as one." Yet she has always been attuned as well to the ties between the political and the personal, the individual and the communal, art and activism. Sanchez's artistic innovations—her aural and visual rule breaking and border crossing—are intricately tied to her dedication to changing both social and educational institutions and the individual consciousness of her reader/listener.

Born in 1934 in Birmingham, Alabama, Sanchez lived with various relatives following her mother's death when Sanchez was only one. She moved, at age nine, with her father to Harlem, and she went on to live in New York City for many years, receiving a B.A. in political science from Hunter College in 1955 and studying writing at New York University with the poet Louise Bogan. A strong female voice in the largely male-dominated Black Arts movement in New York in the late 1960s, Sanchez was strongly influenced by the revolutionary politics and writings of Malcolm X, about whom she wrote a number of poems; but she also spoke out fearlessly about sexism in the movement, as well as in American culture more broadly. As she mentions in this interview, Sanchez was also extremely active as a pioneer in the Black Studies movement, which reconceptualized university curricula with the creation of interdisciplinary Black Studies programs on college campuses across the country. Over the past three decades, she has taught at many institutions, including San Francisco State University, Amherst College, Rutgers University, the University of Pennsylvania, and Temple University, where she held the Laura Carnell Chair in English until her retirement in 1999.

Sanchez's numerous poetry collections include *Shake Loose My Skin: New and Selected Poems* (2000), *Like the Singing Coming Off the Drums* (1999), *Does Your House Have Lions?* (1997), *Wounded in the House of a Friend* (1995), and *Homegirls & Handgrenades* (1984), which won the American Book Award. She has also published books of criticism and children's literature, and her plays have been widely produced and published; her best known, *Sister Son/ji*, was first mounted in 1972. Among other extensive honors and awards, she has been named a Ford Freedom Scholar and a Frost Medalist.

The following interview focuses in part on music in relation to Sanchez's work and life. The interview was conducted by the poet Sascha Feinstein, who edits the journal *Brilliant Corners*, devoted to contemporary music and poetry. The interview took place in Feinstein's home in Williamsport, Pennsylvania, on November 18, 2002, while Sanchez was poet in residence at Bucknell University.

AN INTERVIEW WITH SONIA SANCHEZ
by Sascha Feinstein

SASCHA FEINSTEIN: When did the crossovers between music and literature fully form in your life?

SONIA SANCHEZ: I grew up with music. My father was a drummer and a school teacher in Birmingham, Alabama. He was inducted into the Black Music Hall of Fame. And he taught [the legendary drummer] "Papa" Jo Jones how to play the drums. So I grew up in a house of music. I'd walk into people's homes, they'd have Art Tatum on, and I'd say very casually, "Oh, I love Art Tatum." And they'd say, "What do you know about Art Tatum?" They didn't expect children to *know*. But I grew up on musicians. My father gave up music when he came to New York City because musicians had to travel, and he had a new wife, and she was saying, "If you go overseas, that's it." But he still would do gigs in the Village—for years, until he got too old—and he gave lessons. He gave one of his drums—one of the old-fashioned drums with the pedal—to Max Roach, and I still have his other drums at home. Music has been a part of my life for a very long time, and I think music has helped me to survive for a very long time, too.

I learned about black literature from Miss Hutson—Jean Hutson—at the Schomburg [Library, now the Schomburg Center for Research in Black Culture]. After I got out of Hunter [College in 1955], I needed to get a job, so I answered an ad in the *New York Times*. The ad said the company needed a writer: "Would you please send a sample of your writing and your CV." I did. And I got a *telegram*: "Report to work on Monday at nine A.M." I knocked on my father's bedroom door, showed him the telegram, and said, "See? I *can* get a job as a writer." My father—I will never forget—gave this droll answer: "Well, go try it, but if I were you, I would really prepare to be a teacher." I had *not* prepared to be a teacher at Hunter. I had prepared to go to Law School with no money. (They weren't giving out money at that time.) But being a liberal arts grad, you could always get a job teaching.

Anyway, I go downtown that Monday. I have a blue suit on. Blue shoes on. Blue hat on. Blue purse and white gloves—I *know* I look good. I was there at *eight thirty*. Nobody was there, so I'm standing outside. Then in comes the secretary/ receptionist, and I showed her this [telegram], and she opened the door. I sat down, and I'm thinking, "I can make all this money before I go back to school. I have a chance to really write—they like my writing," because I was a closet writer. About ten minutes to nine, this guy walks up and says, "I'm so sorry, but the job is taken." I looked at my watch and said, "But I wasn't due to report until nine o'clock. How can I not have a job at ten to nine when I wasn't due here until nine o'clock?" He said, "The job is taken." I said, "But I have the telegram." He looked at it, and he looked at me, and his eyes said, "Whoa, did I make a mistake." He raised his voice—"I *said*, the job is taken"—and he walked away. I turned to the secretary, and she looked down; she never looked up. I could see the offices back there, and I said, "You're discriminating against me! I'm going to call the Urban League." The guy turned around to me, like, "The Urban League? So what? What are they going to do?"

I go out, take off my hat, and I get on the train. But I was so angry that I didn't get off at Ninety-sixth, and it went all the way to the East Side. I had to get to the West Side, so I said, "Okay, I'll walk across. I won't pay any more money to go back downtown." I get off at 135th Street and start crossing the street. I look up. I'm hot, I'm sweaty now, and I'm angry. And there's this guy standing out on the steps. I said, "*Schomburg*? What is the Schomburg?" He said, "It's a library. Go and ask the lady inside." So I walked in and saw that long, long table with all of these men— black, white scholars—sitting down like this [*Sanchez bows her head*], working at this long table that took up this whole room.

Miss Hutson was enclosed in a glass office where she could look out. She had her back to me, and I knocked. (She used to tell this story to all my students, and I would be so embarrassed. She used to tell it with this very subtle, sly smile.) She said, "Yes? I'm Miss Jean Hutson." I said, "What kind of library is this? I just got out of Hunter College. I've never heard of the Schomburg." "Oh, dear," she said. "This library *only* has books by and about black folk." And I said, at age nineteen and a half: "There must not be many books in here."

SF: Wow . . .

ss: She sat me down, my brother, and she said, "I'm going to bring you some books." And she brought three books: [Du Bois's] *Souls of Black Folk*, [Booker T. Washington's] *Up from Slavery*, and the top one was [Zora Neale Hurston's] *Their Eyes Were Watching God*. She said [*Sanchez taps the table*], "Okay. For you, dear." I looked around. These men have not looked up yet. Didn't matter who was sitting where. They were working with all these books spread out. I had this little tiny space. I started reading, and then I got into the black English part, and I was thrown for one minute, but I kept reading. And then, I started to cry.

I inched out, knocked on her door, and said, "How can I be an educated woman and not have read these books?" and she said [*Sanchez grins widely*], "Yes, dear. Now go back and read." I inched back in and read some more and came back out again. I mean, I was *stricken* by this, my brother. Then I sat back down, and one of the scholars said [*Sanchez speaks in a gruff voice*], "Miss Hutson! Will you please tell this young woman either she sits still or she has to go!" [*Feinstein laughs.*] And I sat still, and I read those books. I came back every day. I would tell my father, "I'm going to look for a job," but I came to the Schomburg.

I had heard the music of poetry in the black schools of the South—because someone always recited Langston Hughes, Countee Cullen, or Paul Laurence Dunbar. So I knew that existed; I could hear the rhythm. Someone would do Dunbar's [poem, "A Negro Love Song"] "Jump back, honey, jump back." We had heard that. We had heard the music; this poetry had been planted in our subconscious already and in a sense was ready to come out.

I always heard music as I wrote. I ignored it for a long time, or I would write, "To be sung," on the side. Or, "Clap your hands." I would give all kinds of directions. I heard the music at the base of my skull, but I never, *ever* read any of my poems with music until I was making a trek from New York to Brown University, and we got caught in a snow storm and the plane was delayed. (This would have been in the early seventies—I had two books out, *Home Coming* and *We a BaddDDD People* [1970].) I was due to read at eight. The students were told what had happened; they had gone out, eaten, and come back. It is now about ten thirty, and they're ushering me into this packed auditorium. With introductions and all that, I'm reading at eleven o'clock at night. So I said, "I'll give you a good reading."

I did about an hour and a half—from eleven to twelve thirty—because they had waited, and they were so appreciative. And then someone said, "Would you entertain a couple of questions, Professor Sanchez?" I'm thinking, *I'm whipped, and*

I've got to teach a class tomorrow, but I said, "Yes. A couple." And this young African American man said, "Would you read your Coltrane poem?" I said, "I've never read that poem out loud. I've read it silently, but I've never read it out loud." He said, "Yeah, I know—but we waited for you for two and a half hours," and I thought, *Whoa! Okay,* and said, "Give me a minute to look it over."

I had always stretched words out, but that's as far as I would go with the music. I would go, "Ahhhhhhhhh"—merely stretching out the words, in spite of the music that I was hearing, because I didn't trust myself. "I'm not a singer. How can I do this?" In New York, we sometimes would read with musicians and drummers, so my voice was always there, but I had never done a piece like that by myself and made my voice assume all of the instruments, all of the sounds, all of the screams that the [Coltrane] poem encompasses. And when I would read with musicians, I would always be aware that *this* was the poem and *that* was the music.

Well, thank goodness for the Ancestors. And thank goodness for an appreciative audience. When I got to it, I *did* the music. I did Coltrane. The voice did everything. [*Sings a brief, rising tone.*] It just came to me. And from that point on, I was literally released to do whatever I wanted to do with a poem, with music, with sound. I began to investigate different languages as a consequence. I began to notate more—what should be done, what should not be done. I began the whole process of [thinking about] the poem and the music as one.

SF: You've performed with [tenor saxophonist] Archie Shepp. What was that like?

SS: I started teaching at Amherst in 1973, and Max Roach and Archie Shepp were there, as well as the brother who teaches music—Horace Boyer—and I began to do things with them. We did a gig at Boston University [in 1974] that's on the Black Box series. (Someone recorded it and, afterwards, sold it without our permission.) Anyway, Max said, "Why don't we do something together, Sonia?" I said, "Yeah. You want to rehearse?" (I'll never forget that.) And he said, "Oh, no! Just read a little poem. Something short." I thought, "Oh my God . . ." Not that I hadn't done anything with musicians, but we're talking a huge audience: one thousand people! They said, "You go on stage and start reading. We'll come and join you."

Well, I go out there, and, man, all of a sudden, Archie comes out and starts blowing: *Wooooooooooo! Do do do-do do!* And you cannot continue to read as you were before. I had to stop, because the audience clapped, and then I had to fit my voice and these lines over that music so they complemented each other. I truly appreciated jazz singers then. You go to a jazz place and listen, and you think, "Okay. She's singing. She stops. He comes in. Simple." But they made me become a jazz singer on that stage—with poetry—and they also made me direct: "Now I'm gonna do it again as he plays"—whatever. I found myself repeating lines, in the same fashion that I remembered the jazz singers did. Then I'd let him play. Then I'd dip right back in. Then all of a sudden, the pianist came in. Archie changed up with him, and I *couldn't* be left out, so I had to change up with the two of them. Then Max came out and started beating. It was amazing. When I finished, I left and let them play, and when they finished, Max said, "See? I told you it would work," and he threw me up in the air. And you know what it reminded me of? "Papa" Jo Jones. He would come to our house in Alabama for Sunday dinner— he'd come in chewing gum, with that kind of rhythm that he had—and he'd come for us; my sister and I would try to run away. But he'd grab me while talking to my father, throw me in the air, and, at the last minute, he caught me. I just knew he would not catch me, 'cause he was not looking at me. He'd say, "Okay, Sonia! And you know what I think—" and then he caught me. Your heart would be on the floor someplace, and your stomach. . . . [*Feinstein laughs.*] And all the time he was talking, he had his foot moving. It's only been in the last two years that I've stopped doing that, too—tapping my foot. My foot was always moving with a fast beat. When I'd walk with my children outside, I used to walk like my father and "Papa" Jo—*fast*. My children would say, "Ma! Why don't you slow down?" I would say, "Well, keep up!" [*Chuckles.*] It was always some kind of rhythm that was going on, some kind of beat that I kept with me.

Now I find myself always, always, always—in each poem—making the music happen. But then I sometimes had a run-in with the music: I would want to be lyrical as opposed to musical. There was a battle that went on. Sometimes the lyrical would take hold. The music came out, however, when I spoke/wrote in Wolof. My brother, as he moved toward death, began to speak Wolof because the Ancestors spoke Wolof to him. So I would write "to be sung." I allowed the music to come out in that kind of history, as opposed to interfering with the lyricism of the poem. Because the poem took rhyme royal form, the lines that I had that were infused with music weren't working as well. I had to come in and cut the music from them.

I usually do two books at one time because when one's working, the other one's not working. I was doing *Wounded in the House of a Friend* and *Does Your House Have Lions?* I had started *Does Your House* first, but in the middle of this book, there were voices that I heard which were similar to the music. When I say "music"—I would hear music in a different language, and I would call my friends who are African and say, "What is this?" and they would say, "Oh—that's Wolof." I said, "I must have heard someone singing it someplace and picked it up. Tell me how to say this properly. Does this mean what I think it means?" It was a real joy.

When I did a piece for Gerald Penny—one of the young students who drowned at Amherst—I relied a lot on the music. That piece not only had African qualities but Native American qualities as well. I said to someone as I was doing this piece, "In this place it's like *massacres* have been here, so the sounds that I hear I know cannot be African—I know they're Native American," and someone told me about that whole area: "There was a massacre on this spot," and I said, "I know." I mean, I didn't *know*, but I could feel it, feel the chanting.

I believe all of our chants or chanting are the same, anyway. You cannot have people invade—the way the Moors did, get into France, and Italy, and as far away as Ireland—without leaving something behind (part of a language and music, too). The *cante jondo*—the deep song—is in each one of our cultures. One of the *cante jondo* is the blues. The *cante jondo* that became urban—more modern—is jazz, in my head. At some point, when you hear that wail, that song, that fusion, that movement off the ground into the sky—then you know this is ancient and modern at the same time. That's what I try to capture when I chant: a combination of what is ancient and what is modern. Sometimes I do the ancient part by incorporating the African language into it and then the sound. I've done "Middle Passage" [published in *Wounded* as "Improvisation"] in the Midwest, my brother, and I have broken down because I have heard the Native American voices. And I've had Native Americans come up to me and give me something, like a piece of jewelry. They'll say, "I heard our voice in there," and I say, "Yes, because it's the same voice." When you travel and you hear the different cultures, then you know this is indeed the same voice. People have just separated our voices and said, "This one belongs over here—in Ireland. This one belongs in Scotland. This one is only a Middle Eastern sound"—and you know that's not true. These people have moved back and forth and have left their chants, their smells, their sounds, and new people have been born and picked up those old sounds and said, "Oh, look—a new sound." But we know it's the same *old* sound. That's why I'm so amazed when I hear Flamenco. I stop—because it's an old sound, but a new sound. It's in the mountains, but it's also in a bare, urban apartment in Harlem.

That's what I try to do when I use music: I try to make people hear that which they ignore. I try to make people hear that which they would rather not sing. They'd rather *say* it and get it over with, and I'll say, "No—this is a poem that is to be sung. It is to be hummed. It is to be turned over on its side so you can see the juices inside. Sometimes I dry it off and then give it back to you in a dry fashion, but it is still the song and the poem—at the same time."

SF: Etheridge Knight and I were friends, and whenever we were on panels discussing jazz-related literature, Etheridge always mentioned your writing: "Sonia's work *drips* with jazz." How do you think jazz influenced his work?

SS: I think the jazz poems Etheridge did were always in *homage* to someone. He made the line become jazz, but I would never say that Etheridge was a Jazz Poet the way that some of us are. There is so much pain in Etheridge's work that his poems are always infused with the blues life, the blues way of looking at the world. If you do jazz, my brother, you see a win. That's why I love jazz. Jazz musicians, when they play, are saying, "I got it. I see a win."

When I do a blues, and I try to make it "smart" sometimes, I try to infuse an urban style blues, because Bessie [Smith], when she was talking about the rich man in her blues, there was a win there, there was a tartness there, there was a smartness there. And, as much as I loved Etheridge, I think he didn't see a win. There were times when he wrote lines and you wanted to say, "Whip it. Twist it, turn it. Send it up, and then send it back down." But he couldn't do it that way. He did write about jazz—he wrote some exquisite poems with the aroma of jazz—but when you opened it up, it wasn't jazz; it was blues.

SF: Who then—for you—would be among the true jazz poets?

SS: I don't want to say that you have to be in an urban setting to do jazz. That's not necessarily true. But I do think that the people who really *touch* on a jazz motif not only make poems about jazz but create jazz riffs. In other words, the composition of the poem is jazz, the delivery of the poem is jazz, and the juice, infusing it, is jazz. Amiri Baraka does it well. Quincy Troupe does it well. Jayne Cortez does it well. A lot of the younger poets do it well.

There were a lot of jazz poets in *Black Fire* [*An Anthology of Afro-American Writing*, 1968]. You don't see a lot of them now. . . . That was an amazing collection:

---

you saw what they were doing, how they were moving. And that anthology that you did [with Yusef Komunyakaa, *The Jazz Poetry Anthology*, 1991]: you can see that some of the poets in there are really jazz poets, because they not only have the composition of it but I've heard them deliver it, and they're *into* what a jazz poem is all about—from the riff on down to what I call the silences between the lines. That's what I try to do (though I'm not sure if it always works). When you're silent, you let the music resonate from your voice so people hear it, and then you come back in on it. When I stop, I'm saying to an audience, "Come on. Hear it. Come back into it."

I don't always know how one does it, but at some point, once you hear that music, then it's all possible. But you have to hear that music back here, in the base of the skull. I used to ignore it because initially I kept saying, "I can't sing." But it doesn't have to do with singing. So, when I said to that young man at Brown, "But, I've never read that. I don't sing" (and I had *written* "to be sung"), I was limiting myself. I had to leave that arena of limiting myself to being a jazz singer. As a poet performing with musicians, you sometimes have to go back to that arena because you have to do some of the things that a jazz singer would do. But when you're performing by yourself, you don't have to. You accomplish everything. You pull the horn with you. You pull the drums with you.

SF: What would you consider to be some of your representative jazz poems?

SS: Well, obviously, the Coltrane poem. Another jazz piece would be—and no one understands this, but I can hear Coltrane playing behind "I have walked a long time / longer than death." The poem for Ella. The poem "Sequences" is a jazz poem; it's a jazz poem with, like, Rahsaan Roland Kirk playing. It's a jazz suite, something like what Langston [Hughes] did in *Ask Your Mama*. At the core of that is the blues motif, but the execution is jazz.

SF: You got your book title *Does Your House Have Lions?* from Kirk's CD set [*Rahsaan Roland Kirk Anthology*], right?

SS: Yes. I was so stricken by the Kirk anthology. I thought that was an amazing question—"Does your house have lions?"—in many contexts. And so typical of Rahsaan to pose that question that has so many ramifications. ("You're building a house? Does your house have lions?" "What do you mean?" "You know—*lions.*") All the important buildings—libraries, banks—always used to have lions so you knew you were entering a place that was mighty, that was fortified. But if you go back to the continent of Africa and you talk about lions, you're talking about something else, too—the lion as Juba—so that the lion goes back beyond what we see here in the States. And that's why I thought, "What a title!" and I put it in my journal.

As I was writing this book, which is about my brother [dying of AIDS], I didn't have a title. All of a sudden, it hit me: this is what I've been talking about—the idea of a family having lions, the kind of protection that they should have at some particular point. About a country, too, having that kind of protection. So I knew that was the title.

We did this piece [*Sanchez taps the cover of* Does Your House Have Lions?] with music, did you know that? [Tenor saxophonist] Odean Pope, a percussionist, Khan Jamal, and a dancer, Rennie Harris, who danced the part of my brother. I read. We came on stage all dressed in white. It began with the sister's voice, with the brother at seventeen (the dancer) coming out in a green suit. By the time he was getting ready to die, of course, he'd pulled off his layered clothes and was all in white, also. In many societies, of course, people wear white when people die or in celebration of life. Odean did all the music.

sF: What was it like to be one of the relatively few female voices to represent the Black Arts movement of the late 1960s?

ss: [*Laughs.*] It was amazing. People complain and say that Black Arts was sexist. I say to people, "*America* was sexist." All the political organizations were sexist, so that was not just part of Black Arts. But—they weren't sexist on stage. Baraka, Ed Bullins, Marvin X, Larry Neal—I was the only woman on stage with them, and they did not treat me differently. They didn't make me go first, for example, which would have been the completely sexist thing to do.

I always tell this story about Baraka and myself: when we went out to California [in 1965], we thought we were some *baaad* people, know what I mean? And we did our first reading at San Francisco State—just the two of us. We did this reading where he read something and I read something—we did like a jazz thing. He did something, and I answered him with a poem. He said, "Ta doo da doo doo," and I was, "Ta doo da dee dee," and he said, "Ra tuh ta ta," and I was "Dada tatata"—I mean, you loved what you were doing on stage and you understood what the stage was about. And then someone raised a hand and said, "Could you do that again?"—I remember being so taken aback—"You did it so fast. We didn't understand it." Whoa! (I think about the rappers today—talk about *fast* fast.) And we went, "Okay." And so he read, and then I read, but we were self-conscious. That was the first time I understood the difference between the East Coast and the West

Coast, the first time I understood that when you're in different places you have to read things in a different fashion. And it got to be tricky, sometimes, because you always hear the rhythm. You know how you're going to read something, and all of a sudden I heard myself slowing it down 'cause I looked at the audience. "Where are you? Where are you off to?" You had to slow down the beat, just a little bit.

I remember a concert called ToBu—Towards a Black University—down at Howard University, where we honored Sterling Brown in a big gym. I'm trying to remember if there was another woman poet on that program; I don't think so. It was Baraka, Haki [Madhubuti], Larry [Neal], some other poets, and then Sterling at the end. I read right before Baraka—[*Sanchez chuckles*] I *always* read right before Baraka—and then Sterling came on, and the place exploded. And Sterling said [*Sanchez deepens her voice to sound more formal*], "These young poets right here used to scare me."

He was like Dr. Arthur P. Davis—remember that seminal essay where he called us "The Poets of Hate"? (This is an aside but I think it's important because I think that people can change.) I had gone to Howard to do a reading, years later, and there, with his hand up, is Dr. Davis. And I said, "Oops . . ." [*Laughs.*] "How you doing, sir?" He said [*Sanchez imitates an exceedingly self-conscious tone*], "My name is Arthur P. Davis. I was here at Howard for forty-odd years, and I wrote an essay called 'The Poets of Hate.'" Then he said, "I was wrong." It was an amazing moment. We became very dear friends. During the time when he was ill, I used to take the train and read to him once a week. In fact, I started *Does Your House Have Lions?* during the time when he was ill, and I would read to him, and he said to me, "That is a great book." He said, "The thing that I realize is that you have exemplified people starting at one point and continuing to evolve and grow. What I said about all those poets . . . what they were saying, they *had* to say in that way."

No one would have heard us if we had said, "I am a poet. I am here to read you a poem." You had to come out and go, "*Ahhh ah ah!*" because *then* everyone looked up. There was no ready-made audience for poetry. Young people think, "Oh, I wish I had been back there with you." We had to *make* the audience. And you make an audience by learning how to walk a stage: if I came out and stayed right in the middle of the stage, people would look and then look away, but if I came out and moved on that stage, they followed you. People would wonder, "What is she doing?" And if you used a curse word, people would go, "*Oh . . .*" [*Feinstein laughs*].

But you'd never use another curse word, because you'd grabbed them, you'd brought them in. You needed all sorts of techniques to bring people into that arena because people were not interested in poetry.

Baraka probably won't tell this story, but Ed Bullins organized a program for us and there were, at most, twenty people there. We got on stage and started to read, and someone leaned over and said, "What they doing?" Some guy says, "They reading poetry." "I thought they were gonna sing—let's go!" [*Sanchez laughs.*] The whole first row got up and left. But all they did was make us hone our skills, more and more. Hone the music. And it also made us, initially, change to make it slower and then speed it up again. We brought them back with us. We said, "Okay. I gave you a chance to hear it, now come on—ride this way." And then, it made them do what we did: they came at it at another level, at our level. It was an infusion of the East Coast on the West Coast. We were privileged to be a part of the Black Arts on the East Coast and then the Black Arts West in San Francisco. We were there with the Black House when Eldridge Cleaver came out of jail—but I *never, ever* liked that man. I went on record from the very beginning. I mean, the Panthers came to talk to me because I said, "He's not a revolutionary." *That's* when a lot of the sexism came out. A lot of people said, "Well, you know, Sonia, you don't understand. You just a woman," and I said, "No. No no. I might be just a woman, but he is no revolutionary." Haki [Madhubuti] brought me *Soul on Ice* [to review for *Negro Digest*], and—I'll never forget—I stayed up and read that book. The next day, I got up and said, "Haki, when I write this review, the first line will be, 'Eldridge Cleaver is not a revolutionary. He's a hustler.' I come from New York. I've seen many a hustler." I don't know where that review is; back then, you'd send stuff off with no copies 'cause you just knew they were going to print it. But they never printed it.

Many of us were so political that they banned us from teaching in New York. We challenged the universities with the stuff we were teaching in African American studies. I taught [W. E. B.] Du Bois and Marcus Garvey and Paul Robeson out at San Francisco State, and the FBI knocked on my door with my landlord and said, "You should put her out. She's out there teaching Du *Bwah*." [*Feinstein laughs.*] This was 1966 or 1967. People can teach Du Bois and Robeson now, but they were on the banned list then. America said they were Communists; that was what that was all about. But we were such innocents. Young people think of Black Arts and say, "Oh, you knew everything." No! I was a real *inocente*.

sf: Certain qualities to your work have carried over throughout the years, but your poetry, of course, has changed, and your politics seem to have changed as well. I don't see you writing "a/coltrane/poem" at this point in your life.

ss: You're right, but I use Coltrane in my music. That's the difference. Let me put it this way: when you truly are a jazz poet, you don't have to mention Coltrane; people will hear it. I carry the improvisational part of him into what I do. Coltrane is very much a part of "Middle Passage," but it's done in a different way. The music is in the beat, in the repetition.

sf: What about the very conscious fusion of Coltrane and politics, which was a common element of many Coltrane poems from the late 1960s?

ss: This music *is* political. Although Coltrane never came out and said, "I am a political man," he did some music that was political by the very nature of the time and of what he said.

sf: In titles—

ss: In titles. But even when the titles aren't there, the music is still political, because all music, like poetry, is political; it either maintains the status quo or it talks about change. You see, when I first started to write, we had just found out that we'd been enslaved and no one had told us. So coming out of that, we had to say something about being black. If we hadn't done that, we would not have understood our motion and movement. So you had to say, "Wow! I'm a black woman!" "Whoa! They didn't tell us we'd been enslaved!" "Oh my God! These people *did* this to us!" You had to come out slamming everybody and their mama. You had to exorcize that. But in the 1970s, if I happen to still be doing that, there was something wrong.

You meet people. You travel in the world. You read different poets. You get up on stages with people. One of the most important people I met in the late sixties was Paul Blackburn. He was a dear friend. I used to call Paul when he was ill with cancer, and we would talk, and hug over the phone. Paul also had that great jazz sensibility—

sf: "Listening to Sonny Rollins at the Five-Spot"—

ss: Oh, yes. Paul loved that [kind of] poetry. And I looked up to him. And he once said, "I know you're not talking to me when you're calling people 'honkies'—" [*Feinstein laughs*]. I said, "But you have to give voice to these people—you gotta call them *something*," and he said, "But you limited it in your poetry." And I did—it was in, like, two poems that I did, and they were mean poems. So we were laughing about that. But some people came with preconceived notions, and they were surprised if you didn't take crap. I would say to some poets, "I come to you as an equal. I'm no flunky. Don't treat me like a flunky." But Paul treated me as an equal, and as a friend. I read Paul's poetry in my classes—no one's heard of him.

SF: He's just not taught.

SS: I teach him in every class because I think he was such a fine poet and fine human being.

SF: Can you talk a little about your poem for Ella Fitzgerald?

SS: Oh, yes, I've done that Ella Fitzgerald piece on the Academy of Music stage—not with any musicians. I love that piece because I try to make my voice at the end—[*Sanchez sings three notes, the last rising until it's out of her vocal range*]. The Philadelphia musicians who were there were like, "Whoa! We would have come out there with you if we had known you were going to do that," and I said, "Well, I never know how I'm going to do that with her." I just thought it was so important to celebrate that woman.

And I've got to do a Sarah [Vaughan] poem. (I don't have it yet; I've done parts.) Ella was very much of this earth. She was given a voice like no other voice; her voice could travel but, as high as it got, it always stayed earthbound. The beauty of it was that it went *inside* the earth, then came up and out, and then came back down. But *Sarah* left the universe sometimes. Sarah sang so that you would close your eyes and move out of this world into another world. Sometimes she sounded ancient: she went back—really went back—back to Africa, back to India, back to the Middle East, back to Spain. Ella couldn't do that.

I studied [at New York University] with Louise Bogan. Bogan was right about the poet being a universal person, and I began to understand what that was about. I didn't have to change my skin to become universal. The moment you pull out and you give out this sound, this lyricism, these lines that might be talking about my experience in Harlem, or my experience—wherever—someone will pick it up and say, "Oh, yeah. I had a similar experience."

That's what happened when we went out to San Francisco: we left in search of our selves—our history and herstory in the black studies—and we found everybody else, hidden. I mean, I'd be in a classroom and someone would pass by and say, "Sonia, here is a picture. We think this is of a concentration camp for Japanese. You have a couple of Japanese students; bring it up in class." That was how we were teaching. And the students got *mad* at me: "*I don't know anything about that,*

Sonia!" They really got pissed. But I said, "At least ask your parents about this." These eighteen-year-olds came back to class that Tuesday with tears in their eyes. Their parents had told them that they had been *in* the concentration camps, but they had kept it a secret. That's what happened to us: we went searching for ourselves and we discovered other people hidden, too. Japanese. Chinese. Motion and movement. You couldn't teach this and stay in one place. You had to go out.

Bogan was an interesting woman [*chuckles*]. Very aristocratic woman. She's the reason I'm so strict in class. Bogan was strict, too, and I know that that's how I teach because she was my teacher on many levels. I'll never forget asking her, "Do I have any talent?" She said [*Sanchez imitates a slow, haughty delivery*], "*Many* people have talent, Sonia" [*Feinstein laughs*]. I said, "Well, yeah—but I'm not talking about many people. I'm talking about *me*." I wanted to know, should I invest something in this? And she said, "It depends. What do you want to do with it?" And I said, "Well, you just informed me about this, and I don't think I know what to do with it—" and she said, "Yes, you doooo." As I look back on that question that she posed, it might have been a double-layered question because she's looking at me, and I was the only black in that class, right? But in that class, I was the first poet who got published—because Bogan would make you send your work out. And I do the same thing. I say, "Send stuff out. Mention that you're in my class—whatever." So I've had students included in books such as *Confirmation* [*An Anthology of African-American Women*, 1983] on down to *Bum Rush the Page* [*A Def Poetry Jam*, 2001]. I tell my students, "Send stuff in," and they're *in* there, you know? Because this is what this business is about, at some point.

But I'm also amazed by the people who don't have that kind of energy toward this thing that we do called poetry. I teach people who have such egos at such a young age. I say to those people in my class, "You will never, ever *move* with that ego. You've got to drop it." One way to do that is to work with musicians, 'cause you will drop your ego real fast [*Feinstein laughs*] if you're in there for about thirty minutes. They say, "Okay. Show me what you got," and you say, "Oh my God."

At the Painted Bride in Philadelphia, where they have readings and music and dance, we did an evening of poetry and music—[vibraphonist] Khan Jamal, Odean, and a bass player [Tyrone Brown]—and it was really nice. I had given them the poem, and we played with it a great deal and had a lot of fun on stage. When we finished, the people said, "No. You can't get off the stage." We were tired. We had done about an hour. (An hour by yourself is tiring, but an hour with music—

you're very much aware of whom you're dealing with.) But musicians are amazing people, let me tell you. Khan and Odean said, "Come on back, Sonia. Let's do something," and they started playing. [*Sanchez sings musical lines in the spirit of Odean Pope.*] And then Odean came and stood there right next to me. And you can't look at an audience and say, "I don't have anything written. . . ." It got to be funny, so that's when I started with the laughter [*laughs with a staccato sound*], and Odean went [*sings with a similar rhythm*]. That's why when I read "Middle Passage," I start off with laughter. [*Sanchez laughs again, then reads very quickly from "Improvisation" in* Wounded in the House of a Friend]: "It was It was It was It was / It was the coming that was bad." I hear nothing but music in that.

Thank God for the Ancestors. The Ancestors came in and helped me out. That's what they put in my mouth. "It was / it was the coming that was bad." Of course, I added stuff later on, and that's when we started moving on the stage. And Odean really pushed me. He pushed me to such a point that on stage I actually got down to my knees. I have done the piece in other ways, but every time I do it, I hear Odean. That's what I meant about Coltrane and what musicians will do: they cause you to make the word respond to the music until it becomes the music.

SF: Don't you think musicians tend to inspire writing more than writing inspires music? I've published a lot of pieces by writers on music, but very few by musicians on literature.

SS: That's so true. I don't know why that is. I think they probably don't see themselves necessarily as writers, or, if they are writers, they don't feel the need to talk about it. I think if you're a musician, and people can't write what you want, you probably have to write what you need to play, or to hear played. Nobody else is going to do that for you. I think that is what you see—that writing became an extension of the music. And it takes a little genius to do that—a little extra genius to do that: "Now let me sit down and write this, too."

SF: I think music will always have the edge on literature. There are things that I can feel and understand through poetry that I do not understand so absolutely, perhaps, through music—either as a listener or a player—but there's an immediacy to music that literature can only aspire toward.

SS: That is so true. Sometimes you try to make the poem *do* all that, and when I read from *Does Your House Have Lions?* I repeat, I go back, like a musician would do. I'll do it three times. There's a section where I break the form in *Does Your House Have Lions?* where my brother talks about being touched. (I had gone down to take care of my brother and whenever I touched him, he said it hurt. You know, with AIDS patients every time you touch them it hurts, right?) Although I had written the passage three times, I had never read it three times:

hold me with air
breathe me with air
sponge me with air
whisper me with air
comb me with air
brush me with air
rinse me with air.

And I didn't realize until I read with Odean that it needed that repetition. Isn't that something? I mean, that subconscious is a mutha, you know what I mean? [*Both laugh.*] I changed to sound like Odean, like his horn. I broke it up and repeated the lines. People hear the sweet lines, and all of a sudden you don't *want* people to hear the sweet lines. You want them to know how horrific it is, on many levels.

The first time I performed the piece, I tried to stay true to the line, because that's what you do if you're a writer: You don't want to change that line. But if you're working with musicians, you *have* to change it. That's why collaboration with musicians is something else; it changes the poetry so much. But also, the poem can change the music. I would say to Odean, "I hear how you're playing it, but that's not how I hear it." I'd read it, and he would hear what I meant. We both came with an idea of what that book was about, and then we collided—in a nice fashion—and we listened—in a most wonderful fashion—and then it became something else, something completely different.

—a/coltrane/poem

my favorite things
                    is u/blowen
                              yo/favorite/things.
        stretchen the mind
                        till it bursts past the con/fines of
        solo/en melodies.
                              to the many solos
        of the
            mind/spirit.
                    are u sleepen   (to be
                    are u sleepen   sung
                    brotha john   softly)
                    brotha john
                        where u have gone to.
                    no mornin bells
                    are ringen here. only the quiet
        aftermath of assassinations.
                        but i saw yo/murder/
        the massacre
                    of all blk/musicians. planned
        in advance.
                    yrs befo u blew away our passsst
                and showed us our futureeeeee
        screech screeech screeeeech screeech
        a/love/supreme, alovesupreme a lovesupreme.
            A LOVE SUPREME
scrEEEccCHHHHH screeeeEEECHHHHHHHH
        sCReeeEEECHHHHHHH SCREEEECCCCHHHH
        SCREEEEEEEECCCHHHHHHHHHHHH
        a lovesupremealovesupremealovesupreme for our blk
        people.

BRING IN THE WITE/MOTHA/fuckas
ALL THE MILLIONAIRES/BANKERS/ol
MAIN/LINE/ASS/RISTOOCRATS (ALL
THEM SO-CALLED BEAUTIFUL
PEOPLE)
WHO HAVE KILLED
WILL CONTINUE TO
KILL US WITH
THEY CAPITALISM/18% OWNERSHIP
OF THE WORLD.
YEH. U RIGHT
THERE. U ROCKEFELLERS. MELLONS
VANDERBILTS
FORDS.
yeh.
GITem.
PUSHem/PUNCHem/STOMPem. THEN
LIGHT A FIRE TO
THEY pilgrim asses.
TEAROUT THEY eyes.
STRETCH they necks
till no mo
raunchy sounds of MURDER/
POVERTY/STARVATION
come from they
throats.
screeeeeeeeeeeeeeeeeeCHHHHHHHHHHH
SCREEEEEEEEEEEEEEECHHHHHHHHHHH
screeEEEEEEEEEEEEEEEEEEEEEEEE
EECCCCHHHHHHH
SCREEEEEEEEEEEEEEEEEEEEEEEEEEEEEEE
EEEEEECHHHHHHHHHHH
BRING IN THE WITE/LIBERALS ON THE SOLO
SOUND OF YO/FIGHT IS MY FIGHT
SAXOPHONE.

                              TORTURE
        THEM FIRST AS THEY HAVE
                              TORTURED US WITH
        PROMISES/
                  PROMISES. IN WITE/AMERICA. WHEN
        ALL THEY WUZ DOEN
                      WAS HAVEN FUN WITH THEY
        ORGIASTIC DREAMS OF BLKNESS.
                              (JUST SOME MO
        CRACKERS FUCKEN OVER OUR MINDS.)
                                    MAKE THEM
        SCREEEEEEAM
                  FORGIVE ME. IN SWAHILI.
        DON'T ACCEPT NO MEA CULPAS.
                                    DON'T WANT TO
                                    HEAR
        BOUT NO EUROPEAN FOR/GIVE/NESS.
        DEADDYINDEADDYINDEADDYINWITEWESTERN
                  SHITTTTTT
(softly   da-dum-da da da da da da da da/da-dum-da
til it   da da da da da da da da da
builds   da-dum-da da da
up)   da-dum. da. da. da. this is a part of my
             favorite things.
             da dum da da da da da da
             da da da da
             da dum da da da da da da
             da da da da
               da dum da da da da
               da dum da da da da-----
(to be   rise up blk/ people
sung   de dum da da da da
slowly   move straight in yo/blkness
to tune   da dum da da da da
of my   step over the wite/ness

favorite   that is yesssss terrrrrr day
things.)   weeeeeeee are tooooooooday.
(f   da dum
a   da da da (stomp, stomp) da da da
s   da dum
t   da da da (stomp, stomp) da da da
e   da dum
r)   da da da (stomp) da da da dum (stomp)
                weeeeeeeee (stomp)
                        areeeeeeeee (stomp)
                                areeeeeeeee (stomp, stomp)
toooooooday   (stomp.
              day   stomp.
              day   stomp.
              day   stomp.
              day   stomp!)
(soft   rise up blk/people. rise up blk/people
chant)   RISE. & BE. What u can.
           MUST BE.BE.BE.BE.BE.BE.BE-E-E-E-BE-E-E-E-E-
           yeh. john coltrane.
my favorite things is u.
              showen us life/
                          liven.
a love supreme.
           for each
      other
   if we just
lissssssSSSTEN.

—Blues

in the night
in my half hour
negro dreams
i hear voices knocking at the door
i see walls dripping screams up
and down the halls
                    won't someone open
the door for me? won't some
one schedule my sleep
and don't ask no questions?
noise.
        like when he took me to his
home away from home place
and i died the long sought after
death he'd planned for me.
Yeah, bessie he put in the bacon
and it overflowed the pot.
and two days later
when i was talking
i started to grin.
as everyone knows
i am still grinning.

—Sister's Voice
(Read to "'Round Midnight")

this was a migration unlike
the 1900s of black men and women
coming north for jobs. freedom. life.
this was a migration to begin
to bend a father's heart again

to birth seduction from the past
to repay desertion at last.

imagine him short and black
thin mustache draping thin lips
imagine him country and exact
thin body, underfed hips
watching at this corral of battleships
and bastards. watching for forget
and remember. dancing his pirouette.

and he came my brother at seventeen
recruited by birthright and smell
grabbing the city by the root with clean
metallic teeth. commandant and infidel
pirating his family in their cell
and we waited for the anger to retreat
and we watched him embrace the city and the street.

first he auctioned off his legs. eyes.
heart. in rooms of specific pain.
he specialized in generalize
learned newyorkese and all profane.
enslaved his body to cocaine
denied his father's signature
damned his sister's overture.

and a new geography greeted him.
the atlantic drifted from offshore
to lick his wounds to give him slim
transfusion as he turned changed wore
a new waistcoat of solicitor
antidote to his southern skin
ammunition for a young paladin.

and the bars. the glitter. the light
discharging pain from his bygone anguish
of young black boy scared of the night.
sequestered on this new bank, he surveyed the fish
sweet cargoes crowded with scales feverish
with quick sales full sails of flesh
searing the coastline of his acquiesce.

and the days rummaging his eyes
and the nights flickering through a slit
of narrow bars. hips. thighs.
and his thoughts labeling him misfit
as he prowled, pranced in the starlit
city, coloring his days and nights
with gluttony and praise and unreconciled rites.

—A Poem for Ella Fitzgerald

when she came on the stage, this Ella
there were rumors of hurricanes and
over the rooftops of concert stages
the moon turned red in the sky,
it was Ella, Ella.
queen Ella had come
and words spilled out
leaving a trail of witnesses smiling
amen—amen—a woman—a woman.

she began
this three agèd woman
nightingales in her throat
and squads of horns came out
to greet her.

streams of violins and pianos
splashed their welcome
and our stained glass silences
our braided spaces
unraveled
opened up
said who's that coming?

who's that knocking at the door?
whose voice lingers on
that stage gone mad with
      perdido. perdido. perdido.
      i lost my heart in toledooooooo.

whose voice is climbing
up this morning chimney
smoking with life
carrying her basket of words
      a tisket a tasket
      my little yellow
      basket—i wrote a
      letter to my mom and
      on the way i dropped it—
      was it red . . . no no no no
      was it green . . . no no no no
      was it blue . . . no no no no
      just a little yellow

voice rescuing razor thin lyrics
from hopscotching dreams.

we first watched her navigating
an apollo stage amid high-stepping
yellow legs
we watched her watching us

shiny and pure woman
sugar and spice woman
her voice a nun's whisper
her voice pouring out
guitar thickened blues,
her voice a faraway horn
questioning the wind,
and she became Ella,
first lady of tongues
Ella cruising our veins
voice walking on water
crossed in prayer,
she became holy
a thousand sermons
concealed in her bones
as she raised them in a
symphonic shudder
carrying our sighs into
her bloodstream.

this voice, chasing the
morning waves,
this Ella-tonian voice soft
like four layers of lace.

>*when i die Ella*
>*tell the whole joint*
>*please, please, don't talk*
>*about me when i'm gone. . . .*

i remember waiting one nite for her appearance
audience impatient at the lateness
of musicians,
i remember it was april
and the flowers ran yellow
the sun downpoured yellow butterflies

and the day was yellow and silent
all of spring held us
in a single drop of blood.

when she appeared on stage
she became Nut arching over us
feet and hands placed on the stage
music flowing from her breasts
she swallowed the sun
sang confessions from the evening stars
made earth divulge her secrets
gave birth to skies in her song
remade the insistent air
and we became anointed found
inside her bop
> *bop bop dowa*
> *bop bop doowaaa*
> *bop bop dooooowaaaa*

Lady. Lady. Lady.
be good. be good
to me.
   to you.   to us all
cuz we just some lonesome babes
in the woods
hey lady. sweetellalady
Lady. Lady. Lady. be gooooood
ELLA ELLA ELLALADY
> *be good*
> > *goooooood*
> > > *goooooood . . .*

leslie scalapino

A profoundly philosophical, spiritual, and political poet, Leslie Scalapino traces many of her formal and thematic preoccupations to Buddhist thought, particularly the anti-Cartesian notion that "appearances" (i.e., the external world) are the same as consciousness: appearances are manifestations, or projections, of the mind in action. This paradox illuminates her view of reader and text as conjoined in a continual present tense. Scalapino's interest in the "motions" of a text—its evolution in the act of being read—emerges from a conviction about the unfolding of the present moment, which is at the heart of her poetics. At the same time, Scalapino holds that contemporary culture reproduces itself in what we perceive as our own deepest identities. Accordingly, Scalapino replaces conventional subjectivity in her work by what she calls the "tiny self," an ego diminished, though not denigrated— restored to its place in an infinitely vaster phenomenological scheme. Scalapino's language suppresses affect and remains provocatively flat. Small blocks of text, set amid the often impinging white space of the page, unfold in textures of repetition and permutation, a serial form of potentially infinite, discrete, and repeating units. For Scalapino, seriality is inseparable from a poetics that documents minute acts of seeing, as in the title of one of her critical works: *How Phenomena Appear to Unfold* (1989).

In addition to being a poet of complex linguistic surfaces, Scalapino is a highly visual writer, using the spatial elements of the page and experimenting as well with images, particularly photographs, as in the title poem of *Crowd and not evening or light* (1992), which is excerpted here and discussed in the interview. Scalapino has also collaborated frequently in both texts and avant-garde theater. The recent book-length cross-genre work *The Tango* (with the visual artist Marina Adams, 2001) extends her inquiries into language and image in a photo-text that reveals both her interest in collaboration and her provocative visual poetics.

As she notes in the following interview, Scalapino was introduced early on to Asian cultures and non-Western thought, and the exposure sparked a lasting interest that continues to inform her poetry. She was born and raised in Berkeley, California, where her father was a professor of East Asian politics at the University of California. On two occasions—when Scalapino was seven and then fourteen—the family traveled for several months throughout south and southeast Asia and in the Middle East. After earning a B.A. from Reed College, Scalapino received an M.A. in English from U.C. Berkeley, which she describes as an "awful" experience, one that may have cemented her career-long quarrel with social and literary conventions; she notes that she started writing only after she left graduate school.

In the mid-1970s, Scalapino published several short sequences, most of which were collected in her first major volume, *Considering how exaggerated music is* (1982). That book has been followed by numerous experimental works, each of which challenges generic boundaries among fiction, poetry, drama, artist's book, and literary/cultural criticism. These include *Zither & Autobiography* (2003), *Dahlia's Iris: Secret Autobiography and Fiction* (2003), *The Public World/Syntactically Impermanence* (1999), *Defoe* (1994), *Green and Black: Selected Writings* (1996), *Objects in the Terrifying Tense/Longing from Taking Place* (1993), and *way* (1988). She is also the the founder and editor of the press O Books, through which she has championed the publication of new avant-garde writing since the mid-1980s.

This interview, with the poet-critic Elisabeth A. Frost, took place on July 9, 1993, at Scalapino's home in Oakland, California. It was edited over several months, and in August 1995, Scalapino addressed additional questions by correspondence.

AN INTERVIEW WITH LESLIE SCALAPINO
by Elisabeth A. Frost

ELISABETH FROST: I'd like to start with an idea you've written about—that style is "cultural abstraction."

LESLIE SCALAPINO: In various works I've written, beginning with *The Return of Painting, the Pearl, and Orion: A Trilogy* (1991), I was getting into the notion of using a visual cultural form, like action films or the comic book. These are cultural abstractions as current forms that embody the conflicts going on in any period of time. In my book *Defoe*, I was taking literary objects—Richardson's *Clarissa* and *Pamela*—not mentioning those in particular but creating sequences that duplicate Richardson's plot: the woman is kidnapped and is being prevailed upon but is resisting in a similar mode. I wanted to take erotica as the thing that it is—a form or genre that consists of particular actions—because it can't be anything else and isn't a symbol of anything. The movements are indistinguishable when the woman is with her kidnapper and when she's with her lover, except that she resists the kidnapper.

The text of *Defoe* brings something to the simplest movement, so that as the writer I was supposedly removing the social construction or interpretation of it and the reader is experiencing the action without that interpretation. The text has only that simple movement. The plot does not conceal or "symbolize" anything. I wanted to see if I could get a text that would be still, where it would come to a balance, that there is in its form something else besides the plot as a motion that you don't understand and really can't articulate in any other way.

EF: Would you say, then, that you're elaborating on form itself in *Defoe*, because the movements are the same with the lover and with the kidnapper—in other words, that the "action" is the same in both cases?

LS: The delineation of motions only, made by the couples, motions that are qualified specifically by the dawn or dusk sky, birds flying, et cetera—these are a "stilling" of plot to the degree of "finding" the place where action is without the imposition of interpretation. Where that interpretation hasn't occurred yet, as text, is the place of finding something about the shape or nature of oneself and occurrence. In *Defoe*, the violence of war, motions in fighting (such as people being thrown through the air), and the motions of "love" appear to be outside, yet they are effectively "inner" events in the writing.

EF: Would you consider your own formal choices, particularly those that alter traditional language, as expressions of a sociopolitical vision?

LS: Yes, everything expresses a social or political vision. My writing is fabrication of self, of subjectivity (which itself is seen to be "cultural abstraction"), yet in it the "self" is not separable from its own illusion. I want to get the writing to come to that point where you perceive people's motions as not separate from occurrence itself. For example, writing a brief description of *The Pearl* recently, I noted that in this work in which one-line paragraphs are the same as poems with line breaks, one's physical motions, such as running (as an extended shape in motions that are the text), are the same thing as their mental conception. Fictionalizing overtly is the same as living. Both, when they're the same movements, are serene and free: one's movements have the effect of being ahead of one, in some part of the writing that one has not reached in the present reading. In another work, *The Front Matter, Dead Souls* (1996), I expressed this as "reading as apprehension per se, so it is slow / has no content but that."

Any form one is using somehow has a shape and a sound to it that is a way of seeing what something's actual movement is. That's different from a political theory that has a particular polemics and imposes that view on phenomena—having a dogma and wanting the work to express that. I want the writing simply to be finding out. I want to get to the inner relation of events.

EF: Formally, your work often involves juxtaposition, particularly between what seems to be private, or erotic, and what happens in public spaces. In "The floating series," one of the sequences in *way*, you juxtapose a sexual encounter between a man and a woman with events going on outside—opening up a small store, the issue of rents, people on the street.

LS: I'm interested in the idea of small points, many encounters, tiny movements that are very particular—many people in interactions on this huge span— and seeing a kind of impossible place where the motions are similar, how these things are arranged in writing as a place that is unknown, without imposing a form or a format that would link them artificially. I was asked to write something about *Defoe* for *Conjunctions*, so I wrote this about it: "Positions of erotica occur in this which are like them in those exact minute motions. These have a rhythm of presentation in this that occurs in spurts and not planned. When it is subject to only its movement it has no other reflection. It isn't social perception, or rather is it only. What's that?" A space of the text has a reflection that's only its own movement and not what is called a social perception. It's as if the perception were solely that—social.

EF: So it's that same idea of things happening simultaneously as parts of—not exactly a whole, in the sense of being complete—but part of a large pattern.

LS: Yes, so that what's left out—which is vast, which is everything—is implied in the movement. I like Richard Tuttle's description of his aim "to make something which looks like itself" [*Chaos, die/the form* (Edition Cantz)]—that is, his interest lies not in representing something but in creating new "things" that have never existed before. This is akin in *Defoe* to "making" historical actions.

EF: You've written about your use of erotica as a specific genre—with its own rules and conventions. In "Note on My Writing," you describe erotica as something "artificial which can 'comment on itself' as a surface" (*How Phenomena Appear to Unfold*).

LS: I've used it in different ways, yet my writing is not itself genre. Rather it is commenting on that as a view of itself. For example, in *Defoe* I wanted to make erotica that is somewhat explosive—as simple action, not given any cultural meaning or interpretation, but there as the motion in the text. Erotica would be completely revealing about people's social positions, while being itself "neutral," and at the same time what I wanted to do in that whole book—as an extended piece—was to get at some sense of what love is, palpably. That it has nothing to do with those motions and at the same time is those motions because that is all that is there, even though I'm giving no emotional meaning or even counterpoint. I wanted to know whether the text could do this itself, simply in its particular movements.

In *that they were at the beach: aeolotropic series* (1985), there is a piece called "A sequence," where people are seen as having leopard parts. It was making something be unromantic and essentially not palatable erotically. It's as though it were just erotica, with no point in it where you are describing any theory of what you're doing or any purpose—so that it would be completely identifiable with that genre.

It would be revealing because of that. It's almost like working against either the notion of an emotional description of what happens between people or a description of class or sex or any kind of domination. I didn't want there to be any kind of violence or domination occurring in it, and at the same time to reveal something of the nature of that because it isn't that. The text is completely deadpan, flat. Somebody said to me that he didn't like it, that it wasn't erotic, and I thought, that's right. I wanted it to be removed from a level of conflict and tension, yet be something that you are apparently taking seriously—I can't describe it.

EF: That seems just right to me. There's an absence of strangeness in what's happening. The human bodies are described as having leopard parts for their sexual organs, and for the speaker, this somehow relates to sexual arousal. But the strangeness of all that isn't part of the writing—it's taken for granted.

LS: It's as if in music you could get a deadpan, a neutral tone, and actually do something with that neutral tone, if such existed. It seems always to stay that same thing, but it produces responses in you. It doesn't have depth, and because it doesn't have depth, you have a reaction to it. That's what I think about Cindy Sherman's work, for example. There's something interesting about giving a surface that doesn't have depth.

EF: Part of it may be that as a reader or a viewer you get disoriented. Whatever you expect to be able to plumb isn't there. With Cindy Sherman, you realize that it is and isn't her in those poses, and that calls into question your position as a viewer. Maybe that's part of what happens in reading your poetry.

LS: It may elicit a different level of emotional response.

EF: Different from what viewers normally experience from conventional art?

LS: In both Sherman's and my work, there is and is not the expectation of that being the "real" person.

EF: I was wondering whether you think of the newspaper or TV news as a kind of serial, or infinite, form—a form you've used often in your writing. This kind of news seems to reflect such a basic aspect of our culture that we take it for granted. We're part of it, and yet we're distanced from it, too.

LS: Yes, it's the idea that you're watching history in the form of an action taking place that is in some way connected to you, though you feel completely isolated from it, and which is also totally fabricated as an action.

EF: In the television form?

LS: That's the form in which action on a worldwide level is being presented to you. You are totally isolated from it, watching this thing that is deliberately, completely separated from you as if it were not happening or as if you were not happening. It proposes that dichotomy. Where does the action start? Mental action is the same as reality. Living in the imagination is as real an event as anything else.

EF: Is there a relationship between the erotic and the serial?

LS: Yes, but I don't know what it is. There is something interesting about the serial form, almost as if it were soap opera. Except I hate soap operas and I never look at them. But it's the idea that something could go on and then start again and keep going, and it would always reproduce some of the information that's core information so that you could come into it at any point. It implies that there's no end to this and also that people are attending to very intricate but essentially delicate, small things that they're doing. There's something about that that's satisfying, but definitely not at all satisfying in soap operas.

EF: Maybe it's the idea of not ending that has an erotic charge.

LS: Yes, right, and that you can feel comfortable and relaxed in something. For me, "The floating series" in *way* has that sense. You actually could just enjoy something.

EF: And without that determinate structure of beginning, middle, and end. On the other hand, a lot of people associate with traditional poetry the pleasure of closure. A sonnet, say, and the way that it closes.

LS: I don't know. Writing a form that implies closure in conventional works that I've heard or read—I find that completely stifling. You feel that you're trapped and dead. I have a reaction of total claustrophobia.

EF: Has the amount of traveling you've done—being immersed in different cultures as a child, in Japan and in the Middle East—affected your view of American culture?

LS: Yes, because of coming back. Coming back was always difficult.

EF: You went back and forth a lot?

LS: Only a few times when I was a kid, but it was very important. Also as an adult, traveling to Japan, Bhutan, and Thailand recently. I went to India as well, in 1987. I'd been to India twice as a kid for three-month periods. Coming back from those trips was an absolutely devastating experience, because I was looking at something that seemed so flattened and subdued here, where there was no connection between people that one could find. Everything seemed isolated from everything else and somehow subdued in hiding what's actually occurring, which is living—the fact that there are connections to organisms and dying, et cetera, so that we don't know anything about our being alive. It's as if somehow in America we'd subdued things, to the point where we can't see anything about ourselves because we have no connection to it. So one is using up one's life without seeing it.

EF: Somehow that sanitary surface of things is very comforting to many Americans.

LS: But it's mystifying why. It's terrifying. You're not seeing something that is inevitable.

EF: There's a comment you make in your trilogy, in *Orion*, that a person who's rebelling is often called alienated. Does this imply to you that whatever that person does is perceived as her or his own existential problem rather than a political act?

LS: In poetic terms, one must be very critical of the "romantic" position of rebel as self, egoistic illusion. It's necessary to criticize that without invalidating the real experience in the exterior world. The process of sanitizing has to do with saying that one's objections are to something that is "whole." During the bombing of Iraq [in the 1991 Gulf War (—ed.)], I was here in the Bay Area, where there were various large demonstrations. Then I went to the East Coast. There were demonstrations in New York and Washington. The newspeople were pro-war and were not adequately covering any protest. When I was in Massachusetts, they flashed an instant of a demonstration in San Francisco, saying, "But the Bay Area has a tradition of peace movements." As if the demonstration was invalid because these people were biased—but also possibly that it wasn't abhorrent because it was their tradition.

EF: I wonder how that kind of political awareness enters your poetry. I was interested in your exchange with Ron Silliman, concerning a piece he originally wrote for the *Socialist Review*.[1] Silliman seems to say that there's one kind of change, from people who are already in the system, which involves breaking it down. And then there's change from people who are disenfranchised entering the system. That, say, writers of color want to have their stories told, and that's a way of entering a system that is already in place—

LS: Yes, of course, but what is problematic to me is the idea that telling one's story (whatever that is) is itself a conventional narrative (those were the words Ron used). In order to get at what you're seeing as oppressive, the writing must be aware of the way in which one (and the writing) is formed and reformed by exteriority, the solidification of a pattern coming to "one" from the exterior world. The writer may express the difference between what's interior (different from what's "socially" articulated) and what is being shaped, which is itself a reintegration vis-à-vis the "whole," placing the person (again) in a conventional relation to that supposed whole. In a lot of my earlier work, I was concerned with the solidification of that pattern coming to you from the exterior world, that no matter how you try to express the difference between what's interior and what is being shaped for you—what is regarded as convention—it would be remolded so that you would be interpreted in that old shape.

The point I was making in the exchange with Ron Silliman was that any narrative in which one describes that difference (of "one" from the outside) would have to be a change of that conventional language. No one enters the "system" without being it. Ron's position is that white men in avant-garde groups, removed from the pressure of the necessity of social change, are freer to investigate poetic form. My position was that under duress, change in form is a necessity.

My position on that point is not entirely accurate. And his isn't either.

In this period, the conversation amongst writers about "emotion" has tended toward the stringent in saying that emotion is simply personal, confessional, which is a conventional form, rather than a form that is investigative. But I think emotion is as interesting and as objective as anything else. It's a reflection on that which is exterior and also a reflection on one's own psyche.

EF: So there's too often a conflation of emotion with confession?

LS: The idea is to have the writing be almost like a sheet or screen on which things register. It's like a reverberation of a motion (or emotion) on that supposedly still sheet. You can see something on it, the way you put a ripple on water. As such, delineation of emotion has nothing to do with the confessional.

EF: Is syntax something you see repeated in various writers' works—that in a sense it becomes a convention of its own?

LS: This is true of any group or period of time. For example, the New York School—one hears a certain sound pattern or shape which in the best works is terrific and interesting; then there are people who are imitating that. It's not one thing, but it's identifiable; you're in that language and its sense, and for some reason it comes up and is done for a while and is meaningful to people. Similarly, the

Beat poets and the Language group have an identifiable syntax, which if you've read the work of that period you can identify immediately—you've heard that sound.

Recently a poet sent me something he had written about measure and the sound of a work, and he was criticizing Language work as not being interested in measure—maintaining that this is associated more with a Williams preoccupation. He quoted Charles Bernstein as saying that he is not interested in predictable sound. I recalled going to readings hearing what I'd say is an "establishment" sound, whatever that is—one wouldn't think it would be one thing, but there is a particular sound, a way of breaking the line and a polished smoothing of active engagement that conveys a settled, predictable sense. I don't think that there's anything that could be done at this point within that establishment sound or pattern that one hasn't heard many times. I think the criticism of that is just necessary.

EF: How much do you feel yourself affiliated with Language writing?

LS: People see a certain sensibility occurring which is a generational thing—there's something that's formed in terms of your preoccupations and your ways of seeing things that presumably happens when you're a kid. It's neither here nor there whether you're in a particular group, because your work is reciprocal and is carrying on a dialogue.

EF: Yes, although Language writing did emerge as a very self-conscious movement. Did you feel a part of that agenda, that group?

LS: No. I liked conversing with them. With some individuals' views, I wanted to change them, but that didn't occur. I thought it was fun to try.

EF: It seems that, for you, the sense of dialogue you just mentioned includes people like [Robert] Duncan and also H.D., both of whom you wrote about in *How Phenomena Appear to Unfold*. H.D. appears more recently as well, as a subject in *Objects in the Terrifying Tense/Longing from Taking Place*. What other writers are particularly important to you?

LS: Well, many writers—Murasaki, much Japanese medieval work, certainly Robert Creeley and Philip Whalen. Virginia Woolf was important in my early work. In regard to *How Phenomena Appear to Unfold*, some of the things that are in there were written for particular occasions, particularly the one on Duncan. I listened to his readings and his lectures, and I got a lot out of them, particularly because he was so generous and interesting and lively. But I think that my sensibility and way of writing, preoccupations and personality are quite different from his.

EF: What about Stein? I understand you taught a course on Stein.

LS: There's something about Stein's perception that is very modern, something we already know even before we read her—which is one reason why, I believe, as time goes on people find Stein more and more approachable, which was the case with the students in my class. They were inclined at first perhaps to be prejudiced against her because they wanted the writing to be visionary, having to do with myth; she completely goes against that. But she has a sort of phenomenological approach. I took her writing as not describing, but having to do with wanting to be able to write the essence of something, of an emotion or a person—

EF: Or a thing.

LS: Yes, an object, and that's impossible; she's fully aware that it's impossible, so she's in a mode of conjecture about things, a curiosity and experimentation.

EF: You wrote about Stein's idea of the "continuous present." It's a concept crucial to your own work as a whole, isn't it?

LS: I'm smiling because I wrote a play that's called "The Present." Also, I recently finished *The Front Matter, Dead Souls*, in which I had the idea of a serial work that would be published in a newspaper. I began to write it as fast as I could at the beginning of the 1992 election campaign and sent out a very small version of it to different newspapers to try to get it published. It was the idea of doing a political cartoon in a sense, a cartoon in language, taking images as wild as possible, as extreme as possible, to be totally an expression of the actual event of the present time. Basically, I think that's similar to Stein. It's similar to the continuous present, but also to her portraits of objects and people in trying to get the present time's reverberation of something. It strikes me that things that are difficult like that are the only things interesting to do.

EF: In *Orion*, where you use the comic book as a form, you imply that there is no such thing as historical experience at all. Do you feel that there is no experience outside of convention, period?

LS: In *Orion* and *The Pearl*, I was playing around with the idea that there is no experience outside of convention, meaning the concept of experience and history is "theirs," and a fabrication. If you perceive something in a given way, and you're constantly reinterpreted in terms of it, and you're not alone, somehow this is something that we're calling "the social community." One is outside of convention, actually. If it is theirs, you could be free from it because you'd be outside of experience itself, in a realm that's totally quiet and peaceful and pleasurable.

EF: That almost sounds like a Buddhist position, being outside of experience, outside of time or sequence.

LS: I think a Buddhist position would be to be only inside experience, which is nonexistence?—which may be the same as what you just said. I interpret it as, when you're walking inside your skeleton, you're actually doing something that is the only motion that there is for you at that instant. You're not up against that whole political thing in the writing of these things—getting yourself up against an insurmountable problem where there is no relief available because you cannot defeat it or see all of it. Occasionally I come to the conclusion that I'm proposing a problem that I could simply drop. If I dropped it, I could get to an area in the form of what I'm writing that would be completely free of the problem, a free zone. You're not standing on a point and making a doctrine. You're not failing to observe yourself or imposing yourself on it. It's really a sort of impossible place, but that's what I want to try to do.

EF: In *way* you have a piece called "no(h)-setting." It involves a number of discrete descriptions of street scenes. Could you talk a bit about your use of No in that piece?

LS: I don't know very much about No except for the sense of movements (as writing). I was in Japan not long ago and saw some No drama. The recurring minute motions—seeming almost the same and appearing as the actors were performing a series of plays—were themselves the occurrence of the different stories. That fascinated me.

When I was a kid, we lived in Japan for a while, and my parents took us to No drama and to Kabuki. My sense of it at that age was of listening to incredibly strange cries and strange motions associated with these cries. I enjoyed it. Later on I read Antonin Artaud's *The Theater and Its Double*, which I found really beautiful and suggestive. When sound doesn't have a meaning, it's all the more interesting because you're hearing it in a way you couldn't if you attributed meanings to those sounds.

EF: There's a great deal of playfulness and pleasure with the comic book form that also comes up in the way your poetry works—small units of text in blocks on the page.

LS: I even like the idea of the visual shape of the comic book being those different boxes that are all over the place. For example, *The Front Matter, Dead Souls* is a novel, really a poem, to be published in a newspaper. I had the idea that it could be done on billboards, that all of it would just be one sentence, one paragraph; there's no reason you would necessarily have to follow it from beginning to end, but it involves close reading.

EF: The billboard makes me think of a number of feminist visual artists who use mass forms like that, especially Barbara Kruger. Kruger, though, has more affinity for the images that come from mass media: she takes them whole, so even though she uses them on her terms, she still repeats the language and images of advertising.

LS: Right. What I want to do in *The Front Matter, Dead Souls* is in some ways the opposite—trying to get to an imaginative realm that is vivid by creating images that are very extreme and contain a totally disruptive element at every point, but that also on some level offer the satisfaction of beautiful little objects—which itself is an illusion. I want the reader to feel that "inner" satisfaction and to be aware of the illusion at the same time. Barbara Kruger obviously takes something straight as exterior and doesn't let go of the original.

EF: I'm interested in your use of photographs and visual images, especially in *Crowd and not evening or light*. You use a series of black-and-white pictures of beach scenes, and you've inserted handwritten phrases in script below and around them. Did you take the photographs?

LS: Yes. In *Crowd and not evening or light* I took a lot of photographs. I also collaborated with Norman Fischer. We both took photographs, wrote phrases, and then exchanged the photographs. Neither one of us is a photographer. I was using a cheap camera that focused automatically, and I'd not taken many pictures before. In *Crowd and not evening or light*, I was trying to photograph people standing in the ocean—something that fascinated me was watching them as herds, a crowd of people, just standing and chatting with each other. I simply stood in one place and kept snapping the camera and didn't do anything to organize it. I wanted to capture this really strange, mysterious scene. The terrain is completely flat, and so are the photographs. They give the impression that everything's flat, that there's no inside to them. It was as if they give the inside of something else. I also wanted the photos to be a nonverbal surface that cannot be separated from the writing.

EF: The idea of surface is interesting—and neither language nor image is privileged. I also see the photographs in *Crowd and not evening or light* in the opposite way from those of someone like Sherman or Kruger because they look like family photos: they're so obviously not posed, not produced in any way. And the appearance of the handwritten captions underneath and along the margins leads you to think that they'll say "Venice Beach 1990" or "Uncle so and so." But there's really nothing personal about them—that's where the disruption, the confusion, comes in.

LS: Yes. Sometimes I wanted to convey the feeling of seeing those early photographs that were almost like paintings, in which you'd have an object that appears to be a kind of romantic image, an interior expression, but which is a mechanical image that wasn't posed. The photograph that's on the cover of *The Return of Painting* is an example of that. It's a landscape with a nude person standing in it, the way the Hudson school would have one figure standing in this huge expanse of nature. So in a way it's like a painting.

EF: The cover of *way* has two photographs, juxtaposed. One is captioned "Couple dancing in bar" and shows a man and a woman embracing; the other says, "Men fighting on sidewalk," and shows a similar pose—but a violent one— between two men. The cover almost appears to be an introduction to the book. How did you select those images?

LS: I chose those photographs because I just happened to see them—on a postcard—and I liked the idea of using street scenes that were very localized and specific. I wanted to counteract the idea of "the Way" as something exalted and to suggest "the way" as something not exalted—it's just what anybody is doing. I wanted that idea to be very simple, like something that would be on a postcard, which it was.

EF: And in terms of the erotic moment being juxtaposed with the violent moment—was that in your mind?

LS: No, not really. But people of course have remarked on that. One person said it looks as though the two couples are doing the same thing, and it's okay if that's what people see.

EF: I wonder how you feel about the position or lack of position of poetry in our culture, especially nonmainstream poetry, which has a sort of nonposition.

LS: As many people say, it's a good thing in a way, because poetry can be totally free and concentrate on an aim that's noncommercial. For example, in publishing, frequently the question comes up, How can we make this accessible, in distributing and selling the book?—accessible to people who hate this kind of stuff. That doesn't make sense, because you will never make it palatable to someone who wouldn't look at it to begin with. Also, it raises the question of why you would want to model yourself on that idea, why being known to a person who has no interest is a good thing, something that you would want. It's not something you wouldn't want, but it's irrelevant. People have to do what interests them.

EF: You were talking earlier about how living in the imagination is real in an important sense. It brings to mind the issue of the inside/outside dichotomy that dominates most Western thinking. Is this basically a false distinction?

LS: Yes. I think that it has to do with the fascination of seeing that your mind and an action really are the same thing. Even though someone else doesn't perceive you, they perceive their mind doing an action. It's like trying to get into the time you're in, as Stein was saying.

EF: Do you consider your work to be feminist?

LS: I certainly consider my work to be feminist. Writing considers gender perceptions. At the same time, insofar as gender roles are social creations, one's identity as that is an illusion. My articulation of feminism is in the gesture of trying to unravel how something is packaged or mirrored back to me—as part of the whole web of what's around us—and how we can be attuned to seeing social creations of ourselves and others. You have to have the most subtle responses that are sometimes mirroring the social almost exactly, so that you can hardly see the difference. But that enables you to see that difference—to get to the place where you are created as a social being.

EF: So if we adhere to the dichotomy of gender difference that's constructed in our culture, we inevitably participate.

LS: Related to the form of writing—it's a matter of not making assumptions beforehand. One's decisions about what one is as a formed being, as a woman for instance, are like placing the conclusion or the hypothesis on something before one has done it. It's a process of unraveling the hypothesis and the conclusion—there should be no hypothesis. Which is impossible because you hypothesize when you go down to the grocery store that it will be there. My sense is that the intention should be not to make a placement of yourself psychologically.

EF: How can you reconcile that with having to exist in this culture with its perceptions and roles? You're using your text to try to get to this place before the hypothesis existed, but we can't do that on a daily basis, in our lives as lived.

LS: I think one can; sometimes one can't. It's very difficult, painful, especially when you're placed against something when there's no way out. One can quit a job, for example. It's that pressure that actually causes one to find a way to get to a goal and to let go of something. I had the view for years of wanting to focus on this subject as a matter of interest (as writing and as experience), to see how one is being socially created, at every point—in the instant it occurs, in the most minute things, like conversation. The book I was writing at that time was called *Considering how exaggerated music is.* I practically went crazy in this total constriction of pain in having to come right up against this thing, seeking this very thing that is barring you. And to look at it—even your perception of people's perception causes it to occur more so. I was having a lot of trouble functioning at all.

At some point I was sitting and talking to some women whom I didn't know very well, and one of them remarked to me, "You're having a lot of trouble; you've got to just stop reacting, stop responding and they'll stop doing that." It struck me as fascinating that that would be noticed. That was precisely the thing: I had decided to respond to something, therefore causing it to happen. I had responded to various restrictions being placed on me, interpretations, the constant definition of me as a woman or as a social being. These women were noting the fact that you have to stop the reverberations coming from you in noticing them, and then the reverberations will stop. What I found fascinating as writing was that I was trying to see this thing, and the more one observes it, the more it happens. The only way to stop it from actually happening is to have your mind drop it. It struck me—the idea that your mind is action is absolutely the case.

EF: You've told me that you'd like to discuss the connections I've made between your work and Stein's.[2]

LS: The nature of Stein's work is to see character or mind as action, not entity. This might be described as disrupting a sense of the unified subject, which was broached by many Western artists and writers in the twentieth century. But this is a view traditionally known—rather than being disruptive—in Asian cultures. I certainly agree that Stein's work is of great interest. However, my primary influences have been from other sources.

Phenomenology and Stein's view of the continuous present and her view of perception have some similarity to views of perception and phenomena in Tibetan and Zen Buddhist philosophy (such as that of the early Indian philosopher Nāgārjuna), which writings seem to me far more radical than Stein's and which had already influenced me before I came to read her. I began to investigate various texts after my father, when I was thirteen, assigned a book on Buddhism; my sisters and I were out of school traveling with our family in Asia.

Nāgārjuna's propositions, for example (which I read as an adult), are a logic of phenomenal emptiness. A phenomenon hasn't inherent existence, as it is not based on a single moment of a mind, nor on successive moments of a mind, as such moments arise dependently (don't exist inherently, not being that phenomenon itself—though appearing to be). In other words, the apprehension of the "moment" of the mind appears to be the phenomenon itself which the mind itself is seeing.

As nothing has inherent existence, in that it is dependent on other factors, it can't begin or have an ending as an inherent object; nor can a view of its nonexistence be accurate either. Poetically, this implies change/transformation being the principle or "structure" itself (as from all points or perspectives) of the writing.

Regarding influence on the process of writing, one is engaging "the present" in the act of writing more than one is "conveying" themes. Granted all writing is exchange, and exchange is active in finding out what the present is. This description of writing could very well be a paraphrase from Stein's "Composition as Explanation." It comes from the process itself.

Notes

1. Silliman, "What/Person: From an Exchange" (—ed.).
2. See Frost, "Signifyin(g) on Stein" (—ed.).

—as–leg

walking on the street – to try
to be calm – and in a light – couples arm-in-arm
embracing, who seemed to beam at me – going by
as a grace – mercy – but which one
wouldn't want – to have to get – not from them – but
in that

> the couples – have a
> blissful – time – not from that
> – though it is from that – as
> the criticism

> a bursting –
> with my chest not being able
> to contain myself – not it

when as not any custom
– of driven out to walk down the street
– to try to be calm – with their strolling seeming serene
happening to be couples – but not coming from anything
in the sense of their smiling to me, when my chest
was bursting in a physical state – from lack of sleep

and the couples were swept up – embracing
arm-in-arm – in a beautiful light – as
if floating toward me – when I'd gone down
the street and was returning,
coming toward them

> there's nothing to
> fight in that – in the superimposed of

the couples on the street – being there – or
their appearing to float up the street – walking –
which was toward me – in my wrestling not
from them

not returning – without there being
anything for them – long times spent
isolated – but wrestling miserably without comprehending
it – but there being love between men and
women – for one thing – not from parents

it's sort of pushed out
the other side – from such
being serene – but not comprehending
anything about it – having to go down the street to
try to be calm – and separately,
the couples – strolling – there only being love
between men and women

woman – in cart
but then killed for some
reason – by the men shouting
spitting – rubbed with shit – the women having been enslaved after
the war, the men dead – suffering, brutalizing
– humiliated, all of them – the
woman in the cart – as some forgotten

woman – carried off, separated from
the others – their crying to her – some dying
jumping

not concentrating on certain wrongs – not having anything
to return to – savage – people who may go after
– others – in the street – so frightened –

and suffering as not the sense of custom or wanting
that

people finding out what
they are – because they don't have any
custom any longer – we don't
not from suffering – though going on
or their finding out, the women having been enslaved
the men dead – custom – suffering
made to be that

        children – outside
        all crying, as some
        game – at once – like birds, or for some
        occasion – whaa – hear
        from an
        apartment – city

     not rowers – not written – seen – as being
     the bourgeoisie – from a
     mentality – not ours
     warriors – rowers – on the
     blue – sea

     – of – rowers
     men – on the –
     sea – ours – as not
     to return to that – more inactive
     taking a longer time – and
     blue

        men – with
        chains – in subway
        threat – who

are either inactive
as that

    the same – as – the
    action – rowers – on
    the blue – stowaway – being
    rowed to the other, freighter –
    not from that

not to return to
stowaway, falling in – when
being in the rowboat – going – to the other
freighter – or warriors – rowers – on
the – blue – ocean

man
with blue hair – some
shaved – ear
rings – nose ring
in subway – from
city – hear

man
with shaved hair
chains – come in
 – subway – as finding out
 – suffering – of them – or from – whether
 – city – that is

    not to return to
    the mood – theirs – of people who
    happened – to be strolling – embracing
    in light – when I was coming to them –
    again – as – struggling

which isn't – their, the couples
– seen – strolling – an
indication of anything – my – and wouldn't
or wasn't thought to
be such

not in that –
though it is –
and – held to it
to   man fast
                                asleep
                                in subway car
                                – out

        sun – driver
        of taxi hailing me – who's walking,
        I must look like – someone – who needs – or
        would – take – or wants
        a taxi

                                making jokes
                                out
                                 – not in that
                                view
                                though it is

—Crowd and not evening or light

crowd and
not evening or light

not scratched
on it

wading in the grass - it is like an elephant
trunk extended
on the trunk

wading on the grass — trunk of woman on the grass
in it

drunks who were homeless
and not excrete
something

not quite that
not quite that
not quite that

c. d. wright

INTRODUCTION

C. D. Wright has been critically associated with many movements in contemporary American poetry (Language writing, elliptical and analytic lyric, feminist), yet her work belongs wholly to no school or aesthetic. Wright's poetry in the last fifteen years has been markedly exploratory, characterized by an intellectual relationship to its roots in a southern storytelling heritage—resisting the strong narrative pull without utterly forgoing it. Her investigations of poetic language and structure/ formal invention expand the formal range of the postmodern lyric.

Wright has, as she describes in the interview that follows with poets Charles Jensen and Sarah Vap, "an affinity for the other arts." Like other poets included in this volume with strong musical and visual elements in their work (Kathleen Fraser, for example, and Mei-mei Berssenbrugge), she has investigated not only the dynamics of looking ("the one watching the other," as a prose poem in *Just*

Whistle: A Valentine puts it) but also the relationship between poetic and visual arts, using space on the page more actively and allowing verbal and visual languages to touch. Wright calls *Deepstep Come Shining*, her 1998 tour de force book-length sequence (a selection of which is included here), her "rapture." In that work, visual and linguistic elements interact, revising, commenting on each other, in a sustained series of untitled poems that alternate between prose and lyric poetry. We have added a bullet to designate separate poems.

Wright's formal explorations build on some of the constant elements in her work: muted, unassuming tone and spare understatement, witness, cataloging, and a willingness to juxtapose fierce, social indictment with lyric observation and an at-times elliptical narrative. In one of Wright's earliest collections, *Translations of the Gospel Back into Tongues* (1982), a woman who may be Billie Holiday is humming "Strange Fruit," Holiday's signature song about lynching. As Wright quotes from a poem that explores a representative moment of unconscious and casual racism, which she discusses in the interview that follows at some length, a southern librarian is asked whether the library has any "black literature," and she responds, "We used to have *Little Black Sambo*." Such critical moments hover without comment in the larger lyric structures like nested—and passing (pun intended)—remarks. Wright's poetic contemplation of social justice has produced recently a groundbreaking collaboration (with photographer Deborah Luster), *One Big Self: Prisoners of Louisiana* (2002), a collection of poems and photographs based on years of interviews with both male and female prisoners.

Wright grew up in Arkansas, where her father was a judge and her mother was a court reporter. She completed her B.A. at Memphis State University and attended one semester of law school, before dropping out to pursue a life as a poet. She is the author of ten volumes of poetry, among them *Steal Away: Selected and New Poems* (2002). She is the recipient of two National Endowment for the Arts Fellowships in Poetry, a Whiting Foundation Award, a Guggenheim Fellowship, and most recently, a MacArthur "Genius" Award (2004). From 1994 to 1999, she served as the State Poet of Rhode Island and is currently the Israel J. Kapstein Professor of English at Brown University.

This interview was conducted at the Arizona Biltmore in Phoenix, during Wright's week-long residency at Arizona State University, November 2003.

AN INTERVIEW WITH C. D. WRIGHT
by Sarah Vap and Charles Jensen

CHARLES JENSEN: You've said you came to poetry later in life, thinking initially that you wanted to work in the arts but unsure of where. Do you feel like these other artistic endeavors, like playing saxophone, which is one of the things I read you did—

C. D. WRIGHT: Yes, very badly—

CJ: [*Laughs*] Okay. Do those other arts maintain an active presence in your work?

CDW: No, what I have is an affinity for the other arts. I imbibe other arts, so I think very indirectly they're influential and sometimes more than indirectly. I might use something that seems sympathetic to a particular song or film or exhibition. Even the title of the selected and new poems, "Steal Away," comes from an old spiritual. It's not an especially informed borrowing, it's just the liking, liking some of the language, liking some of the movement. The visual arts are probably the most influential for me at this time.

CJ: So whatever sticks to you is what you take away?

CDW: That's right, yes, what doesn't steal away—being aware of musical qualities in other people's writing, then trying to find a quality akin to that music in my native tongue.

SARAH VAP: Speaking of that, what do you usually start with for a poem? For me, it's always an image, and I know that for some of the other poets here in Tempe it's probably more of a sound that they start with. Do you know, is there anything that consistently moves you into a poem?

CDW: I don't think so. I start with the words. In the past a title alone has been very generative for me. I still like to have a title, at least a working title, for an overall project, a place to touch, to keep me in contact with the field I'm working. *One Big Self* was Deborah Luster's title, which she took from a Terrence Malick film— he has only made three marvelous films. The Malick film was based on the book *The Thin Red Line* by James Jones, but the phrase, "one big self" is only in Malick's screenplay. I don't usually say this of films, but I would say that film is a kind of poem. We went back and forth between my text having a separate title and her titling the book *One Big Self* and then neither of us would let it go, you know, and the argument dissolved around, well, better to have one "big" title.

cj: What is it about Malick's film that you feel is poetic?

cdw: Maybe that it's elliptical. It's not a straightforward feature; it does not a documentary make. There is not a lot of language in it—the language feels very chosen, and somewhat artificial, but chosen and crucial to the construction of the film.

sv: If title is a place you return to during your process of writing a poem and you use it to bounce off of, what sort of way are the titles themselves composed for you? Or even the "King's Daughters" title—your titles are very distinct, and many of them seem to have elements of irony, like *Just Whistle: A Valentine*.

cdw: I think *Just Whistle* is the title in which irony is really present. And actually a lot of orphanages were called "King's Daughters." Old orphanages. Titles are just something for me to work, work against and work toward, and in my head the title is at the center of the poem, and once I know what the center is, I can go in any direction and for any period of time away from the center. This is how I imagine a good title functioning.

sv: What are you working on right now?

cdw: Debbie and I are scratching our way into a new project. I have a habit of talking about what I'm working on prematurely, dissipating the focus before it is achieved.

sv: I definitely connect to that. What was it like for you when you were starting out as a poet? I think that Charlie and I have a lot of questions along these lines because this is the place we're at. What were some of your early challenges or early successes?

cdw: The first remarkable fortune for me was meeting Frank Stanford, because I suddenly came face to face with a poet from my part of the world—a poet my age, who spoke my language, who knew what to do with it. That made a huge difference for me. Then writing was no longer an idyll. It also seemed as if he might take the whole thing, you know, because there's an encyclopedic scope to his work—I thought there would be nothing left for me, just, you know, the out-of-date preserves at the back of the pantry. [*Laughs.*] So coming face to face with Frank's work was also my first challenge, because I had to grow in the shadow of it, write through the shadow of it, partly because the work was big—big, romantic, funny, dark, anarchistic, intelligent. It was delta dirt rich. Also because the poet committed suicide in 1978, I had to write my way through that too, both on a personal level and as a poet, to get back, to begin again. Traces of Stanford are still visible in my work, and I honor them when they occur when I recognize them, but for several collections of poetry they were more than just traces—I was eclipsed in the shadow. But in the wake, the whole thing got serious for me. Then the dream and the responsibility were real. There really was such a poet and such a poetry, and then I knew what I was aspiring to.

CJ: You mean after you met him or after he died?

CDW: Actually before I met him but after I read his first book, *The Singing Knives*, and then after I met him and found out there were four or five more collections, little collections, and his tome, *The Battlefield Where the Moon Says I Love You*. I read everything.

SV: Did you ever consider leaving poetry since that seriousness took hold?

CDW: Yes, often and so forth. It used to be a stimulus for me to write the next book, to put the last book behind me. Because I work in the negative. By and by, I reached a point where I started feeling proud of some of my projects and I would think I could never get there again. I'm through, because I don't want to start becoming a bad imitator of myself or start doing things that are not as good as what I just did. So I'm always saying, "That's all she wrote." After about the last four books I feared I couldn't get there again, I couldn't hit that note again, or keep getting up on that one. Then something happens, and I go on. Also true I don't know what else to do. I'd like to do good deeds, but you need a lot of money to do really good deeds. And since I do not expect to be a minor saint, I will just be an inconsistently good egg and the best poet I can be.

CJ: That's really interesting because Sarah and I both feel a sense of awkwardness and maybe a little bit of embarrassment about our own past work.

SV: We're just now getting to the space where we can have relationships with past work because it exists.

CDW: That's not a bad position to be in.

CJ: But they're not nice relationships.

SV: They're sometimes awkward relationships. We were thinking that the scope of what you do is amazing, and project to project you often tackle completely new ideas, and so, if I'm as uncomfortable as I am with some of my past work and learning how to have relationships with it, I'm wondering how doing so many different kinds of things, how do you negotiate those relationships?

CDW: If I have a foothold or just even a toe, even a little toe into a new project, then I get excited all over again about the possibilities and start hoping that I can do it a little bit better this time. Or, at least if not better, I can do it differently enough that it will be compelling.

cj: Do you feel a sense of detachment from any of your old work? Like, "Who is this poet?"

cdw: The more work you have behind you, the more detached you get from it. You go through a point where you can't stand it because you're tired of it or you can't stand it because it seems so rudimentary, and then enough time passes and you make a peace with the fact that you were once young and wrecking-ball your way. [*Laughs.*] You can never be that innocent again, so you lose things; you lose the freshness that goes with the innocence and you lose some risk taking that sprang from ignorance.

sv: We were wondering about the way line works in some of your poems. I'm very drawn to how a poem looks on a page. It seems as if you pay a lot of attention to that in your poems, and even in some of them approach some of the questions that May Swenson was thinking about with the way a poem looks. She was definitely considering line in extreme, such as in her *Iconographs* she's thinking about lines all over the page. Could you talk a little bit about the way your poems look or what you do with line and materiality with your poems?

cdw: It's a good question. In terms of lineation I think I have a more developed sense of the visual field of the poem than I do of the aural field. Although I'm very conscious of the cadence and sounds inside the poem, internal to the poem, I don't have a strong enough sense of lineation. I notice that when I read aloud, I often read as a corrective to what is on the page. A more developed lineation is something for me to study because learning is always cool. I do, however, have a good eye for how I want people to read it with their eyes. But I have to coordinate those two to a higher degree.

sv: I love the way your poems look. In particular in *Deepstep Come Shining*, I mean—it seems as if the layout was done on a very intuitive level. Some of the poems start near the base of the page or just the text running on the side of some of the pages, the line breaks—each poem seems to really attempt something unique in terms of what it's doing, materially.

cdw: Some of that was the designer. I really scored there. When I turn a manuscript in, I provide them with a crude facsimile of how I want it to look. I don't want the designer to be slavish to my manuscript because I am not a graphic designer; I do not know how it should ultimately look. *Deepstep*'s "aboutness" concerns vision, so naturally everything regarding its look was very important to me, and the designer laid out the visual layers I had in mind. For instance, I don't think in my manuscript there were passages at the bottom of the page. I wasn't working the white space. And when I turned in the stenotype, these long ribbons of scattered type, of my mother's transcriptions of the prose passages, I put them on transparent sheets, sort of hoping they would print transparent overlays in the book. What the designer did was to reproduce the actual stenotype. Not only a less expensive but a far better design choice.

sv: It's such a beautiful book.

cdw: Which is why it's so much fun to work with Debbie Luster. The cover comes from another project we did together, a totally different project. I answered some questions this week for an art critic writing about Debbie's work. The art critic had stumbled upon Debbie's pictures because she saw *Deepstep Come Shining.*

cj: Yes, you mentioned earlier today that the cover comes from a series of poems, the *retablos,* which you did in collaboration with Deborah Luster. How did you arrive at the form of the *retablos?* Does it communicate directly with the work that Debbie did or was it really just your response to it?

cdw: The *retablo* poems were responses to individual images, which is the one and only time I ever worked that way, attempt particular poems to particular images.

cj: What I thought was interesting about it was that it is among the few times in your work I ever saw a foreign word creep in and play such a prominent role— like *chuparosa.*

cdw: We wanted to avoid mimicking or raiding a wonderful Mexican art form, so we had to do something that was ever so slightly related. I found the sound of the word *chuparosa* irresistible.

cj: Over the course of your work, what do you think has remained the most constant in your poetry? You do seem like a poet who tries to challenge herself as she goes along, and as you said, you try to leave projects as you go and move firmly ahead into the next project. Is there anything that continues along with you?

cdw: Who I am. I've always been pissed off. I've always been interested in matters of justice. I've always had a homemade, somewhat ugly relation to beauty. I've always used humor as my weapon. The latter I didn't learn to use in the poems for some years. I don't like funny poems per se. I also tend toward a fairly mean-sided humor. I use the humor as a wedge. Also, idiom. I've always loved idiom, wherever I've picked it up. Of the smatterings of French and Spanish that I know, the first things I learn are idiomatic—what gives the color to people's language, a kind of cultural specificity.

sv: Could you say a bit more about how your poems work politically? Perhaps they are political through their narrative—their act of witness, the idea of witness as a political act.

cj: Is representing people like the prisoners a political act?

sv: The poem where the child asks for black literature and they say that they used to have the book *Little Black Sambo*, it's just inserted and then walked away from in the poem. These gestures of what I would call witness seem very related to your political beliefs or your sense of justice or maybe things you're trying to remind people of. How are these moments working in your poetry? Are we supposed to understand them politically?

cdw: I know you can easily write bad politically motivated poetry. It's always problematic, knowing that I feel very strongly about things, that I think that if I leave that out, then what am I doing here in this language if I'm leaving that behind because the poetry authorities say it doesn't belong here. Someone once told me that politics is not a subject but an aspect. That was useful to me. There is nothing that politics doesn't enter into. And determining those parts of yourself that are so much a part of you—your humor, your political anger, your passions, everything that converges into your critique of life—this is where you rise up and where you go deep. Then you have to find the language; then the form that carries the whole body of thought and feeling forward. Some writers seem to find a form very early on in their writing. Some would say this is just repeating yourself, but I think the impulse is deeper. Once a form was plumbed for their language, they could say everything that needed saying, more or less pour it through that form providing they knew how to render it flexible, mutable. I felt whatever I took up next had to witch out its form. This little construction that I built for one book can't cross this body of words in couplets, and so on.

sv: It seems that a big element of your process is courage or belief in yourself, to be able to walk away from a form and be willing to leave something behind it, to see something brand new all over again and find its form. Is that what happens with each project that you take on?

CDW: Yes, but total reinvention is an illusion. You think you've totally left all the elements of an earlier work behind, but it's readily recognizable to other people. You are just reusing some parts and not others, creating room to come upon alternative measures.

SV: I am, along with being ADD, a little compulsive and so I list. I love lists, any list, and two things that seemed to be a long-term instinct in your work are the idea of listing and the idea of witness. I wonder if you think these observations are on or off and if you could say something about either of them?

CDW: There are lists and there are *lists*. Some are pretty banal; it's what's lodged within the banalities that makes the list worthwhile. But it is always a transparent exercise, the list. Best used sparingly.

SV: Witness seemed to be the other long-term instinct—the sort that comes through in *Deepstep Come Shining*—a lot of personae or voices, giving voice to people; there seems to be so much going on in the act of seeing.

CDW: I do not *feel* as if I were giving voice to people who don't have a voice, if that is what you mean by witness. I am simply interested in what is actually said. If I am the beneficiary of hearing something telling, then I will make a record of it. I could put what I have heard into other words, put it more artfully, but if I judge the outcome would not yield something more significant than what I heard spoken, I quote.

CJ: I think that we feel that it has to do with witnessing because those moments in your work lack judgment but they carry weight. In the poem about *Little Black Sambo* you present the snippet of this scene of two people talking, and there's no criticism about the people involved—it's just there. But as a reader, it's hard to walk away from that without making judgment ourselves about it. I think that you ask the reader to consider the evidence and then make a decision.

CDW: That seems a very judgmental poem to me now. I mean, it definitely conveys my attitude toward the librarian's remarks. At that time I was a summer Vista Volunteer in southern Arkansas, and I was gunning for every white person I talked to—I couldn't escape my own skin. I find what people say to be pretty interesting. It betrays their biases; putting it down in a certain context betrays my biases. I am not a neutral observer.

SV: In a previous interview, you said, and I love this, "There is at the very bone of collaborating a willingness to make mistakes—after all, no one is in total control" (Johnson 350). You were speaking of your work with Deborah Luster. I am so

---

drawn to this idea of mistake, and I have this suspicion that you mean something really beautiful by it. Could you speak about what you meant by mistake?

CDW: Giving up control *is* being willing to make mistakes, and it is indicative of a willingness to go places where you wouldn't have gone on your own. Braver in numbers. The mistake is often the very thing you were about to overlook; you slipped, pratfalled. Suddenly it was under your hand or at eye level. Aesthetically, it may be not so much in the making of a mistake, but in the letting one stand. I wrote a little bit about this in "The Box This Comes In." The authenticity of the box had as much to do with the pleasure as the gift of the box. The workmanship shows, and other things—someone laid a cigarette on the lid and left a scar; the lid doesn't close quite right. You feel contact with the one who made the box because you could see the flaw; you knew it wasn't made by machine. It calls up Brecht's alienation effect—where you are shown the bones of the drama—as in where you put tape on something so the audience can see you've taped this cloth back so it will fall a certain way. The tape is all-important. It's real.

CJ: Earlier when we looked through *One Big Self,* you said you were planning more collaborations. One thing I noticed about your work was that sound was really right there, the sounds of the words you choose and how they are spoken. Then there's this really fragmented imagery—in some poems it's really choppy and startling. Because of those images, I can understand your impulse to work with a visual artist, but how about an audio artist? Is there a collaboration that you'd like to do that would involve sound more than the visual?

CDW: We are going to add sound for exhibition purposes of *One Big Self.* The entire work is being acquired by the San Francisco MOMA but is, in the meantime, still scheduling exhibitions. Text in an exhibition space has limited appeal because most viewers will not stand in one spot and read for long. I run through exhibitions myself. Art long, life short. We will find a way to bring the text in that draws people further into the whole work.

CJ: So your part of the collaboration becomes the sound part of the exhibition?

CDW: Yes, for exhibition purposes. The book is there anyway, so the text has its time-honored forum. But for exhibiting collaboratively, we have to reinsert the voice.

SV: There's an essay we read recently by Donald Hall, and he says that anything that deeply affects us in our poetry is connected to something in childhood. I love this quotation: "Every present event that moves us deeply connects in our psyches with some thing (or things) in the past" (142). It seems as if you negotiate your childhood very differently in your poetry than most poets do, or negotiate the personal differently in your poetry. We were wondering if you could comment on that.

CDW: I was talking to Aishah Rahman, a playwright at Brown, talking about my son (because I am always talking about my son), and she said she hated being a child, that she couldn't wait to be an adult. Hearing this, I realized, I did not much like being a child either. I didn't make a good child. I always wanted to be an adult. So, I am not nostalgic about my childhood—not that it was a bad childhood, I just did not like who I was as a child.

CJ: I also felt that as I was growing up—I was a very independent child, and I think part of it is having siblings who are so distant from you in age and maybe being that last child; there are different expectations about what kind of involvements you need. Having older siblings, I felt like I wanted to be doing what they were doing instead of the things that everyone had already done.

CDW: My brother was older, and I thought he was amazing—he introduced me to Bob Dylan when he went off to college and I was still in elementary school; that shivered my timbers.

SV: I felt as a child so old—I never felt like a kid.

CDW: Yes, I think I was an elderly kid.

CJ: I think adopting the taste of your older sibling also makes a disconnect between you and other people your own age and pushes you outside that group.

CDW: It is not that I matured any faster than my peers—I didn't. But I remember people coming to my dorm room and talking to me as though I were wise, you know, when I had the sense of a turkey. [*Laughs.*] Nevertheless, I would dispense wisdom. Preposterous. And the personal—is not personal for long. After it's happened, and once you tell it, even if to a couple of friends, half-sober—you tell this thing that happened—it's no longer personal, it's a story. You are already embellishing, coloring, to make it more interesting, as you're telling it. Turning it into a story detaches you, period. And poetry breaks the story down much further than recounting.

SV: The word "uncategorizable" has been used about your work. But it seems as if people try to or would really like to categorize your work. There are elements in a few things that you've done that maybe look like you're thinking about the same questions that some Language poets are thinking about; a few things you've done that seem like you're thinking about the same questions narrative southern story-telling tradition would be thinking about, and so on. There's really something about your whole body of work that's simply unlike anyone else's. We were wondering if you could comment on that. Yesterday when [the poet] Caroline Berry asked you about her potentially being categorized as a "southern poet" or "woman poet," you said to her, "Don't sign up." I loved that, to not sign up to be a member of any group willingly. Maybe you could say something about that, if that seems correct or incorrect?

CDW: I think I would be a much lesser poet but for the Language poets. It would be laughable to dub me a Language poet, certainly by them. Those poets identified the burning issues in poetry, bonded around them, gave articulation to the issues, and created serious challenges to prevailing paradigms. Over time the Language poets became very independent of one another, and some became oppositional toward one another. But in its overall effect, Language poetry was energizing to the entire genre. I can't join a team. I always end up "riding the pines," as I heard a young benchwarmer say about his position on a baseball team. I have to go my own way, and I think it's very important that poets "follow the lights in their own skull." I don't think there is anything wrong with finding a temporary captain to follow, learn from, even imitate, as long as such adherence does not turn into your whole writing life or you'll never get to be grown up. Trends, tendencies, currencies, and to some degree "schools" of writing will form—you become sort of infected with wanting to sign on because it's exciting, it's new, and that's healthy. But it may not last you.

SV: Maybe along those lines, what is your poetic community? And I think this is maybe something Charlie and I or anyone who's graduating from an MFA program wonders about—the thought of leaving and having no poetic community again is sort of heartbreaking. I wonder how you've created yours, or what is yours?

CDW: Community is important for poets. I live in a town where there's a fairly active literary community—we do talk to each other and we socialize, but I have lived in a lot of places where there was no such critical mass, and then I did it through the mail. Or there was one person to talk to. When Forrest [Gander] and I lived in Eureka Springs, Arkansas, we worked in a tiny room with a frightful gas heater and worked at a partner desk, facing one another. It was fine. We work in different buildings now and couldn't do otherwise. It can be alienating to live where there's nobody to talk to, but again I would say, you only need one person to validate your undertakings.

sv: How do students figure into that community? Do they provide anything in terms of your poetry?

cdw: Sure. Students are good because you're curious about each other, and the students are always on the hunt, so they save you some of that trouble because they bring it right to your door, and you don't have to be stalking all the time anymore. Students are a source of renewal, and you're a source of fuel for them. There are times when it would be good to be student free, but I get those times, I can find those times. I would much rather spend my time talking to students than spending my time in meetings, even though I love my colleagues. But administrative meetings, I'd much rather spend my time with students. It's not the same as peer relationships; those get dispersed because people have to move around and find jobs and wrestle with their lives. When I first got out of school, I wasn't publishing or career bent, and I stayed on in Fayetteville, Arkansas, for several years after I graduated. A lot of people in town were cooking in the arts. It was a good time and a good place to "woodshed," that's what we called it, to stay and work and get some chops—and then within a year of Frank Stanford's death there was a diaspora, people went to the cities. Even for cruddy jobs, I mean, we didn't have "futures" as such, but a couple of friends went to New Orleans, a few more went to Houston; I went to San Francisco. People went to the cities because the college and the college town cannot sustain you forever. Frank can be seen as a catalyst for that sudden movement. More than likely his death was coincidental for everyone striking out. It was the next stage, toward learning how do you ground this in the world, in the other world, the nonuniversity world?

cj: Along with Frank, who would you say have been the most influential members of your own poetry community as you've progressed through your career? Who's really stuck with you or really played an important role at a particular time?

cdw: Forrest Gander's work of course. There are critical things we've learned from each other, and because we do not write the same way, we are very good "outside" readers of each other's work. There are many, many poets whose books are sourceworks for me—poetry by Evan S. Connell, Bernadette Mayer, George Oppen, Lorine Niedecker, Michael Ondaatje, Ron Silliman, David Antin, Arthur Sze, Mei-mei Berssenbrugge, James Agee, Keith and Rosmarie Waldrop, and a hundred and seventy or so others.

SV: Charlie loves any poem about Minneapolis because he's from Minneapolis. And I immediately connect with any poem or any poet from some place with a humungous mountain. Is it inevitable that a poet is going to have some sort of connection to particular geographic or elemental things? And another question related to that, is Lake Return a real place?

CDW: Is Lake Return a real place? No. Yes. [*Laughs.*] There is a hand painted, arrow-shaped sign for Lake Return that I pass every time I go to my hometown from the regional airport. I also pass a fighting-cock farm, and I have stopped there to take pictures. I can never believe what I am seeing. And there is another sign for Dogbranch Cemetery near Lake Return. Next time, I always say to myself, I am going to follow those turnoffs. Deepstep is a town for which I saw a sign. I was on a road trip with Deborah Luster. I think we were in Georgia. Later, Debbie told me she was looking in a Deepstep phone book and she noticed there were a lot of Veals in Deepstep, and I used that "a lot of Veals in Deepstep." I don't know where she picked up the directory. Probably from her husband Mike, a folklorist, a pack rat, book rat, record rat, et cetera rat. You mention anything about anything, and whoosh he hands it to you wrapped.

CJ: I think it's really interesting that places you don't go are the places that travel with you. And for us it's the places that we've left that are there.

CDW: The places you have left that really matter to you, they ghost you for a long time, and it's not until they stop ghosting you that they start worming their way into your work in a way that's anywhere near effective.

SV: That's so true. I didn't write about Montana when I lived there, but now I do. Did you write about Minneapolis when you lived there?

CJ: Not about the city itself.

SV: And I live in the desert and I don't write about it.

CDW: It might even be not until Minneapolis or Montana has let go of you that you really start getting it, until you quit thinking about it. Rosmarie Waldrop said (as was said to her), "Don't worry, your obsessions will always resemble you."

SV: What are your obsessions?

CDW: Justice. My boy. [*Laughs.*] Arkansas—less so. I think I'm writing my Arkansas, but I know it's not the place that I am trying to relive. It may be a life I am trying to rewrite. In a poem in *Tremble* I write, "Those dark Arkansas roads, that is the sound I'm after," quoting Miles Davis, who was from St. Louis, whose grandfather lived in Arkansas. Think about Miles Davis, the quintessential urban-cool musician, *that* was the sound he was after, the sound from his grandfather's farm—*Core* music. After you have been to every corner of the world and done everything else you could imagine.

sv: Do you use your dreams in your poems?

cdw: Once in a blue, blue moon. I seldom remember a dream. I know Bernadette Mayer has long kept dream logs, and her dreams figure into thousands of her lines.

cj: I feel like there's a lot of dream logic at work though, especially in terms of listing—one thing that leads you to the next thing, not related on the surface, but related because they make sense deep down. I think the same thing about fragmented imagery, too; the way you use it in your poetry is very dreamlike.

cdw: The connections are only clear to the writer, and so you just take this leap of faith that either that connection is accepted by the reader or they just think, "I'll just let that one go, I'll just pretend that never even happened."

sv: In the introduction to *Further Adventures with You*, you say, "Writing is a risk and a trust." We were wondering what you risk in your poetry and what you trust?

cdw: Well, I think I said the best of it always lies yonder or something like that. The only place I'm willing to risk everything and anything is on the page. Otherwise I am an unadulterated chicken shit. Trust is a good place to be in—that perfect, beautiful space. Getting there is the risk.

—*from* Deepstep Come Shining

In the seclusionary cool of the car the mind furnishes a high-
ceilinged room with a white piano. Seldom struck. Color
sensations. In which the piano floats on a black marble lake,
mute swan in a dark room. Beyond the windshield the land
claims saturate levels of green. Illuminating figures and
objects. Astonishing our earthliness. I was there. I know.

```
        H.    E          L
              E    R          S
T  P  H
T.    H     E                 S
      P    A          R    TS
K
      P  H  A              B  G
         W     O          PB
         H     O          L
               O       R
TK          E              T
      HR    EU
            EU       L
                  F  P  L  T
T. P                          T
S.    W   A              P  L
                         P
TW.    R
       P              E    PB
S                     EU       L   S
              A
S                     E    R
                      EU         S
                   F
       RA                 PB
TK          O             P  L.
T  P  H          U   P  L   S
            O
S           O
    PW      O             PB    S
                   U
K           O
      W              EU  PB
K      A             R  B
            O        R
         A
K           O             PB
S.    R    E    R       T
                EU    BL
                   F  P  L  T
T. P              U  R
TKPW             EUF
                 E    PB
   T. P  H  A          P  L   S
         P          E    PB
S.                  EU       L   D
                 O
              A
ST.     R   EU  PB  G
                 F
            R   EU    B    S
                   F  P  L  T
         W   A      FR       T.
S.    W  A          P  L
                    P
TK.   R
S.       A                    S
                      F  P  L  T
         K     O       P  L
      P  HR    EU
                   F  P  L  T
      WH A
```

Healers in these parts can make one WHOLE or deathly sick. If the swamp doctor pencils a series of random numbers on some bones you could win cash or a convertible. If your given name is penciled on a string of ribs. Whatever the swamp doctor says. Comply. Whether a believer or not. Remember Pascal shewed our very air has weight. It can be measured.

First visual memory: one of vagrant white splotches in a
clearing, a fat, diapered baby in a field of timothy chasing
another diapered bottom through the timothy. Last visual
memory: one of vagrant white splotches in a clearing, a fat,
diapered baby in a field of timothy chasing another diapered
bottom through the timothy. When it's mowed, and the
fodder's fresh. I remember. I was there. No other features
vex the view: Not the barn, the Gold Bond Medicated
Powder sign fading from its highway plane. The black dog
tearing after us. (*Night*, the black lab, the family's ecstatic.)
The specific lighting from the sky never impinged upon the
eye. Not individualized rocks. Split-rail fencing edged with
fleabane. The proximity of a neglected pitchfork. Never
never never . . .

.

There are enough signs. Of the lack of tenderness in the
world. And yet. And yet. All you have to do is ask. Anyone
here can extol the virtues of an onion. Where to get barbecue
minced, pulled, or chopped. The hour of the day they have
known the thorn of love.

.

In the ceaselessly decomposing smoke of a pool hall. Seven
green tables are racked under seven naked bulbs. The jukebox
in the din calls the man a blanketyblankblank. If not the exact
words the exact tenor. The plate glass casts glimpses of
everything that has ever happened. The genesis of direction
breaks and scatters.

.

In the living room of a saint. Watching television. With an
ice-cream headache. Assume lotus position. A documentary
in black and white. Of young men and women with AIDS.
Preparing to die. Communicating, wanting above all to be
able to communicate, the alpha and omega of all things
unfamiliar to us: Visions ringed with seas. The hatching of

supernovae. Deep music. Balanced between two tones. July
by lotuslight. Poetry at a standstill.

.

Early every evening she sits on the steps of her trailer. The
dirt yard raked. Caterpillar fording the furrows. Mercy,
Louise. If it wasn't hot hot hot. Cornlight. Eyes drink the
color and are refreshed. Images seen but not interpreted.
Thanks to her lovely twin trees the water she drew was cool.
Cool the water she drank from the pump.

.

Private-party love. By one sixty-watt bulb. And it be blue.
The cool produces a halation. The couple standing
underneath stir the floor as one. Some modeling on the side
of the face. When directly below the bulb. All other detail
dropped out. The eye gradually grows accustomed to this.
The music circling. Huge and dark. *Eroico furore*. Supremely
insane. Accelerated arpeggios. Unchain a cruel streak. Breath.
Nerve. Mind. Pain. Teeming tonal centers. D-state. Nocturnal
emission of sperm. Corner of Hamlet and Bridges. And in the
last year. They say he did. See angels. A synergism of cancer
and dwelling in musical extremis.

When the aim is to feel wholeness itself. She laid her hand on
the deeply furrowed bark, groping for the area of darkest
color. The trunks would be painted with a palette.
Solids would develop from the center outward. Avoiding any kind
of line. The body pressed against the trunk until she were
certain of being extinguished by the darkness. One achieves
a concealed drawing. Which is most like night.

First the light sinks to shadows. The shadows become
flooded with broad washes of dark. Watch. As the dark
comes entirely into its own. Watch. The light being eaten.
Devoured. Sonorous certainty of the dark. What sets the
hangers in a closet singing in unison. The light murdered,
that the truth become apparent.

```
ST  P  H          F  P  L  T
ST  P  H          F  P  L  T
 T  P          EU  R      S
                          T
       HR   EU            T
 S          EU   PB  G  S
  T      .O
 S    H  A                   D
         O                   S
              F  P  L  T
 T
 S    H  A                   D
         O                   S
      PW              B  G
 T P  HRAO                   D
                             D
      W
      PW  R  O               D
        W   A     R  B
                             S
              F
 TK      A    R  B  G
              F  P  L  T
      W  A    R  B
              F  P  L  T
         A              S
                        T
 TK      A    R  B  G
  K      O       P  L  S
          E   PB
 T            EU  R
      HR   EU
 T P  H
 T       O              TS
         O
      PB
              F  P  L  T
      W  A    R  B
              F  P  L  T
 T
      HR   EU        T
                 B  G
         E          T
         E   PB
              F  P  L  T
 TK           E
 S    R  O  U  R         D
              F  R  L  T
 S       A
 T P  H  O    R
              U         S
 S       E    R    T
         EU
              F         T
 TK      A    R  B  G
              F  P  L  T
      W  A
 S       E          TS
                    T
      H  A    PB  G
         E  R         S
```

Branches drop without warning. Clouds accumulate around a
kind of idea akin to sonic weight. Progressive darkness. 250
miles offshore with winds at 105 MPH, Bertha turns inland.
Multitudes of windows crossed with masking tape.
Evacuation mandatory in the low-lying areas. Contrasts
annihilated. Concealing loneliness and fear. As when the lens
opening is too small. Taken too late. Or too early.
Uncharacteristic silence loading the car. Worry over
maundering. Hunger over worry. Tranquilized with a private
jukebox in formicalight. Endless refills. Pigs-in-the-blanket-
and-grits-on-the-side time. Beats the bejesus out of Bertha's
maw. Now do you know where we are. My over-air-
conditioned-and-caffeinated love.

.

The scrape of chairs on a stone floor. A sack of birds escaped
in the house. Fleshy, velvety dampness. Panic. Time lapse. Silence.
That they think only of sight while they chew. Slowly the hand
unwraps the bandages. Until the night shuts like a door. And
the light slams from his face. Interrupting the flow of stimuli.
It is all whiteness, he says, even this sightlessness.

.

Don't touch that dial. Here's the rest of the story: These three
ladies they had been into all manner of wrongdoing. They
were wearing the evil one's varsity jacket. They were hot for
god and they were on fire. That night they were thrown to
the ground under the power. That night the glory cloud filled
the church. The prayer line stayed open that night. A real
hard light, sharp, cold as a nail, split right through the boards.
Angels went to banging around in the rafters like a sackful of
birds. We'll pick up at the next chapter, dearly beloveds . . .

In the hither world I lead you willingly along the light-bearing
paths. In the hither world I offer a once-and-for-all thing,
opaque and revelatory, ceaselessly burning. Anyone who has
ever been through a fire knows how devastating it can be.
The furniture lost, books collected over thirty years, the
mother's white piano. I was there. I know.

```
        PW  A        R   G
    .    P  A                TS
                   F  P  L  T
  T  P  H                   T
         H      E U          T
                E   R
         W   O      R   L   D
                E U
             O     F R
         A
         W   O         P B   S
         A O  E U
                      P B
         A O  E U
  T  P       O     R
         A O  E U
         A               L
  T    H      E U
                  R  B  G  S
         O
    P    A               B  G
         A               P B

         R     L  F
               E
      H R A
  T          O     R
             E U
                   R  B  G  S
  S            E             S
       H R     E             S
       H R     E U
  P W          U  R P B  G
                   F  P  L  T
  T  P  H      E U
         W   O         P B
         H   O               S
              F R  B
  T     H R   U
         A
  T  P        E U  R
  T  P  H  O                 S
         H   O   U
  T K         E  F
  S T    A                 T
                           G
  . T
    K                 B
                   F  P  L  T
  T
  T  P         U  R P B
  T            U  R
       H R  O                S
                   R  B  G  S
       P W   A O       B  G  S
    K  H R     E       B  G  S  D
         O    F R
  T    H      E U  R        T
              E U
    K  W  R   E   R      . S
                   R  B  G  S
  T
```

barbara guest
and kathleen fraser

INTRODUCTION

Barbara Guest has steadily emerged in the past fifty years as one of the most important experimental American women poets of the latter half of the twentieth century. The joint interview with Kathleen Fraser, conducted by poet-critics Elisabeth A. Frost and Cynthia Hogue, comprises one of the few interviews Guest has given during her long career, and it is all the more significant for its being the last she was able to give before a debilitating stroke in 2004.

Guest grew up in California, attending the University of California at Berkeley before moving to New York in the early 1940s. There, she soon met Frank O'Hara, and along with James Schuyler and John Ashbery, became known in the 1950s as a member of the New York School of poetry. These poets took witty issue with confessional and closed-form New Critical aesthetics then dominating poetry. While working as a writer for *Art News* magazine, Guest began to craft the distinct work for which she has become renowned: abstractly visual (what Fraser aptly calls a "painterly witness"[1]), nonlinear, and conceptually musical. In her final works, Guest continued to take poetic risks, exploring the possibilities of syntactic openness, assemblage of lyrically intense fragments and perspectives, and improvisation. She importantly collaborated as well with such women artists as Grace Hartigan and Mary Abbott.[2]

Like that of the other New York School poets, Guest's poetry was deeply influenced by the abstract expressionist and action painters of the 1950s and 1960s (especially Willem de Kooning, Jackson Pollack, and Larry Rivers), as well as by surrealist poetry. In *Forces of Imagination*, Guest describes her feeling of coming of age "in the shadow of surrealism," reading the French poets Apollinaire, Éluard, Valéry, and Breton: "[T]here was no recognized separation between the arts. . . . One could never again look at poetry as a locked kingdom. Poetry extended vertically, as well as horizontally. Never was it motionless[.] . . . Assisting in this poetic mobility would be an associative art within whose eye the poet might gaze . . . for a glowing impersonal empathy." Guest learned from the Surrealists how to make a poem move in ways other than by linear narrative: by introducing a mobile, associative element into the poem, a sense of the "magical" originating force from which the poem derived, and a blurring of boundaries among the poetic, musical, and visual (even plastic) arts. Although the romanticized image of Woman was foundational to the surrealist project—as Rachel Blau DuPlessis observes, its "marvelous" was decidedly gendered—it afforded Guest the all-important intellectual "liberation" of "breaking rules."[3] But as Guest herself wryly recalls of the gender dynamic in the heady artistic world in which she moved in her youth, she was redolently aware of how women had to negotiate being both "object" and peer to their male contemporaries, a difficult balance at best.

Guest's many books include the novel *Seeking Air* (1978), a recently reissued biography of H.D., *Herself Defined: The Poet H.D. and Her World* (1984), and twenty-six collections of poetry, among them *The Red Gaze* (2005), *Miniatures and Other Poems* (2002), *Selected Poems* (1995), *Defensive Rapture* (1993), *Fair Realism* (1989), and *Türler Losses* (1979). Her honors include the 1999 Robert Frost Medal for Distinguished Lifetime Achievement from the Poetry Society of America. She lived in Berkeley with her daughter, Hadley, until her death in 2006.

Kathleen Fraser has been recognized in the last three decades as a writer whose poetry, criticism, and crucial contribution as founding editor of a major avant-garde feminist journal have been a driving force in defining the project of women's innovative poetry in North America in the postmodern era of the last century. During the late 1970s and early 1980s, Fraser increasingly noted the exclusion of most experimental women poets from anthologies and serious critical treatments. In 1983, seeking to create a place for women poets writing outside the dicta of both second-wave feminist poetry and the inheritors of male-centered modernism, Fraser founded the groundbreaking journal *HOW(ever)*. In its seven years as a paper journal, *HOW(ever)* became an important forum for innovative women poets, critics, and scholars interested in modernist/postmodernist directions in women's poetry in the twentieth century. Reclaiming an obscured tradition of women writers engaged in language experimentation (Gertrude Stein, H.D., Lorine Niedecker, Mina Loy, and Guest, among others), the women who published their work in *HOW(ever)* conducted extensive investigations of the relationship of language to gendered experience. It was Fraser's objective that the theoretical interest in poststructuralist literary problems would carry over into the investigation of current poetic practice and its intentions.[4]

Fraser grew up in Oklahoma, Colorado, and California. After moving to New York (a "smaller New York," as she recalls in this interview) for a career in magazine writing, she was soon on the poetry scene, publishing her work in the *Nation*, *Poetry*, the *New Yorker*, the *Hudson Review*, and many small-press journals associated with Black Mountain and New York School poets. Among her honors are an NEA Young Writers Discovery Award, a National Endowment for the Arts Fellowship in poetry, and a Guggenheim Fellowship. In 1972, Fraser returned to California to direct the Poetry Center at San Francisco State University, where she founded the American Poetry Archives. She has published seventeen books, including *Each Next* (1980), *Something (even human voices) in the foreground, a lake* (1984), *Notes preceding trust* (1987), *When new time folds up* (1993), *WING* (1995), *il cuore = the heart: Selected Poems, 1970–1995* (1997), and *Discrete categories forced into coupling* (2004). Important critical essays by Fraser that articulate approaches to understanding avant-garde women poets have been collected in *Translating the Unspeakable: Poetry and the Innovative Necessity* (2000).

Recognized as a major poet with a significant body of work, Fraser is known for her reinvention of inherited language structures, sometimes playfully, always attentively, listening for "the mysteries and 'mind' of language to come forward and resonate more fully," as she puts it in "The Tradition of Marginality" (*Translat-*

ing 33). In this interview, Fraser specifically discusses the quality of attention to language's mysteries that she brought to bear while writing one of her most significant serial-assemblage pieces, "Etruscan Pages." She characterizes a more recent poetic project as "a kind of action-collaging, . . . using my own already written text instead of found material"—giving readers insight into the exploratory poetic process that she continues to investigate and to further. Engaged in a visual as well as feminist poetics, Fraser offers in her work ways to think through how formal strategies interact with lived experience, encouraging us to consider the engagement with formal structures not just as a method of representation in poetry but as a mode of experience.

The following conversation/interview with Kathleen Fraser and Barbara Guest took place on a brilliant fall day over four intensive hours at Guest's home on October 16, 2003.

AN INTERVIEW WITH BARBARA GUEST AND KATHLEEN FRASER
by Elisabeth A. Frost and Cynthia Hogue

CYNTHIA HOGUE: Elisabeth and I have looked forward with great excitement to this occasion, which brings together for a conversation two women poets with avant-garde East and West Coast associations, both of you with a deep interest in the visual arts, both of you beginning your distinguished writing careers in a New York that has certainly disappeared. How was it to begin developing as poets so wonderfully and richly in touch with the other arts?

BARBARA GUEST: New York then was a mixture of arts. And if you walked down the street you were liable to bump into other artists. Everything was new to me. New York was so new and so modern. I only knew one person to contact when I arrived in New York. I immediately got pneumonia, and she rushed to my hotel room and said, "You're coming home with me." We had never met. New York had an openness that only major cities have. And they all have it. But when I first arrived there, it was the war, and many refugees were in New York.[5] We were saved by these artists. We were taught so many things. All this wisdom that came over. I met many people then who had come here to escape Hitler.

CH: This was the early to mid forties? America is in the war and the refugees are arriving, the artists, gathering in New York?

BG: Yes, and they were all out at midnight to get the newspaper. I had never known people who rushed to get a newspaper at midnight. And then they met each other on the corner of Eighth Street [Greenwich Village] and talked. There you saw all these famous men who had escaped. There was a different idea of time during the war, especially for the Europeans. They talked and talked into the night. And that was an indication of what they were going through.

KATHLEEN FRASER: That hunger for news and the need to discuss it connects with my sense of many parts of Europe still today—in cities and villages, particularly in France and Italy, where I've spent more of my time. The café is so much a part of daily life, a source of primary information, where people are trying to figure out what's going on politically and socially, often when it comes to things that may have an impact on their survival. It's really different. What you're describing is something that wasn't really a part of American life until these immigrants arrived in New York, don't you think?

BG: It took a great city. Because they had come from great cities.

CH: How were they wise?

BG: Well, for one thing, they read the newspaper. I had never known anybody who read newspapers all day long. Or talked as much as they about events. It was all "foreign-speak" to me, in a way. You'd meet with one person and then another person wanted to meet you. In a sense, well, I was an object. I mean, they really wanted to see a young American woman.

KF: In Europe, women would seldom have been out on the street so late—or part of such discussions—unless invited along with their companion as part of a very particular group. [addressing Guest] Tom Hess's magazine [Art News] was a rather unusual collaboration, wasn't it, so many poets doing that much art writing and thinking about contemporary art? I was wondering how you began there, and how much of your time you spent doing that work, and if they gave you regular assignments?

BG: Yes, they did. But, by then we're in another year, another era. And the war is over. Tom wrote to me and others [John Ashbery and Frank O'Hara], and he hired us because he said he wanted some poets. Things aren't done that way now so you can't imagine it. I can't either! But it instilled in me this tremendous affection for the arts.

CH: Barbara, you said in your book *Forces of Imagination* that growing up under the shadow of the surrealists opened your eyes to a different way of writing and a different way of seeing. As you put it, it gave you "an associative art within whose eyes you were able to gaze" at the writing of the poetry. You talk about surrealism as "unlocking the kingdom of poetry" in the 1950s. We wondered if you could talk a bit about what that was like, the poetry that you found you could unlock through this introduction?

BG: It's curious. I never believed that I'd be writing surrealism today, because it was a foreign subject.

KF [*addressing Guest*]: It's your term "associative work" that really seems most to pertain or carry through, rather than what we tend to attribute to the pro forma European surrealist vision. The *associative* art strikes me powerfully in your work.

ELISABETH FROST: The other aspect of that which is so interesting, in light of what has happened in the years since, is this idea of unlocking something that was too locked up among the writers or the poets.

BG: Yes, I was talking recently about why I left the university and went to a junior college. Because I wasn't learning anything [at UCLA] because they had these rigid rules and wouldn't teach modern poetry. I wanted to know about a poet, and nobody knew him at the university. He was really unique, the opening of modern poetry. He was T. S. Eliot. I had never seen poetry that way. And nobody could tell me about it. So I thought, I'll go to the junior college and see about that. And sure enough, I went in the classroom and I asked, and the professor told me all about T. S. Eliot. I said, "How do you know about him?" He said, "Oh, my wife's a poet." It was that wonderful unfamiliarity [of Eliot's language] that changes everything.[6]

KF: *Forces* demonstrates a similar immediacy, writing not shaped by an academic demand but rather from your more immediate connection to the subjects you were thinking about. I experienced a similar frustration to yours in what I was *not* getting from my formal education in literature. I attended a very good liberal arts school in southern California [Occidental] but couldn't find any courses in modernist or contemporary poetry. Actually, the subjects I was genuinely excited about were my painting and sculpture classes, and the sciences. I'd spend hours alone, or with one other person, working silently in the art studio with clay or paint. There were two records they piped in repeatedly over the loudspeaker system in the Arts building—Stravinsky's "Rite of Spring" and Vivaldi's "Four Seasons." We got sick of them, but they seemed to produce a kind of work-zone atmosphere.

Eventually I began reading the prescribed books for an English literature major and uneasily noting the attitudes one was supposed to adopt toward specific genres and texts, depending on the views and training of your professors. There were no living authors, no modernists or French symbolists on our reading lists, but a few exciting poets began sneaking into my reading through my friends' enthusiasms. My friends gave me T. S. Eliot's *Collected Works* for my birthday my senior year, as well as Garcia Lorca's *Selected Poems*, W. C. Williams's *Asphodel, That Greeny Flower*, and e. e. cummings's *Six Non-Lectures*.

BG: That's a *very* cummings work.

KF: It is. I remember how thrilled I was with that book. I'd already discovered poems of his hanging like little scrolls on the wall of a new friend's room. His eccentric syntax and inventive page space and peculiar punctuation immediately intrigued me in a way that didn't happen in my seminars. All of this *unofficial* writing was distracting me from what we were exposed to in the classroom. I believe my idea of moving to New York City began at that point; I knew I wanted to be where I imagined all the really modern artists and writers were living and working.

EF: So how did you ever end up finding the New York School poets?

KF: Well, soon after I moved to New York, I signed up for a summer workshop with the poet Daisy Alden (thinking to study with a woman). But she became ill, so Kenneth Koch was called in to take her place. It was through that workshop that I met second-generation New York School poets Tony Towle, Alan Kaplan, and James Brodey and, later, Joseph Ceravolo and Hannah Weiner. Hannah and I were the only visible "second-generation" women poets around the New York School scene at that time. This was several years before Anne Waldman, Bernadette Mayer, and Maureen Owen appeared as a three-way force at the St. Marks Poetry Project, where we all hung out [Alice Notley soon joined this trio; see interview in this volume (—ed.)].

Kenneth taught a night class at the New School, which I wanted to take after that summer workshop sample. He gave us provocative assignments that unlocked a lot of silly stuff in me. I loved discovering that poetic language could include humor. Kenneth's teaching stance was something like that of an improvisational stand-up comedian, but he could be publicly nasty when he didn't like a student's work. I'd go home from his classes confused by his harsh mockery of some beginning poet's attempted assignment that he found dull and predictable. But at the same time I was dying to begin experimenting with his outrageous ideas for opening up the poem. What he thought was most interesting was how you put language together. Good poetry for him always involved surprise.

BG: He was a very good poet.

KF: Well, he wasn't my favorite poet, but he was a very generative teacher. I was completely intrigued and inspired by his teaching.

CH [*addressing both Guest and Fraser*]: Did it feel like there was the space for you as women poets in this very rich artistic scene in New York, to grow and explore and experiment? You had a kind of confidence, it sounds to me, that gave you the courage to begin to expand, to transfer some of the methods of the surrealist and abstract expressionist artists into the poetry. How did this start?

BG: Well, everyone was so close. We were close to the artists, and they were close to the poets. I think that the closeness of the poets and the artists was very, very significant, because we were exchanging ideas all the time. We knew each other's work.

KF: I remember reading with friends from the New School classes, in one of the coffee houses where the poets hung out, and noticing that the painters whom we admired were actually coming to hear our work. To find myself in the company of New York School painters was great fun and completely inspiring, feeling this exchange of edgy, unpredictable work and seeing that they took our words as seriously as we did their painting.

CH: Did Kenneth introduce you to Barbara?

KF: No, the person who set up my introduction to Barbara was Frank O'Hara's roommate [and partner, the artist], Joe Le Sueur, a very kind person. One night, we were at a big party in someone's loft, and Frank said to me, "You know who you have to meet? You have to meet Barbara Guest." So he went off to look for her, but it turned out she wasn't there that night. Joe decided that I should meet her anyway.

CH: Why did he think you should meet Barbara?

KF: Probably because she was *the* female poet figure in their group and maybe because of our common interest in painting. I'd met a number of the guys—first- and second-generation poets—and had gone to readings and gallery openings with them. I think Joe just felt that Barbara and I might enjoy talking with each other, but as much as I liked the idea, I was too shy to make any contact. Something happened, because about a month later, she wrote me a very friendly note and invited me to come for a visit—she was living uptown in a big apartment with her husband, Trumbull—and I remember being very thrilled that an older, established poet would take the time to talk with someone just starting out. I was worried that I wouldn't appear sufficiently sophisticated, even though I was reading fiendishly and looking at paintings during all my lunch hours. But of course a conversation with Barbara cut right through all that.

CH: What was striking about Barbara's work when you first encountered it?

KF: That in no way was it "obvious" or like anything I'd ever read. The poems continuously invited me into her very precise and shifting sense of the mystery of "the real"—very exact and abstract relations, without telling one what to think. No *interpretation*. There was always a word lure suggesting something more—in the way that a small area of a painting may lead you into the larger work. I was always intrigued. *Always*. But I did not think, "I want to write like this," for Barbara was so clearly an original. It was more that her work put me in touch with the intriguing possibility of discovering my own peculiar diction, as well as attracting me to a far more interesting reading/writing agenda than I'd been presented with up to that time. Something in her work pulled me forward, the way a particular music pulls you to it. There was also the intriguing work of my most admired peer and friend, Joe [Joseph] Ceravolo, who died way too young and whose poems deserve to be noted here even though his work has not yet been sufficiently studied.

CH: Some of the other first-generation New York poets do seem so much more direct, but your work [*addressing Guest*] has been so evocative from the first, and that indirectness that Kathleen was talking about *is* so mysterious. Did you feel that you knew what you were doing from the beginning or did it feel like a kind of exploring?

BG: I was fortunate in that I was able to rent an apartment away from my home as a writing studio, where I could really go inside. A friend rented it for me, and I think that the separation was crucial, that I was able to get away to write. Because I never wrote at home.

CH: A room of one's own.

KF: Oh, and full of paintings by your friends. It was so beautiful!

BG: It looked out over the East River. It was nice, and I had it for quite a while. And I was able to write so much there. I wrote the H.D. book there [*Herself*

Defined]. I was pretty worn out by that book. I really was. I just broke down. The place that I was in had a little walk around it, and I would walk out there on the terrace.

KF: That terrace appears in *Seeking Air* [Guest's novel], doesn't it?

BG: Yes, that particular place made me want to write prose. I do think you have to get away. I think it's the real solution. The way a painter goes into the studio to work.

KF: I agree. I wish that luxury—which is really a necessity—could be built into more of our lives. I had the experience for the first time, two summers ago, of being away from home, in a little cabin on a cove in Maine, living and working alone for a month, learning to take that time to read and write without needing to accommodate the habitual expectations of the daily. Last summer, I shared a house with my sister—only for a week—on the Oregon coast, where we could both assume our own independent schedules during the day but share evening meals and a walk on the beach. I got more work done in those seven days than in a period of months at home—particularly the kind of revision work that takes (for me) a fierce, unbroken concentration. I worked in a very ordinary room. It had a desk and a big wooden chair on which I had to stack pillows to make it tall enough for me to write at my laptop. But this inconvenience was nothing, given the heaven of not having to think about meals and telephone calls. To be there with only the goal of writing, reading, and walking made all the difference.

EF: Cynthia just mentioned Woolf's famous phrase, and I wonder whether it remains particularly urgent for women—who are often surrounded by others' domestic needs—to have the space.

CH: And to dare to have that courage, isn't it, to separate oneself.

BG: Yes, because you cease being a good mother. Automatically. I was fortunate to have had somebody to be there, with the children in the apartment. But it certainly separates you from home. At first, I did try to write at home. I remember there was an extra room, and I tried to write at home. But the work was just awful.

CH: Because your concentration kept getting interrupted?

BG: Yes. And also I didn't want anything around me, and I still don't. I didn't want anything that brought congestion.

EF: Do you have a space here now?

BG: I have that room now. It's small, but I've written a lot of books in it. I like it small.

CH: You've brought up your H.D. biography and mentioned that your first husband told you that you reminded him of H.D. What made you decide to write a biography on H.D.? What is your connection to her work?

BG: I always loved her poetry. And I had to really hunt for it, because it wasn't readily available. But I found it. I thought she was completely marvelous.

EF: Was it important for your own work?

BG: I read her thoroughly when I was a young poet. And I was impressed by the meter and the precision of her images—oh, there were all sorts of things that I liked in her work.

KF: Was she being presented as an *imagiste*? Represented by that particular group of her earlier poems, when you read her? That is to say, did your reading include works like *Trilogy* or the later epics?

BG: No, no. I read them all. She's a good poet, and she gets better all the time. I went to see Bryher in Switzerland. I telephoned her and went over. I went back three times, and all three times Bryher said, "Oh, I have a new stove I want to show to you." So we had to go down in the cellar each time and look at the stove. This woman had millions. She had never cooked or kept house.

KF: But she was so happy with her new stove! [*Everyone laughs.*]

Did you call her because you were thinking about writing the H.D. book?

BG: No, she intrigued me in her own right. She was extremely intelligent. In spite of all that money, which confused her, she was very, very intelligent. And she saved H.D.'s life.

CH: Did "Türler Losses" come out of those trips to Switzerland? Because although one can't see Bryher in that series, the kind of word play, the kind of unpacking of the idioms that you do in that poem, in such witty and such incredibly moving ways by the end, resonates with H.D.'s work.

BG: Yes, that poem did come out of those trips. And I did drop the watch.

EF: Did the poem develop over time? You lost two watches, made three trips to Switzerland.

CH: Yes, I said to Beth, "I bet there's a literal context to this poem. I bet she lost the watches, the Türler watches, and had to buy a couple of Timexes." [*Everyone laughs.*]

EF: I love when the Timex comes in.

CH: The poem is so witty about loss, and toward the end so beautiful:

my image against your shoulder, the homespun
logic of our twosomeness, a fabric time
will displace the threads, a shrivel here,
there a stain, the rotting commences like lanes
of traffic hurtling into air as the sun comes down.

It moves out of the word play into this incredible intensity of emotion there.

BG: I remember that was a very haunted house, where I wrote that poem [in Bridgehampton, Long Island]. There was something there. It was an old farm-house.

EF: You've spoken about how important that house was for you, as a writing space.

BG [*reading the end of "Türler Losses"*]: "A wrist for every watch / releasing doves // In the blown haze / a search for crystal // Broken glass."

CH: The layerings of time in this poem, of course, remind me of H.D.'s method of the palimpsest that you've written about, Kathleen.

KF: Yes, but discovered in such a different way—Barbara's references aren't so intentionally "instructive" as H.D.'s.

CH [*addressing Kathleen*]: It seems to me as though temporal "layerings" or time shifts have been a chosen construction in your own work—I'm thinking of your enjambment of time frames.

KF: I think that's true, but I can't necessarily claim it as a preexisting inten-tion—at least not in every case. In this particular context, I'm thinking of a poem I wrote—"Electric railway, 1922, two women"—inspired by the railway poster that illustrates the jacket of Barbara's first edition of *Herself Defined*, that links or com-presses the "embodied" experience of being female through five generations of women writers. In this poem two women are riding inside the safety and comfort of a first-class compartment on a train, looking out at the passing "film" of moun-tains curving around a lake, with a passenger boat coming into the harbor.

My original interest—beginning the poem inside this frame—wasn't pursued as a "method" but felt more like an impulse to connect with a deceptively simple scene and the feeling of impending violation that it invited me to recognize. The poster's code of physical luxury and its scenic lure of the unknown led to a set of unplanned perceptions and memories (a palimpsest, if you will) recalled by the passing view, but finally linking five women writers traveling on this "same" journey—in physical and mental time layers—each preceding image unfolding to and commenting on the others: H.D., Bryher, Barbara, myself, and Susan Gevirtz [poet and Fraser's close friend], who was traveling alone in unfamiliar territory during the time I was working on that poem. I was feeling very aware of the ambiguous position of a woman who wants to travel independently yet who appears, by her very solitariness, to be a vulnerable target.

I began with what you see in the poster, two women—Bryher and H.D., in my imagining of it—returning home from Italy to Switzerland. I thought of them pronouncing Italian—the very same words I'd struggled with, myself, on a similar train ride in another layer of time. That, in turn, invoked the present moment, in which travel posed a less protected and more vulnerable reality:

Cielo magnifico!
    "Az-zu-ro"
    "Ce-les-te"
    [. . .]
A life is out the window and you are pulled through it.
All you worry about diminishes you. At every moment
a body is being violated,
although the mahogany window frame was designed for safety
when you chose this method of seeing.

BG: Yes, the poster was meant to represent H.D. and Bryher (but it wasn't they in real life).

KF: But in a way, that doesn't matter since we keep erasing and adding in slightly different permutations of human alarm and pleasure when we rewrite our version of a story.

EF: As in H.D.'s own use of the palimpsest—that juxtaposing of past texts and voices, the uncovering of them, sometimes mourning the absence of them. I'm thinking of what you [*addressing Fraser*] do in "Etruscan Pages," for example.

KF: There are certainly ghosts and presences "layering" those Etruscan burial sites.[7] Being among them marked one of the few times I'd ever felt truly transported outside of "normal" time. I'm not sure that I would have been available to the resonance of the *necropoli*—or the Etruscan culture, in general, that catalyzed the poem—without having read H.D. years before and having felt connected to her visionary experience within the context of Egyptian hieroglyph and artifact. Clearly, a larger sensing was available. Once there, I didn't want to talk—nor to talk about that interlude when we left the Maremma coast to return to Rome. The contact was too powerful and I had no language for it.

EF: How did you happen to go there? Did you have a preconceived idea that those sites would be important to you?

KF: Actually, my friend was due to visit, so we used that opportunity to make the journey with her to the tomb sites at Norchia, Tarquinia, and Vulci—because I knew she'd be interested in them, but also with a bit of the feeling of an intellectual obligation, these sites being part of Italian history, archaeology, et cetera. But very soon after we got there, I felt infected by something unexpected and very powerful. Perhaps it was the fact that Norchia was not written about in the guidebooks and hadn't been officially groomed as an archaeological site for tourists, as Tarquinia had. I didn't believe I'd ever be able to write anything out of the experience; it was just too nonverbal. But its effects wouldn't leave me.

I had this sense of a profound loss, a deep sadness for everything that had once existed there. The Etruscans had been such a living and erotic and celebratory culture. I'm sure that the experience of being in those burial grounds with much-loved friends heightened my awareness of the fragility and preciousness of being alive and of having that life taken from me.

CH: Interesting that you experienced the catalyzing events of the poem physiologically, that you experienced it at a level of heightened consciousness. I think of those lines of H.D.'s about "infectious ecstasy."

KF: It would not let me be. During the period of writing the first sections, I had two different dreams, both recounted in the poem. In the first dream, I'm trying to understand how to get from "this world" to "the other." I notice that there are layers of white cloth around me and explain to Susan that you just keep wrapping yourself in them until you get from one world to the other. In the second dream, two nights later, I was with my friend Norma [Cole]—a painter and writer—who invited me, in the dream, to work with her on a lithographic project, clearly a metaphoric parallel to the Etruscans' habit of scratching their names into the burial tombstones and painting them with red and black dyes. In the dream, I began scratching into a lithographic stone with my red and black ink. It was clearly about assembling evidence, presence—literal, psychic, and historic—and about finding my own writing implement to do my work, but in collaboration with a friend, to discover that there is, in fact, an evolving being inside us. Breathing.

EF: That's such a wonderful visual image you write of in the poem, the descent to the tombs! It's so graphic, that sense of many levels of time being present as you climbed down to find the antique burial site, and the loss of the coherency of that language.

KF: Yes, the loss of coherency, and yet, somehow—in the way we were talking about paintings or when I was speaking about the beckoning of Barbara's mysterious language—I did feel a similar powerful connection to the Etruscan language and its alphabet. When we returned to Rome, I went back to revisit the Etruscan collection at the *Villa Giulia*, where there are displayed two beaten-gold tablets covered with beautiful Etruscan letters and words pressed into the thin gold. There was something so palpable also about the ancient letters carved into the porous stone lids of their burial vaults (coffins). After seeing their alphabet, I began to draw my own letters as a kind of code and to insert handwritten Etruscan words and images into the spaces of the poem text I was still working on. I wanted their graphic presence.

EF: Talk about palimpsest! Barbara, that image seems a central one for you, too, of the notion of palimpsest, from H.D. Does it come up consciously in your writing, that you are engaging with a layering of voices, of languages?

BG: Yes. And no.

CH: Sometimes you move into a very visual, almost "cubist" moment in your poems, that shift of perspective. Sometimes they're so associative that, as a reader, I have the experience of trying to reinvent the original associations to follow the poem. To take an example, "The Rose Marble Table" opens with the shape of the shadows:

Adoptive day replenished by shadow
chooses octagonals such as chatter
and swimsuits at an angle
where smiles become orange.

That's the first stanza. Then the point of vision shifts from the near to the far, to the sea in the second stanza:

Sea whose translucence disturbs inferior atoms,
that passage from ice to shallow removes familiars
as glass changes to foam, the parallel lake diminished,
combs drop into fur.

That stanza seems to start moving from an exterior to a more perceptual, interior landscape, doesn't it? And then the poem continues: "Between sea and lake a shape . . . ." And then we're back to the notion of form, of shape.

EF: I've noticed the quickness of the changes that you orchestrate, line by line, almost phrase by phrase. The jumps. We wondered whether as you write you are following your mind's own jump-cuts or whether there is a more willed after-thought to that construction. I guess we're asking you how you compose.

BG: [*Laughs.*] Yes, I guess you *are* asking me that. Each poem is composed com-pletely differently. It's what I call "shuffling mind." I go a good deal by sound, and I mean I can write *on* sounds. I guess you can say I write by ear. That's really what I do.

CH: Is it a kind of aural intuition?

BG: That's a very nice phrase. I do write with a kind of aural intuition. In *some* poems [*laughs*].

CH: Yes, that's right. With *some* poems—because I'm following the music. If I try to parse these lines, I can come up with any number of speculative readings, but if I just read them following the music—"adoptive day," "replenished by shadow," "chooses," "chatter," "swimsuits," "smiles," "sea," "translucence"—then I start to see that aural patterning.

BG: That is the way it should be written. The way you added up those words is the way it should have been written.

EF: Omitting the in-betweens?

BG: Yes. Funny, I'd like to do that.

CH: You *have* done that. In *Seeking Air*, you have that beautiful section, "Lus-trous Polychromes," that opens as a list poem:

Cypress, eucalyptus, magnolia, oak, olive, palm, sycamore,
orange, lemon, jacaranda, pine, yucca

Bougainvillea, gardenia, geranium, camellia, rose, oleander,
succulent, begonia, sage, thyme, heather, pansy, pink

Fog.   Sun.   Heat.   Coolness.

Mountain.   Sea.   Canyon.   Desert.

Dry.   Parched.   Green.   Watered.

Smudge pots.   Acqueducts.

Porch.   Balcony.   Grill.   Gates.   Hedge.   Stucco.
Tile.   Wall.

Deep shadow.   Ardent light.

My first response to it was, "Oh, this is a beautiful section of the novel," but I hadn't brought it into my intellectual articulation to say, "Oh, this is an aural intuitive pattern." You wrote about that section, Kathleen, in your essay on *Seeking Air*.[8]

EF: Barbara, a lot of your recent work has that kind of density that leaves out the unnecessary just in your sudden use of white space, without punctuation. The air around the words is breathing, in that passage from your novel, and also in your more recent work, like *Miniatures*, for example.

BG: That's, for me, very experimental.

EF: It feels sort of ekphrastic, but at a tremendous slant, so that the poems are finally more abstract than visual. They're never descriptive. But I like that effect in *Rocks on a Platter* as well, which is more descriptive, more discursive.

BG: It turns out now at this late date to be more descriptive. Before, it wasn't.

EF: Just in comparison. But the white space is so important, it's so beautiful, and there's so much breath in it. I like the balance between the discursiveness and the minimalism in this book.

BG: I think that was my favorite book until now. I left out so much in this last book, *Miniatures*. I went through it and deliberately left out, and I found that extremely satisfactory. I think I was beginning to despair, because I didn't like what I was doing. And the leaving out has helped me. Now I believe it's always more powerful when something's left out. But it's very hard for me to know when to stop.

KF: I know what you mean. I had a similar experience last spring, while writing a poem for Norma Cole. She'd had a stroke just before I left for Rome, and we were unable to be in touch because she couldn't speak or write e-mails at that time. I was trying to describe for her what it was like to be inside an Italian ritualized family situation—both its moving and its comic aspects, in this case taking place over the weekend of *Pasqua* and *Pasquetta* [Easter and the Monday just after it, "little Easter"].

I began the poem on Easter day and continued to work on it when I returned to Rome, but by the time I'd "finished" it, I was very unhappy because it didn't resemble anything I'd hoped to capture—the confusion of contemporary Roman TV Easter with ancient religious rites; the physical alarm of having one's speech or memory taken away with no warning; the war raging, not so far away[9]; and the loss of four friends unexpectedly dying in the space of a few months.

One morning I decided to blow up the "finished product" and to force its materiality to come forward. I completely severed its intended meanings by enlarging the type and cutting into it. The composing process resembled a kind of action-collaging, except that I was using my own already-written text instead of found material. I decided to make a series of discrete wall pieces composed from phrases discovered swiftly and without plan, inside the rejected whole. I suppose you might call it an intentional defragmentation. I determined to use all the words and all the letters from the original finished draft.

I was sitting on the floor cutting away, and soon I began composing, literally, on a white throw rug as if it were my big page or my canvas. When I found what interested me, I would paste those words and letters onto a piece of paper. Eventually I reformatted these individual pieces into visual/typescript pages for a chapbook, *hi dde violeth i dde violet* (2003).

But the process of revising was about that dissatisfaction Barbara was speaking of. I don't mean to compare it exactly to hers, but rather to talk about the experience of dissatisfaction and cutting into, or out of, the arrangements that words find themselves in when their use has become habitual, even musically so, or in some way shaped by an assaultive and banal soundtrack crowding in on you—the sound of language sets that repeat themselves in the daily press or come into your ear from television. I was trying to break these patterns apart because it was so deeply upsetting to have written an overly smooth, highly controlled narrative poem when it did not express the urgency nor the assaultive quality of life I'd been experiencing and wanted to give accurate visual form.

CH: Barbara, you spoke about how *Miniatures* came to you, and the terms in which it came to you, that had to do with how you had conceived of it, imaginatively, and then how you executed it.

BG: I think I've been very fortunate in that I've had a real easeful time in construction, and I don't have it now. I just have a lot of difficulty. And I have to regain something that I've deposited somewhere else.

KF: I remember when you were talking about how interested you were in Anna Marie Albiach's work at a certain point. When one is suddenly struck or entered by another's work, it can't help but begin to make you want to find out what that's about.

BG: She uses vocabulary in a totally different way than she used to. It's completely original. I want to go back and find out. She did something to the alphabet that nobody else had done. I really admire that.

CH: You started in *Miniatures* with the medieval discourse.

BG: Yes. It was medieval. And it turns around and is either very contemporary words or it goes back to the medieval. Which are the periods I chose. But I had a lot of trouble with it, and it wasn't until "Coal" that I felt that I really was on easy ground, because that's when I brought in my grandfather. And he helped me.

CH: So it was a kind of discovery as you went along.

BG: Yes, the night was very deep in "Coal," and I was able to go way back, as if one were in a coal mine. And that was a great relaxation, because I was stuck. It's not an easy thing to do. There's one that I like very much, "Petticoat," the poem with the word "Leviticus" in it. I love that word *Leviticus*. "She ran down the middle of the road" [*starting to read, she stops, and asks Fraser to read for her*].

KF: [*reading with high comedic drama*]

She ran down the middle of the road throwing her hands up to Heaven.
Longinus, Leviticus, mathematical wonder.
            She believed whole buildings might fall on top of her.

                    Pollen filled the air.
It was her duty to plunder the ant of air, beasties of calico.

The Morse Code arrived in petticoat blue, the steam engine.
  She read Liebnitz before she visited the pastor.
[*Everyone laughs.*]

KF: This connects for me, way back, to the playfulness in your work.

CH: Which takes one by surprise. It just erupts there. It's something that one of your artist friends, Willem De Kooning, said to you, which you write about. He talks about keeping the work alive through that challenge to keep exploring.

EF: Concerning a different aspect of the visual, I'd like to ask about the cinematic ideas of cutting and montage. I'm struck by the elliptical narratives in *Seeking Air*, Barbara—the way the movies determine the point of view at times in those prose poems:

Life's cinema aspect. Remarked on elsewhere. It begins to unroll from my windows overlooking the city streets. There a man enters a store. A car turns left onto a street. Cars wait for lights. A bus stops. A yellow cab cruises. A light changes. The pace of the cars is faster. Slower. Water tanks top buildings. Windows cleave to them. A door is an entrance. A person crosses at a diagonal. A bench is empty. Someone sits on a bench. A person moves quickly. A person stops. Except for a parked car there suddenly is an empty street. I ask if this is a French, Spanish, Algerian, English film. The subtitles will give me the answer.

Seeing is directly linked to the cinematic here, and the perceptual shifts are like long shots and jump cuts.

BG: Yes, it's the sense of watching a *scene* the window frames. I grew up around Los Angeles. The movies were everywhere. But here the eye sees from another film tradition. It's an American scene, but it's not an American film.

EF: And Kathleen, I was reading your new book [*Discrete categories forced into coupling*], which could refer to either collage or a cinematic coupling. I'm also struck by your cinematic metaphors in a poem like "Bresson Project," written much earlier:

he is violent   ultra-
violet   She is
the wow of his silver screen

cinnamon queen with
freckles, she's so fine,
so fi-yi-yine
[. . . . .]

> This is the working medium between them, out of the
> mouth of Bresson, into the spoon of his reader, which we
> swallow the contents of. We make that effort. This is real,
> as a popular love song we remember from our childhood
> is real when it wets the heart with satisfying equations.

Both of you evoke *motion* pictures in your work—a medium quite different from
the stillness of the canvas, which is also so important for you both.

KF: For me, using film imagery or its technical vocabulary was not really a conscious project or decision but came from the parallel gestures and metaphors that
link one's life to the films you see, how they enter you. It just seemed to come up
in relation to the situation being explored. In the longer prose piece, "Soft Pages,"
from *Discrete categories*, there are a number of "cinematic" sequences. At one point
the narrator—and reader—enters a theatre and there is a speculative passage that
follows:

> It had happened, had been happening. An incremental shaping, a turning
> movement. You could also say that something suddenly leapt forward in the
> dark theatre and that what had been the curb now became a screen with her
> foot projected onto it just as it was lifting and setting itself back down. The
> screen was carried inside her, it having already installed itself, forming its con-
> tours again and again, but the light falling on her foot, as it appeared to lift of
> its own volition—as a separate animal, even—made it seem as if the projector
> were also hers, illuminating the moment which had been gathering in her, yet
> not hers, until now.

Its genesis was a photograph I'd looked at for three years, propped up in front of
me on my desk in Rome. It was a slightly blurred image of people walking, and
there was a man's foot moving into the frame from the left edge, then a woman in
motion, and then a foot raised in the air, left behind by someone else rushing out

---

the right side of the photograph. Eventually, this photograph on my desk—this moving picture—started entering into the writing. The foot keeps arriving in different ways throughout this piece.

Thinking back to the sixties in New York, I realize how very important film was to me, in teaching me the breakdown of movement. I began to see how differently one's vision might be constructed—the tempo of it, the speed of image arrival. Stan Brackhage was showing a lot of speeded-up footage then, in one of the small art-film theatres downtown, and uptown John Cassavetes's films were slowing everything down to "real time," pulling meanings beyond their economic compressions. It made a new kind of sense if you were thinking of what was going on in jazz and "new music"—all those jump cuts delivering meanings outside of the linear narrative which, normally, had provided one's main frame of reference.

It was an enormous relief to shed—or at least to extend and improvise on that received familiarity authorized by the mainstream models: how things ought to be if you were going to write a "good" poem. Sound *was* involved in the jump cut, but there was also the odd gap and exposure of filmic splicing (space). That incredible freedom is what Barbara—and other New York School poets gave me access to through their work. Freedom and pleasure. Pleasure is a great part of it.

CH: And, as you mentioned earlier, playfulness.

EF: It also sounds like an aspect of relinquishing control.

KF: Exactly! The control of others' limits. You finally do bring your own shaping to what you do. In the revision process itself, there is an artistic control that is demanding and particular, but the poem is leading you to it.

BG: To that place where the poem lies waiting for you.

Notes

1. See Fraser, "The Tradition of Marginality" in *Translating* (29); also quoted in "The Gendered Marvelous: Barbara Guest, Surrealism and Feminist Reception" by DuPlessis, in Diggory and Miller, *Scene of My Selves*, 189–213 (—ed.).
2. For a rich discussion of Guest's relationship with these two women Abstract Expressionists and the contemporary visual arts scene more generally, see Sara Lundquist's groundbreaking essay "Another Poet among Painters: Barbara Guest with Grace Hartigan and Mary Abbott," in Diggory and Miller, *Scene of My Selves*, 245–64 (—ed.).

3. See DuPlessis's "The Gendered Marvelous" for a trenchant analysis of Guest's gendered relationship to Surrealism (—ed.).

4. *How(ever)2* was resurrected in 1999 as an electronic journal (currently published out of Royal Holloway University) and archived at Arizona State University's Virginia G. Piper Center of Creative Writing (—ed.).

5. Fraser queried Hermine Ford, daughter of painter Jack Tworkov, about this time in New York. Tworkov, like many of the artists Guest knew, arrived in New York around 1940, and Ford grew up among them. In an e-mail to Fraser dated January 23, 2004, Ford writes: "Yes, there were of course many artists who came to NY because of the war. . . . DeKooning came in the 30's, Cavallon, Gorky, Duchamp. Mondrian. Albers. Quite a few architects especially from the Bauhaus. . . . The composer Stefan Wolpe . . . and the Surrealists André Breton and André Masson. . . . And of course there were other immigrant artists who had arrived before the war, to escape poverty, and/or anti-semitism in Europe. . . . [T]he feeling and excitement of the cultural capital of the (western) world shifting to NYC just before and after the war . . . was very very palpable."

6. Guest eventually transferred to the University of California at Berkeley, where she completed her B.A. before moving to New York.

7. We have done our own palimpsestic "layering" at this point in the interview: what follows on "Etruscan Pages" is a collage of Fraser's actual brief comments and our questions during this present interview and a condensed excerpt from Hogue's earlier interview with Fraser, which could not be included for reasons of space limitations (—ed.).

8. See "'One Hundred and Three Chapters of Little Times': collapsed and transfigured moments in the cubist fiction of Barbara Guest" in *Translating the Unspeakable* (161–73).

9. The time to which Fraser refers is the U.S.-led invasion of Iraq in the spring of 2003.

—Parachutes, My Love, Could Carry Us Higher

I just said I didn't know
And now you are holding me
In your arms,
How kind.
Parachutes, my love, could carry us higher.
Yet around the net I am floating
Pink and pale blue fish are caught in it,
They are beautiful,
But they are not good for eating.
Parachutes, my love, could carry us higher
Than this mid-air in which we tremble,
Having exercised our arms in swimming,
Now the suspension, you say,
Is exquisite. I do not know.
There is coral below the surface,
There is sand, and berries
Like pomegranates grow.
This wide net, I am treading water
Near it, bubbles are rising and salt
Drying on my lashes, yet I am no nearer
Air than water. I am closer to you
Than land and I am in a stranger ocean
Than I wished.

—An Emphasis Falls on Reality

Cloud fields change into furniture
furniture metamorphizes into fields
an emphasis falls on reality.

"It snowed toward morning," a barcarole
the words stretched severely

silhouettes they arrived in trenchant cut
the face of lilies. . . .

I was envious of fair realism.

I desired sunrise to revise itself
as apparition, majestic in evocativeness,
two fountains traced nearby on a lawn. . . .

you recall treatments
of 'being' and 'nothingness'
illuminations apt
to appear from variable directions—
they are orderly as motors
floating on the waterway,

so silence is pictorial
when silence is real.

The wall is more real than shadow
or that letter composed of calligraphy
each vowel replaces a wall

a costume taken from space
donated by walls. . . .

BARBARA GUEST AND KATHLEEN FRASER

These metaphors may be apprehended after
they have brought their dogs and cats
born on roads near willows,

willows are not real trees
they entangle us in looseness,
the natural world spins in green.

A column chosen from distance
mounts into the sky while the font
is classical,

they will destroy the disturbed font
as it enters modernity and is rare. . . .

The necessary idealizing of you reality
is part of the search, the journey
where two figures embrace

This house was drawn for them
it looks like a real house
perhaps they will move in today

into ephemeral dusk and
move out of that into night
selective night with trees,

The darkened copies of all trees.

—The Rose Marble Table

Adoptive day replenished by shadow
chooses octagonals such as chatter

and swimsuits at an angle
where smiles become orange.

Sea whose translucence disturbs inferior atoms,
that passage from ice to shallow removes familiars
as glass changes to foam, the parallel lake diminished,
combs drop into fur.

Between sea and lake a shape manneristic residence
of blue, pool waits the diver shock. Sylphs
luxuriate in ripples seasonal branches they tease
the spread of trained water, their silks reply yes then no
their dive provokes,

Gentle disruptions on certain days ruminating in
clear water, thoughts trailing the slap integrating
there with east of lake the westerly sea at heel
pool repeats an omen in sky dip,

Emotive waters possessed by bodies their octaves
glide on marginal air, light weighing its touch
here and thither to an arc of shapes and drips
from wings. Couperin wades to his rock,

Branches graze and sink, an unsettled stress
pleads antic decline, let the dead limb fall
imminence remains arms flung into dirt alarms.

Creative soul you hesitate, I with my hand
on the rose marble table, like you a difficult creature
ignoring the universe, igniting shadows. Gulls
over porches, bamboo familiars mine.

Ultramarine is cold it shivers
until the scumbled white of foam distributes

wilfully from sea to lake to pond we watch
heads revel in occasional dips
while background thoughtful water frames sestinas
they repeat a sobriety like a rose marble table.

Supple nature declares texture lends
formality to words a flight of marble
can rearrange the speed of waters,
we pass hands upon its surface and embrace
the creative object, throbbing waves fly over.

—Spirit Tree

LO! It shakes boughs Spirit Tree.

Plenty of wonder here and miraculum.

Pleaseth shade with lark!

Immortalis makes entry.
Small feet carry chalice, Domine.

    Swete be sound and soothing.

Lady and gazelle, amitié.

—Turret

    What is your version, raking hay, reading law
    In turret, transferring documenta?

What is origin of miscellany, misdemeanor,

from whence doggerel?

Whose profile in margin

where small animals lie, toad, minnow, book of Saints,
olives.

—Petticoat

She ran down the middle of the road throwing her hands up to Heaven.
Longinus, Leviticus, mathematical wonder.
        She believed whole buildings might fall on top of her.

        Pollen filled the air.
It was her duty to plunder the ant of air, beasties of calico.
        The Morse Code arrived in petticoat blue, the steam engine.
        She read Liebnitz before she visited the pastor.

—Noisetone

    Each artist embarks on a personal search.
        An artist may take introspective refreshment from green.

Or so they say in Barcelona when air is dry.
        In our country it is a water sprinkler that hints, "rinsed green."
        Colors often break themselves into separate hues

of noisetone.　　In a Barcelona cabaret when green is overtaken,
it is stirred into the mint color of drink.

The spirit is lifted among primary colors. Nine rows of color.
The future writ in white spaces.

—*from* "Türler Losses"
　　"Though nothing can bring back the hour"[1]

What was the other look you brought?
Houses with gardens, laughter like
the necessary wreath?

Wearing your Timex you gathered the October harvest.

Every inch dowsed by rain
pumpkins rotting and corn,
no tassel there, no sheaves
coves windswept. That summery wristband
blue and yellow faded like folded skin
voices overheard pacing acres
in the archery mud.

"We've all got to take our lumps."

You made the autumn ginger cookies

Sniggered like mules, kind of a dumb show.

Let that embrace last on the rim of the inkstand.
Wearing a white collar and the weight of it
holds you down like glaze, like Zurich.

You are creating two watches.

You enter the laboratory. Look out for the watch
called "Never Loses."

(Later they embrace as winter slides over the sill.
outdoors we would wear snowcaps on our skulls.)

Don't interrupt.

Continued in the kitchen under the Seth Thomas.

.

Seemingly realistic codes have pointed to other
levels of images beyond their limits, ice
permitting time to decorate a block.

.

Likely rivers graduating into lakes the desolate curve
my image against your shoulder, the homespun
logic of our twosomeness, a fabric time
will displace the threads, a shrivel here,
there a stain, the rotting commences like lanes
of traffic hurtling into air as the sun comes down.

.

Subterfuge
When the tribal months
come trooping over the clocks

I'll have mine plain
or I'll wear the brown.

Another old magazine while something
darts into the shallows

.

Tensions as the clock strikes
muttering envelopes, envelopes
"clouds surround their faces."

Seeking the chute or drifting
these rafts hourless in the breathing
admire the quarter hour
brave sofas surround

Breathing test while we waltz
a curious toe pointed toward hours

Eyes with negative irises shutting
as the minutes fly
birds crossing the deep chambers

Shoes at the fireplace or homogeneity
decided while the drops
elaborated before our envious vision

A child entered the room
wearing a clock costume
A child of pigmy size
unmodified by time's blisters

And time's throat burrs and time's screens
across which time's numerals

Flash ruptures

"Look now forwards and let the backwards be"[2]

1

Frost villages on the slope
that's the bell peal
icy mountain time!

Scampering to the inn carrying our pumpkins
best not to be late in this region
rites are observed
habits called "old as time itself"
women go coiffed.

2

Arriving at sea level he hands her a Valentine
named "Coast,"
the sky is white and grey like February
the waves whiter while reflecting the sky
in patches of thickness that beat
on the coast with timely strikes
preparing sand exits.
She holds this landscape
the wet snow falls over it.

3

There were movements
in the garden with leaves and bicycles

Torpors suffered under cellophane
ripening and grasping

4

A bride and groom wait
beneath a canvas, cellophane

separates them from elements,
the groom steals a look at his watch
he would like to ride off
into the far bicycle spring.

5
Autre temps, autre mœurs

Yes I'd like to reorganize
the way it was in the October scheme.

A wrist for every watch
releasing doves

In the blown haze
a search for crystal

Broken glass

_____

[1] Wordsworth
[2] Ouspensky

—Norchia *from* "Etruscan Pages"

A The letter A is a plow
(mare pulling into *mare*)
    horse plowing sea
    Maremma

    Was A
    where
you made and
    unmade your mind . . .

first hesitation

    when you doubted
   what you
    thought you
   were
   looking for?

  .

alpha. aslant. alien. appall. answer. anodic. alum. *A.*

stooping. struggle. squeeze of light. sling. slate. shut.
scrutiny. *S.*

ropy. *R.* viscous. *V.* overhang. *O.* hold. hover. *H.* boar. *B.*
follow. flush. *F.* herbaceous. *H.*

.

"we know what each mark is equal to, but in retrospect . . ."

red paint or black

.

another progression of ants across dry mud ruts

this abandoned road mapped with their cultivated huts and paths

they continue in dry weather in wind

deliberate burdens through the temporal

He isn't here, nor his page of exertion
No close-written excavation of particulars

to inscribe a limit
Footstep's parallel replica

such breathing

(still, a pressing flutter climbs with us
down and through stone)

Lava revetments
retain precipitous bluffs—

(ashlars compose a frame for each entering dead one)

lintel of their own Alpha

Tombs carpentered shut
as if made of wood

(scrutiny of stone mason
eyeing his painted house
on ravine's opposite bank)

rooms carved with tools

For the journey
ductile metal
malleable gold fibula
gold spiral for curls

bronze mirror
(stooping, Thetis
curves P. close behind)

. . . a Gr. story
but an Etruscan has scratched
    Herecele + Mlacuch

---

over it
in her own hand

.

Death imagines us into pleasure. We want to continue

We stand in front of the dark abandoned tunnel
a tomb where all has been emptied and carted
to the villa—

a thick glass door we will open
(the museum keeper's blink)

Leaves are massing, green speeding up

We are not dressed in wide straw hats with grosgrain bands
our make-up is not elaborate

but we want a record of us where there is "nothing"
as if by holding each other's waists, we could
find the border and lose it

No plan for this bargain   Take our picture   ˙

.

14 . June . 1991

Dear Susan,

"An isolated fact, cut loose from the universe, has no significance for the poet. It derives its significance from the reality to which it belongs." (Wallace Stevens, "On Poetic Truth")

    The night after you left for Paros, I dreamt I was lying on a stone slab at the base of the cliff tombs at Norchia, preparing to make my transition from "this world" to "the other." I was thinking about how to negotiate the passage, when it came to me—the reason for all the layers of fine white cloth arranged and spread around me. I said to you (because you were with me), "You just keep wrapping yourself with white cloth and eventually you are in the other place."

I wanted to write about the trip but I couldn't find words for those places at once so peaceful and full of what was & wasn't there. Two nights later I dreamt, again, of Norchia. This time Norma had come there to work on engravings. She asked me if I'd work on them with her. I began assembling evidence after that, scratching with my red and black ink down the pages of the new ledger you'd given me . . . all fragmentary . . .

Today—exactly a week since your face went by inside the window of the cab—a classical archeologist phoned up to have a look at our place (he'd seen our rental announcement). He knew Norchia and the cliff tombs and we talked about the mystery surrounding the Etruscan language. "We still have no idea . . . beyond family names and lineage or sometimes an inscription to a particular god or goddess . . . one doesn't have much to go on, with tombs as your main reference." Then he recalled several other sources under study—two plates [rectangles] of fine-beaten gold, covered with text, found in the temples at Pyrgi (very near where we were, but closer to the sea . . . I saw the plates at the Villa Giulia in Rome on Sat. and they are the size of letter pages with nail holes distributed around their edges, as if pounded into a wooden door or wall).

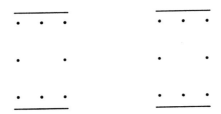

The other source is the "mummy wrapping," linen originally from Egypt (probably hauled on trading ships), and covered with formulaic and repetitious Etruscan religious precepts—written "retro" (right to left). Even though there are over 1,500 words covering it, the total lexicon is barely 500. The mummy text is preserved in the museum in Zagreb, YUG., thus "The Zagreb Mummy." When they found her in Etruria, her body had been wrapped in this shroud made of pieces of linen, written on through centuries . . . used as "pages" for new writing whenever the old text had faded. Her family had wrapped her in this cloth, this writing, because it was available.

I have no letter from you yet. Margy's daughter, Ariana, comes tonight for supper with a friend (a little like having M. here) . . . Arthur will make his famed *spaghetti vongole*—"*per morire*" (to die for)

With dreamed stylus in wakeful hand—and many empty pages—I send you love, imagining you half in, half out of the water.

K

—*from* "Wing"

I. The Underdrawings

The New comes forward in its edges in order to be itself;

its volume by necessity becomes violent and three-dimensional
and ordinary, all similar models shaken off and smudged

as if memory were an expensive thick creamy paper and every
corner turned now in partial erasure,

even bits of pearly rubber, matchstick and lucent plastic
leaving traces of decision and little tasks performed

as if each dream or occasion of pain had tried to lift itself
entirely away, contributing to other corners, planes and
accumulated depth

.

the wing is not static but frayed, layered, fettered, furling and
stony

its feathers cut as if from tissue or stiffened cheesecloth
condensed in preparation for years of stagework

attached to its historic tendons; more elaborate
the expansive ribcage, grieving, stressed, yet

marked midway along the breastbone with grains of light

.

there are two men, they are tall men, and they are talking softly
among the disintegrating cubes

II. First Black Quartet: Via Tasso

A cube's clean volume shatters and reassembles
its daily burnt mark the New is used and goes
backwards into match sticks one struck at each
day's oxygen, common pinched breath and nerve
the remaining light bricked-up Now melt with
nothing changed yet he persists as does pain
have a way of crash ing in on you, swimming

through matter heart rate in each cell There
are two men turning their limit of blanket
that one particular evening appears in reds
to unfold in expand ing brilliant traces or
stars: "that which is known to us" or just
improvised on deep kitchen floor meanwhile
picking, pecking at our skins ghost or angel
sent to tell us what we didn't want to know

III. Wing: Via Vanvitelli

It can happen that the intoxicating wing will draw the mind as a
bow   The cubic route of wing falls backwards with light
leaking through at the edge   The cube is formally particular
and a part of speech and lost   it looks for like kind,
regardless of function, and attempts to replace itself   The
square root of anything captures and holds, seeming to be final,
and we are grateful   We see the delicate marks along the
feather and we follow, now to define or depict the outskirts of
meaning   A plume of smoke or any of the growths which cover
the bodies of birds   To form a model of the wing's surface,
the cube arrives on a day called "the darkest day"   Its
likeness consists of strength, atonality, pigment, emptiness and
shafts partly hollow   I put my mouth just at the opening where
a steel edge gives way to an angle   from which light emerges
along its soft narrow barbs   If the wing had a voice it would
open through a shaft   *I am not of that feather*

VI. Crossroads

He extends thus into plumage as fruit rubbed from walls soaks
inward

.

Your mango human skin doth beckon overlaps against the larger
screen

.

Where floods our night hike, features of body assemble
their hawkeyed distance

abnormally retaining jet-liner lure

.

yet wanting the same thing always: your innocence
dressed in red anterior borders

pinion and spur, my teeth which may fit the angel's gear

.

having seen thy ancient ground

messenger: ἀγγελος : wing

X. Vanishing Point: Third Black Quartet

forward edge itself to be volume by necessity as if partial   erase
edge itself to be volume by necessity as if partial erase   other
itself to be volume by necessity as if partial erase   corners
to be volume by necessity as if partial erase   planes
be volume by necessity as if partial erase   accumulate
volume by necessity as if partial erase   depth
by necessity as if partial erase   condensed
necessity as if partial erase   in
as if partial erase   preparation
if partial erase   stagework
partial erase   historic
erase   tendons
of   elaborate
pearly   ribcage
lucent   marked
decision   midway
and   with
little   grains
tasks   of
of   light
pain   talking
had   softly
tried   among
to   disintegrating
lift   cubes
to lift   the
tried to lift   falling
had tried to lift   wing
pain had tried to lift   will
of pain had tried to lift   draw
tasks of pain had tried to lift   the
little tasks of pain had tried to lift   mind
and little tasks of pain had tried to lift   as
decision and little tasks of pain had tried to lift   a
lucent decision and little tasks of pain had tried to lift   bow

itself   the   wing   not   static   but   frayed,   layered,   fettered,   furling

CONTRIBUTORS

SASCHA FEINSTEIN won the Hayden Carruth Award for his poetry collection *Misterioso*. He is the author of two critical books, including *Jazz Poetry: From the 1920s to the Present*, and coeditor (with Yusef Komunyakaa) of *The Jazz Poetry Anthology* and its companion volume, *The Second Set*. He is a professor at Lycoming College, where he codirects the Creative Writing Program and edits *Brilliant Corners: A Journal of Jazz & Literature*.

ELISABETH A. FROST is the author of *The Feminist Avant-Garde in American Poetry*. She serves on the editorial advisory board of the feminist journal *HOW2* and is the recipient of grants from the Rockefeller Foundation–Bellagio Center, the MacDowell Colony for the Arts, and the University of Connecticut Humanities Institute, among other foundations. She is associate professor of English at Fordham University, where she serves as director of Poets Out Loud.

JEANNE HEUVING is the author of the critical study *Omissions Are Not Accidents: Gender in the Art of Marianne Moore* and of the cross-genre experimental work *Incapacity*, which was a Small Press Traffic Book of the Year in 2005. She has received grants from the National Endowment for the Humanities, Fulbright Foundation, Simpson Center for the Humanities, and the Beinecke Library. She is on the editorial advisory board of *HOW2* and a member of the Subtext Collective in Seattle. She is an associate professor at the University of Washington–Bothell and on the graduate faculty in English at the University of Washington–Seattle.

LAURA HINTON is the author of *The Perverse Gaze of Sympathy: Sadomasochistic Sentiments from Clarissa to Rescue 911* and coeditor of *We Who Love to Be Astonished: Experimental Women's Writing and Performance Poetics*. She has published creative nonfiction in *September 11: American Writers Respond* and prose poetry in *HOW2, Bird Dog,* and *Feminist Studies*. She is an associate professor of English at the City College of New York.

CYNTHIA HOGUE's most recent collections of poetry are *Flux* (2002) and *The Incognito Body* (2006). She is coeditor (with Laura Hinton) of the anthology *We Who Love to Be Astonished: Experimental Women's Writing and Performance Poetics*. She has received NEA, NEH (Summer Seminar), and Fulbright fellowships and was the 2004–2005 H.D. Fellow at the Beinecke Library at Yale University. She is the Maxine and Jonathan Marshall Chair in Modern and Contemporary Poetry in the Department of English at Arizona State University.

CHARLES JENSEN is the author of the chapbook *Little Burning Edens*. His poems have appeared in the *New England Review,* the *Journal, Quarterly West, Washington Square,* and *West Branch*. He works for the Piper Center for Creative Writing at Arizona State University and teaches film studies at Rio Salado College.

ANALOUISE KEATING teaches women's studies at Texas Woman's University. She is the editor of Anzaldúa's *Interviews/Entrevistas* and coeditor with Anzaldúa of *this bridge we call home: radical visions for transformation* and *Bearing Witness, Reading Lives: Imagination, Creativity, and Cultural Change*. Her books also include *Women Reading Women Writing: Self-Invention in Paula Gunn Allen, Gloria Anzaldúa, and Audre Lorde* and *EntreMundos/AmongWorlds: New Perspectives on Gloria Anzaldúa*.

CLAUDIA KEELAN is the author of four books of poetry, including *Utopic* (Beatrice Hawley Award, 2000) and *The Devotion Field*. She directs the creative writing program at the University of Nevada–Las Vegas, where she also edits *Interim*.

LYNN KELLER is professor of English at the University of Wisconsin–Madison. She is the author of *Re-making It New: Contemporary American Poetry and the Modernist Tradition* and *Forms of Expansion: Recent Long Poems by Women* and is an editor of the Contemporary North American Poetry series, published by the University of Iowa Press. With Cristanne Miller she coedited *Feminist Measures: Soundings in Poetry and Theory*.

CRISTANNE MILLER, chair and professor of English at SUNY/Buffalo, is the author of *Cultures of Modernism: Marianne Moore, Mina Loy, and Else Lasker-Schüler*, *Marianne Moore: Questions of Authority*, and *Emily Dickinson: A Poet's Grammar*. She has also coedited several books, including *The Selected Letters of Marianne Moore* with Bonnie Costello and Celeste Goodridge and *Feminist Measures: Soundings in Poetry and Theory* with Lynn Keller.

SARAH VAP is the coeditor for *42opus*. She teaches poetry in the Phoenix public schools through Arizona State University's Young Writers Program. Her two collections of poetry, *American Spikenard* and *The Dummy Fires*, are forthcoming.

WORKS CITED

Allen, Donald, ed. *The New American Poetry, 1945–1960*. New York: Grove P, 1960.

Anzaldúa, Gloria. *Borderlands/La frontera: The New Mestiza*. San Francisco: Aunt Lute Books, 1999.

———. *Friends from the Other Side/Amigos del Otro Lado*. San Francisco: Children's Book P, 1993.

———. *Interviews/Entrevistas*. Ed. AnaLouise Keating. New York: Routledge, 2000.

———, ed. *Making Face, Making Soul/Haciendo caras: Creative and Critical Perspectives by Feminists of Color*. San Francisco: Aunt Lute Books, 1990.

———. *Prietita and the Ghost Woman/Prietita y la llorona*. San Francisco: Children's Book P, 1995.

Anzaldúa, Gloria, and AnaLouise Keating, eds. *this bridge we call home: radical visions for transformation*. New York: Routledge, 2002.

Anzaldúa, Gloria, and Cherríe Moraga, eds. *This Bridge Called My Back: Writings by Radical Women of Color.* New York: Kitchen Table, Women of Color P, 1981.

Armantrout, Rae. "Feminist Poetics and the Meaning of Clarity." *Artifice and Indeterminacy: An Anthology of New Poetics.* Ed. Christopher Beach. Tuscaloosa: U of Alabama P, 1998. 287–96.

Baraka, Amiri, and Amina Baraka, comps. *Confirmation: An Anthology of African-American Women.* New York: Quill, 1983.

Baraka, Imamu Amiri, and Larry Neal, eds. *Black Fire: An Anthology of Afro-American Writing.* New York: Morrow, 1968.

Bedient, Calvin. "The Solo Mysterioso Blues: An Interview with Harryette Mullen." *Callaloo* 19.3 (1996): 652.

Bernstein, Charles, ed. *The Politics of Poetic Form: Poetry and Public Policy.* New York: Roof Books, 1990.

Berssenbrugge, Mei-mei. *Empathy.* Barrytown, NY: Station Hill P, 1989.

——. *Four Year Old Girl.* Berkeley, CA: Kelsey St. P, 1998

——. *The Heat Bird.* Providence, RI: Burning Deck P, 1983.

——, with Richard Tuttle. *Hiddenness.* New York: Library Fellows of the Whitney Museum of Art, 1987.

——. *Nest.* Berkeley, CA: Kelsey St. P, 2003.

——, with Richard Tuttle. *Sphericity.* Berkeley, CA: Kelsey St. P, 1993.

Caputi, Jane. "Interview with Paula Gunn Allen." *Trivia* 16 (1990): 50–67.

Cortez, Jayne. *Coagulations: New and Selected Poems.* New York: Thunder's Mouth P, 1984.

——. *Jazz Fan Looks Back.* Brooklyn, NY: Hanging Loose, 2002.

——. *Pissstained Stairs and the Monkey Man's Wares.* New York: Phrase Text, 1969.

——. *Somewhere in Advance of Nowhere.* New York: Serpent's Tail/High Risk Books, 1996.

Dahlen, Beverly. *A Reading 1–7.* San Francisco: Momo's P, 1985.

——. *A Reading 8–10.* Tucson: Chax, 1992.

DeKoven, Marianne. "Male Signature, Female Aesthetic: The Gender Politics of Experimental Writing." *Breaking the Sequence: Women's Experimental Fiction.* Ed. Ellen G. Friedman and Miriam Fuchs. Princeton: Princeton UP, 1989. 72–81.

Deleuze, Gilles. "Literature and Life." *Essays: Critical and Clinical.* Trans. Daniel W. Smith and Michael A. Graco. Minneapolis: U of Minnesota P, 1997. 1–6.

Diggory, Terrence, and Stephen Paul Miller, eds. *The Scene of My Selves: New Work on New York School Poets*. Orono, ME: National Poetry Foundation, 2001.

DuPlessis, Rachel Blau. *Drafts 1–38, Toll*. Middletown, CT: Wesleyan UP, 2001.

———. *Drafts: Drafts 39–57, Pledge, with Draft, Unnumbered: Précis*. Cambridge, UK: Salt Publishing, 2004.

———. *Genders, Races, and Religious Cultures in Modern American Poetry, 1908–1934*. New York: Cambridge UP, 2001.

———. *H.D.: The Career of That Struggle*. Bloomington: Indiana UP, 1986.

———. *The Pink Guitar: Writing as Feminist Practice*. New York: Routledge, 1990.

———, ed. *The Selected Letters of George Oppen*. Durham, NC: Duke UP, 1990.

———. *Tabula Rosa*. Elmwood, CT: Potes and Poets P, 1987.

———. *Writing Beyond the Ending: Narrative Strategies of Twentieth-Century Women Writers*. Bloomington: Indiana UP, 1985.

DuPlessis, Rachel Blau, and Peter Quartermain, eds. *The Objectivist Nexus: Essays in Cultural Poetics*. Tuscaloosa: U of Alabama P, 1999.

DuPlessis, Rachel Blau, and Ann Snitow, eds. *The Feminist Memoir Project: Voices of Women's Liberation*. New York: Three Rivers P, 1998.

Falon, Janet Ruth. "Speaking with Susan Howe." *The Difficulties* 3.2 (1989): 28–42.

Feinstein, Sascha. "Interview with Jayne Cortez by Sascha Feinstein." *Brilliant Corners: A Journal of Jazz and Literature* 3.1 (1998): 52–71.

———. "Interview with Sonia Sanchez by Sascha Feinstein." *Brilliant Corners: A Journal of Jazz and Literature* 7.2 (2003): 64–98.

Feinstein, Sascha, and Yusef Komunyakaa, eds. *The Jazz Poetry Anthology*. Bloomington: Indiana UP, 1991.

Finch, Annie. *A Formal Feeling Comes: Poems in Form by Contemporary Women*. New York: Story Line P, 1994.

Fraser, Kathleen. *Discrete categories forced into coupling*. Berkeley, CA: Apogee, 2004.

———. *Each Next*. Berkeley, CA: The Figures, 1980.

———. *hi dde violeth i dde violet*. Vancouver: Nomados, 2003.

———. *il cuore = the heart: Selected Poems, 1970–1995*. Hanover, NH: Wesleyan UP, 1997.

———. *Notes preceding trust*. Santa Monica, CA: Lapis P, 1987.

———. *Something (even human voices) in the foreground, a lake*. Berkeley, CA: Kelsey St. P, 1984.

———. *Translating the Unspeakable: Poetry and the Innovative Necessity.* Tuscaloosa: U of Alabama P, 2000.

———. *when new time folds up.* Minneapolis: Chax P, 1993.

———. *WING.* Mill Valley, CA: EM P, 1995.

Frost, Elisabeth A. *The Feminist Avant-Garde in American Poetry.* Iowa City: U of Iowa P, 2003.

———. "An Interview with Harryette Mullen." *Contemporary Literature* 41.3 (2000): 397–421.

———. "An Interview with Leslie Scalapino." *Contemporary Literature* 37.1 (1996): 1–23.

———. "Signifyin(g) on Stein: The Revisionist Poetics of Harryette Mullen and Leslie Scalapino." *Postmodern Culture: An Electronic Journal of Interdisciplinary Criticism* 5.3 (1995): 40 paragraphs. <http://www3.iath.virginia.edu.pmc>.

Frost, Elisabeth A., and Cynthia Hogue. "Barbara Guest and Kathleen Fraser in Conversation with Elisabeth Frost and Cynthia Hogue." *Jacket* 25 (February 2004). <http://www.jacketmagazine.com/25/guest-iv.html>.

Fulton, Alice. *Cascade Experiment: Selected Poems.* New York: Norton, 2004.

———. *Feeling as a Foreign Language: The Good Strangeness of Poetry.* St. Paul, MN: Graywolf, 1999.

———. *Felt.* New York: Norton, 2001.

———. *Palladium.* Chicago: U of Illinois P, 1986.

———. *Powers of Congress.* Boston: Godine, 1990.

Garber, Linda. "Spirit, Culture, Sex: Elements of the Creative Process in Gloria Anzaldúa's Poetry." Keating, *EntreMundos* 213–26.

Guest, Barbara. *Defensive Rapture.* Los Angeles: Sun and Moon P, 1993.

———. *Fair Realism.* Los Angeles: Sun and Moon P, 1989.

———. *Forces of Imagination: Writing on Writing.* Berkeley, CA: Kelsey St. P, 2003.

———. *Herself Defined: The Poet H.D. and Her World.* Garden City, NY: Doubleday, 1984.

———. *Miniatures and Other Poems.* Middletown, CT: Wesleyan UP, 2002.

———. *The Red Gaze.* Middletown, CT: Wesleyan UP, 2005.

———. *Rocks on a Platter.* Hanover, NH: Wesleyan UP, 1999.

———. *Seeking Air.* Santa Barbara, CA: Black Sparrow P, 1978.

———. *Selected Poems.* Los Angeles: Sun and Moon P, 1995.

———. *Türler Losses.* Montreal: Mansfield Book Mart, 1979.

Hall, Donald. "Goatfoot, Milktongue, Twinbird: The Psychic Origins of Poetic Form." *Claims for Poetry*. Ed. Donald Hall. Ann Arbor: U of Michigan P, 1982. 141–50.

Heuving, Jeanne. "An Interview with Rachel Blau DuPlessis." *Contemporary Literature* 45.3 (2004): 398–420.

Hinton, Laura. "Three Conversations with Mei-mei Berssenbrugge." *Jacket* 27 (April 2005). <http://www.jacketmagazine.com/27/hint-bers.html>.

Hinton, Laura, and Cynthia Hogue, eds. *We Who Love to Be Astonished: Experimental Women's Writing and Performance Poetics*. Tuscaloosa: U of Alabama P, 2002.

Hogue, Cynthia. "An Interview with Alicia Ostriker." *Writer's Chronicle* 35.5 (March–April 2003): 5–9.

———. "Interview with Harryette Mullen." *Postmodern Culture: An Electronic Journal of Interdisciplinary Criticism* 9.2 (1999): 36 paragraphs. <http://www3.iath.virginia.edu/pmc>.

———. "An Interview with Kathleen Fraser." *Contemporary Literature* 39.1 (Spring 1998): 1–26.

Howe, Florence, ed. *No More Masks! An Anthology of Twentieth-Century American Women Poets*. New York: HarperPerennial, 1993.

Howe, Susan. *The Birth-mark: unsettling the wilderness in American literary history*. Hanover, NH: Wesleyan UP, 1999.

———. *Defenestration of Prague*. New York: Kulchur Foundation, 1983.

———. *The Europe of Trusts: Selected Poems*. Los Angeles: Sun and Moon P, 1990.

———. *Frame Structures: Early Poems, 1974–1979*. New York: New Directions, 1996.

———. *The Midnight*. New York: New Directions, 2003.

———. *My Emily Dickinson*. Berkeley, CA: North Atlantic Books, 1985.

———. *The Nonconformist's Memorial*. New York: New Directions, 1993.

———. *Pierce-Arrow*. New York: New Directions, 1999.

———. *Pythagorean Silence*. New York: Montemora Foundation, 1982.

———. *Singularities*. Hanover, NH: Wesleyan UP, 1990.

———. "Statement for the New Poetics Colloquium, Vancouver 1985." *Jimmy & Lucy's House of "K"* 5 (1985): 13–17.

Jensen, Charles, and Sarah Vap. "A Risk and Trust: An Interview with C. D. Wright." *Hayden's Ferry Review* 34 (Spring–Summer 2004): 120–34.

Johnson, Kent. "Looking for 'one untranslatable song': An Interview with C. D. Wright." *Jacket* (December 2001). <http://jacketmagazine.com/15/cdwright-iv.html>.

Keating, AnaLouise, ed. *EntreMundos/AmongWorlds: New Perspectives on Gloria E. Anzaldúa*. New York: Palgrave Macmillan, 2005.

———. "Interview with Gloria Anzaldúa." *Frontiers: A Journal of Women's Studies* 14.1 (1993): 105–30.

Keelan, Claudia, and Alice Notley. "A Conversation: September 2002–December 2003." *American Poetry Review* 33.3 (May–June 2004): 15–19.

Keller, Lynn. "An Interivew with Susan Howe." *Contemporary Literature* 36.1 (1995): 1–34.

Keller, Lynn, and Cristanne Miller, eds. *Feminist Measures: Soundings in Poetry and Theory*. Ann Arbor: U of Michigan P, 1994.

Kinnahan, Linda A. *Lyric Interventions: Feminism, Experimental Poetry, and Contemporary Discourse*. Iowa City: U of Iowa P, 2004.

Kristeva, Julia. *Revolution in Poetic Language*. Trans. Margaret Waller. New York: Columbia UP, 1984.

Lazer, Hank. "The People's Poetry." *Boston Review* (April–May 2004). <http://bostonreview.net>.

Lunsford, Andrea. "Toward a Mestiza Rhetoric: Gloria Anzaldúa on Composition, Postcoloniality, and the Spiritual." Anzaldúa, *Interviews/Entrevistas* 251–80.

Luster, Deborah, and C. D. Wright. *One Big Self: Prisoners of Louisiana*. Austin: U of Texas P, 2002.

Medina, Tony, and Louis Reyes Rivera, eds. *Bum Rush the Page: A Def Poetry Jam*. New York: Three Rivers P, 2001.

Miller, Cristanne. "An Interview with Alice Fulton." *Contemporary Literature* 38.4 (1997): 586–615.

Mullen, Harryette. *Blues Baby*. Lewisburg, PA: Bucknell UP, 2003.

———. *Muse & Drudge*. Philadelphia: Singing Horse P, 1995.

———. "She Swam on from Sea to Shine." *Callaloo* 19.3 (1996): 648–50.

———. *Sleeping with the Dictionary*. Berkeley: U of California P, 2002.

———. *S*PeRM**K*T*. Philadelphia: Singing Horse P, 1992.

———. *Tree Tall Woman*. Galveston, TX: Earth Energy Communications, 1981.

———. *Trimmings*. New York: Tender Buttons Books, 1991.

Neile, Caren. "The 1,000-Piece Nights of Gloria Anzaldúa: Autohistoria-teoría at Florida Atlantic University." Keating, *EntreMundos* 17–27.

Notley, Alice. *"Close to me & Closer . . . (The Language of Heaven)" and "Désamère."* Oakland, CA: O Books, 1995.

———, ed. *The Collected Poems of Ted Berrigan*. Berkeley: U of California P, 2005.

———. *Coming After: Essays on Poetry*. Ann Arbor: U of Michigan P, 2005.

———. *The Descent of Alette*. New York: Penguin, 1992.

———. *Disobedience*. New York: Penguin, 2001.

———. *Mysteries of Small Houses*. New York: Penguin, 1998.

Ostriker, Alicia. "Beyond Confession: The Poetics of Postmodern Witness." *American Poetry Review* 30.2 (March/April 2001): 35–39.

———. *The Crack in Everything*. Pittsburgh: U of Pittsburgh P, 1996.

———. *Dancing at the Devil's Party: Essays on Poetry, Politics, and the Erotic*. Ann Arbor: U of Michigan P, 2000.

———. *Feminist Revision and the Bible*. Cambridge, MA: Blackwell, 1993.

———. *The Little Space: Poems Selected and New, 1968–1998*. Pittsburgh: U of Pittsburgh P, 1998.

———. *The Nakedness of the Fathers: Biblical Visions and Revisions*. New Brunswick, NJ: Rutgers UP, 1994.

———. *No Heaven*. Pittsburgh: U of Pittsburgh P, 2005.

———. *Stealing the Language: The Emergence of Women's Poetry in America*. Boston: Beacon P, 1986.

———. *The Volcano Sequence*. Pittsburgh: U of Pittsburgh P, 2002.

O'Sullivan, Maggie, ed. *Out of Everywhere: Linguistically Innovative Poetry by Women in North America and the U.K.* London: Reality Street Editions, 1996.

Ramos, Juanita, ed. *Compañeras: Latin Lesbians*. NY: Routledge, 1987.

Rankine, Claudia, and Juliana Spahr, eds. *American Women Poets in the Twentieth-First Century*. Middletown, CT: Wesleyan UP, 2002.

Rayor, Diane J., trans. *Sappho's Lyre: Archaic Lyric and Women Poets of Ancient Greece*. Berkeley: U of California P, 1991.

Rayor, Diane J., and William W. Batstone, eds. *Latin Lyric and Elegiac Poetry: An Anthology of New Translations*. New York: Garland Publishing, 1995.

Sanchez, Sonia. *Does Your House Have Lions?* Boston: Beacon P, 1997.

———. *Home Coming*. Detroit: Broadside P, 1969.

———. *Homegirls & Handgrenades*. New York: Thunder's Mouth P, 1984.

———. *I've Been a Woman: New and Selected Poems*. Chicago: Third World Press, 1985.

———. *Like the Singing Coming Off the Drums*. Boston: Beacon P, 1999.

———. *Shake Loose My Skin: New and Selected Poems*. Boston: Beacon P, 2000.

———. *We a BaddDDD People*. Detroit: Broadside P, 1970.

———. *Wounded in the House of a Friend*. Boston: Beacon P, 1995.

Scalapino, Leslie. *Considering how exaggerated music is*. San Francisco: North Point P, 1982.

———. *Crowd and not evening or light*. Oakland, CA: O Books, 1992.

———. *Dahlia's Iris: Secret Autobiography and Fiction*. Tallahassee, FL: Fiction Collective Two, 2003.

———. *Defoe*. Los Angeles: Sun and Moon P, 1994.

———. *The Front Matter, Dead Souls*. Middletown, CT: Wesleyan UP, 1996.

———. *Green and Black: Selected Writings*. Jersey City, NJ: Talisman House, 1996.

———. *How Phenomena Appear to Unfold*. Elmwood, CT: Potes and Poets P, 1989.

———. *Objects in the Terrifying Tense/Longing from Taking Place*. New York: Roof Books, 1993.

———. *The Public World/Syntactically Impermanence*. Middletown, CT: Wesleyan UP, 1999.

———. *The Return of Painting, the Pearl, and Orion: A Trilogy*. San Francisco: North Point P, 1991.

———. *The Tango*. New York: Granary Books, 2001.

———. *that they were at the beach: aeolotropic series*. San Francisco: North Point P, 1985.

———. *way*. San Francisco: North Point P, 1988.

———. *Zither & Autobiography*. Middletown, CT: Wesleyan UP, 2003.

Silliman, Ron. "What/Person: From an Exchange." *Poetics Journal* 9 (June 1991): 51–68.

Simpson, Megan. *Poetic Epistemologies: Gender and Knowing in Women's Language-Oriented Writing*. Albany: SUNY P, 2000.

Sloan, Mary Margaret, ed. *Moving Borders: Three Decades of Innovative Writing by Women*. Jersey City, NJ: Talisman, 1998.

Stein, Gertrude. *Tender Buttons*. Los Angeles: Sun and Moon P, 1991.

Tate, Claudia. *Black Women Writers at Work*. New York: Continuum, 1984.

Vickery, Ann. *Leaving Lines of Gender: A Feminist Genealogy of Language Writing*. Middletown, CT: Wesleyan UP, 2000.

Wright, C. D. *Cooling Time: An American Poetry Vigil*. Port Townsend, WA: Copper Canyon P, 2005.

———. *Deepstep Come Shining*. Port Townsend, WA: Copper Canyon P, 1998.

———. *Further Adventures with You*. Pittsburgh: Carnegie-Mellon UP, 1986.

———. *Just Whistle: A Valentine*. Berkeley, CA: Kelsey St. P, 1993.

———. *Steal Away: Selected and New Poems*. Port Townsend, WA: Copper Canyon P, 2002.

———. *Translations of the Gospel Back into Tongues*. Albany: SUNY P, 1982.

INDEX

aesthetics *(continued)*
258–60; Sanchez, 5–6, 276–77, 279,
281–82, 288–91; Scalapino, 5, 303–4,
308–10, 312–14, 318–19; of silence, 156,
160; of sound, 372; Wright, 5–6, 7,
329–31, 339

African American poetry and literature, 70;
anthologies, 77, 283–84; black dialect,
190, 199; militancy of, 77–78; Mullen on,
189, 192–93, 199, 205–6; radical poetry
in Sanchez, 275. *See also* Black Arts
movement

African motifs, 203, 205, 281–82, 284–85,
291

Agamben, Giorgio, 99–100

AIDs, 285, 292

Albiach, Marie, 369

Alden, Daisy, 357

Allen, Mimi, 51, 53

Allen, Paula Gunn, 24, 25

American mainstream poetry, 128–29, 225

American Poetry Review, 252

Amherst College, 74–75

Ammons, A. R., 130–31

Amos 'n Andy, 199

ancestors, 281, 291

Anderson, T. J., 206

anti-intellectualism, 166

anti-war demonstrations, 310

Antin, David, 109

Anzaldúa, Gloria Evangelina, 11–42;
aesthetic influences, 5–6, 12; on alternate
states of being, 17–18; *Borderlands/La
frontera*, 12, 18–21, 24, 26, 28n1, 28n4;
Chicana activism, 7, 11, 18, 22, 25;
childhood, 21–23; death, 13; "El Paisano
Is a Bird of Good Omen," 16; *Haciendo
caras*, 21; *Llorona*, 26; poetic structure, 7,
11, 12, 26–27, 28n1, 28n3; *Prieta*, 16, 17,
28n6; publications and awards, 12–13; on
sexual orientation, 18–21; themes, 12, 13;

This Bridge Called My Back, 7, 13, 21; on
vulnerability, 23–24; writing process, 12,
26–27. Works included: "*Cihuatlyotl,
Woman Alone*," 29–30; "*Del otro lado*,"
30–32; "Don't Give In, *Chicanita*," 32–33;
"Interface," 14, 34–39; "Poets Have
Strange Eating Habits," 40–42

Armantrout, Rae, 48–50, 109

art and artists, 55, 157–60, 354–58, 373n5

Art News, 351, 355

Artaud, Antonin, 314

Ashbery, John, 97, 351, 355

Asia/Asian philosophy, 52, 309–10

Auden, W. H., 252, 256

audience for poetry, 54–55, 286–87. *See also*
readers

aural intuition, 366

autobiography/biography, 135–36, 172–73,
260

autohistoria-teoría, 12, 28n3

avant-garde movements, 4–7, 9n8, 304. *See
also* Black Arts movement; Language
writing/Language Poetry; New York
School; objectivism

Baker, Josephine, 198, 201

Baraka, Amiri, 69, 76–77, 283, 285–87

Barnard, Mary E., 137–38

Beat poets, 312

Benjamin, Walter, 171

Bernstein, Charles, 97, 163–64, 312

Berrigan, Ted, 219, 221–22, 228–31

Berssenbrugge, Mei-mei, 43–68; aesthetic
influences, 5–6, 43–44, 47–48, 50–52,
54–55; "Audience," 54; childhood, 44;
Empathy, 50, 52; on fragments, 49, 54;
Hiddenness, 56; on importance of
mystery, 50; *Nest*, 48, 52, 53–55; poetic
structure, 44–45, 47, 49, 53–54; on
poetry, 9n9, 45–46, 50–51, 53; political
activism, 49; publications and awards,

44; *Four Year Old Girl*, 45; themes, 43, 44–45; writing process, 44–45, 49–50, 52–54. Works included: "Chinese Space," 57–59; "Empathy," 59–62; "Honey," 64–68; "I Love Morning," 53, 62–64

98–99; "For the Etruscans," 97; Judaic heritage, 100–1; "Language Acquisition," 97; on long poems, 104–5, 108–9; "Memory," 94; on motherhood, 96, 104; on Objectivism, 101, 103, 105, 107; poetic structure, 96–99, 102, 104; on poetry, 98, 101, 103–9; political activism, 94; publications and awards, 94–96; splay in, 96–97; *Tabula Rosa*, 94, 96; *The "History of Poetry,"* 104; *Wells*, 103; *Writing Beyond the Ending*, 96; on writing "Drafts," 96–103, 108, 109; writing process, 94–100, 102–3, 107–9. Works included: *from* "Crowbar," 104, 110–11; "Draft 27: Athwart," 112–17; *from* "Draft 52: Midrash," 97, 101, 117–20; from "Writing," 94, 96, 104, 111–12

Eckhart, Meister, 222, 223
Edwards, Melvin, 71–72
ego, 290, 303
Eliade, Mircea, 227, 235
Eliot, T. S., 257, 356–57
elliptical narrative, 370
Ellison, Ralph, 205
emotion in writing, 133–34, 138, 311
erotica, 305–9, 316
Eshleman, Clayton, 109
essays/essays-in-verse, 12, 26, 97
essentialism, 15, 126
ethics, 6, 7, 254
ethnic identity, 6, 11, 25–26
Etruscan culture, 364–65
etymology, 99–100, 102. *See also* language
expatriates, 225
experience, 313–14
experimental poetry: Berssenbrugge on, 9n9, 50–51; interest in, 2–4, 8–9n5; listserves, 8n3; style aspects, 165–66, 367; women writers and tradition, 48–49
expressionism, 352, 358

Falon, Janet Ruth, 160
Feinstein, Sascha: Cortez interview, 71–78; Sanchez interview, 277–92
Feld, Merle, 259
femininity, 24–25, 55, 197–98
feminism: activism, 94; black feminism, 70, 190; and diversity, 6, 7, 12, 197–98; ethics, 6, 7; feminine cultural model, 55; feminist theory and poetry, 97, 165; First Woman concept, 233; Fulton on, 127; and Judaism, 249, 259; literary criticism, 103–4; postcolonial, 14–15; and race, 6, 197–98; Scalapino on, 317; sexuality and, 6; sociocultural change, 93, 97, 107. *See also* second wave feminist poetry
Feminist Dictionary, 199
Feminist Studies, 97, 107–8
fiction in poetry, 135–36, 232
field poetry, 5, 104
film imagery, 370–72
Finlay, Ian Hamilton, 164
Firespitters, 75
First Woman/First Man, 233, 234
Fisher, Norman, 315
Fitzgerald, Ella, 289, 299–302
"fold" as poetic device, 98–99
folklore, 192–93, 195, 205
Ford, Hermine, 373n5
Foucault, Michel, 171
Fourçade, Dominique, 168
fragments/fragmentary style, 49, 54, 97, 194, 368
France, Marie de, 228
Franciscans, 221
Fraser, Kathleen, 351–95; aesthetic influences, 4–5, 6, 356–57, 362–65, 371–72; "Bresson Project," 370–71; on dreams, 364–65; and DuPlessis, 108; "Electric Railway, 1922: Two Women," 362–63; on Guest, 358–59, 363; *hi dde violeth i dde violet*, 368; interest in poetry

Fraser, Kathleen *(continued)*
of, 8–9n5, 327; poetic structure, 49, 354, 362–66, 368–72; publications and awards, 353; on revision, 368–69, 372; St. Marks Poetry Project, 357; "The Tradition of Marginality," 353–54; use of palimpsest, 362–63; writing process, 354, 360, 362–65, 368–69, 371–72. Works included: "Norchia" *from* "Etruscan Pages," 354, 363–65, 385–90; "Soft Pages," 371–72; *from* "Wing," 390–95

free verse, 253

Freelon, Nnenna, 206

Frost, Elisabeth A.: Guest/Fraser interview, 354–73; Mullen interview, 191–207; Scalapino interview, 303–19

Fulton, Alice, 121–53; "About Face," 129; aesthetic influences, 5–6, 122, 126–27, 131–32; "Between the Apple and the Stars," 124; on betweenness, 123–24, 126–30; "Cascade Experiment," 136; "Cusp," 137; *Dance Script with Electric Ballerina*, 123–24; double equal sign/bride sign, 121–22; "Duty-Free Spirits," 125; "Echo Location," 124–25, 134; "Fair Use," 122, 136; *Feeling as a Foreign Language*, 127–30; *Felt*, 121, 122, 125, 135, 137, 140n3; "Immersion," 121; on inconvenience of knowledge, 134, 140n3; "A Little Heart to Heart with the Horizon," 129, 132–33; "My Last TV Campaign," 137; on meaning of "fair," 125; "A New Release," 130; poetic structure, 121–25, 126–31, 129, 138; on poetry, 128–30, 132–39; "Point of Purchase," 139; publications and awards, 122–23; on race, 122, 125–27, 139; "Some Cool," 122, 134, 136; "Split the Lark," 134; "To Organize a Waterfall," 131, 139; on writing about pain, 134–35; writing process, 121–23, 125, 129–31, 137–38.

Works included: "= =," 138, 141–42; "Fuzzy Feelings," 131–32, 142–46; *from* "Give: A Sequence Reimagining Daphne & Apollo," 122, 130, 137, 146–51; "The Permeable Past Tense of Feel," 134, 151–53

function words, 129

Gander, Forrest, 338, 339

Garber, Linda, 28n4

Garvey, Marcus, 287

gender: approaches to writing, 48–49; cultural aspects of, 95, 97, 352; and energy, 24–25; Howe on poetry and, 172; identities, 6, 51, 123–26; language aspects, 353; Language writing, 165, 172; and oppression, 19–20, 49; poetic voice, 122; posthumanism, 96; power, 19–20, 124; power constructs, 124; Scalapino on perceptions of, 317; ungendered characters, 123–24

genocide, 101–2

Gervitz, Susan, 363

Ginsberg, Allen, 104, 228, 250, 252, 254

Glassgold, Peter, 163

globalism, 189

Goya, Francisco de, 50–51

grace, 173

Greenwald, Jed, 159

Guest, Barbara, 351–95; aesthetic influences, 5, 7, 351–52, 354–58, 361, 369–70; "Coal," 369; *Confetti Tree*, 370; death, 8; DuPlessis on, 97–98, 352; *Forces of Imagination*, 352, 356; Fraser on, 358–59, 363; on H. D., 359–60, 361, 365; *Herself Defined*, 359–60, 362; "Lustrous Polychromes," 366–67; *Miniatures*, 367–68, 369; poetic structure, 352, 365–67, 369–72; publications and awards, 352; "Rocks on a Platter," 367; *Seeking Air*, 360, 370; on surrealism, 352,

musical elements in poetry: Cortez, 69–78; Guest, 352, 366–67; Sanchez, 279–80; Wright, 327, 329
mythology, 125–27, 137, 234–35, 258–59

narrative poems, 53, 233
Native Americans, 234–35, 282
Navajo creation cycle, 234
Neal, Larry, 196, 285
neplanta places, 21, 26
New Age awareness, 15
New American Poetry, 104
New Critical aesthetics, 351–52
New York School (of poets and artists), 4–7, 44, 220, 228–29, 311–12, 351–53, 357–58, 372
Nietzsche, Friedrich Wilhelm, 220
Notley, Alice, 219–47; aesthetic influences, 5, 6–7, 219–20, 222, 224, 227, 229–30; "Change the Form in Dream," 225; *Close to me & Closer*, 223, 224; *Coming After*, 228; *The Descent of Alette*, 222–24, 226–28, 233–35; on dialogues with men, 229–30; *Disobedience*, 224–25, 229, 232, 233, 234; on drugs, 230; DuPlessis on, 98; on military service, 231; *Mysteries of Small Houses*, 228–30, 232, 234; on mythology, 234–35; on novels, 233; on poetic structure, 220, 233–34; publications and awards, 220–21; St. Marks Poetry Project, 357; themes, 221–23, 226, 230, 234–35; on theorists, 227–28; workshops, 223–24; writing process, 220, 224, 228, 232–35. Works included: *from "Désamère,"* 220, 222–24, 228, 230, 236–47
Nozick, Robert, 48

O Books, 304
objectivism, 4, 17, 101, 103, 105, 107
O'Hara, Frank, 229, 351, 355

O'Keeffe, Georgia, 44, 48
Oliver, Douglas, 220–24, 227, 229, 233
Olivier, Laurence, 162
Olson, Charles, 5, 104, 158, 164
ontology, 101–2
Oppen, George, 5, 94, 104–8
orality, 191, 193
Ostriker, Alicia, 249–74; aesthetic influences, 5–6, 7, 250–53, 258–60; "The Book of Life," 259–60; "Cambodia," 261; *The Crack in Everything*, 260, 261; *Dancing at the Devil's Party*, 249, 254, 256; "Everywoman Her Own Theology," 254–55, 256; Judaic motifs, 258–60; "The Leaf Pile," 260; on mastectomy, 260; on mythology, 258–59; poetic structure, 250, 254, 260; on poetry, 249–50, 256; prose poems, 261; publications and awards, 250; *Stealing the Language*, 258; *Vision and Verse in William Blake*, 251; on relationship with God, 259; writing process, 250, 253–54, 260–61. Works included: "About Time," 265–66; "The Class," 253; "The Eighth and Thirteenth," 260, 262–64; "I Brood about Some Concepts, for Example," 255; *from "The Volcano and the Covenant,"* 250, 259, 260–61, 266–74
Other, 136–37, 139
Otis, Johnny, 73
Oulipo, 190
Owen, Maureen, 163, 357

Pack, Robert, 104
page design, 7, 160–61, 332–33, 367
Painted Bride (Philadelphia), 290–91
painting, 157–58, 160, 316
palimpset, 362–66
Parker, Charlie, 70
patriarchal institutions, 19, 49
Patterson, Raymond, 76

Penny, Gerald, 282
performance art, 44, 276, 279–81
perspective, 47, 49
phenomenology, 303, 312, 318–19
Phillips, Little Esther, 74
philosophy, 6, 48. *See also* theorists
photography, 197, 315–16, 328, 371–72
Plumpp, Sterling, 76
poetic structure: Anzaldúa, 7, 11, 12, 26–27,
    28n1, 28n3; Berssenbrugge, 44–45, 47,
    49, 53–54; Cortez, 69–78; DuPlessis,
    96–99, 102, 104; Fraser, 354, 362–66,
    368–72; Fulton, 121–24, 126–31, 129, 138;
    Guest, 352, 365–67, 369–72; Howe,
    156–57, 160, 161–62; Mullen, 190, 192,
    194, 199, 201–3; Notley, 220, 233–34;
    Ostriker, 250, 254, 260; Scalapino, 304,
    306–9, 311–12, 313–16; Wright, 328,
    329–30, 332–33, 354
poetry: as a calling, 166, 173; and art,
    157–60, 336, 354–58;
    autobiography/biography in, 135–36,
    172–73, 260; categories of, 2, 3, 4, 52–53,
    192; epistemological, 122; experimental/
    innovative, 2–4, 7; formal attributes of, 4;
    and history, 158; hybrid genres of, 52–53,
    97, 157; second wave feminist, 4–7, 249,
    353; signature poems, 71; voice-based,
    123, 128, 192. *See also* sociopolitical
    poetry
poets: identity as, 251; interest in power,
    230–31; as medium, 173; poet-critics,
    109; predominantly male, 252–53;
    Romantic, 128, 172; sense of community
    with artists, 354–58
political activism: Anzaldúa, 7, 11, 18, 22,
    25; Berssenbrugge, 49; DuPlessis, 94;
    Sanchez, 275–76; Scalapino, 306, 313
politics, 190, 254, 306–8, 310–11
polyphonic poems, 123
Pop Art, 157

Pope, Alexander, 97
Pope, Odean, 285, 290–92
portal poems, 96
postfeminism, 127
posthumanism, 96
postmodernism, 43, 108–9, 122, 233, 260,
    327, 353
poststructuralism, 9n14, 171, 189, 254–55,
    353
Pound, Ezra, 94, 105, 130, 172, 257
poverty, 221–22
Powell, Bud, 77
power, 19–20, 124, 133, 230–31
pre-Columbian worldviews, 12, 14, 16
Price, Sammy, 73
prose poems, 7, 166–68, 192, 261, 327–28,
    371
publishing: in anthologies, 3, 163;
    pages/page design, 7, 160–63, 332–33,
    367
Pueblo culture, 47
punctuation, 102, 121–22, 192, 367
Puritanism, 158

quatrain, 202–3
queer theory, 11

race/race identity, 6, 122, 125, 126–27, 139,
    197–98
Rahman, Aishah, 337
Rainey, Ma, 74, 196
rap, 77–78
Rayor, Diane, 194, 199, 201
readers, 25–26, 49–50, 166, 171–72, 303.
    See also audience
reality, 16–18, 27, 96, 204
Reed, Ishmael, 53
refrains, 72
Reinhardt, Ad, 157, 160
religion: Buddhism, 54, 222, 250, 303, 314,
    318–19; Christianity, 221–23; Judaism/

voice in poetry: identity, 122–23; multiple layers of, 161–62; voice-based poetry, 123, 128, 192; women's voice, 98, 104, 107, 108, 165

Waldman, Anne, 220, 357
Waldrop, Rosmarie, 340
Walker, Alice, 201
Walker, Madame C. J., 203
Ware, Wilbur, 74
Washington, Booker T., 279
Watts Repertory Theatre Company, 70
Weinberger, Eliot, 107, 108
Whalen, Philip, 228, 312
"Where Lyric Meets Language," 9n6
Whitehead, Alfred North, 229
Whitman, Walt, 252, 254
Williams, Mary Lou, 73
Williams, William Carlos, 104–5, 108, 130, 232, 357
Wittgenstein, Ludwig, 48
"Wom-Po," 8n3
women: black female body as motif, 201; identity with ethnic writers, 25–26; Notley on world role of, 224; subjugation of, 127; and travel, 362–63
women's voice, 98, 104, 107, 108, 165, 252
Woolf, Virginia, 98, 107, 164, 171, 260, 312
words: as images, 160; list poems, 158–59, 335, 366–67
Wright, C. D., 327–49; aesthetic influences, 5–6, 7, 327, 329–31, 339; "The Box This Comes In," 336; childhood, 337; cross-genre work, 336; *Further Adventures with You*, 341; interest in social justice, 328, 335, 340; *Just Whistle: A Valentine*, 328,

330; "King's Daughters," 330; on obsessions, 340–41; *One Big Self: Prisoners of Louisiana*, 328, 329, 336; poetic structure, 327–28, 329–30, 332–33, 354; on poetry, 331–32, 335–36, 340–41; publications and awards, 328; *retablos*, 333; "Steal Away," 329; *Translations of the Gospel Back into Tongues*, 328; *Tremble*, 340–41; writing process, 328–30, 333–35. Works included: *from* "Deepstep Come Shining," 328, 332–33, 335, 342–49
writing: gender approaches to, 48–49; new forms of, 50; as profession, 221–22; Scalapino on engaging the present, 318–19. *See also* poetry
writing process: Anzaldúa, 12, 26–27; Berssenbrugge, 44–45, 49–50, 52–54; Cortez, 70, 72–73; DuPlessis, 94–100, 102–3, 107–9; Fraser, 354, 360, 362–65, 368–69, 371–72; Fulton, 121–23, 125, 129–31, 137–38; Guest, 359–60, 366–67, 369; Howe, 155–56, 160–62, 166–68, 170–71; Mullen, 189, 192, 194, 197–99, 202–5; Notley, 220, 224, 228, 232–35; Ostriker, 250, 253–54, 260–61; Sanchez, 279, 282, 286; Scalapino, 303–4, 306, 313, 315–16, 318; Wright, 328–30, 333–35

XCP: Cross-Cultural Poetics, 8n3

Yeats, William Butler, 257
Young, Al, 77

Zolbrod, Paul, 234
Zukofsky, Louis, "Mantis," 97